Praise for
NO LONGER ENEMIES,
NOT YET FRIENDS

"Powerful and thought-provoking. . . . The tough-minded narrative has a full measure of acute observations on latter-day Vietnam. . . . A masterful storyteller's clear-eyed tribute to the postbellum reconciliation."

—*Kirkus Reviews*

"Amid the lengthening list of return-to-Vietnam accounts, this is one of the most memorable . . . distinguished. . . . The story of Downs's coming to terms with his former enemy is both moving and instructive."

—*Publishers Weekly*

"Superbly rendered flashbacks to the war. . . . Downs's own growth, from rabid anti-Communist soldier to a partner in breaking down political barriers, is well told."

—*San Francisco Examiner & Chronicle*

"A book filled with poignant and resonant scenes. . . . A powerful and searing odyssey."

—*Baltimore Sun*

"Fred Downs proved his courage and his love of country on the field of battle during the Vietnam War. *NO LONGER ENEMIES, NOT YET FRIENDS* exhibits no less courage and patriotism, perhaps of an even harder sort. It is a stirring work that points the way to how men and nations may heal their wounds."

—W. E. B. Griffin, author of
The Brotherhood of War series and *The Corps*

"Fred Downs may have lost parts of his body in Vietnam, but he has the eye, ear and heart to capture pieces of war and humanity everyone else has missed. *All* of his books are essential to understanding the Vietnam War—and war in general."

—Joel L. Swerdlow, coauthor of
To Heal a Nation: The Vietnam Veterans Memorial

"NO LONGER ENEMIES, NOT YET FRIENDS is remarkable for its candor, insight and feeling. . . . One of the most thorough portrayals of the dismal reality of Vietnam today. Downs writes with the instincts of an infantryman, the eye of a reporter, and the heart of one hell of a human being."

—Laura E. Palmer, author of *Shrapnel in the Heart: Letters and Remembrances from the Vietnam Veterans Memorial*

Books by Frederick Downs

The Killing Zone: My Life in the Vietnam War
Aftermath: A Soldier's Return from Vietnam
No Longer Enemies, Not Yet Friends*

*Published by POCKET BOOKS

No Longer Enemies, Not Yet Friends

AN AMERICAN SOLDIER RETURNS TO VIETNAM

FREDERICK DOWNS

POCKET BOOKS

New York   London   Toronto   Sydney   Tokyo   Singapore

This book is dedicated to my extraordinary wife
MARY BOSTON DOWNS

POCKET BOOKS, a division of Simon & Schuster Inc.
1230 Avenue of the Americas, New York, NY 10020

Copyright © 1991 by Frederick Downs

Published by arrangement with W. W. Norton & Company, Inc.

ISBN: 0-671-79513-9

First Pocket Books printing September 1993

10 9 8 7 6 5 4 3 2 1

POCKET and colophon are registered trademarks of
Simon & Schuster Inc.

Cover photo by Thomas Braise/Tony Stone Worldwide

Printed in the U.S.A.

Acknowledgments

★ Writing is late nights, missed weekends and holidays, and no free time without a nagging sense that one should be working on the book. Writing is a shared experience at times when clarification of episodes and dates has to be checked, facts verified, and support and encouragement are needed. I want to thank my friends and others for their assistance and contribution to any or all of the above.

Paul Mather and Bill Bell did yeoman work reading and rereading the drafts, making corrections, and offering comments and observations. These two are a wealth of practical knowledge about Vietnam. Charlie Twining gave the draft a close scrutiny and provided me with his sage advice. Andy Gembara's review of my work and his friendship and support were much appreciated. My wife Mary did her usual masterful task of reading and criticizing the first draft. Johnie and Sherry Webb provided valuable information and a couple of good meals. Jim Grady was a jewel when I needed help or somebody to talk to. André Sauvageot was another ace with Vietnam facts and practical knowledge. Pat Patrick had a lot to offer.

Another group I particularly want to say thanks to are

Acknowledgments

John Connor, Bill Cowan, Don Morrisey, Vaughn Forest, Bob Kerrey, Gerry Byrne, and Curt Suplee. You covered my flanks even when some of you disagreed with me.

In a class by himself is Gerald Howard, my editor, who did a magnificent job on the manuscript.

General Vessey's executive assistants, Colonel Bill Mayall, Colonel Frank Libutti, and the rest of his staff have stood up through some fire storms, and I thank them for their steadfastness.

★ Contents ★

First Trip to Vietnam
★ August 1987 ★

August 21, 1987

★ Vietnam! The word is one I have lived with ever since I joined the Army on February 14, 1966. Now I was on a Boeing 747 United Airlines aircraft flying back to Vietnam, twenty years to the month since I first flew to Vietnam as a twenty-three-year-old infantry lieutenant on my way to war.

Then I had been flying in a Continental DC-8, in a window seat toward the front in a cramped military-chartered contract flight. We had departed from San Francisco, made a fuel stop of forty-five minutes at Wake Island, and landed at Tan Son Nhut Air Base outside of Saigon. The flight had been almost twenty-four hours long. We arrived at night close to 2300 hours (11:00 P.M.). It was the first time I had been west of the Mississippi River. Wild horses could not have kept me back. I wanted to go to war in Vietnam more than anything else in the world.

This time, as I sat in the 747 at 39,000 feet above the Pacific, racing with the sun, listening to the steady muted roar of the engines, feeling the rhythmic vibrations of their power, I was caught up in a web of powerful memories. I thought of the men I had known, the sacrifices made, the

1

death and the pain and the misery. But also the good memories and good friends from those times.

As with my first trip to Vietnam, I was eagerly looking forward to my arrival. I would not have missed it for the world.

The difference was that now, at the age of forty-three, twenty years after being sent to Vietnam by my government as a young combat officer to kill Vietnamese, I was being sent by my government to Vietnam to help the Vietnamese with their humanitarian needs.

The circumstances that brought me back to Vietnam this time, though, were considerably different from what they had been in 1967. The impetus for this trip had started in February 1987, when the former chairman of the Joint Chiefs of Staff, General John W. Vessey, Jr., U.S. Army (Retired), was appointed by President Reagan to be his presidential emissary on prisoner of war (POW) and missing in action (MIA) matters. This move was fully supported by the National League of Families of American Prisoners and Missing in Southeast Asia, whose members had fought long and hard to keep the American government's attention focused on the bitterly contentious issue. In fact, the League had been made a member of the Interagency Group that was developed to coordinate strategy within the government for dealing with the POW/MIA issue.

The Vietnamese had never fully cooperated with America on POW/MIA issues after Operation *Homecoming* in 1973. Vietnam for years had rebuffed American attempts to resolve the POW/MIA questions; it allowed only a few MIA remains to be returned to America, and then only when it served Vietnam's interests. In an attempt to get the Vietnamese to address the POW/MIA issue in a more forthright manner, General Vessey was appointed by the President, at the urging of the National League of Families, to strike up a dialogue with the Vietnamese.

Working throughout the spring of 1987, an advance team

sent to Vietnam to get agreements on Vessey's upcoming visit to Hanoi was successful in one significant area—a key never before utilized. The Vietnamese government agreed to a visit by General Vessey for discussion of the POW/MIA issue as a *humanitarian* issue, separate from and not linked to the political or economic issues that divided America and Vietnam. The separation of these matters was the key both sides needed in order to go forward.

The Vietnamese acknowledged America's claims that resolving the POW/MIA issue was a humanitarian matter. However, they said America had been too one-sided; that Vietnam also had humanitarian issues resulting from the war and they would like America to address these as well.

The immediate problem for the Reagan administration was the danger of people in America perceiving that the Vietnamese were using the humanitarian issues as a way to "buy" economic aid or political concessions by linking those issues to any progress on the POW/MIA issue.

Secretary of State George Shultz stated his concern about this on July 18, 1987, in a speech before the National League of Families in which he said: "Humanitarian reciprocity is one thing, but any attempt to trade information on our missing men for economic aid is another. We cannot agree to this."

The stage was thus set for the next round between the two adversaries, America and Vietnam.

Before leaving for Vietnam, General Vessey met with President Reagan, who charged him to "attempt to get agreement from the Vietnamese government to resume and accelerate progress toward the fullest possible accounting of prisoners and missing in Vietnam." General Vessey was also charged to raise other humanitarian concerns such as the Orderly Departure Program, Amerasian children, and reeducation-camp prisoners if it appeared that progress could be made on these issues as well.

And the President authorized General Vessey to listen to

Vietnam's humanitarian concerns. They could be expected, of course, to bring up other issues, political and economic, which could be reported back to the President; but Vessey was not to engage in any dialogue on these issues.

With these instructions in hand, General Vessey left the States for Vietnam. On August 1 through 3, 1987, Vessey and his delegation met in Hanoi with Vice Premier Nguyen Co Thach and the Vietnamese Delegation.

General Vessey outlined American objectives for the return of any live Americans, the resolution of discrepancy cases (that is, those cases of Americans for whom there was strong evidence that they survived their crash or ground action and were captured or otherwise came under Vietnamese control, or about whom the Vietnamese authorities should have information), the died-in-captivity list, crash-site excavations, repatriation of remains, and the fullest possible accounting of America's POW/MIAs.

The Vietnamese responded by asserting that they also had humanitarian concerns: 1.4 million disabled, 500,000 orphans, and many destroyed schools and hospitals. They stressed that these too would have to be addressed if there was to be progress on the humanitarian concerns of the U.S. side.

Vessey responded by making it clear that the United States could not and would not attempt to solve all of Vietnam's problems stemming from the war, but he acknowledged there were some areas we could help them in. He reiterated that any steps the United States did take would have to be consistent with the legal, political, and policy constraints governing America's current dealings with Vietnam.

What that basically meant was he was reminding the Vietnamese that America does not recognize Vietnam, and does not have diplomatic or trade relations with Vietnam (which means, among other things, that Americans are restricted from having any commerce or dealings with

Vietnam as it would constitute a violation of the "Trading with the Enemy Act").

From that definition of ground rules, the two sides began to determine parameters within which both could work. In subsequent discussions, the U.S. side sought to define the Socialist Republic of Vietnam (SRV) definition of humanitarian concerns to bring the problem within limits the United States could address by concrete steps. This was eventually achieved and an agreement was reached containing these elements.

- A Socialist Republic of Vietnam (SRV) commitment to resume cooperative efforts to account for Americans missing in action, with an initial priority on resolving discrepancy cases, including those listed by the Vietnamese as having died in captivity.
- A reaffirmation of U.S. readiness to assist Vietnamese efforts to account for our missing men, including the training of search/excavation teams, the provision of needed excavation equipment, and orientation-training visits by Vietnamese forensic experts to the Central Identification Laboratory in Honolulu.
- A U.S. commitment to address "certain urgent humanitarian concerns" consistent with legal, political, and policy constraints.
- An agreement to meetings of two separate groups of experts to be held on August 25–28, 1987, in Hanoi; one to discuss the POW/MIA issue, and the other to examine Vietnamese humanitarian concerns, with a particular focus on their need for prosthetics.

Pursuant with the agreements, two teams were scheduled to travel to Hanoi. The POW/MIA technical team would consist of four people: the commander of the Joint Casualty

5

Resolution Center (JCRC), the chief of the JCRC liaison office in Bangkok, the commander of the Central Identification Laboratory in Hawaii, and a casualty resolution specialist, a position that requires Vietnamese-language capability.

The second expert, humanitarian team was to be composed of Dr. Carlton Savory, an orthopedic surgeon and a Vietnam veteran; myself, as director of the Veterans Administration's Prosthetic and Sensory Aids Service, and a Vietnam veteran who had lost an arm during the war; and as a representative of a nongovernmental organization, Food for the Children, Larry Ward, Ph.D., who had traveled to Vietnam many times on humanitarian missions.

At the time I had no idea these events were transpiring. It was only during the first week when General Vessey returned from his August trip that I had an inkling of what was to come. I received a call from the Administrator's Office of the Veterans Administration and then a call from the State Department, both asking me if I would be interested in going to Vietnam as part of an official U.S. government team.

I was momentarily taken aback by this call out of the blue. First was my surprise at the U.S. government choosing me, and second was the thought of returning to Vietnam. All my adult life has been affected by Vietnam the country, and Vietnam the war. My wife asked me once, not too long after I had given a speech on combat leadership, if I would ever be able to let go of Vietnam. I was surprised at the question. I had never thought about it that way. I had often wondered about the question from the other side, though: Would Vietnam ever let go of me?

Did I want it to? I thought not. Once a man has contributed his blood and his honor to a country, he is always a part of what it becomes. And of course there is always the fact that one's duty to one's own country never ends.

So of course I answered yes, I would be honored to be a

member of an official U.S. government team going to Hanoi, where we would meet with the Vietnamese Delegation to discuss and review the problems they were having in providing prosthetic limbs to the Vietnamese people. Within a matter of days, we were on our way.

Little did I know what I was in for. When I returned from Vietnam in 1968, I was criticized by some people as a fool for doing what my country had asked me to do. When I. returned from this trip in 1987, I would also be criticized by some people as a fool for doing what my country wanted me to do.

Luckily for me and for the others who would comprise the mission, our leader, General John Vessey, Jr., was to prove more resourceful and tenacious in carrying out the mission than its detractors were in trying to stop it. He would pull us through each time the mission was in danger of faltering.

General Vessey had been chairman of the Joint Chiefs of Staff during President Reagan's term. He was well known and respected by all those he dealt with. Like all leaders he had his share of detractors and critics, but few, if any of those, knew him personally.

John Vessey had started out his military career as an enlisted man in World War II. He is one of the few men in American history who had worked up from the enlisted ranks to become a four-star general. He is of medium size and a little on the wiry side. He has silver hair, wears glasses, and does not look as tough as he really is. He inspires great loyalty in those who work for him, and I am no exception. He is a down-to-earth kind of guy and we got along from the beginning. His strength and belief in those who work for him got us through some of the low points.

When President Reagan asked General Vessey to be his presidential emissary to Vietnam on POW/MIA affairs, he undertook the task because he felt a strong commitment to the families involved. He was hopeful from the start that he could make a contribution to getting the issue back on track.

At the time the President asked Vessey to do this, eighteen months had passed with no real movement on the talks. There was a good deal of discouragement among the families as a result.

The task was devilishly complicated, and Vessey knew it. He told us he had three goals in mind: Get the talks back on track; expedite the resolution of POW/MIA cases; and use the humanitarian issue as something that would reenergize the POW/MIA issue to get the Vietnamese to resume and accelerate their cooperation.

General Vessey was the right man for the job, but even he did not realize how difficult his mission would become. Fortunately, the Vietnamese had respect for him as a warrior and an elder statesman—and there would be times when his credibility with them seemed to be the only glue that held the talks together.

I thought about all the astonishing events that had brought me to this point as I sat in a row seat toward the tail of the aircraft in the smoke-filled economy section. The passengers seemed to be mostly Oriental back here, and they all smoked like fiends. There were lots of family groups with babies. The Department of Defense people who had arranged our travel had said we would be traveling in business class because of the length of the trip and our status as Vessey's expert team. However, some travel clerk in the bowels of the Pentagon did not recognize our exalted status, so we were in economy class. I was more cramped on this trip than I had been on the military charter twenty years earlier.

Along with me on this flight was our team leader, Carl Savory, who is over 6 feet tall, slim and gangly. Carl has a wonderful sense of humor, and no patience. He had two combat tours in Vietnam: once as a platoon leader with the 173rd Airborne Brigade and a second as a company commander of a Long Range Reconnaissance Patrol. He was wounded once. When he returned from Vietnam, the Army sent him to medical school where he became an orthopedic surgeon and decided to stay on and make the Army his career. He had retired last year as a full colonel and was now living and practicing in Columbus, Georgia. Carl was sitting in an aisle seat on the other side and was so pissed off about being in economy, I thought he was going to have apoplexy.

Both of us struck it right off. We seem to be of like temperament and attitude, and share many of the same beliefs: get down to basics and get the job done. We traded war stories the whole trip.

The third member of our team was Larry Ward, an older man in his sixties who is short, balding, and overweight. Carl and I were the medical experts and Ward was the expert on nongovernmental organizations, the nonprofit groups who do humanitarian work. If the American government decided to allow humanitarian aid to be provided to Vietnam, it would be the nongovernmental organizations that would be tasked with the job. Ward has been to Vietnam numerous times and was someone the Vietnamese were familiar with. He was the friendly, gregarious sort, who had been performing "dogooder" work for at least thirty years. Larry claimed to have made 109 trips into Vietnam; he talked all the time and seemed to know everybody.

The fourth member of our traveling group was Laurence M. (Larry) Kerr, a tall, big-boned, well-built redhead—a witty and erudite man who is the Vietnam/Cambodia/Laos desk officer at the State Department. He also had two tours as a combat officer in Vietnam. He was to accompany us as far as Bangkok, where he would work in the embassy until we "came out."

The trip took forever. My body was not twenty-three anymore, it was forty-three, and my butt and legs are full of shrapnel and covered with scar tissue. Sitting in the narrow, cramped seats became excruciatingly painful. Finally I told the stewardess I was going to lie down on the floor. There

9

was room next to the rear door. I lay down, but then I started to freeze. The seal around the door at 39,000 feet is not that tight, and it was drafty as hell. The stewardesses felt sorry for me and threw more blankets on me. In spite of the cold I felt so good at being able to stretch out that I determined to stay there until we landed.

I spent a number of restless hours trying to sleep and being prodded every once in a while when a stewardess would push a cart in next to me. Finally a stewardess shook my shoulder and told me we were preparing to land in Hong Kong to refuel and lay over for three hours. Three hours—Jesus, what a miserable trip! Almost six hours from Dulles International to San Francisco, two hours layover there, 13.5 hours from there to Hong Kong, now another three-hour layover, and then two hours on to Bangkok. I was exhausted, and we were not even to Bangkok.

Because of a two-hour delay in Hong Kong we actually had to wait five hours on the ground. By comparison, the flight to Bangkok seemed short at only two hours. I was aching and tired beyond belief, but I excitedly stared out the window as the 747 started to let down through the dark sky above Bangkok, Thailand.

I was surprised at what a modern airport Bangkok had. There were long lines of 747s painted with the colors of airlines from all over the world parked along the tarmac. The terminal was brand new and seemed to spread for miles. All signs were in Thai and English. Soft music played through excellent speakers. The well-lighted, spick-and-span baggage area was at least two football fields long.

There were plenty of Customs booths manned, even at 0030 hours (12:30 A.M.). All of the Customs men were neat, clean, and well dressed in pressed uniforms. At the booth I went up to, the officer was very courteous. He was a small-boned, slightly built man about the size of a young teenager, who could not have weighed more than 110 pounds soaking wet. It turned out all the Thais are small-boned. They seemed like a delicate race of people. Later on I would find out they had been fighting wars for thousands of years in this part of the world. They may have been small but they were tough as nails.

The terminal was air-conditioned, I noticed. When we had gotten off the aircraft to load onto the buses for the trip to the terminal, the weather was warm, with high humidity. It was a reminder we were now in the tropics.

The baggage showed up with no problems. Everything worked like clockwork. The Joint Casualty Resolution Center team—consisting of Joe Harvey, Paul Mather, and Bill Bell—were there to pick us up, as they had an office at the American Embassy. They introduced themselves and assisted us through Customs.

Next, the JCRC team loaded us into their van for the trip into Bangkok. There were three rows of bench seats for us to sit on. However, the van was Japanese-made, tailored for the small bodies of the people of this part of the world, so we had to sit sideways—there was no room for our legs.

On the drive into Bangkok, I was amazed at how modern everything looked. The road was a superhighway with four lanes running in either direction. Street lamps lined the road. Traffic even at that late hour was heavy. Well-lighted buildings and factories stretched along both sides for as far as I could see. Paul Mather, who has lived in Bangkok for eleven years, said that ten years ago the area between the airport and the city had been rice paddies, but it had all filled up now with commercial development.

Part of my surprise at everything I saw from the airport on into town was that in my guts I had expected dirt roads, grass, mud buildings, and a somewhat primitive society. Intellectually, I may have known better, but still I had never expected this level of development.

We were taken to the Regent, which was magnificent, a white seven-story building. Two small white cement elephants stood to either side of the front steps, and there were

11

a number of bellmen wearing white pith helmets and dressed in white uniforms who greeted us as we left the van. In the lobby 30- by 40-foot murals covered the ceiling and high walls. A thick royal blue rug stretched over a huge white marble floor. Exquisitely carved teak paneling was tastefully used throughout the hotel, including the elevator.

My guestroom itself was a wonder. A dark teakwood desk with brass lamp sat along the wall next to a dark teak entertainment center with roll-desk doors. There was a small, fully stocked refrigerator in a teak cabinet behind louvered doors. A speaker system piped music into a bathroom of clear cream marble. An umbrella, hair dryer, suit tree, shoeshine kit, and slippers completed the amenities.

I threw down my bag. I had been traveling nonstop for almost thirty hours and I felt like hell. No wonder twenty years ago, when I got off that military charter flight in Saigon, I was ready to kill somebody.

I slept until eleven-thirty local time. There is exactly twelve hours difference from Eastern Standard time so I did not even have to change my watch. Somewhere over the Pacific we crossed the international date line, so it is a day later here. Strange, I thought. When I flew to Vietnam twenty years ago, either I did not realize I had crossed a date line or I did not care. When I was there I did not really think about it being a different day back home in Indiana. I knew it was nighttime but I just did not think about a different date.

The reason this trivial thought crossed my mind was the realization that all the significant events in Vietnam happened one day different from the date the folks back in the States were on. A son reported killed on the 11th was killed on the 10th U.S. time. I had not thought about it before.

After I got out of bed, I decided to go jogging in a park about half a kilometer from the hotel. There was a lake with a fountain of water shooting up in the air. The park was clean: families strolled around the road which circled the park, lovers lingered under the bushes, soldiers sat around enjoying the girls, small groups of young men and boys were playing a kickball game.

The people would unobtrusively sneak a look at this one-armed man wearing a T-shirt with "USA" across the chest jogging by them, and then go on about their business. The course was only a kilometer around so I did a number of laps. A group of Thai soldiers lounging near one of the bridges watched me a few times and then applauded me on one of my passes. I was pleased at this unexpected display of respect from what I thought of as the uncaring Orientals.

I was still thinking the way I had always thought. This was my first trip to this part of the world since Vietnam. I had been in the job of killing "dinks" then, and I still had a low opinion of Orientals who lived in this part of the world. Not loathing or fear—I just thought of them as people who did not have a high regard for life. They were not Christians. They worshipped things, not God. They were a people I had no respect for.

After returning from my run, I showered and went down to meet Carl and the leader of the JCRC team, Colonel Joe Harvey. He was stationed in Honolulu but had flown in so he could be in charge of the JCRC team that was going into Hanoi with us. As agreed by General Vessey and Vice Premier Nguyen Co Thach, both the humanitarian team and the POW/MIA joint recovery team would meet with their respective counterparts at this first meeting.

The leader of our team, Carl Savory, and the JCRC team leader, Joe Harvey, discussed how the teams should react in Hanoi. The question from the beginning of this trip was, were the Vietnamese serious? All of us were skeptical. We did not trust the Vietnamese and we were leery of their motives. We figured they would jack us around. There was a strong possibility the Vietnamese were somehow going to use our visit as a propaganda opportunity to make themselves look good and cause America to lose face. The position was strongly held by our group that the Vietnamese government did not give a damn about humanitarian aid to its people. They had not cared about it before, why should they change their minds? We did not believe they had, but Carl and Joe said that regardless of what the Vietnamese pulled on us, we would do our job the best we could. The consensus of the group was that the Vietnamese were treacherous and guilty of duplicity, as proven in their past dealings with America. But we resolved to deal with them honestly and straightforwardly. If these talks failed, it would not be for want of trying on our part. On this note the meeting ended.

It was Sunday and the embassy was closed for business, so after lunch Carl, Larry Kerr, and I rented a car and driver from the hotel to go sightseeing. We visited the Grand Palace, temples, and pagodas. We saw Bangkok as the cosmopolitan city it has become, complete with shopping malls. The city is bright with colors and fresh sweet-smelling flowers, and its aura is one of vibrant, energetic growth. The atmosphere reminded me of New York City. Cars, vans, motorcycles, buses, and trucks filled the streets, flowing in rhythm with traffic lights and billboards. We had a good time and were impressed by the city.

That evening, Carl, Larry Kerr, Larry Ward, and I went to Neal's Café; they served American-style food, and although we would have loved Thai food, none of us wanted to go into Vietnam with an upset stomach. Our only concession to foreign food was to drink the Thai beer, Singha.

Afterwards, Carl and I wanted the group to go to Pat Pong Street, which was famous during our Vietnam tour. Neither Carl nor I had ever taken R and R (rest and relaxation) in Bangkok, but we had heard plenty of stories from the men who had. They said you could buy a fantastically beautiful young woman for 15 U.S. dollars to spend the whole five days of your R and R with you. They told of stories where you could go into a bar and get a blow job at the bar while drinking a beer. They said you could buy three women to make love to at one time and it would only cost $5.

The stories were too wild to be true, but to young men in the jungle the fantasy was too good to destroy. Imagine my surprise when the guys now said it was all true. The only difference was that inflation had driven the price up to $20 for a body massage and an all-night stand.

Well, we were not young troopers anymore, but we did want to at least see this street. We took a cab to Pat Pong Street and it was like a scene out of Sodom and Gomorrah. Europeans and Japanese had replaced the American soldiers of long ago in the bars and on the street, but other than that Larry said it was the same.

It was like going back twenty years. Half-naked women stood in the open doors of bars, hawkers ran up to us with propositions, women walked down the street flirting with any man passing by. Lights blazed and noise cascaded out onto the street from competing bars playing the latest rock music. We went into one of the bars and the women immediately swarmed around us.

If we had been single, younger, and didn't give a damn about all the sexually transmitted diseases, we could have been entertained all night long. The women were beautiful and childlike in their demeanor toward us. They coyly touched our legs and asked us to buy them a drink. Just like the Saigon tea the girls used to ask us to buy them in Vietnam. Saigon tea was just regular tea, but we were charged a full alcoholic-drink price for it. The bar girls could drink gallons of it as long as we had the money to buy it. Some things do not change at all. The girls of course seemed to be very interested in our well-being, but we were in our forties and much wiser now. We bought them Bangkok tea without feeling anything but relaxation at having a good time and joking with each other about what this would have been like twenty years ago.

The girls would come off the dance floor and make a pass at us. We were rich Americans and not to be ignored. A couple of the old mama sans came over after the girls reported who we were and reminisced about the "war days" against Vietnam, when there were so many American soldiers.

The girls were fascinated by my artificial arm, especially the mama san who was in charge of them. One of the bar girls had lost the first couple of knuckles on her right hand, and so she was sent back to us time and time again. Finally the mama san realized we were a lost cause and came over to raise hell with the girls to chase them away.

Back out on the street again, I noticed an old crone dressed in dirty black pajamas and wearing a ragged conical hat squatting by the curb tending a cauldron of boiling grease. I stopped to watch—wondering what was deep frying. She looked up and smiled. Holding her hat on with one bony hand, she used a foul black iron rod to pull up a wide wire tray full of fried grasshoppers. There must have been hundreds in there. I shook my head, but a passer-by dug in his pants for money and bought some. She put them in a piece of newspaper and handed them to him, whereupon he started munching them like nuts. I was actually tempted to try them, but I did not. It was not the grasshoppers I was afraid of but the unsanitary conditions in which they were cooked. Later I learned that the people who sell grasshoppers to the vendors don't crawl around on their hands and knees all night catching them; they spray them with insecticide.

The next day would be a heavy work day to prepare for the trip into Vietnam, so we decided to call it a night. We all agreed the local economy must have suffered greatly when the Americans pulled out of Vietnam; and they were not making any money from this group of tired Americans. It was still early as we headed back to the hotel. We reflected happily that by going to Pat Pong Street after all these years

we had closed a little gap on our past experiences in this part
of the world.

August 24

★ I got up early to go running, and immediately noticed the
difference in the large numbers of people who were in the
park exercising. Sunday had been a rest day, but today was a
work day. The streets were jammed with traffic and the park
with people. There were hundreds of men and women of all
ages exercising in groups all around the park. The most
popular activity seemed to be Tai Chi, a sort of slow-motion
Kung Fu maneuver. Another group was doing aerobics to
loud rock music blaring out from a tape deck. Every group
had a leader. There were so many runners on the path it was
like being in a race. We had to weave around the exercisers,
who were in the middle of the road.

After my run I cleaned up and went downstairs to meet
the others at the entrance to the Regent. We rented two cars
and convoyed to the American Embassy where we would
make final preparations for our trip into Hanoi. We left the
cars at the armored front gate and went through the first
security checkpoint at the booth by the gate. That involved
showing our ID, signing in, and having someone in the
embassy come get us.

I have only been to American embassies in the Third
World, and each one has always been like a fortress. In El
Salvador there are guard towers with machine-gun nests on
the wall around the embassy compound. Here there was
only a wall and a reinforced gate. But the wall was high and
there were guards spread round the compound. The wall
surrounds a large, 10-acre spread on which the embassy and
outbuildings are set.

After we were cleared through the gate, we walked up a

gently curving path bordered by flowering shrubs to the front door. The embassy is a modest white three-story building with a driveway in front and a small pond across the road. A pagoda was being built in the middle of the pond. Beyond the main building were a series of outbuildings used for administrative functions.

Immediately inside the front door, behind bulletproof glass, was a Marine security station. We slipped our ID through a slot at the bottom. I failed the metal-detector test because of my artificial arm and was hand-searched. After we were cleared, we were taken up to a conference room where we dumped what we were carrying and went down to the cafeteria for breakfast.

The ambassador had the designated smoking area for the cafeteria outside on the patio, which in this hot, humid climate was not the best place to be. I thought how American it was that the government smoking policy in the States would extend to our embassies worldwide. It seemed to me something the British would do.

Later, at the meeting upstairs in the conference room, we discussed our roles on the coming trip. Carl and I were confident and eager to attack the prosthetic problems in Vietnam. However, we were concerned that the Vietnamese would want to link anything we did directly to political or economic aid; we were worried as well that our own countrymen would see this mission as the Vietnamese trading American bones for prosthetic limbs.

I felt no love for the Vietnamese and thought of them as the enemy, the "dinks" I used to fight against who had killed and wounded so many of my friends. I believed they did want to trade the bodies of our missing in action for assistance from the United States, and I found the idea repulsive. To my way of thinking, the Vietnamese were evil ghouls who for years had continued to torment the families of our missing in action and prisoners of war.

I had hated the Vietnamese for years. Their refusal to

return our MIA bodies had been like salt poured into our wounds. I thought of those MIA/POWs as comrades in arms. It was our duty to return these men from the battlefield if we were to have any honor as a nation.

As the meeting in the conference room proceeded, I wondered why I should help the Vietnamese. I had consented to come because it was my duty and I was curious: I wanted to see what Vietnam was like now. I assumed that our purpose was related to getting our MIAs back, reason enough for the mission.

The uncertainty of knowing what the Vietnamese were up to bedeviled us. As we left the aircraft, we wondered, would the Vietnamese attempt to put the two teams, the humanitarian aid team and the POW/MIA negotiators, together so that the photographers could take pictures of us as one group, thereby linking the two together? This was a real concern because their propagandists could then claim the Americans were providing reparations as a trade-off to solve the POW/MIA issue.

How would they seat us at the discussion tables? Would the teams be together or separate? Shades of the Paris Peace Talks, I thought. It took months for them to work that out to everyone's satisfaction. Now we were going to be on their home turf, so they could try anything.

This all would sound very paranoid except for the fact that the history of our dealings with the Vietnamese had proven that matters between the Americans and the Vietnamese were always in jeopardy of falling apart either through design or through misunderstanding.

The State Department representative had said that once we landed at Hanoi, we would be out of touch until we returned to Bangkok. There would be no way to communicate. If there was an emergency, we could go to the embassy of an ally and use their communication devices, but that should only be in cases of extreme duress.

It seemed an ominous statement. Anything could happen

to us here. This was a country that America did not yet recognize and had no official communication with, so what exactly were we getting into, anyway? This was a deadly serious business involving relationships between two countries that had never resolved the animosity between them.

How did I feel about entering the country of my enemy? I had very mixed feelings. Vietnam was a Communist country. It represented everything I had been brought up to hate and to fight against. I had given my all for the benefit of the South Vietnamese people. In the process I had been wounded four times and had lost my arm near Tam Ky. As a warrior I felt tied to the country, as if I had a vested interest in its well-being. The fact that the North Vietnamese overcame the South did not diminish the importance of my efforts, my sacrifices on its behalf. Perhaps it was wrong of me to be so arrogant in that belief, but I truly believed (and still do) that my purpose was correct.

In short, I felt strangely drawn to Vietnam, and I wanted to help the Vietnamese people just like I started out to do twenty years ago.

Before we left the briefing, we were told that if the Ministry of Labor, Invalids, and Social Affairs was in charge of the meeting with the humanitarian team, then the Vietnamese would be serious, because these people are believed to be truly concerned about their countrymen. However, if the Ministry of Foreign Affairs was in charge of the meeting with the humanitarian team, we would know the Vietnamese were not serious. The director of that ministry was in charge of the Ministry of Foreign Affairs for North America, headed by Mr. Bai, who was reported to be a very tough man. It was alleged by some people that he did not have a humane bone in his body and that if he was in charge, we were doomed to failure from the beginning.

On that happy note we ended the meeting. We went next door to the fiscal officer to get a cash advance because the Vietnamese would demand U.S. dollars in payment for everything we used there, including van rental and quarters.

They are so desperate for hard currency they will accept neither their own money nor Russian rubles.

Next stop was the commissary, which we had special permission to use as nonembassy people. I bought toilet paper (a must when traveling in Communist countries), soap, a wash cloth, towel, and other odds and ends that I thought would be useful. Larry Ward bought a small jar of instant coffee, which would turn out to be a wonderful idea.

August 25

★ We got up early at 5:00 A.M. in order to be checked out and ready to fight the traffic out to the airport. Larry Ward and Carl Savory were waiting for the van out front, along with Joe Harvey and his colleague Johnie Webb. The rest of the JCRC team would meet us at the airport.

Thai International Airport serves both the civilian and military traffic. Today, the van took us over to the military side and we proceeded to the small hangar rented by the U.S. government to house our Defense Attaché Office aircraft. We were going to fly to Hanoi in the DAO's C-12, which is the military version of the Beechcraft King Air.

The twin-engine, propeller-driven aircraft sat outside the hangar while a three-man crew finished the preflight checks. Carl and I remarked that they could take all the time they needed as long as they were thorough. We had no desire to have anything go wrong while flying over the trackless jungle. I hold a pilot's license and I love flying, but the old saw about an airplane being a collection of parts flying in close formation is a sober reminder that it is only a piece of machinery. Although the turbine engines on the C-12 are quite reliable, Murphy's Law says anything can go wrong.

The DAO aircraft was painted in the official U.S. colors of white and gray separated by blue and gold trim. UNITED STATES OF AMERICA was printed in bold letters along the length of the fuselage. The sight of the official markings underscored the importance of our mission, and at the same time provided us with a reminder of home.

Over to the side of the tarmac was one of the ubiquitous Huey helicopters. Inside the hangar was a modified Thai military twin-engine four-blade helicopter belonging to the king of Thailand. It is used for trips "upcountry" and can also be used to evacuate him from the palace grounds in the event of a coup or an uprising. I had been told by a congressional friend back in the States that America maintains "escape" helicopters for our allies and their families in much of the Third World. I was also told that more than one leader has an escape chopper parked in his yard, ready for instant departure. This is one of the perks we offer for being America's friend.

We were introduced to the crew, all American, of course. The two pilots were military, clean cut, neat, and looked to be in their thirties. One was dressed in gray and the other in khaki. The crew chief was a civilian contractor who was dressed informally in a short-sleeve shirt and trousers. He was swarthy, dark-haired, and wore a short trimmed beard.

We gathered along the side of the plane near the rear door for a group photograph on what we considered to be the beginning of an historic trip. That accomplished, we loaded onto the aircraft and buckled in. Sweat was pouring off of us, but the pilots assured us we would cool off at altitude.

There was a single row of seats on each side of the cabin. We were all tight but not uncomfortable. I explored the seat pocket in front of me and found a Chinese folding fan—the air conditioning while on the ground. A small door with a curtain separated the cockpit from the cabin, but the curtain was tied securely out of the way so we could converse with the cockpit. On the right side of the cabin, starting at the front, was Colonel Joe Harvey, commander and team leader of JCRC. I was next in line. Behind me was Larry Ward, and behind him was the crew chief. Colonel Paul Mather, JCRC deputy stationed in Bangkok, sat in the front seat on the left side. Behind him and across from me was Dr. Carl Savory, and behind him Colonel Johnie Webb, the director of JCRC's forensic section. Last in that row was Bill Bell, the JCRC team's interpreter.

The pilots fired up the engines and at 1030 hours we taxied out to the active runway for takeoff. We lifted off into a hazy, bright sky and headed north while gaining altitude. The Thailand landscape spread out in a perfectly flat, water-soaked sea of light green rice paddies as far as the eye could see. Brilliantly colored golden pagoda roofs dotted the sea of green.

We climbed up through thin broken clouds; to the north we could see clouds building up into possible individual storm cells. The pilots reported rain in Hanoi. Typhoon Carrie was sweeping through central Vietnam and the weather was unsettled all along our course. We were above most of the clouds, and we flew around the really tall ones. I could see the sweep of the radar across the green-colored screen in the middle of the panel between the pilots. The storm cells showed up as irregular dark blotches, which the pilots pointed to with their finger and then calculated routes around.

Sun streamed in the window at my right shoulder. A small sign in the corner of the window said:

Notice: Direct
Viewing of The Sun
May Be Harmful.

We may have been on the other side of the world, but there was no way to escape the little idiot pearls of wisdom Americans dream up to protect themselves against the obvious.

The roar of the turboprop engines vibrated through the fuselage as we settled back for the two-hour, forty-minute flight to Hanoi. The flight plan called for us to fly north up into Laos and then turn east on a heading for Hanoi. As a pilot myself, I was interested in all aspects of the flight and asked to see the air maps and route we were flying. The pilots obligingly handed them back for me to study. The first thing to catch my eye was a forbidding boxed notice outlined on the air map of Vietnam, Cambodia, and Laos. It read:

Warning
Aircraft Infringing Upon
Non-Free Flying Territory
May Be Fired Upon
Without Warning.

Yeah, well, this is no game, I thought to myself. The warning served to bring into focus what we were about.

Carl and I were sitting across from each other and the plane was insulated enough so we could carry on a conversation at a comfortable level. Neither of us could believe we were actually flying into Vietnam, especially Hanoi, on official business.

I suppose those few veterans who have returned on tours must have the same types of feelings we had: trepidation, disbelief, wonderment, unreality, and a mystical sense of longing to return to the country that so drastically affected our lives.

At a certain point the pilots got busy with the radio and started scanning the sky around us and looking down at the ground. They told us Vientiane, Laos, just radioed to ask what type aircraft we were and what was our destination. The pilot yelled back at us that he wanted to radio back that we were a Bravo-52 heading for Hanoi, but he had refrained from doing so. We all enjoyed the joke. Everyone on board except for Ward had served in combat in Vietnam during the war.

The pilot then signaled us that we were crossing into Vietnam. I looked down at the terrain below and weird feelings churned through me. Beneath us was rugged mountainous jungle, and as I stared down at the inhospitable terrain I thought back on humping similar mountains with a 70-pound pack on my back, leading my platoon up and down the ridges for days and weeks looking for the North Vietnamese Army (NVA) regulars and the Viet Cong (VC).

I thought of the war as I knew it. The fierce firefights and ambushes in those jungle mountains, the men on both sides killed and wounded, the months of sleeping in the jungle, the heat, humidity, bugs, snakes, thorns, ants, bees, leeches, jungle rot, diarrhea, mosquitoes, gnats, cuts and scrapes, falls, rain, sleep deprivation, long exhausting marches, fear-filled days and nights, hunger, thirst, filthy bodies, the cold and wet, the gagging stink of decomposing jungle or a dead body, the danger of malaria—and losing my arm.

Below me was the land of my enemy. I felt strange. It had been so many years now. It seemed hard to believe all that happened twenty years ago. It seemed even stranger to still be involved with it. What was my dad doing twenty years after his war, World War II, was over? He sure was not involved in returning POW/MIAs.

Where were the surface-to-air missiles (SAMs)? We were in enemy territory and any foreign aircraft over Vietnam is in harm's way. I looked down at the verdant jungle growth and realized if we crashed in that craggy mountainous terrain no one would ever find us, and the North Vietnamese knew our flight plan. I wondered how many of our MIAs were lying on the sides of mountain jungles, forever lost to us.

Carl, Paul, Joe, Johnie, Bill, and I had been telling war stories, talking about the books and movies out on Vietnam. Our attention then turned to the Vietnam of today. We wondered what it would be like. The old hands on board said the Vietnamese were unpredictable. Even they didn't know how the Vietnamese would behave this time.

We started to let down for our approach to Hanoi's international airport, Noi Bai. The clouds had cleared off around Hanoi, and the sky was sunny. We had good visibility in spite of the humidity. We eagerly looked at the land below. There was so much water flooding the rice fields it looked more like an island sea. Hanoi was off to the right, sitting next to a large, red silt-filled river. The Vietnamese name for the river is Song Hong, but we called it the Red River during the war. It was easy to see from the air how it got its name.

The plane bumped through heat thermals as it lost altitude. The sudden movement knocked my forehead against the porthole window as I strained to see everything. I wanted to be oriented when I got on the ground, and most of all I wanted to absorb every aspect of this unbelievable trip.

I could see the infamous Long Bien (or Paul Doumer) Bridge our airplanes spent so much time bombing. Or at least I thought I saw it. There were two bridges across the Red River from Hanoi, so I was unsure which was which. Then I saw two lanes with a railroad track between them on the north bridge; that one must have been the Long Bien.

Hanoi was smaller than I had imagined it to be. From the air it reminded me of Terre Haute, Indiana, where my mom lived. They were about the same size and Terre Haute sits next to the Wabash River. The big difference was all the water surrounding Hanoi. Of course, I figured during a flood the farms around Terre Haute would look about the same.

Hanoi passed behind us as we flew to the Noi Bai Airport located about 30 kilometers north of the city. As we crossed over the rice paddies, the old-timers pointed out "Uncle Sam's Duck Ponds." That is the name given to the water-filled bomb craters still left over from the war when B-52 bombers and other American aircraft attacked Noi Bai Airport. There seemed to be hundreds, perhaps thousands of bomb craters spread around the ground. Some were spread out in long parallel lines where sticks of bombs had fallen in very orderly fashion; others were scattered haphazardly throughout the rice paddies. Bill Bell said many of the bomb craters were left unfilled for use as ponds. Anywhere you have seasonal rice with a dry season you must have little ponds to retain water for seed rice, in order to be ready when the rains come. They raised fish in them also.

So much for precision bombing. Of course it was hard to maintain a heading when someone was shooting SAMs at you. Just as I had this thought, someone shouted, "SAM site off to the right." Jesus Christ! Goose bumps raised the hair on my neck as the shout drew my attention to the lethal nest of missiles sticking their pointed noses up out of a bunker next to a group of trees. We were on final approach, close to the ground. The missile site passed quickly behind and I could catch glimpses of the runway threshold approaching. There was only one runway at Noi Bai and it was laid out northwest to southeast.

1310 hours, touchdown in North Vietnam. I felt adrenaline surge through me, and I got that strange nervous weakness I used to get when I heard the sounds of the helicopters coming to pick us up to carry us into a hot landing zone. Butterflies.

MiG-21s were lined up in revetments along the runway; I counted at least fifteen. The old terminal building with its control tower was pointed out by Johnie Webb. It was deserted, also a casualty of the war. Its windows were all shattered and the walls were pockmarked by shrapnel from the bombing.

I gloated over the damage. It was strange, though, to still be able to see it. The last bombing had been during Christmas 1972, fifteen years ago. You would have thought everything would have been repaired by now. I wondered why it wasn't.

The roar of the reversed propellers slowing us down subsided as the pilot turned off the active runway onto a taxi way opposite the blasted terminal building. Paul Mather explained that a new terminal had been built some years ago on the other side of the field with the help of one of the Eastern Bloc countries allied with Vietnam.

I snapped some pictures of an Aeroflot twin-engine pas-

senger jet sitting close by the terminal. The red Soviet flag
was painted high up on the tail. I had been taught all my life
that the Russians were our enemy. Not without good cause: I
was wounded in the Vietnam War with weapons supplied to
the Vietnamese by the Russians. The Russians as enemy was
not an abstract notion to me. Funny, though, this was the
first time I had ever seen a Soviet flag in the wild.

Two Vietnam Airlines twin-engine passenger jets sat close
by the Russian jet. The red Vietnam flag with a golden star
in the middle was also painted high up on the tails of these
aircraft. We were definitely in enemy territory.

I loved the fact we were in an official aircraft with UNITED
STATES OF AMERICA written across both sides. The American
flag was painted high up on our tail as well for all to see. I
hoped it galled them to see it.

There was a delegation standing on the tarmac waiting for
us as we taxied to the ramp and shut down the engines. Six
or seven seemed to be with the press, complete with movie
cameras and press IDs hanging from their belts. Off to the
side, standing with their hands behind their backs, were
three or four soldiers in green uniforms and visor caps
watching us shut down. In front of those two groups were
about four or five men and one woman, all dressed in
tropical civilian clothes. This last group was obviously the
welcoming committee.

"Goddamn, don't you wish you would have had these
guys in your sights twenty years ago?" I exclaimed to Carl.

"Yeah," he answered. "We might still wish that if this
mission goes belly up."

When the crew chief opened the rear door, which was
hinged at the bottom to swing down for use as stairs, a
palpable wave of intense heat and humidity swept into the
cabin. I thought I had remembered how hot and humid it
got in Vietnam, but my memory was no match for this.
Sweat started running freely from every pore. There was
also the smell of the tropics—wet, rotting vegetation. Not as

strong as in the jungle but still there, underlying all other smells.

Joe Harvey and his team exited the aircraft first and moved over toward the tail to give our team room to gather separately out by the wing tip as we came out. We stayed in two distinct groups as the hot sun beat down from above and reflected up from the concrete below.

I was surprised and slightly embarrassed to find that my legs were weak and shaking as I went down the steps. I kept a tight grip on my shoulder bag and held tightly to the hand cable so I wouldn't fall. When my feet touched the concrete and I let go of the cable, I discovered my hands were shaking and my knees were trembling. The adrenaline was rushing through me.

I could not suppress the powerful feeling of being in enemy territory. I was surrounded by North Vietnamese. The shock of feeling this so strongly after twenty years was eerie and unexpected, and I was taken aback at my reaction. I had left Vietnam in a drugged, pain-filled stupor, having lost my arm on the battlefield while trying to kill these kind of people. I had hated them for twenty years as the epitome of evil communism. The shock of stepping out of the plane into the presence of my enemy brought all my past crashing into my present.

However, my confidence and my ability to deal with adversity had stemmed from my total belief in myself as an infantryman, and from the self-discipline I developed as a soldier and then strengthened as a patient in the hospital. Now I drew on that inner strength again. I looked at all those people and smiled right at them. I had a mission, I had a duty, and nothing was going to stop me from carrying them out.

The reaction passed quickly as my reflexes were calmed by the action of walking across to the wing tip. Butterflies had always bothered me before any action, but they left as soon as I started the task before me.

The cameras were rolling, pictures were taken, and the press introduced themselves but asked no questions. This press created no mob scene as one sees in free societies, but was polite and reserved. The foreign press was represented by what appeared to be Australians, Japanese, Chinese, and Europeans.

This seemed unusual to me because the first two countries were our allies, and Vietnam considered China its enemy. When I asked about this later, Bill and Paul said the Chinese was the loneliest reporter in Vietnam—the Vietnamese steadfastly ignored him. As for the Australian and the Japanese, we would see plenty of other American allies in Hanoi.

The welcoming group spread out to introduce themselves. Mr. Le Bang from the Ministry of Foreign Affairs was in charge. He was, as are all Vietnamese, small-boned and slightly built. When I introduced myself, he looked at me more intensely and smiled even more. He said to me in good English, "Oh, you are Mr. Fred Downs of the Veterans Administration." I was surprised, in spite of the fact we had been told that in all probability a dossier had been drawn up on each one of us. The Russians probably helped them do it, Carl and I agreed.

There were two protocol officers with Mr. Le Bang, Ms. Ha and Mr. Luong. Ms. Ha was a young, good-looking woman who got down to business by asking for our passports as we were being introduced in the hot sun. She did not waste any time. She gathered all our official passports, got into a car, and was driven over to the terminal.

Meanwhile our luggage was piled into a van, as were we, for the short drive over to the west side of the terminal where all of us were escorted into a VIP holding area while Customs and administrative procedures were facilitated. I looked back one last time at our aircraft with the beautiful logo across the side and the flag on the tail.

We went through a glass door into a short hallway with

doors off to either side. We were ushered into a room on the left at the end of the hall. This was the front of the terminal; through a hall window I could see a mob of people milling around on the sidewalk.

The section of the terminal we were in was a year old. The narrow room was air-conditioned, which was a relief, and had a high ceiling. Two rows of chairs faced each other across an Oriental rug. One chair sat at the head of the room.

We made a point of keeping the teams separate, one on each side of the room. The team leaders were given forms to fill out, listing our luggage, cameras, tape recorders, electrical equipment, and all amounts of currency we were carrying. The dong was so artificially low that the black market exchange rate was 840 dong to the U.S. dollar, in contrast to the official rate of 80 dong to the dollar. Consequently the government strictly controlled the whereabouts of all dollars brought in.

I was sitting next to the door. Mr. Le Bang arrived after arranging for refreshments, and we made small talk while waiting for the paperwork to be filled out. After my rush of adrenaline out on the ramp, I became involved with the mission and found it only a little peculiar to be talking face to face with a genuine Communist.

He asked me if I had ever been to Vietnam before. I smiled and answered, "Yes, I was an infantry officer in the South in 1967 and 1968."

He sort of nodded his head and said, "Oh." That seemed to be the end of that subject.

We asked about each other's families and showed the pictures of our wives and children we were carrying in our billfolds. He mentioned his wife and said he had two sons, the allotted number for a good party member. His wife had wanted a daughter but it was not to be; they had had their limit of children. He remarked that all couples should limit themselves to small families, but the "country people"

31

resisted such thinking. Large families were traditional in Vietnam, but there were too many people now and the population kept growing. This was bad for the future.

I was surprised at his statements—they were so forthright and he sounded so sincere. Of course I suspected that anything we heard from these people would be a Communist trick, so I had resolved to take anything we were told with a grain of salt. However, it was interesting to talk to a real Communist, even if he was probably lying.

The refreshments were brought in by two women and set on small tables between the two rows of chairs: large bottles of beer, bottles of water, and fruit. The beer looked good but Carl and I stuck with the water as being safer to drink. Bell and Webb, the old hands, didn't hesitate as they poured themselves a glass of beer. I had to admit to myself, as I sat back in air-conditioned comfort drinking a glass of water, that the VIP treatment was the way to go through Customs.

Once the administrative details of our arrival had been taken care of, Ms. Ha came back with all our papers except our passports, which she said would be returned later. We were then escorted out the front to a white van where our luggage was loaded in the back and both teams climbed into the middle seats. The driver and one of the men from the Ministry of Foreign Affairs rode in the front.

We were an object of curiosity for the sixty or seventy Vietnamese milling around out front. Some were dressed in peasant garb of black pajamas and black or white shirt, especially the older ones, but the rest were dressed in regular trousers and short-sleeve shirts. To my eyes, there did not seem to be much difference in the clothes of the men and women. Everyone was wearing thongs. The Vietnamese women did not wear skirts, but many wore the conical white straw hats I remembered so well.

They were all waiting for relatives to clear Customs. One of the Vietnam Air or Aeroflot passenger jets had discharged passengers and I could see through an open door the chaos of uniformed soldiers checking through luggage. I was certainly glad we had not had to go through that mess.

As we drove out of the airport onto the road to Hanoi, the people and the scenes around us caused a variety of feelings. Euphoria and *déjà vu* bubbled up inside of me. I was here and yet I was back in time and space twenty years earlier. Nothing had changed! Everything looked the same. There was no difference between North and South. The women wore black pajamas and conical hats, bicycles clogged the road, water buffalo toiled in the rice paddies, cone-shaped bamboo fish traps were placed in every drainage point in the fields and ditches, children played alongside the road, adults squatted in the doorways of their dwellings.

Yet something *had* changed, but it did not register with me at first, it was so obvious. What was it? Finally it struck me. There were many young men mixed in with all the people. They were doing the same things as the other people around us, going about their business. In South Vietnam I did not often see young men: they were either in the South Vietnamese Army or they were with the Viet Cong. I remembered that when we were on patrol near Duc Pho, young men were so rare that the one time we did see one in a nearby village we captured him as a Viet Cong suspect. It turned out he was a South Vietnamese soldier home for his wedding, but we did not know that until later.

Another shocker for me was to see the men on the road wearing army uniforms complete with red stars on their epaulets and headgear. Some wore caps, but pith helmets were more the order of the day. They were not carrying weapons nor moving as a unit. These were individual soldiers walking or riding bikes or motorscooters mixed in with the rest of the road traffic.

When I was here last time, these men and I would have tried to kill each other. Now we calmly studied each other, wondering where the other fellow came from and where he was going.

I looked at the red star on their uniforms and thought what a great souvenir they were in the old days. I remarked to the rest of the guys about it, and they agreed it used to be greatly coveted by American GIs. In those days you got one when you took it off the body of a man you killed. So, if a GI had one, it was a sign of honor because it had been taken in battle.

I wondered out loud if one could be bought. Bell said, "No. The red star on the cap or hat badge is an issued item, just like a weapon, and cannot be bought or borrowed. The star insignia is worn by all ages if they are on active duty. It is illegal to wear it if not on active duty. This is one way to distinguish between active duty soldiers and former soldiers who just wear the uniform because that is all they have to wear."

I ruefully wondered what the North Vietnamese considered was the best souvenir to get off an American soldier. Hell, we carried so much gear and personal items it must have been like a pygmy bringing down a bull elephant. There was an embarrassment of riches.

I knew if anyone could have read my thoughts during these moments they would have wondered at my sanity, but I could not help it. They were not frivolous or irrelevant, or sick. It was just that they were all connected to the most significant, intense, and violent period of my life.

Carl and I were snapping pictures as we rode along. We were immersed in Vietnam and there was so much to see. There were plenty of buildings along the road. Single-family dwellings were being built along both sides. The houses crowded right up to the edge of the narrow, bumpy paved road in order to take advantage of the high roadbed. The rice paddies started at their back doors.

Brick is used to build most buildings, Paul explained. The soil is of such a consistency it needs only to be dug up, shaped into rectangles, and fired in a kiln to make bricks.

There were many homes in various phases of construction; most were two stories tall. The finished ones were given a coat of a pastel color. Right below the eaves of the roof, or sticking up above the roof in some cases, the year the building was constructed stood out in colored block numbers. Most of them on this stretch of road read "1987."

This was rice country. The rice paddies at the back of the homes spread out for as far as the eye could see. The rice stalks were a beautiful bright green at that time of year, and the fields contrasted beautifully with the azure sky.

Water was everywhere. It is the lifeblood of the area. Not only is it used to flood the rice paddies but it feeds innumerable fish ponds, and I discovered from Bill that fish were also raised in the flooded rice paddies. In the middle of one five-acre pond I saw a sign with a skull and crossbones painted on it. At first I thought it meant danger, but Mr. Le Bang said it was a warning to others that the fish in this pond were spoken for.

Another food-bearing activity connected to the water was the raising of huge gaggles of ducks. Many times I saw a farmer herding ducks along a dike or path or across a rare dry field with nothing more than a long, thin switch. Back during the war I seldom saw even one duck in South Vietnam except on the rare occasion when someone going to market would have one tightly bound in a bamboo cage. The villagers must have hid them from soldiers.

Water buffalo! They were in the fields, they were on the road pulling carts and wagons, they were standing in streams and in front yards. I had never seen so many water buffalo.

There were multitudes of people in the fields working, on the road going somewhere, or standing in groups talking. Everyone we saw looked industrious.

I compared what I was seeing with what I remembered from the war-torn South I patrolled. There were never any new buildings being put up. Out in the countryside a brick structure was always a well-marked place on the map that

Americans could use as a reference point when firing artillery or calling in air support.

We would burn down hootches on a search-and-destroy mission or forcibly enter a village hootch to search for weapons and roust the people out to search them. If we found males, we tore off their shirts to see if we could find evidence of pack straps on their shoulders. If they looked of military age and could not prove why they were in the village, we tied them up and took them back as prisoners.

We rarely found anyone of military age.

When we were on patrol in South Vietnam we used to see the fish traps at the drainage areas, but we did not know the Vietnamese raised fish in the paddies, nor did we know they raised fish in ponds. It never occurred to us there were a large number of fish in the water around us. We only saw an old fisherman occasionally, and he would be using a net suspended with cord at four corners and tied to a single pole that he raised and lowered into the stream.

It was war, and we were suspicious of everything and everybody, so we did not have the time or the inclination to be interested in the people or the land. Our only interest was in surviving. Our thoughts were constantly preoccupied with the question, Can it kill us or hurt us? Any time we lost our concentration, then one of us would be killed or hurt by a booby trap, land mine, or gunshot. We could not speak the Vietnamese language, nor did we understand the Vietnamese culture. We were not tourists. We were soldiers, who had been sent to kill the enemy, and he was all around us. Our environment was treacherous and we responded in kind. We would often destroy the fish traps because we figured the Viet Cong were using them. Sometimes we took one because they made great souvenirs.

Once while guarding Bridge 101 on Highway One, a few of my men threw hand grenades in the water to stun fish. They were doing it for fun until the villagers came over to barter for the fish. Grenading fish was against the rules, so when I found out what they were doing I made them stop. We never thought we were destroying one of the villagers' food source.

Water buffalo in South Vietnam had a reputation for hating all Americans. The legends grew in our battalion of the Vietnamese water buffalos' ability to smell Americans, after which they would lower their heads and charge. During bridge duty we would be wary when the village children brought the water buffalo down to the stream to drink. The children had them under control, but we were prepared to shoot the buffalo if the kid lost control. We did not trust the evil-looking creatures. The kids did not seem to be afraid of them, though. They rode on their backs and twisted their tails.

On one search-and-destroy mission I watched a water buffalo being used for target practice by Charlie Company. It was the last day of a long four-week operation and the battalion was spread out on a low chain of foothills above the flat rice paddies. Our attention was drawn to Charlie Company's line, which was down on a dam along a small stream bordering the rice paddies. A water buffalo was running back and forth on the other side of the stream with its nose in the air preparing, we thought, to charge across the stream at Charlie Company. Somehow he must have gotten left behind when the people streamed out of the valley earlier upon our approach. In the morning from our spot in the higher mountains we had seen the people hurrying away, driving their livestock before them and carrying their belongings on the ends of those long poles they used. Getting left behind was the buffalo's bad luck. This was a search-and-destroy mission anyway, so everything was fair game. One of Charlie Company's M-79 grenade launcher squadmen fired a round at the water buffalo, hitting it in the side and knocking it down. We all cheered, but amazingly the water buffalo jumped up with a loud bellow of pain and charged across the stream. An M-60 machine gun opened up along with M-16s to pour a hail of lead into the animal, which made it across the stream before falling dead in front of Charlie Company. We thought it was great fun.

Another contrast between the war years and now were the large numbers of people around us traveling and working. I could see hundreds as we drove. In the South only a small number of farmers would work in the fields—old men, children, and women of all ages. Many of the fields had been dry and dormant. Some had the scars of harassment and interdiction (H and I) fire: artillery and mortar rounds fired at night at suspected trails, intersections, clearings, or areas where Viet Cong or NVA might be located. Any area within the radius of an American base camp was subject to H and I fire. No one knew how effective it was, but it was fired every night, all night long. If nothing else it gave us a sense of security, however false.

I even had my own form of H and I fire when we were in static positions guarding the bridges. We were attacked on a regular basis so I was allowed to use my platoon's M-79 grenade launchers as H and I fire at night.

There was a problem caused, though, by unexploded ordnance out in the flooded rice paddies. Sometimes the explosive M-79 round would not go off when it fell into the soft mud and it would lie buried a few inches under the water and mud. We made it a point to stay out of the rice paddies in the radius around our position as much as possible. When we did have to go through them, we stepped lightly. The villagers, on the other hand, would go out to work in those paddies during the day at their own risk, which they did every day. We never warned them. They lived right next door and heard what we were doing, so they must have known there was danger out there in those fields. But all the people around us were Viet Cong sympathizers, we had been told. We had no feelings for these people. Whatever happened to them was their own bad luck, we figured.

One day a convoy of American Armored Personnel Carriers left the road to dash across the paddies and one of the trucks hit an unexploded M-79 round. It wasn't powerful enough to hurt the APC, but the shock of the explosion caused an American soldier riding on top to flip off into the muddy water. He was unharmed. We all thought it was funnier than hell.

There were quite a few unexploded artillery shells fired from Fire Base Thunder out there in that soft mud. We had heard them smack into the mud at night with no explosion. If an APC ever hit one of those big rounds, it would be a different story.

Reflecting back on those days, I thought that it was no wonder there was a dearth of people around us or in the fields. We were Goddamn dangerous. We knew the Viet Cong deliberately terrorized the people, but in our own way we were dangerous simply because we did not much care for nor were we concerned about the people. No wonder we did not do a good job of winning the hearts and minds of the people. I shuddered—I was thinking blasphemous thoughts.

Back in the present, I was beginning to think I had survived the war in South Vietnam only to die in the traffic on the roads in North Vietnam. Carl and I were unprepared for the way people drove. The driver had one hand on the horn, one on the wheel, and his foot on the gas. He did not let up on any appendage. The road was paved but barely wide enough for two vehicles to pass. It was bumpy, with many dips, depressions, and holes. These combined with the weaving-and-rolling motion of the van as the driver passed with abandon and fearless disregard of oncoming trucks, bicycles, people, water buffalos, carts, and motorcycles to create the feeling of being at sea during a storm.

Indications of the French presence were part of the landscape. There were little foot-high dilapidated red-and-white mile markers off the side of the road at each kilometer, giving the name of the next town, with the remaining mileage painted below the name:

HANOI
15 KM

At a curve on Road QL 3 (QL stands for *Quoc Lo*, or National-level Highway), the bare turret from an old French tank was set in concrete on a berm from which the gunner could have commanded both approaches. It had probably been abandoned since the war with the French. The sides were shiny from where kids had been playing on it for decades. A group of children were sitting on it as we careened around the curve.

The remnants of French concrete bunkers stood at both ends of the bridges across the Ca Lo and Duong rivers. One of them was split open from the powerful explosive used by the Viet Minh to root out the French soldiers defending the bridgeheads over thirty years ago. The bunkers were lonely testimony to the battles fought for control of this land.

I had noticed as we left the airport a walled enclosure out in a field. The walls were about 5 feet high and were white or cream in color. In the middle of the enclosure was a tall 20-foot white pillar with a red star embossed on the top. Within the walls surrounding the pillar were rows of white tombstones with red stars embossing their tops. There were many of these enclosures spread here and there out in the rice paddies during the trip. After I had spotted the fifth one sitting way off in the distance, I asked about them. The JCRC team explained that they were "Hero" cemeteries— the graveyards of the soldiers who had died in the war with America or were dying in the present wars along the borders in Cambodia or along the northern border with China.

I was pleased at the large number of Hero cemeteries. They were proof we had hurt them badly during the war. I wondered how many we had killed. I had heard or read they had lost over a million men.

The JCRC team pointed to the north out of the left side of the van and told us there was the wreckage of a B-52 located beyond the horizon. The Vietnamese have never allowed the JCRC team to go to the site. I wondered why the Vietnamese continued to be so mean-spirited about letting us retrieve our dead.

At a major turnoff the JCRC guys breathed a sigh of relief. They told us if we had turned right, it would have meant the Vietnamese were going to put us up at the Thang Loi Hotel. It had been built by the Cubans and its name meant "Great Victory." It was a place the JCRC team preferred not to stay because it was on the northern edge of town and isolated. By going the way we were, it was more likely we would be staying in downtown Hanoi, which was the preferred place to be.

We were getting close to Hanoi. Off to the left I saw a biplane flying just above the trees and a herd of water buffalo working nearby. The sight of a biplane above a water buffalo looked incongruous, like so much of what I had seen in Vietnam. The Gia Lam airport, which must be the biplane's base, was off to the left. Even though it was used as a MiG base during the war, Washington refused to let it be bombed because it also doubled as Hanoi's international airport. The same could not be said for the railroad switching yard across the road. It was a target site and had been blown to hell.

The village we were in was between the airport and the large, walled-in railyard on the right. Bill Bell, as part of the American team present for the release of live U.S. POWs, was here in February and March 1973 right after the big B-52 bombing strikes in 1972. This was the Christmas bombing raid ordered by President Nixon to force the Vietnamese back to the peace table, and Bill said the whole area was devastated. Rails were twisted like pretzels and scattered everywhere. Locomotives were standing on end. Nothing was left standing, including the town we were in.

Bill said it was precision bombing at its best. The raids were designed to punish Hanoi and convince its leadership that America could make life very difficult for them. The raids worked, but our side also paid a price. I had read that the United States lost fifteen B-52s over Hanoi during the Christmas bombing. The White House and the Pentagon insisted on the bombing, and the Strategic Air Command planners in Omaha used tactics developed in the safety of those closed rooms far from the battlefield that sent those pilots and crews to their destruction.

Bill Mayall, a navigator on one of those B-52s that was shot down, was now General Vessey's executive assistant. Bill had explained to me what it was like. As I remembered his story, I wondered where the wreckage of his plane was in relation to where I was right now, sitting in this village and waiting for traffic to move.

Bill said they had taken off from U-Tapao Air Base, Thailand, late in the evening of December 21, and he was shot down around 0400 hours on December 22. The area around Hanoi had been fortified by the North Vietnamese into history's most heavily defended area against aerial attack. No aircraft had ever before had to fly over a target so well defended.

The B-52s, known as BUFs (Big Ugly Fuckers), had six-man crews. In the front cockpit was the pilot and co-pilot. Behind and below them were the bombardier navigator (Bill Mayall's position) and the radar navigator. Behind the pilot and co-pilot was the electronic warfare officer. Bill was in an older "D" model, so the tail gunner sat in a turret in the tail of the plane.

It was a night-bombing raid involving thirty B-52s. They were flying in a long chain of ten cells, three bombers to a cell. Bill's airplane was toward the end of the string, in the eighth cell. The aircraft flew across South Vietnam and turned north, where they flew almost to the Chinese border.

Then they turned south and flew in a long line toward Hanoi. It was the fourth night in a row that bombers had flown this mission. The first three nights they had been flying at set altitudes on set courses and had been ordered not to deviate from their course even if they were shot at with SAMs. It was pure hell. As the bombers approached Hanoi, the Vietnamese sent the SAMs up in droves. They had had three nights to practice on the bombers, which had flown the exact same pattern. The same altitude, the same speed, the same direction.

The bomber crews had raised so much hell about the rigid tactics that on this night they had been told they were allowed to maneuver in the target area. But by this time the Vietnamese had the range. When Bill's aircraft, at the back of the strike formation flying at 34,000 feet, reached the target area, three B-52s had already been shot down, one of them from the seventh cell, just in front of them.

On the approach to Hanoi, his bomber was struck by a tremendous blast from a SAM exploding under the nose near the crew compartment. Almost a split second later the B-52 was rocked by another SAM exploding in front of the navigator's compartment, wounding Bill in both legs and the left arm. All communication was knocked out. Bill and his partner looked at the bailout light to see if the pilot had signaled the crew to eject. The light came on and the radar navigator signaled Bill to bail out. They were buffeted by noise and they had their helmets on, so without communications working they made hand signals. The crew mate made a motion, "After you," whereupon Bill reached down and pulled his ejection lever. He pulled it right out of the housing—a severed cable dangling from the end where it had been cut by the explosion. His seat failed to fire.

Bill held the useless handle up for the other navigator to see and motioned for him to try his. Bill said the guy reached down, pulled his lever, and disappeared, just like that. In their position in the bomber the two navigators are ejected downward out of the bottom of the B-52. Bill looked over into the hole where the guy had disappeared. The aircraft was still flying level, although added to the other noises there was a loud whistling roar coming from the hole left by the ejected navigator. Bill unhooked himself from his ejection seat, refastened his parachute, and crawled over above the hole. Squatting by the edge, he tucked in his arms and rolled out into space.

When his chute opened in the pitch darkness, he saw an awesome sight. His B-52 was aflame from wing tip to wing tip and nose to tail. It continued to fly majestically out into the darkness where it descended slowly into a fogbank. An eerie glow showed its path through the fog until a brilliant flash marked its crash into the earth.

Bill descended alone. His crew would be remarkably lucky in that all six of them would survive—the only crew who bailed out in the Hanoi area during the Christmas bombings to do so. He found out later that the electronic warfare officer had ejected first, followed closely by the pilot and co-pilot, who had ejected almost immediately after hitting the bailout light. Next was the other navigator, and then the tail gunner. The tail gunner felt the blasts and knew the plane was hit, but the bailout light did not go on, the backup bailout light was dimly flickering, and the communication system was knocked out. He looked out the turret to check what the problem was and saw the airplane engulfed in flames. He lost no time in ejecting the turret glass and jumping out, the standard escape for a tail gunner.

Bill was the last man out. Consequently, he was separated from the other crew members by a distance greater than the others were from each other. The sky was beginning to get a touch of gray from the early dawn when Bill landed in a rice paddy, No one seemed to have seen him come down. He quickly discarded his chute and helmet, but before he could move he heard excited voices. He dropped into a little canal between two rice paddy dams and hugged the earth as a group of Vietnamese civilians and military jumped the canal at a run going in the direction of the crash.

44

Bill thought he had escaped detection, but one of the Vietnamese, slower than the group, came behind the others and looked both ways for a spot to cross the canal. He spotted Bill and called to the others, who started yelling and firing their rifles at him. Bill hugged the earth as bullets cracked in the air and smacked into the dirt and water around him.

Finally they stopped firing and Bill stood up with his hands in the air. The Vietnamese ran up to him and stripped him down to his underwear. They then tied him up and took him to a village, where he was thrown to the ground. After a couple of hours, he was taken to an army camp a mile or so away and loaded onto a truck containing the co-pilot and tail-gunner. Then they were taken to a field where they thought they would be executed. After an interminable wait another truck drove up with the other members of the crew in the back. They were all taken to Hoa Lo Prison, the infamous Hanoi Hilton.

Bill's legs and left arm had been severely damaged by the SAM explosion, but the Vietnamese refused to treat his wounds. After a number of days the arm had become so infected that Bill fell deathly ill. A Vietnamese doctor came into the prison: without giving Bill anything to dull the pain, he removed a piece of shrapnel and drained the wound. Bill recovered and was repatriated with the other POWs.

How ironic that Bill was now the executive assistant to General Vessey, the man leading the humanitarian effort to help Vietnam. How much more ironic it would be if the B-52 crash site over the horizon to our left was his aircraft.

Everything in Gia Lam had been rebuilt. Large modern buildings to house the locomotives, railcars, and workshops could be seen jutting up behind the high brick fence enclosing the railyards. The village was all rebuilt. The houses had "1981" and "1979" on the roof.

We were sitting still waiting for a traffic jam to clear. This made for a good opportunity to watch the people. There were people squatting in the open doors of their houses and sheds tending to their duties in a mixture of activities along the street that encompassed their lives. Little stands made of wood sold one or two products, usually cigarettes or something in a bottle to drink. The proprietor and his friends or customers were sitting under a woven reed mat suspended at its four corners by thin bamboo poles.

In the side lots I saw many rusty, greasy mechanical parts and engines in various stages of being stripped down. I also noticed something which I would see again many times. Wherever or whoever is working on a whatever, there will always be a number of his friends sitting around on their haunches passing the time of day with him and with each other. Lots of people are out of work. But still, throughout my trip there was always a feeling of industriousness on the part of the Vietnamese.

Finally the traffic jam broke and we moved forward. There was a large pond at a fork in the road between the village and the railroad. I wondered if one of those bombs dropped from a B-52 was a dud and was still lying under the water or mud unexploded. It would be a shame in this peaceful setting. Seeing the mudbank made me recall the dormant H and I rounds in the mud around our perimeters in the South.

We took the left fork, which led to the new bridge over the Song Hong into Hanoi, the Chuong Duong Bridge. Joe Harvey said it was a much faster way to cross than the old bridge, which we saw a kilometer upstream. The infamous Paul Doumer Bridge (the Vietnamese Long Bien Bridge) was named after the French governor general of Indochina when it was built at the turn of the century. Doumer's name occasioned a famous joke in Vietnamese classrooms. A teacher asked a student a question and the kid couldn't answer. The teacher said he would ask him one more question, and if he did not answer he would be in trouble. He then asked the student who built that bridge, and the student, frustrated, simply said, *"Du Me* (Motherfuck!),"* and the teacher said, "That's correct. It was Paul Doumer!"

During the war with the Americans, the 5,532-foot bridge was the only bridge across the Red River within 50 kilometers of Hanoi. Consequently, it was a prime target. It had been successfully blown up five times. The Vietnamese had it surrounded with over one hundred antiaircraft guns and further protected it with SAM sites.

It looked like it had caught hell. With all the various bridge parts used to patch it up, the Doumer Bridge looked like an old warrior, a crazy quilt of a bridge. The Vietnamese traffic had to constantly change directions in the two lanes, one going into and one out of town, to keep the bridge from weakening on one side. This may have been due to movement or the weight of the loads (in full, out empty), or both. Looking at it across the water was like being back in the war.

Joe Harvey told us that before they built this new bridge, they would get stuck on the old bridge for hours. It had one lane running each way with a railroad track down the middle. If someone's oxcart broke down in the middle, there was no way to go around.

The one we were on looked like an old steel-frame bridge built in America in the early part of this century—tough and durable.

I looked down at the silt-laden water rushing by a few feet below and saw again why this was called the Red River. It was the same color as the bricks used in the buildings. In a moment of reflection I glanced back at the rice paddies and felt relieved not to have to worry about taking fire from the treeline. I turned my attention to what was ahead.

It had taken twenty years, but at last we had arrived in Hanoi. When I was a soldier we had wanted to invade Hanoi, and here it was finally before us. Suddenly we reached the end of the bridge and were looking out over the city from atop a levee about the height of a big oak. The view was of a peaceful pastoral setting.

Hanoi spreads out on the west side of the river and looks

like an old faded painting of a French provincial town. Crowded French-style buildings two to three stories high, with roofs of weathered, blackish-red tile, line the narrow, tree-shaded streets. The stucco-covered buildings were painted in peeling pastel colors and had fancy ornamental ironwork balconies projecting from the second and third stories. Louvered shutters covered the windows and doors or stood open to admit the light and air. The haze of the hot August afternoon sun lent the city a Monet quality. I found it difficult to imagine B-52 bombers or other fighter bombers over the city.

The van turned left down off the levee onto Tran Quang Khai, the wide main street running along the river. We were immersed in the hustle and bustle of Hanoi. The street was crowded with traffic and lined with shops, many of which were for bicycle repair.

Within three blocks the van turned right on Tran Nguyen Han Street, went a short block, then turned left onto a wide boulevard, Pho Ly Thai To. Ahead of us on the next block stood a massive stone building that looked like it could be a bank building back home. It was an imposing French-colonial building, with wide steps and tall Greek columns in the front. A large billboard was built onto the front of the roof with a gigantic head-and-shoulder picture of Ho Chi Minh looking out over the city.

I asked what that important-looking building was. Probably party headquarters, I figured.

"It is the bank," Joe answered.

There was a park across the street and the driver turned right onto Le Thach Street, bordering the park. Midway down the block he turned left into a driveway, went through a gate with two soldiers standing guard, and pulled up to a six-story apartmentlike building. The JCRC team said this was a good sign because it was the government guesthouse, the best place in the city the government can put guests in.

The walled compound of the guesthouse enclosed a

quarter of a block. The guesthouse itself was located at the back of the compound, and a magnificent three-story yellow French colonial-style home was located in the front. It looked out onto Ngo Quyen Street, which angled off the street in front of the bank. The two buildings in the compound were separated by a nicely kept flower garden. A small motor pool was located over against the far wall. A huge tree higher than the roof stood in front of the guesthouse.

We entered through large, curtained glass doors opening onto a white marble-floored foyer. To the right of the foyer was a big meeting room with a double row of chairs facing each other. We went in through a set of glass doors framed in dark wood.

Mr. Le Bang, Ms. Ha, and the other Vietnamese who had met us at the airport were sitting in one row; we sat down in the other row, facing them. The chairs had wicker backs and bottoms and were low and long in the seat. Water was brought in and placed on end tables between the chairs.

Mr. Le Bang told us it was late in the day, so the Vietnamese Delegation would meet with us tomorrow. We had braced for many hostile actions or attitudes from the Vietnamese but so far they had been very friendly. Carl asked him who would be meeting with our team. We were worried the Vietnamese Delegation would not have medical people meeting with us, only politicians. Le Bang assured us that a number of medical people would be attending the meetings.

He smiled and said, "Of course, some Foreign Ministry people, including myself, will be there to guide them. I will be a guided missile." He laughed in a good-natured way.

Le Bang said all our meals would be served in the dining hall across the foyer and we were free to do as we wished until 0830 hours on the 26th, the next day. Whereupon we all stood, shook hands with each other, and prepared to go up to our rooms to unpack while they filed out to the two small black Russian cars, Ladas, and sped away. A larger Russian car, a Volga used by VIPs, was parked over by the side of the motor pool.

I peeked into the dining room. The room was a mirror image of the meeting room, except it had tables set for meals and there was a kitchen through a doorway at the back. Meals were served at specific times, so we had better not miss them, Joe and other members of the team told us.

Both of the large rooms on the ground floor had air conditioning which overflowed into the foyer, helping to keep it cooler than outside, which was brutally hot.

We were given our room assignments by one of the employees of the guesthouse. There was no elevator in this building, so we picked up our luggage to carry it upstairs to the second floor. I walked up the marble steps, passing from the layer of cool air in the foyer up into the hot, muggy air of the mezzanine. What miserable weather! The next flight of steps took us up into the even hotter, muggier air on our floor. Sweat poured off us. There was not a dry spot on my clothes.

Our team was in the rooms down the left hallway. I was in Room 105, Carl in 109, and Larry in 106. Joe, Paul, Johnie, and Bill were down the other hallway.

An old-fashioned skeleton key was in the lock of my room. I pushed open the door, after first nodding at the man and woman who were standing at the end of the corridor watching us. Their job was to police the hallway, clean the rooms, and change the sheets. We kidded among ourselves that they were also responsible for changing the tapes on the recording machines we suspected were hidden in our rooms.

My room opened into a 5-foot-long passageway with a bathroom door to the left. I stood in the doorway trying to take it all in. I was in Hanoi! I took my stuff in and started unpacking. The room was spartan but neat and clean. A freestanding wooden clothes closet stood against the wall next to the door. Next to the closet was a small brown refrigerator. It was empty. Beside it stood two wicker-bottomed chairs with a wooden table between them. A light green bottle of water sat on the table, accompanied by two water glasses. A cone-shaped paper cup was upside down on the bottle.

I was dying for a drink but I was suspicious as hell of any water. I picked the paper cone up to see if the bottle was sealed. It wasn't. I thought about it for a few minutes, then decided it wasn't worth it. I would wait.

Against the opposite wall were two single beds made of wood. Above each bed pinned to the wall was a folded mosquito net ready to be pulled down to drape over the bed. A wooden nightstand with a dainty lamp on it stood between the beds. Between the second bed and the outside wall was a simple wooden desk and chair. Another dainty lamp stood on the corner of the desk. The light bulbs were only about 20 watts and both of the lamps had tiny red shades. The red corrugated shades made the room look innocent in a homey sort of way, like a child's room.

The outer wall of my room was floor-to-ceiling glass panels in wood frames. A wood-framed glass door led out onto a cement balcony. Heavy dark curtains hung over the windows but not the door. My room was on the front side of the guesthouse. When I went out onto the balcony, I could look down into the courtyard and across into the back of the yellow French-colonial house. Ho Chi Minh smiled at me from his vantage point on top of the bank.

An air conditioner in the panel next to the door was laboring mightily, rattling with a noise close to what a Harley Davidson motorcycle with straight pipes sounds like as it goes down a steep grade in low gear. The whole glass wall vibrated. All to no avail, for the air in the room was suffocatingly hot. A thin stream of air was pushed out in a trickle from the machine, but the heat was so intense it smothered it. Three feet in front of the machine there was no breeze.

Sweat poured off me in rivulets as I unpacked my suitcase. I wondered if the Vietnamese were bothered by the heat.

51

Strange that I should have that thought now. I had never cared before how the Vietnamese felt about anything.

On the desk I laid out my paraphernalia: paper, pens, camera, address book, and two special talismans. One was a little American flag and the other was a picture of my two-year-old daughter Kate and twenty-one-year-old daughter Teri. I sat at the desk looking at both and thinking of all that had passed these last twenty years. And I pondered the thoughts I had had as I rode in from the airport.

I did not feel like a stranger in a strange land. I was glad to be here. I felt different than I thought I would feel. Were these people really still my enemy? I had never entertained this question before.

I got up and went into the bathroom to see what it was like. The bidet, commode, sink, and tub were of a heavy white porcelain style from the thirties. A glass shelf ringed by a chrome bar was set above the sink. A 10-gallon hot-water heater hung from the ceiling behind the door. Like everything else I had seen, it looked old. The shower was a chrome hose hooked to the tub, there was no shower curtain. A wooden grate was on the floor next to the tub. Two thin hand towels were hanging on the towel rack and there was a gaily wrapped bar of soap in the soap dish. A bottle of water stood on the glass shelf. It was stoppered with a plastic cap, so I decided to take a chance and drink from it. Oh, it tasted good in that heat. I prayed I wouldn't get diarrhea.

A cockroach the size of a mouse was the king of the bathroom. He was not afraid of me and I did not mind his company. I hated the thought of stepping on him in the middle of the night, though. He wasn't the type to run away just because he heard me coming to the bathroom. I resolved to turn the light on before I stepped into the room.

I was totally drenched with sweat when Carl knocked on my door. We were eager to explore the city around the guesthouse. Contrary to what we had expected, Mr. Le Bang had said there were no restrictions on our activity. The

JCRC team confirmed that they roamed the city freely and it was safe to do so. We banged on the door for Larry, and headed off to see what we could see.

We walked out the front of the guesthouse and turned left to walk out of the gate. Three young soldiers were at the guardhouse at the entrance. Their uniforms were sea green with red epaulets; gold stars lined the epaulets, the number of stars varying according to rank. They each wore a green cap with a black visor, and at their hip a pistol in a black leather holster with a flap strapped to a black belt. They were in sandals. The uniforms looked clean, but worn and slightly shabby.

We turned left out of the gate onto Le Thach Street to walk the half block to Dinh Tien Hoang, a wide boulevard bordering the east side of Ho Hoan Kiem, the Lake of the Restored Sword. When we reached the corner we could see the Nephrite Pagoda, "the Turtle Pagoda," in the middle of the lake. At the north end we could see the Hue Bridge (Sunshine Bridge) connecting the shore with another pagoda, the Ngoc Son Pagoda.

Bill Bell had told us the name of the lake and the pagodas when we arrived. All Vietnamese know of this lake. There is a legend, Bill said, that long ago, when the Vietnamese people were suffering under the harsh yoke of the Chinese Ming Dynasty, a blade was provided by the waters of the lake. On the blade was an inscription: "Obey the Commands of Heaven." General Le Loi took the blade and matched it with a sword handle inlaid with nephrite that he had found hanging in a tree in the jungle.

This sword became a terrible weapon in the hands of General Le Loi, enabling him to destroy Vietnam's enemies without mercy. With the help of this sword, the Vietnamese drove their conquerors from the land. After the wars, when General Le Loi was boating on the lake, a great golden turtle rose to the surface next to the boat and told the general that he must return the sword to the King of Dragons. General

Le Loi delivered the sword back to the waters of the lake. The Turtle Pagoda was built in the lake to commemorate this event.

A street vendor on the corner was selling postcards, envelopes, note pads, and other gee-gaws. Her stand was a wood box with an umbrella over it to provide shade. We tried to buy postcards with U.S. dollars but she kept shaking her head. She refused to accept anything but dong, which we did not have. We had to give up, which was a disappointment because the post office was next door. We could have mailed cards out immediately.

We stood on the curb just to watch the people for a few minutes and to get our bearings. Bicycles, bicycles, and more bicycles. There were a couple of motorbikes, a very few cars, and once in a while a truck would drive by. The vehicles all had one thing in common: they were all old and beat-up-looking. It was amazing they were still in working order, they looked so dilapidated.

Everything and everybody seemed drab, which added to the ancient look of the city. There were no brightly colored clothes, vehicles, or buildings. All the colors were muted, with a grayish dusty overtone. Whenever a young lady dressed in bright colors did come by on a bicycle, she stood out starkly.

The city was shabby and obviously poor. Streets, curbs, sidewalks, and buildings all had cracks and holes in them and were in need of repair. The high temperature and humidity is brutal, which may be the reason in this tropical climate everything looks faded. It takes money to keep paint looking good and to repair streets and buildings. This was an economically depressed country with no money to spend on upkeep.

Before I left the States I read that the United Nations had just ranked Vietnam 162nd out of 164 nations as to level of prosperity. The poverty was evident all around us and would become more so during our visit.

The busy streets were strangely quiet. The thousands of

bicycles were silently pedaled by Vietnamese intent on going somewhere. There was no conversation between the riders, just concentration on the road ahead. Many of the bicycles had passengers, though, and they didn't seem to mind looking around. We saw one bicycle that had a man pedaling with a child on the handlebars and a woman with a baby in arms riding sidesaddle on the rear fender seat.

To be in a city of 2 million people in which traffic is so quiet was an eerie but pleasant experience. There were, of course, hundreds of people walking. The fact that everyone walks or rides a bicycle makes Hanoi a very human city. This became more evident as we strolled around the lake. What a contrast to Bangkok's cacophonous environment!

Not all was sweet silence, however. The occasional car or truck could be heard well before it was seen. The horns on all vehicles in Hanoi blare, beep, or honk in a continuous and raucous machine-gun staccato as they bully their way through the crowd. It was a good thing there were not more vehicles, or the noise would have been deafening.

We watched the traffic pattern for a while before trying to cross the street, but finally we just started out. This was tricky business. Crossing the street was a game of chicken for us until we got the hang of it. The traffic moved on the right side just like in the States, but halfway across, Carl and I stopped and sort of pulled in our stomachs from the traffic coming the other way. At the same time we kept an eye on our asses stuck out in traffic behind us. While we had lost courage and were stalled out at the middle lane, roly-poly Larry sailed serenely across like a barge crossing the bay. We couldn't stay where we were, so we started on. We learned that if we kept moving at a steady pace, the bicyclists could accurately judge how to pass by us with inches to spare and continue on their merry way.

We discovered later that major intersections were an intriguing phenomenon to watch. There were only a few stop lights and signs in Hanoi, so everyone was on their own except at rush hour, when a traffic cop tried to control a few busy intersections. There were solid streams of bicycles that a city of 2 million produced.

A cement walkway of about a mile's length bordered the oblong lake, and we turned right to stroll to its northern side. There were lots of people around the lake sitting, playing, and talking, just like any other park in the world.

In one little grassy section containing a couple of dozen flowering bushes, three or four enterprising young men had set up individual photography businesses, taking portraits. They were competitors, and each had a 3-by-3-foot board displaying examples of his work. Business seemed to be good.

Several girls were waiting their turn while others prepared to have their picture taken. They had gotten some rouge and lipstick somewhere and they had on their best blouses, usually a brightly colored one or a new white one with a colorful scarf. They were combing out their hair and fussing with themselves like any Western girl preparing for a date. One or two of their friends would be shyly laughing and giggling while helping each girl to prepare.

When her turn came, the girl would sit in a demure pose next to one of the flowering bushes while the cameraman snapped her picture. It would be interesting to know where these guys got their cameras because they were working with some real antiques. One had an old Brownie box camera, one an old Kodak, and so on—old tourist cameras. From the evidence of the pictures on their display boards, they did pretty good work.

Later on, Bill and Paul explained to me how the girls acquired the make-up they were using. This society was so poor and the shortages so great that there were few cosmetics in Hanoi. Existing cosmetics were so rare they were used with frugal care and were the basis for doorway businesses.

Lipstick and rouge were sold by the smear: a shop set up in an open doorway on the street would sell a smear of lipstick or a smear of rouge. The girls lined up outside one of these shops and paid their money to the old lady behind the door. The old lady would then put a smear of the lipstick or rouge on the girl's lips and cheeks. There was a mirror next to the door which the girl used to smooth out the cosmetics evenly. Then off she went.

Bell had told us the three biggest businesses in Hanoi were refilling ballpoint pens, fixing flats, and selling lipstick by the smear. I thought he was kidding until we started walking the streets of Hanoi.

I was fascinated when I first saw one of the doorway shops that specialized in refilling ballpoint pens. The shop was typical of those found all over Hanoi. A half door or low shelf in the doorway provided a table on which the proprietor's tools of his trade were laid out. A light-colored cloth covered the shelf. Two or three well-used and empty ballpoint plastic ink tubes were lined up on display in a neat row on the ink-stained cloth. In one corner of the shelf stood an ink bottle, and next to it, an old-style hypodermic needle. A scribbled-on paper pad used to test the refilled pen lay in the middle of the shelf. Occasionally complete pens were also laid out for sale.

I stood by the doorway to watch the process of refilling. The inkman would pull the ballpoint out of the end, insert the hypodermic needle into the inkpot, and pull up on the plunger, sucking ink into the container. Then he would hold the ink tube with one hand and insert the needle into the length of the tube. As he slowly withdrew the needle he simultaneously pushed the plunger, thereby filling the tube up with ink. Afterwards he would reinsert the ballpoint back into the tube and scribble on the pad until the ink started running. Voilà! A satisfied customer.

Christ! I swore to myself as I walked away. We Americans take so much for granted. I was carrying in my shirt pocket two cheap, perfectly functioning ballpoint pens that I would just nonchalantly throw away when they ran out of ink. A couple of borders away in Bangkok, a country with a capitalist economy, I could buy new pens as cheaply as I could in the States.

I never saw so many flat tires in my life as I did in Vietnam. From the time we left Noi Bai Airport until we returned there four days later, there would inevitably be someone in our vicinity working on a flat tire. I once worked for a year at a truck stop on Highway 41 in West Terre Haute, Indiana, fixing flat tires, and I never saw such a stream of flat tires as I did in Vietnam. They use inner tubes in Vietnam; a tubeless tire was as unheard of here as it was in America fifty years ago. Vietnam's rough roads and inferior tires made a tubeless tire useless. In Hanoi they did not have new tires for sale, nor would anyone have the money to buy them if they were available. The tread on most of the commercial vehicles I saw had what my dad used to call "mouse bellies." This was a tire so worn through that the wrapping forming the core of the tire showed its different layers. It made no difference how worn the tire was, the owner was forced to keep repairing and reusing it until it was impossible to repair.

Even then they would not throw it away. The Vietnamese would always find a use for whatever remained. I remembered during the war in the South a great souvenir to take off of a dead NVA soldier was his pair of Ho Chi Minh slippers. This was the name we gave to the sandals the NVA wore. The soles of the sandals were cut from used tires, and strips of used inner tubes were used as straps to hold them on the feet. The tire tread on the bottom always provided us with the opportunity to joke about the mileage a soldier had gotten before we killed him. I noticed that a few people in the streets still wore Ho Chi Minh slippers.

Again and again I was to see examples of how the Vietnamese used everything until it simply disintegrated. Then they would use whatever was left to repair something else. Bill Bell made a remark later that explained it perfectly: "These people are too poor to generate trash."

Carl, Larry, and I were dripping sweat from every pore as we walked the pathway, observing the people and in turn being observed by them. Three Americans strolling along the Lake of the Restored Sword was not an everyday sight. The kids were fascinated by my hook, as kids are everywhere. They bravely gathered around us, their faces expressing curiosity, awe, and wonderment. They would politely follow along with us for a short distance until their watchful parents called their names.

This was in stark contrast to when I was in the South during the war. There the children in the villages close to the American camps and along the main roads would flock around begging for cigarettes, food, candy, and money. A few of them would pimp for the girls. It was always startling to see a four-year-old child squatting in the dirt, puffing away on a cigarette he had bummed off a GI. They were notorious thieves and we learned to hate the little bastards when they wouldn't leave us alone. They would scream obscenities at us and say we were "number fucking ten" when they didn't get what they wanted from us. If they were happy with us, they said we were "number fucking one." That didn't happen very often. When we were in convoy riding on the road, the kids would hear us coming and would run up to the side with their hands out, begging for goodies. They would wave their middle finger at us in what they thought was a form of friendly American greeting. Sometimes the soldiers would maliciously throw heavy cans of C-rations from the speeding vehicles at the outreaching children. More than once I saw a child knocked down from the force of the blow. It was his own hard luck, for the other kids would swarm toward the can, fighting for it. The dazed kid never even got to share in the booty, near as I could tell. I ordered my men never to do that and none of them ever did to my knowledge.

The children out in the country villages away from the main roads and the influence of the Americans were much nicer because they acted like normal kids and did not beg or plague us with shrill demands to buy this or that. Not being around Americans, they couldn't understand or speak any English. I always remembered that those kids were afraid of us and would hide behind their mothers and grandparents when we went through their villages looking for the Viet Cong, or evidence of their presence. If we were in the mood while on patrol through a village where the kids were nice, we would hand out cigarettes and candy to them to show them we were nice guys and not to be frightened of us.

We reached the north end of the lake. Tracks for a trolley line ran along the road bordering the lake. About twenty people were sitting at an open-sided shelter waiting for the trolley to arrive. This area formed a large intersection where five streets branched off. Shops occupied the ground floor in the three-story stucco French-style buildings facing the intersection. We could see the bustle of people wandering in and out of shops along the street.

The late-afternoon sun was still above the rooftops. Its rays struck full force into the open area of the intersection at the end of the lake, baking the concrete. The air did not stir, a haze of dust hung low in the sky, and glints from multitudes of insects sparkled against the sun. Time seemed to slow almost to a halt as the Vietnamese in the shaded shelter spotted us, stopped talking, and turned to look at us for a moment. We noticed a stillness in the lull of traffic. The sense of being in the early thirties sunk in as I registered the French buildings, the berets on the waiting passengers, the quiet bicycles, an antiquated French trolley pulling into the stop, and a very old Mercedes-Benz.

I think we all felt it, and I attributed it to the hot sun and the lack of a drink of water. I walked over to the lake to see what the water looked like. I had seen a father with his child squat by the edge and cool himself and his child with water he scooped up in his hands. I was curious as to the lake's cleanliness.

The water was cloudy, with the dirty gray look of sewage and runoff from gutters. I was to find out later that polio and other infectious diseases were rampant throughout Vietnam. I remembered the father and child at this lake when I heard this report. Although we Americans are properly afraid of the water in countries like Vietnam because of the danger it holds for us, we often forget or do not realize the water is just as dangerous to the people who live there.

The unsanitary-looking and smelly water did not invite one to cool off. I shuddered to think how sick it could make me. The sight and smell of it reminded me of the rice paddy water we used to drink when on patrol or an operation. We knew the Vietnamese peasants fertilized their fields with animal waste and their own feces because we had observed them doing this many times. However, our desire for water during the hot season when we were out on a mission overcame our abhorrence of the rice paddy water, sometimes the only water we could find. We would put a half package of Kool Aid in a canteen to hide the taste and a couple of iodine tablets to purify it as best we could. In spite of the iodine tablets I still got five separate infections during my six months in the field. Afterwards in the hospital the medical staff got rid of most of those little microorganisms, but it took Fitzsimons Army Hospital in Aurora, Colorado, five years to purge my system of worms.

We continued our walk on around the lake to the western side, which was shaded by tall trees and the late-afternoon shadows cast by the buildings across the street. It was cooler here in the shade, and the number of people taking advantage of the coolness was evident.

It was on the western side of the lake, as we walked through the park watching the activity around us, that a latent thought unexpectedly struck me. I noticed all around me a number of fathers who had their son or daughter with them on an outing or spin around the lake. A father dressed in his Sunday best would be riding his bike, with his child sitting in a seat on the rear fender, or he would be walking alongside his bicycle pushing it while his child rode up on the seat. Both the father's and the child's faces showed obvious delight at this activity.

A great deal of love, affection, and pride was evident. I did not expect to see this from a hard-core Vietnamese. "Hard-core" was the term we used to describe the tough Viet Cong or the North Vietnamese Army soldiers. We believed they felt life was cheap and meant nothing. Life was nothing, so death was nothing, or so we thought. In fact we thought all Orientals were like that in disregarding the value of human life. That was one reason it was easy to hate them. There were plenty of stories about how the Oriental thought his water buffalo was more important than a human life. One common rumor during the war was if you were in a vehicle that hit and killed both a buffalo and a man, then you had to pay $400 to the family for the water buffalo but only a few bucks for the man.

If Orientals' lives never meant anything to them, then it was easy for us to rationalize that they sure as hell didn't mean anything to us either. This made it easier to kill them. It also made it easier to deal with the noncombatants because they were all the same. Dinks. Gooks.

This is a common mind-set in wartime and is practiced by both sides to develop hate and focus on the enemy. Obviously, though, I had not shed those hateful thoughts and emotions after the war. Even though I considered myself a well-balanced person, I was shocked to find within myself such limitations that I would be surprised to see love for a child on the face of my former enemy.

This realization would bear considerable contemplation on my part. Somehow I was not deprogrammed from my feelings about the Vietnamese left over from the war. It probably had a lot to do with America's negative feelings against Vietnam veterans for so many years. Going through a war was bad enough, but having your own country blame you for it afterwards was doubly hard to take.

These were good thoughts to be thinking. I was working through some things in my mind and I was feeling exceptionally good. Looking around at the big trees we were walking under, I felt comforted by their presence. They were like the oak trees back home and gave me a sense of security.

About halfway around the lake we met the one and only

beggar child we saw in Hanoi. He was more ragged than the other children, who were wearing clean and neat clothes. I discovered later he was probably an orphan without any family to take him in. The Vietnamese, I was also to discover, traditionally have a very close-knit family and feel a responsibility to take care of family members, but they do not feel responsible for others outside the family. If you have no family, then you are on your own. There is much disease in Vietnam and so there are many orphans with no place to go or no one to care for them. There are some orphanages, but they are few and overloaded.

This particular child was quickly scolded by a teenager wearing a white blouse and a red scarf. She gave us an embarrassed smile as she shooed him away. Carl said she was probably a Red Pioneer, which was a Communist youth group.

We completed our walk on the west side, and then crossed the street through heavy bicycle traffic to visit what Larry said was the major department store in Hanoi. We walked into the big open double doors across a cement threshold. The air inside was so heavy and stagnant with the heat and people milling around, I felt like I couldn't breathe.

The store reminded me of a large warehouse sale in the States at the end of a successful day. There was hardly anything on the shelves. The floor was littered with dirt and the walls were cracking and peeling. The display counters were sixty years old if they were a day. Anything on display was behind dirty glass panels. What there was didn't look like much. There would be three soap boxes stacked in a pyramid. One sweater. One hat. One pair of plastic sandals. Five bottles of different-colored liquid.

Most of the items were unobtainable. Everything is distributed on a quota system, and the stores can only sell so much of an item, if they have it at all, each day. We decided we didn't see anything we couldn't live without, so we decided to return to the guesthouse for dinner.

When we left the store, six young soldiers were lounging

on the corner. They were dressed in green uniforms and caps and wore sandals. They had no weapons. They were very friendly and let us take their picture as we walked by, crowding around in poses for a couple of shots. They seemed remarkably young.

Most of the soldiers we saw did not carry guns. I noticed this right away because in my mind's eye I always pictured the Vietnamese with a gun in hand. In the South, of course, during the war all soldiers, American and Army of the Republic of Vietnam (ARVN), were always armed, and all propaganda from the North always showed everyone armed, even the peasants. That image had always stuck with me: Vietnam as an armed camp. It now seemed like a normal country.

To our left as we walked up the street was the park across from the guesthouse. A large, grass-covered air-raid bunker sat in the park across the street from the back door of the post office. There were entrances sunk into the ground on two sides of the bunker. Air pipes stuck out of the top near the back. The closed steel doors were rusted, and the neglected entrances filled with the litter from blowing leaves, branches, and dirt. We could see concrete edges, but grass had grown over most of the dirt-covered bunker, giving it a gentle appearance.

I looked around at the buildings and thought of the people running for cover during an air raid. Even though the United States did not directly bomb Hanoi, the people would not have known that ahead of time. There were some accidents from misplaced bombs, and it had been dangerous in the city with all the falling shrapnel from antiaircraft guns, spent bullets and shells, and exploding SAM missiles. Also, the occasional American jet crashed into the city.

More than once I had been in a bunker under attack and I knew for a fact it was not a pleasant experience. But at least I was armed and could fight back. More than that, I was a soldier and war was my job. The civilians who used this bunker must have felt totally helpless. My wife's godparents lived in London during World War II and I would have them explain it to me some day. I personally never liked the feeling of being in a readymade tomb.

We turned into the gate to the compound and met up with the JCRC team coming back from their foray. They were carrying something wrapped in newspapers. We asked what it was and they told us it was beer. These old hands had been coming to Hanoi for years and they had their priorities straight. While we had been out sightseeing they had been tracking down every beer they could to store in the room refrigerators.

As we went up the stairs I asked where we could go to get beer. The guys said nowhere. All the places had already sold their quotas, there wasn't any beer to be had. We could go try if we wanted. Maybe we could find some if we looked hard enough. What the hell, I thought, I have to go on a scavenger hunt to get a beer?

Bell said that each place that sells beer gets only a certain quota for any one-time period, be it a week or whatever. Therefore the shopkeeper divided his quota into so many bottles a day so he could have a little beer to sell each day until the next quota was delivered. Shops and offices normally choose one person to get off early and go to the bar and order many glasses of beer before everyone gets off. They put all the glasses in the center of the table until everyone shows up after work.

The meals were served only at specific times, so we washed up and went down for our first meal. When we entered through the dining-room doors, we saw our table set for seven. The JCRC team sat on one side and our team sat facing them; that is how we sat for the rest of the meals.

We were fed like kings. There may have been people starving in Vietnam but the kitchen didn't show it. They brought out course after course of Vietnamese-style food. The chef was excellent. Besides the food, there was beer and bottled water on the table.

The nuoc mam sauce made from fermenting fish smelled so strong it almost gagged Carl. Bell and Johnie showed us how to mix it properly to use with the food. Carl said there was no way he was eating that foul-smelling stuff. It smelled the way we remembered it in South Vietnam. In the platoon we often claimed we could smell nuoc mam sauce a couple of kilometers downwind. However, the sauce in the Vietnamese restaurants in the States did not smell bad, so my wife had wondered why I talked about it smelling so strong. I had wondered about that myself, so I asked Bell.

He said that there were two basic versions of nuoc mam, one cut with water, sugar, and sliced carrots, which was the one served in American Vietnamese restaurants, and another that was full strength. Even though the full strength smelled a little stronger, it was no worse than tabasco sauce or garlic sauce. However, most GIs who recall the strong smell of nuoc mam were actually remembering when it was being used as a cooking oil. The aroma of nuoc mam is amplified about a hundred times if it is placed in a hot pan and evaporated into the air. Add a little garlic and it is worse. An American soldier never forgot its malodorous smell, and for some, even the mild smell of the table version would upset their stomach.

Chopsticks, rice, and tea were part of the table service. But the one thing which was a pleasant surprise was the white bread served to us. It had sort of a smoky, musty flavor, but it tasted good. It tasted so good we ate a lot of it to offset the very Vietnamese flavor of the food. The bread was wonderful, but inside were crunchy black specks about the size of poppy seeds. When we asked what that was, the JCRC team to a man gleefully informed us those were weevils which live in the flour and are baked right along with the bread.

"Adds protein," Joe chuckled.

I paused with a slice of bread halfway to my mouth and studied the slice. Yeah, those black things did look like insects. I remembered my queasiness when reading of

Horatio Hornblower eating weevils in his biscuits. It didn't bother Hornblower. I bit into the bread and finished it off. The bread did taste okay, especially with butter. You just had to ignore the cracking sound the baked weevils made when you crunched them between your teeth.

After dinner, the two teams went for another walk. The night gave us a different perspective. The heat had not let up a bit, though; if anything the air was more oppressive. The humidity was so high, sweat wouldn't evaporate and our clothes were wet rags on our bodies. Worse was the sticky, clammy feeling on our skin. The stump of my arm stuck to the sides of the prosthesis and the socket cut into my armpit. I decided August was not a good tourist season for Vietnam.

We went past the guards at the gate and walked toward the lake. We turned left toward the intersection and rambled along while the JCRC team members told us about Hanoi and what we were seeing. The real bonus for our team on this trip was having the JCRC people with us. They have been going into Vietnam for years, ever since the Paris Peace Accords in 1973, and they definitely know the ropes.

Bill Bell had gone "native," the other members of his team good-naturedly kidded him. He was that rare American who knew the language fluently, both written and spoken. He was always going into Hanoi bookstores to browse and buy Vietnamese magazines and books and he never missed an opportunity to read a Vietnamese newspaper. He said the Vietnamese party was now allowing constructive criticism to be printed in the newspapers. His favorite feature was the letters-to-the-editor column where the average Joe could write in and complain about or report waste and abuse. Sometimes actual names, positions, vehicle numbers, and the like, were reported and he believed it was authentic. Bill claimed to get a good feel for what was happening in the country and to the people by reading the newspapers.

Bill's involvement with Vietnam started in 1966 when he was an airborne-infantryman in his first tour with the

1/35th Infantry battalion of the 25th Infantry Division. He came back for a second tour with the 101st Airborne Division, and in 1967 he transferred to the 525th Military Intelligence, where his ability to speak Vietnamese was a great asset. He stayed on in Vietnam. In January 1973, when the Paris Peace Accords were signed, there was a provision for a Four Party Joint Military Commission whose task it was to carry on the search and account for missing individuals. The members included representatives from the United States, the Republic of Vietnam (South Vietnam), the Democratic Republic of Vietnam (North Vietnam), and the Provisional Revolutionary Government (Viet Cong). Bill was assigned to that team, and at the end of the war his title was Chief of Liaison, U.S. Delegation, Four Party Joint Military Commission. He was responsible for liaison between the U.S. Delegation and the other three delegations, plus the various delegations to the International Commission for Control and Supervision (ICCS). This commission was an international supervisory force formed as a requirement of the Paris Peace Talks. The ICCS was a miserable failure. It was supposed to stop violations made by both the North and South Vietnamese.

During the war, Bill was married to an American and they had lived with their two children in Saigon in the seventies when he was working liaison with the various delegations involved in the ceasefire mechanism. As South Vietnam crumbled from North Vietnam's spring offensive in 1975, Bill's wife had volunteered to work with a joint U.S. government and private group to fly thousands of Vietnamese orphans to America for adoption. When the first load on a U.S. Air Force C-5A took off on April 4, it was carrying 243 South Vietnamese babies and 62 adults who were being evacuated from Vietnam. Bill's wife, ten-year-old son, and five-year-old daughter were on that flight. Tragedy struck a half hour later when the plane's aft pressure door exploded while the pilot was trying to return to the airport because of decompression problems. The C-5A crashed into a rice paddy close to the Saigon River near the airport, killing over two hundred children and all but a few of the adults. Bill's wife and son were killed.

As an odd twist of circumstances, I would later find out that a good friend from my platoon in OCS, Andy Gembara, who was a special operations officer in Vietnam at the time of the crash, was good friends with Bill and his wife. Andy had visited them in their home just a few days earlier. He happened to be in the area of the crash of the C-5A and was one of the first to reach the scene. There were some survivors, but Andy said it was the grimmest sight he had ever confronted. Bill had returned to the Defense Attaché Office from a liaison visit to the NVA and Viet Cong when he saw Andy and several others rushing out to a vehicle, so he knew something was wrong. But he had no idea his own family was involved.

Bill was now married to Nam Xuan, a Vietnamese woman he had met at Fort Chaffee, Arkansas, in the refugee camp established there after the fall of Saigon. He was working for the Defense Intelligence Agency to debrief refugees escaping from Vietnam in order to gauge the amount of war materiel and classified material abandoned, and to evaluate the POW/MIA information brought out by refugees. He provided an overall analysis of the Vietnamese Communists' future intentions and capabilities to wage war. Xuan had come out of Vietnam with her family. Bill had hired her father, who was a well-known ARVN lieutenant colonel and graduate of the National Military Academy, to assist in the security preparation for the visit of President Gerald Ford to Fort Chaffee in June 1975, and later to debrief refugees of criminal and intelligence interest to the United States. Bill and Nam Xuan were married and had two children: a seven-year-old son, Scott, and an eight-year-old daughter, Elisabeth. They lived in Bangkok. Bill's older daughter, the one who had survived the C-5A crash, was in the States, where she was preparing to enter college in the fall.

Paul Mather, the chief of the JCRC Liaison and stationed in Bangkok, was an Air Force lieutenant colonel also married to a Vietnamese. Paul had lived in Bangkok for eleven years; he had been an original JCRC member from its inception in 1973.

Joe Harvey, a lieutenant colonel in the Army and the commander of JCRC stationed out of their headquarters near Honolulu, had been a member of the team since 1981. He had been in Vietnam during the war as a specialist in air defense.

Johnie Webb was a lieutenant colonel in the Army and commander of the Central Identification Laboratory in Hawaii. His division's job brought together the skills of the archeologist and the forensic experts. They would go out to a crash site or suspected burial location, retrieve what they could, and bring the remains back to Honolulu to their labs for identification. Johnie had been in charge of petroleum truck convoys in Vietnam during the war and had been with the Central Identification Laboratory since 1982.

All of these men had worked with the Vietnamese, North and South, longer than any other Americans. They knew the Vietnamese as much as it was possible for an American to know them. In addition to their time in South Vietnam during the war years, Bell and Mather had been coming to Hanoi for fifteen years, Webb and Harvey for six.

As we walked the streets of Hanoi, their familiarity and knowledge of the city and its people were evident as they pointed out the nuances only an experienced hand would catch.

One constant subject was the poverty. For instance, there is very little soap in Vietnam, which probably accounts for the colorless drabness of the clothing. Consequently, the team told us, when they have stayed at various hotels in Hanoi used to house foreigners, the soap they brought with them and left in the soap dish would be shaved a little each day. The maids took the shavings home so they could use it to do the laundry. One of the items we had brought with us was our own soap. I resolved to check my soap dish each night.

I recalled how twenty years ago in South Vietnam, my soap bars would disappear if I turned my back for just a moment while bathing in the stream next to the village. The kids were clever at stealing things like that, but we never understood why they would take risks to steal a lousy bar of soap. Back then none of us realized just how poor the Vietnamese were, especially the peasants living in the villages close to our locations on the bridges.

The team also told us that besides the soap getting shaved, they noticed the level of their aftershave lotion would go down. The maids would pour out a tiny amount to take home because they used it as perfume.

Selling cigarettes was a booming business in Hanoi and everywhere outside the city, from what we had observed. Street vendors and door stores would be located two or three to a block selling cigarettes. Each vendor had an inksize kerosene lamp burning with an open flame next to the cigarette display. I asked Bill why there was an open flame in this heat. Bill answered, "They sell cigarettes by the package or one at a time. The buyer will not buy a cigarette if he can't get a light from the vendor because the buyer will have neither matches nor a lighter. The buyer is too poor to afford them, and besides that the lamp is much cheaper than matches."

I had never been in a Communist country before, especially the poorest one in the world, and although I had read about shortages of consumer goods in Communist societies, I had never really grasped what it meant. Lipstick by the smear, lack of soap, no perfume, cigarettes sold one at a time, no matches and no place to buy them. What a situation for a group of people to be in.

"Christ," Carl exclaimed. "This country is really fucked up!"

To which I readily agreed. "Yeah, we can't buy a beer, and if we did find one it would be warm because they can't afford a refrigerator nor the electricity to run it."

Carl looked around us at the poverty and asked me, "How did they beat the South, anyway? They don't have anything."

"Beats hell out of me. It sure makes you wonder, doesn't it?"

The seven of us strolled south on Hang Bai Street in groups of two and three along the badly lit sidewalk. There were few street lights and they were very dim. The city was dark, and in the middle of the block where the lights did not reach, it was black. This made walking difficult because of the disrepair of the streets. Cracks, holes, upheaved or sunken bricks made it easy to trip in the dark. In those sections where the street lights did not work, whole blocks would be dark.

But even so, the bicycles streamed by in multitudes. They had no lights; like phantoms they glided out of the darkness to silently brush by and disappear back into the darkness. There was a great deal of traffic going both ways, so crossing the street in the dark was a tense exercise.

At first glance the traffic at night seemed impossible, but somehow it worked. At least most of the time. Bill said someone would occasionally write an editorial berating those irresponsible drivers of vehicles who would drive with their lights on, especially those who used bright lights. As these vehicles moved through traffic they would leave a wake of bicycle wrecks behind them, because the vehicles' lights destroyed the bicycle riders' night vision. The editorial would point out that a good driver only used the parking or running lights at night in the city. Of course a full moon was heaven for bicyclists. Bill told us the white stripes painted on the trees helped to guide the drivers through the night. This technique had been used on the Ho Chi Minh Trail.

* * *

The JCRC team asked us if we would like to see the Hoa Lo Prison, the infamous "Hanoi Hilton" where many of America's POWs were kept during the war. Carl and I immediately agreed.

An electric surge went through me at the mention of that malevolent place. It symbolized POWs and those Americans who never came back after the Vietnam War. To me the Hanoi Hilton was the one permanent symbol of the cruel victimization of our prisoners by the spiteful Vietnamese.

I never imagined so notorious a structure would be within walking distance of where we were staying. I knew the prison was supposed to be in the center of Hanoi, but I didn't perceive it as part of a neighborhood. I envisioned it as a monolith in the middle of a plain.

We walked west on Hai Ba Trung Street in the direction of the prison. Each block we walked became darker as the few working street lights spread further apart. This was a residential neighborhood and it was early, but there were no discernible lights in the homes.

After we had gone four blocks in deepening shadows, a massive wall loomed ahead in the gloom. The Hoa Lo Prison. This place of misery was simply named for the street on which it sat. The Vietnamese meaning, however, underlined its hellish purpose. *Hoa Lo* means "Fire Furnace" or "Fire Oven."

We stopped on the corner across from the prison. Carl and I apprehensively looked up at the wall, starkly lit by the weak street light at the end of the block. The stone walls were about 20 feet high and the top was covered with an 18-inch mass of large shards of broken glass embedded in concrete. Above the glass were six strands of electrified barbed wire.

We moved slowly down the dark, deserted street past the solid, double-door front gate set in the middle of the block. The only light within was shining through an open office window on the second floor above the front gate. Not a sound came from the ominous, massive structure. We were

73

hesitant to cross the narrow street to stand next to the gate or the wall. There was no one around and no guard in evidence. However, this was no place to make a misstep. I did not know what the laws were in Hanoi about hanging around prisons at night, but I did not want to tempt fate. I didn't relish the idea of trying to explain to a low-ranking non-English-speaking guard what I was doing around his prison at night.

Joe assured us it was perfectly safe; after all, this was the middle of a city, and people were free to use the streets around the prison. It was just another building in the neighborhood. We talked in low tones as we finally decided to cross over and stand beside the wall. We slowly paced along it to the far corner on Ly Thuong Kiet Street. When we peeked around the corner, we saw the back wall of the prison cut back at a 45-degree angle. Tho Nhuom Street went through the block at an angle, making Hoa Lo Prison into a trapezoidal building, and not a rectangle as I had assumed.

I walked out into the single lit intersection so I could stand back to get a better perspective on the prison. I could do this because for the first time since our arrival in Hanoi, there was little traffic. The other streets were busy, but not this one. Maybe this area at night was like a graveyard back home in Indiana at night. Your mind said it was okay, there was nothing to be afraid of, but your guts said this place was spooky and stay the hell away.

I looked back down Hoa Lo Street where the 20-foot-high front wall of the prison ran the length of the block. On the other side of the street facing the prison wall was a 7-foot wall which also ran the entire length of the block. It formed the side of a compound within which sat a large French-colonial building which, I was informed, was the site of the Ministry of Justice. The long wall was unbroken, but in the middle, opposite the prison gates, a shed with open sides was built against the wall. Later on, during the daylight hours when we drove along the main street I discovered this was a shelter for lines of Vietnamese waiting to enter the prison. A few vendors hawked their food products to the waiting people. But tonight it was empty and silent.

We started down the street bordering the back wall of the prison. As we moved away from the lighted intersection into increasing darkness, my Irish and Welsh heritage exerted itself, enabling me to sense a presence. The other men moved ahead and I stopped alone to look up at the prison. It looked evil sitting there in the dark: an island of dread in a city of life. The island was like a black hole in space, its gravity so much stronger than what was around it that nothing escaped—neither light, nor sound, nor hope, nor human being.

As I stared up at the wall I was reminded of the fear I felt as a child staring through the darkness at an old house rumored to be haunted. I was alone and late coming in from the fields, and I was hurrying in the evening dusk along the gravel road past the long-abandoned weathered wooden house set back from the road in a stand of old trees. My young and active mind imagined all sorts of horror in that place and I felt afraid.

Now I felt the same kind of fear as I imagined what went on behind those prison walls. Hoa Lo is still an active prison. That is what the French built it for, and that is what it is used for. It did not seem strange to me here to feel the same kind of helpless fear I had felt on that gravel road so long ago. The reality of what had happened within these walls was a child's horror-filled imaginings come true.

I went up to within a few inches of the stone and arched my neck back to scan the lethal shards of glass and barbed wire on top. Up this close the sense of a force emanating from the stone was so strong I felt a suction like an undercurrent pulling me into the wall.

Startled, I stepped back. The wall was inanimate, but I felt it would crush me if it could. It had leeched a bit of life from every man within its walls in the eighty years since the French had built it as a prison.

Before World War II the prisoners were Vietnamese, put there by the French; during World War II the prisoners were Vietnamese and French, put there by the Japanese; during the Indochina War the prisoners were again Vietnamese, put there by the French; after the Viet Minh won the war, the prisoners were French, put there by the Vietnamese; during the war with the South, the prisoners were American, put there by the Vietnamese; and now that there was no war, the prisoners were Vietnamese put there by the Vietnamese.

No wonder the wall radiated a malevolent force. That cumulative mass of time lost out of each prisoner's life was what I felt. The walls were a tomb of time lost forever. I looked up beyond the wall, the glass, and the barbed wire to the stars above, to remind myself there was another place besides here.

I broke loose from my reverie and turned toward the other men, who had stopped of their own accord further down the street. I walked toward them, comforted in this alien place by the presence of my own countrymen.

I thought about the Americans who were once within these walls. A few of my friends had spent years in a cell only a few feet from where I now stood. What memories must this place hold for them?

On the other side of the street along this section of the wall was a series of cafés or bars where I could see people sitting quietly in the dimly lit interiors. I made some comments to the guys about how normal life thrived only feet from where our POWs spent years.

My comments were a catalyst to Paul, who responded by telling some stories of former American POWs who had come back to Hanoi on official visits. The JCRC team who had been coming into Hanoi for years was the natural group to escort these guys, and so Paul, Joe, Bill, and Johnie were involved with all the visits.

Paul had walked with Jerry Venanzi to "The Plantation," which was a prison on the north side of Hanoi, on Ly Nam De Street. The railroad that comes off the Paul Doumer

Bridge curves toward the center of Hanoi at the back wall of the prison compound. The two of them had walked there from the Thang Loi Hotel. Paul said Jerry was a little apprehensive outside the prison. He was worried about their being so near the prison and a military compound across the street. Jerry overcame his anxiety and finally did walk in front to stand looking at the prison. Satisfied, he walked away.

I asked Paul what he thought went through those former POWs' minds when they visited the prisons. Paul thought for a few minutes and said he believed it was a catharsis for them. They would stand outside the prison and they knew they could just walk away.

Paul said when he walked around Hanoi with Ray Vohden, a former prisoner of the Hanoi Hilton, Ray was interested in finding out what the sounds were that he had heard outside the prison walls for years. He was curious to go back outside the Hanoi Hilton so he could identify them. There were some he recognized while inside, like children's voices in a playground and traffic, but there were others that had puzzled him for years.

Paul said Ray's curiosity was finally satisfied as he stood on the street during the day outside the prison and saw the hawkers peddling their wares. Hawkers would push their carts along the street, and in order to send an advance notice to the people in the neighborhood that he was coming, each hawker would make a noise peculiar to his product. These were the sounds Ray found so mysterious.

The man who sharpened scissors and knives used a chain and tin strips, which he rattled up and down the chain. The noodle soup vendor used a stick to beat on a hollow wooden instrument a bit like a gourd. He was something like a Good Humor man in that people would hear him coming and their mouths would start to water. Another vendor who sold fish had a stick with notches cut in it, and he would rub a second stick up and down the notches, making a sound like a kid makes running a stick along a picket fence. A third vendor who sold vegetables had a squeeze horn attached to his cart which he vigorously honked. Ray left Hanoi with his curiosity satisfied. John McCain, also a POW, came back to Hanoi when he was a senator. He told the Vietnamese he wanted to see three things. He wanted to see the Hanoi Hilton; the place in Hanoi where his fighter aircraft crashed; and the statue on the shore of the lake he landed in when he parachuted out of his fighter. His likeness is in bas-relief on the statue, which is not a compliment to him, but rather a tribute the Vietnamese put up to honor themselves for shooting his and a number of other American aircraft down over Hanoi.

The Vietnamese complied with Senator McCain's wishes and fulfilled all of his requests.

As Paul related the story, I thought of a picture I had back home. On the day McCain was shot down, a fellow pilot flying above Hanoi at the same time rolled his fighter on its back and with a hand-held 35 mm camera took a photo through the top of his canopy of McCain's A-4 Skyhawk exploding into a fireball as it crashed into a neighborhood of Hanoi. A good friend of mine, Pat Patrick, who had three tours flying fighters off carrier decks during the war, used this photo along with a number of others he had put together as a briefing package for training his fighter pilots.

Pat had shown this photo to me while I was visiting him at his home in Falls Church, Virginia, in 1983, and I was drawn to it for two reasons. One was the fact that McCain's father had been a commander in chief of all Pacific forces during the war. The capture of his son by the Vietnamese was a fearful thing all of us who had been in Vietnam could share with the father, as we imagined the torture the Vietnamese would put the son of an admiral through.

The second thing which intrigued me about the photograph was the group of homes the fireball encompassed as it exploded. I wondered if any of those people were at home when the fighter crashed on top of them.

I stuck my head for a looksee into one of the poorly lit

little cafés across from the prison and then hurried to catch up with the guys, who were almost to the corner. They stood waiting for me on Quan Su, the street which cuts the corner off this edge of the triangle, forming the prison into a trapezoid. We walked up this short street to Hai Ba Trung, the main street on which we had walked up from the guesthouse. The prison wall bordering this street formed the other leg of the trapezoid-shaped prison. We walked along this wall until we reached the corner where we had started. We had completed our circuit of the Hoa Lo Prison.

I was profoundly moved to be here and to have experienced the sensations I felt while circling the infamous Hanoi Hilton—a focal point even today of the despicable manner in which the Vietnamese treated prisoners and their continued meanness on the subject of POW/MIAs.

I thought about my conversations over the years with men who had flown over Hanoi. During my visit to Pat Patrick's house that day, I had asked Pat what he and the pilots thought as they flew their missions over Hanoi, knowing that their friends were down below in the Hanoi Hilton and that they themselves could end up in the same place.

He said his thoughts of the prison and of Hanoi changed during his three tours. Hanoi was always a bad place, but as the war dragged on for years the accumulation in the Hanoi Hilton of friends he flew with made the prison take on a personal nature.

He said wintertime was bad over Hanoi because of the overcast, which restricted flights of sections to only one or two aircraft. This made it easier for the enemy gunners to concentrate on you. During the clear days they would run large Alpha strikes of eight to twelve bombers and four to eight fighter escorts. To have that many aircraft in formation required at least a 10,000-foot ceiling and visibility of 8 miles, which spread things out enough that you had a better chance of surviving.

During the Johnson years, the normal rule was they had to stay outside a 10-mile radius from the center of Hanoi. To hit a target any closer, one had to have clearance from the White House itself. This changed on Pat's last tour, when Nixon put the pressure on the Vietnamese by allowing his military commanders the freedom to make the bombing rules.

Pat told me the two usual targets were the Paul Doumer Bridge and the power plant at the north end of Hanoi on the city limits. When I had seen the bridge today I had an image of Pat diving his fighter bomber toward it, hell bent on destroying it.

Pat's first tour was from December 1967 to July 1968, flying A-4 Skyhawks fighter bombers off the carrier U.S.S. *Ticonderoga*. The briefing when he first arrived on board informed him the losses were awful. This had been McCain's ship and 40 percent of the A-4 attack pilots in Air Group 16 of McCain's air wing had been killed or captured. In the three years America had been attacking the North, 929 aircraft had been shot down and over 700 pilots were killed, missing in action, or had died in captivity.

Pat's second tour was from March 1969 to July 1969, flying A-4s off the carrier U.S.S. *Oriskany*. The war was being Vietnamized, and the American pilots were taking heavy casualties because of increased ground fire while trying to protect South Vietnamese units which were under attack from the North Vietnamese Army. North Vietnam had developed the heaviest air defenses in the history of air warfare. Only a few pilots survived to be sent north to the Hanoi Hilton.

Pat's last tour was from December 1972 to July 1973, flying A-7 fighter bombers off the carrier U.S.S. *Enterprise*. By then all the pilots knew the war was lost. Consequently the Hanoi Hilton became their greatest motivation for bombing the North. Pat had friends, men he had flown with, who were POWs, and anything he and the other pilots could accomplish would help to get their friends out of prison. As far as the pilots were concerned, the POWs were what the war was all about by this time.

Finally they felt their efforts were justified when, as a result of the intense bombing started in December 1972 to force the Vietnamese back to the peace table, a cease-fire agreement was signed on January 27, 1973. All the pilots were informed that after sunset on January 27 there would be no more missions into North Vietnam. Toward evening on that day, while flying their last combat missions over the North, Pat said one of the best guys in the Navy was shot down and killed over the DMZ.

Harley Hall was flying on the last sortie of the day when he got hit. The other pilots reported there were two chutes on the ground and Pat, who was south of the location on another mission, was asked to bring his group up to provide air support while a rescue helicopter went in. The chopper itself was shot down by North Vietnamese at last light and the commander canceled the rescue mission and recalled everyone home. The air war in the North was over. Harley Hall, a former Blue Angel, is still unaccounted for. He is listed as presumed killed in action now, though he had been listed as missing right after he was shot down. His remains have not been recovered.

The most emotional experience of the war came for Pat and the other pilots on board the U.S.S. *Enterprise* when the C-141s flew out of Hanoi with the POWs on board in February and March 1973. The captain announced over the ship's intercom that the C-141s had lifted off from Hanoi. A short time later he announced the C-141s were above the carriers in the Gulf of Tonkin, heading for home. Pat said everyone on board cheered and cheered, but the pilots cheered the longest.

I wished Pat could have been standing with me right then outside the Hanoi Hilton. He could look at the prison and look at the sky and we could talk about it.

We began to walk east down Hai Ba Trung Street back toward the guesthouse. The street was busy with bicycle and pedestrian traffic, and as I glanced back at the prison I wondered if any American had ever escaped. Because if they did get outside the walls, where would they have gone? An American would have stood out like a sore thumb.

This was the middle of Hanoi, which is a very crowded city. There was no place to hide, even at night; every nook and cranny seemed to have a Vietnamese in it. I wondered how I would have fared. The next couple of days I looked for hiding spots and paths an escaped prisoner could travel to get out of the city. Even though I consider myself a pretty resourceful guy, I figured it would be nearly impossible to get out of that city without being seen. Even if I made it outside, it would be hard to remain undetected. Open rice paddies extended for miles into the countryside, with few places to hide.

I found out later that a few men did escape from prisons in the Hanoi area but were quickly recaptured. One of them, Edwin L. Atterberry, an Air Force officer, died from the torture he received after he was recaptured.

The street we were walking on was especially dark. The uneven brick sidewalk was in pitch darkness except for occasional shafts of weak light thrown by faraway lights. Even that light was tricky because of the contrasting shadows it cast on the uneven surface. The sidewalk was in such bad shape from missing bricks and cracks that I was forced to stare at my feet to keep from tripping.

The street itself presented a safer surface but traffic was dangerous, so Bill Bell and I stayed on the sidewalk. The rest of the guys were taking their chances with the traffic because they thought it was safer than tripping. I was walking along the sidewalk talking to Bill while trying to look at everything around me. This was definitely dangerous because negotiating the sidewalk really did demand our full attention.

The danger was dramatically proven. On a particularly dark stretch covered in shadows from the trees, I was looking at the Cuban-Vietnamese Hospital when some primeval instinct made me stop dead in my tracks. When I looked down at my feet, the toes of my cowboy boots actually rested over a black abyss.

82

A hole about the diameter of two manholes opened up in the middle of the sidewalk. If I had taken one more step, I would have plunged to the bottom.

"Jesus Christ! What the hell is that?" I exclaimed. Bill leaned over the hole, lit a match, and dropped it into the pit.

"Must be the sewer down there, smells like," he calmly replied. Bill always seemed unperturbed, which I guessed was a prerequisite to being an interpreter in this environment.

The hairs stood up on my neck as the brief flash of light from the match starkly outlined a jagged edged hole about 10 feet deep. If I had stepped into that, I would have been severely injured. A second match confirmed the existence of broken shards of tile and ragged ends of pipes sticking out of the sides of the hole. Paul asked later if it occurred to me that this was the urban version of a jungle punji stake pit!

I was astounded that this hole was allowed to exist in the middle of the city on a busy sidewalk in front of a maternity hospital. Not only was it not repaired, it did not have a warning sign or barricades to keep people away. I said as much to Bill, who replied there was no money to fix things, plus people who lived in the neighborhood knew about the hole. Strangers were just out of luck.

I backed gingerly away from the abyss and decided to take a chance with the bicycles in the street. The rest of the guys were already in the street, so Bill and I followed them. The walking was a lot easier.

While walking in the streets that afternoon and that night, I made an observation to Bill based on my experience as a big-city dweller from Denver, New York City, and Washington, D.C. I had been on the lookout for dog shit, but I hadn't seen any, or at least I hadn't stepped in any yet.

Bill said, "Don't worry. There isn't any dog shit in the streets because there are no dogs in the street."

Paul, Joe, and Johnie joined in to explain the Vietnamese consider dog meat to be a delicacy, and as with any other livestock they did not let their dogs run loose. A loose dog

83

was fair game for anyone who caught him. A dog running free in the streets was quickly captured for the stewpot.

They asked me if I had seen the dog-butchering shop when we drove into the city that afternoon. I told them I had seen the meat hanging out front of a shop, but I didn't realize it was dog meat.

We walked past the Cuban-Vietnamese hospital and I wondered how one broken-down Communist country could help another broken-down Communist country.

I was curious about health-care systems in Vietnam. After all, that was my job and my reason for being here. As we walked by the gate to that hospital, I was puzzled by the twenty or so women clustered at the entrance. The time was 9:00 P.M. which was late to be accepting so many patients. No one in our group could come up with an explanation except that it was a maternity hospital.

In order to vary our route back so we could see more, we walked north one block to Trang Thi Street and turned right. We reached the lake where Ba Trieu, a cross street, formed a main intersection. There was more light here, which changed the ambiance of the streets.

Our whole walk so far had been a trip through nineteenth-century France. The French-style buildings, the tall trees, brick sidewalks, ornate latticework, and the berets cocked at a jaunty angle on the heads of the Vietnamese men suggested a time long past. But now that we were back in this main section, the Vietnamese influence reasserted itself in the bright lights shining in front of a building on the intersection.

A mixed group of old and young men was gathered there. Of course everyone was smoking. I was reminded of the sidewalk outside the poolhall in Marshall, Illinois, on a hot, humid summer night when I was a teenager.

The old men squatting, chewing, and smoking by the curb were discussing topics of the day in low voices. Meanwhile the younger hot bloods stood in various separate groups, smoking and lounging up against the wall or hanging out close to the bicycle rack. I bet they would have gone nuts over a 57 Chevy or a Harley Davidson Sportster.

We could hear loud music coming from inside the building. I was frankly surprised and asked the JCRC team if we could go in. I wanted to see what all the music was about and I needed a beer anyway.

The light blue double doors were wide open, as were the windows from which the music, a form of slow jazz, flowed. We entered the wide doors into a foyer. The foyer was also the stairwell, which was well lit, with music blaring down.

We traipsed upstairs, talking loudly and laughing all the way. I remarked that this was like a thirties movie: the cement steps, the stucco-covered, green-painted walls, jazz music coming from above, and seven Americans alone in an exotic land, cut off from communication, hot dogs, and baseball. All we needed were brown leather flying jackets and caps with the "30 mission crunch" and we would be in a strip straight out of "Terry and the Pirates." Carl said I was showing my age because none of the younger generation would know what the hell "Terry and the Pirates" was all about.

After about four flights of stairs we reached the top landing. There we were greeted by a pert young Vietnamese lady sitting at a table collecting a cover charge.

"Hah!" Carl snorted. "I bet nobody in 'Terry and the Pirates' paid a cover charge."

We declined paying until we could peek in to see whether the show was worth the price of admission. On the landing were a number of young men and women, sitting alone or in small groups, smoking. Behind the woman collecting the cover charge was an open door through which we could see a large room, maybe 50 by 75 feet. It was well lit, and the walls and ceiling were painted a cream color.

Bill asked the woman if we could go in to look around.

Her face expressed surprise at hearing Vietnamese from a Westerner, but she smiled and nodded her assent. We edged into the crowd.

The room was packed with people in their teens, twenties, and thirties, all sitting at tables attentively listening to a live band. The band was on a low stage against the center back wall. The five musicians were dressed in mix-and-match sports coats and were playing a clarinet, trumpet, saxophone, and a few other instruments.

There seemed to be an equal number of both sexes represented in the packed room. They looked to be hip, and were well dressed by Hanoi standards; light-colored sports coats, open shirts, and trousers, all a bit threadbare.

Every single person in the room and out in the stairwell had a cigarette lit and not a single one of them had a filter. None were smoking American tobacco. The blue haze from cigarette smoke hung in the room like a heavy curtain. The smoke cut my throat and burned my mouth.

There did not seem to be much drinking in the crowd because there were only a few beer bottles in the whole room and a glass or two at some of the tables. Most of the tables looked bare.

I looked around the crowd in wonderment. I just had never expected anything like this in Communist Hanoi. From what I had heard and read, this was a very oppressive society and Western-style music was taboo. Yet here was a very open gathering of people who were having a good time and making plenty of noise about it.

Not that the music was heavy metal or anything like that. It was jazz. Or at least I thought it was jazz. I may have been wrong because it had a weird Oriental twist to it. But I was no expert. If it ain't rock and roll, hillbilly, or country, I don't know what it is.

We looked out over the crowd searching for a seat for all of us, but there was not even space for one of us, let alone seven.

The room was stiflingly hot. The screenless doors and

windows were wide open but there was not a breath of air moving, nor were there any fans. The daytime temperature had been 105 degrees and this room had to be hotter.

While we had been looking the room and the people over, they had given us the once-over also. After turning to glance at us, they returned their attention to the show. They acted as if Americans came by to catch the show on a regular basis. It was only later that I found out they probably thought we were Russians. That's the reason they ignored us; they don't like Russians, and the Russians are cheap-skates to boot.

We all looked at each other and shrugged our shoulders. We would have squeezed in somehow if they had had cold beer, but our quick reconnoiter of the room made us decide to keep walking.

It was with some regret that we left, for I wanted to sit down among Communists to see how they enjoyed them-selves. We waved goodbye to the cover charge lady and went back downstairs outside onto the sidewalk, so my opportun-ity was lost. I resolved to come back to this place some other night.

Bill and I struck up a conversation and fell behind the other men. He had disappeared earlier this afternoon when we arrived at the guesthouse, so he could go to a shop to buy newspapers. Bill said he had read editorials in the Hanoi newspapers in the past couple of months raising hell with the government for not living up to the promises made to their country's veterans. According to the article, the veter-ans were giving the province chiefs hell, and the province chiefs in turn were passing on these grievances to the government bigwigs in Hanoi.

The vets were complaining that they were not getting the prosthetic limbs they were owed to replace those limbs they had lost while fighting for their country. It was a disgrace that those "Heroes" who were most deserving of help from their government were abandoned.

Another big beef written about with increasing frequency

was the younger veterans were complaining that the older veterans had all the good jobs and there were no jobs left for them. These younger men who had gone away to fight for their country now needed a chance to catch up with their stay-at-home comrades.

"Well, now, isn't that interesting," I remarked to Bill. I have been hearing the same kind of complaints for the last twenty years from our own Vietnam veterans.

Strange how it had never occurred to me that my old enemies were suffering the same maladies that we did. Oh, intellectually I could easily recognize they would suffer from the problems of being disabled that the rest of us disabled suffered from. But I hadn't thought about it before because I didn't give a damn before. The Vietnamese had been "dinks" in my mind for twenty years and dinks were not individual human beings. They were an amorphous entity that was the enemy.

This long afternoon had changed all that. The journey from the airport to where I now stood encompassed more than distance. It had brought me to understanding. These were not dinks, these were Vietnamese. No better, no worse than any other man.

I almost felt traitorous not hating them anymore. But I didn't love them either, so that was good. Now I could be objective.

I was in balance after twenty years.

Bill and I were perspiring heavily, and we decided we needed to find a beer. We called ahead to the other men and told them to go on without us. They waved their approval and continued on down the dusty street.

We stopped at various cafés lined along the street, sticking our heads in the open doorways to case them out. None of them had any beer, cold or hot. They were small rooms with enough space for a table or two and always dimly lit by one 20-watt bulb trying to push back the night. Each one usually had at least two customers, generally old men sitting at the tables drinking some amber-colored liquid. The men would always be enveloped in a heavy cloud of cigarette smoke.

There was one place where a younger crowd hung out. The front wall opened onto the sidewalk, making the room an extension of the street. Against the back wall was a counter made of wooden frames in which glass panels were set. A calendar showing a Vietnamese girl in traditional dress hung on the wall behind it. Two women in white blouses sat behind the counter while fifteen or so young men and women sat at wooden benches and low, rough-hewn tables crammed into the available space.

When Bill and I sat down at one of the benches, we almost looked ridiculous. The furniture was not designed to accommodate our larger American mass and longer limbs. I felt like I was sitting at my two-year-old daughter's play table and chairs. My knees felt higher than my chin.

One of the girls came from behind the counter to take our order. Bill talked to her while I looked around at the other customers. They were frankly curious but coolly polite. As the conversation between Bill and the waitress progressed, the crowd discovered we were Americans, not Russians as they had originally believed. Immediately they became much friendlier, smiling and offering us cigarettes. Bill was smoking his own and I don't smoke, so we politely declined. Bill had been trying to cajole the girl into selling us a beer, even though they had sold out of today's quota. He had no luck in talking her into going into the back room to break open tomorrow's beer ration. The large beer bottles we saw on the tables were still being painfully nursed from the late afternoon, when the café had sold out.

The only things they had to sell were bottles of apricot brandy with its distinctive amber color and cigarettes. In fact, those were the only two things most cafés had to sell. Cigarettes were the one commodity in abundance which anyone could buy and sell.

I wondered if there were any Vietnamese who did not

smoke. There sure weren't any nonsmokers in the café crowds. The smoke in this place was thick enough to cut with a knife. I noticed that the cheap tin ashtrays on the burn-scarred table were filthy with little bitty butts. I took that as a sure sign of poverty, because I used to work in a truck stop with a co-worker with eight kids and he always smoked his nonfiltered Camels down to the nubbin like the butts in that ashtray. He supported his wife and eight kids by changing truck tires ten hours a day. He used to tell me between puffs that chain-smoking cigarettes was the only Goddamn pleasure he could afford in life.

It was beginning to look to me as if that was the only thing the Vietnamese could afford also.

Bill gave up trying to get us a beer and we bid the café waitress and café crowd goodbye. The waitress was reluctant to let us rich Americans go, but rules were rules. If she got into the habit of selling tomorrow's beer quota today, she would soon run out completely and would not have any to sell for days at a time. It was better to sell a little beer each day and keep her regular customers coming back than to run out completely and maybe lose those customers forever.

We stood out front on the cement sidewalk and decided not to give up. Finally one café we walked into looked very promising. For one thing, it had decent lighting. It reminded me of a nineteenth-century Western saloon that had experienced hard times. We entered the open front door and a large room spread to our left. Against the far side wall was an ornately carved, dark mahogany bar, complete with a brass rail to rest your foot on. The wood looked faded and dirty and had many scratches on its unwaxed surface, but it was a real bar. Behind it was a full-length mirror framed by two dark mahogany columns on either side. The silver paint behind the mirror had worn off in places, and dirt streaked our reflections and that of the room. On a shelf in front of the mirror were a number of those bottles with the amber liquid, plus a different bottle I had not noticed in the other cafés.

This was a more distinguished bar for a different clientele. When we walked in the front door, a group of thirteen men our age and older were loudly carrying on a discussion. They were dressed in shabby, threadbare dark tropical trousers and shirts. Quite a few of them had on dark berets. They were sitting around a couple of tables they had pushed together. They immediately stopped talking when we entered and watched suspiciously as we walked by them to the bar. We returned look for look and electricity flowed through the air.

Bill and I leaned against the bar, nonchalantly cocking a foot up on the rail and watching their sullen expressions in the mirror. "Old cadre," Bill remarked to me. "Those are men who were soldiers in Vietnam's wars. They're gathered here to talk and tell war stories probably."

"Now isn't that something?" I turned my head to look directly at the group, who had gone back to talking in lower tones. "So those guys are Vietnam veterans? It sounds strange to think of them as Vietnam veterans when all these years we have been Vietnam veterans. We don't look anything like those guys."

Both of us chuckled.

"This has got to be a rarity. Vietnamese Vietnam veterans and American Vietnam veterans sharing the same room. Not exactly a cordial atmosphere, but then again we aren't shooting each other, either."

"Yeah, that's a nice feeling, isn't it?"

The Vietnamese I had seen up to this point had only impersonally represented my former enemies, but here, unexpectedly, were men who actually had taken up the gun against my fellow soldiers. These were real enemy soldiers, who had fought hard battles, suffered deprivation as all soldiers do, and killed Americans.

In another time, in another place, under other circumstances, we would have been violently trying to kill each other. And would have felt gloriously satisfied to have done so. And our individual countries would have rewarded us for it. In fact, the more of the enemy killed, the greater the reward, the greater the glory.

The feelings I experienced were unfathomable. On one hand, I hated them for what they had done; and on the other hand, I begrudgingly had to admit they were only soldiers doing their job. They were probably as proud of their service to their country as I was of my service to my country. If I hated them for killing and wounding my countrymen, they in turn must hate me for killing and wounding their countrymen.

And yet another surprise surfaced within me when faced with the presence of my old enemies. As I looked across the smoke-filled room at these men smoking, drinking, and talking, there was an absence of hate on my part, which I at first found disconcerting. But upon reflection I had to admit my gut reaction was more of an identification with them as soldiers than as enemies. When it was all said and done, the individual soldier did what he had to do. That's the way it always has been with men and that's the way it always will be.

We turned our attention back to our reflections in the bar mirror. After a moment, during which I thought about Bob Hutchinson, Jim Yoder, Greg Iding, Lieutenant Bill Ordway, and a whole host of other men I had known who were killed in this country, perhaps by those very men behind me, I decided to try a shot of that amber-colored liquor. I needed a drink.

The lady behind the bar stood up from the stool she had been resting on and came over. Bill ordered a couple of glasses of apricot brandy and paid her in dong he had brought with him. She set two glasses of dubious cleanliness before us and filled them to the rim. We toasted to the success of our mission and sipped the liquor. Bill knew what to expect, but my taste buds thought I was being poisoned. In the States we would have thrown this stuff out as having gone bad. Here they seemed to relish drinking it.

After the first rush of shivers, I determined to stick with it until it began to taste better—or at least until I finished this glass. As we sipped the sickening, bittersweet liquor, Bill told me about one old North Vietnamese veteran he met in 1973 soon after the Peace Accords, when the JCRC team first started coming into Hanoi. This veteran had related an experience on the Ho Chi Minh Trail to the team.

On one of his trips down the trail, he was driving a truck full of supplies and was strafed by American planes three times. Each time he would get flat tires from the bullets. He did not have any patching material, so after every strafing episode he improvised by hunting around the jungle and catching a bunch of frogs, whereupon he would kill them and skin them. He then used the froghides to patch his tubes so he could reinflate his tires and continue the trek south. This was a real example of field expediency—or else a great example of military folklore.

After we traded a few more stories, we decided to continue our quest for a beer. The stuff we were drinking not only tasted bad, it was warm and unrefreshing, and it made my tongue feel like it had hair on it. We walked out past the old cadre, us staring at them and them staring at us, out onto the busy street, and turned right. Ahead of us at the southwest corner of Ngo Quyen and Ly Thuong Kiet streets was the Hoa Binh Hotel where foreigners stayed, so there was a good chance we could find a beer there. I was so hot and dehydrated the thought of a beer made my mouth water.

The double doors of the hotel were set kitty corner facing the intersection. When we entered the lobby, it was dark. There was no electricity on in the hotel and not even a candle was lit. Bill said it was tough to get candles and they were expensive besides, so most people didn't bother with them.

Some light from the weak street lamp at the intersection entered the open doors and windows, so that our night vision enabled us to make out what was around us. Over to our left was a lobby area where people were sitting in the dark at tables, relaxing with a cigarette and a drink of some kind in a glass. The people all looked European. Even though they were sitting in the dark, they continued about their business as if nothing had happened. Bill told me that the electricity goes out all the time in Hanoi, so people do not become fazed in the least when it happens.

I thought about Pat Patrick telling me the two favorite targets they were always assigned to attack with their fighter bombers were the Paul Doumer Bridge and the power plant on the north side of Hanoi. Here I was seventeen years later and the loss of electricity was so frequent nobody paid any attention, even European visitors. It made me wonder if the loss of the power plant during those attacks made any more difference then than it did now.

We quickly discovered there was no beer here either, but before we left I went into the lobby to look more closely at the people. It was crowded with people who were talking French. As Bill and I walked outside, he told me a lot of French did business in Vietnam.

I was surprised to hear that. I didn't know the French had any interest or desire to be in Vietnam. They had been kicked out as a colonial power, so I hadn't dreamed the Vietnamese would like them either. Bill said no, some of the French still ran businesses in Vietnam. They got along okay here.

More to ponder, but of more moment was the appearance of the rest of the team. They had seen us enter the hotel and had decided to wait outside for us. We all decided to go back to the guesthouse. Although it was early, only 2100 hours, there was nothing to do but go to bed or to read.

On the way back I commented about the electricity being out in the hotel. I had noticed that the electric lines were strung along the street on short metal and concrete poles, not too much taller than we were, that looked like they were constructed from an Erector Set. Each one looked like a miniature radio tower.

The electric wires sagged in the middle down almost to

the level of our heads. On one block that was particularly black under the shadow of the trees a wire sagged down below our necks. I wondered what would have happened if we had blundered into it in the dark. Luckily Johnie Webb spotted it, but if we had gone a few more feet one of us would have become a lightning rod.

I commented on the danger of something like this to people in the area, but we surmised the city had no money to fix it. Besides, like the hole in the sidewalk, this electrical wire must have been known in the neighborhood.

Paul, Joe, and Johnie said it was really something to be in the city when a thunderstorm hit. Live electric wires would break loose and whip around, sparks flying and wires snapping and cracking all over the streets.

The power outage was not uniform; some blocks had power and others did not. As I looked into the open windows and doors of living quarters, I would see an occasional TV set flickering in black and white out of the dark interior of a room.

I stood on the sidewalk outside one open doorway and peered inside to watch a few minutes of TV with the family. They sensed my presence and turned to see who was standing there. They smiled, nodded their heads, and turned back to the TV.

The small 12-inch screen, the black and white picture, and the group of people gathered intensely watching it reminded me of when my dad got one of the first TV sets in our rural neighborhood in Indiana in 1950. Farm families came from miles around to see the marvel. It was a tremendous feat to have a picture beamed through the air into our home. The thrill and excitement of it happening that first day when Dad got it hooked up and turned on is still with me today. These people must have had some of that same feeling not too long ago.

I found out later there was a total of six shows a night beamed from the Soviet Union via satellite, and two shows made in Vietnam. They usually were fifteen minutes in length. The show I was watching looked boring beyond belief. It had something to do with the virtues of a tractor; it was no wonder the shows were only fifteen minutes long. Come to think of it, though, in 1950 we used to watch the Channel 6 test pattern out of Indianapolis, Indiana, because we were so fascinated by a picture that came through the air.

I caught up with the guys and we turned the corner onto Le Thach Street and then into the government guesthouse. When I entered my room, I was pleasantly surprised to see the mosquito netting pulled out over the bed. The room was suffused with a soft glow from the tiny red-shaded lamp at the side of the bed. The room was like an oven in spite of the laboring air conditioner banging away on the far wall. It was simply no match for the heat. I went over and stuck my face to within six inches of the fan and I could barely feel the difference. Was it hot and sticky! How did I ever hump a 70-pound pack and carry a rifle through this heat?

Carl knocked on my door and said to come on with him to visit the JCRC team, who were having a beer in Bill's room. I thought that was a great idea, and we walked down the hall to Room 104. They were lounging around in various chairs drinking the beer they had purchased earlier. They were also listening to Bill's shortwave radio—or at least they were trying to, since Bill had tuned in to a Vietnamese station to get local news.

Every moment of this day had provided me with a sight or sound or smell that had triggered a flood of memories from the war twenty years ago, or from something pertaining to the war in the intervening twenty years. Here was yet another trigger.

I stopped to listen. The last time I had heard a Vietnamese radio announcer had been twenty years ago; when we were guarding bridges on Highway One, south of Duc Pho, we would tune in at night to the only radio station we could pick up. A Communist propaganda radio station had an English-speaking announcer we called "Hanoi Hannah." She was beamed to the South from a powerful transmitter in

Hanoi. She would play a little rock-'n'-roll and then hit us with all kinds of propaganda.

Occasionally we could pick up her competition, "Peking Sally," an English-speaking propagandist beamed to us out of China. But we didn't like to listen to her even when we could pick her up because she played that harsh, discordant-sounding Oriental music.

Hanoi Hannah at least knew what music was popular with Americans. We would have preferred more music, but her version of propaganda warfare was fun to listen to once in a while. Most of what she said was boring bullshit rhetoric, but some of it was entertaining. She would give us soldiers hell for fighting in Vietnam. Rich American bourgeoisie were using us to fight the war so they could make money, she would say.

One night when she said something like that, one of the new men assigned to my platoon, eighteen years old and from a small town in Indiana, looked at me and asked what a "bourgeoisie" was. Being from Indiana myself, I wasn't sure I could tell him, except it was a French word. I thought to myself that that was a good guess because the French used to be here and the Vietnamese probably picked up on some of their words.

Looking back on it now, I chuckled at the memory. If Hanoi Hannah had known two boys from Indiana were so ignorant about the bourgeoisie, she would have been convinced we were being used for sure.

Other memories about her broadcasts were not so amusing. She would tell us about the antiwar demonstrations back in the States and suggest we should join the uprising back home. She never won any converts among us doing that; her comments just pissed us off at the antiwar demonstrators. We believed they were traitors for not supporting us soldiers who were fighting for their freedom. We were always angry at those activists because their activities made our enemies happy. It felt as if we were being stabbed in the back by our own people. This feeling of betrayal became deeper and deeper each time another man was wounded or killed by the enemy these antiwar people professed to love.

The one thing I remembered the most, though, was the inflated figures she used each night in describing the American "losses" caused by the "victorious" people's army. One night she said ten thousand American soldiers had been killed that day and fifty airplanes had been shot down. These numbers were so outrageous we wondered why they bothered to read them. They didn't think we would believe that stuff, did they?

The night I heard that particular broadcast I was leaning on the railing of the Bailey Bridge, which we were guarding with nine men. Part of the original bridge lay in twisted pieces in the rice paddy next to us. The American engineers had dragged them there after the Viet Cong had blown it up. I was looking across the wreckage as I stared out over the terrain lit by a full moon, thinking these dinks were crazy to believe they would ever beat us.

None of these ridiculous broadcasts ever did what they were designed to do, like cause us to desert. But they did add to our anger when Hanoi Hannah would read the American-published articles against the war. We were not angry at her for reading them. We were angry at those Americans who had written them. They were just like the demonstrators.

Somebody in our high command must have been even more angry. I read years later that American aircraft were given the mission of destroying the radio transmitter. They bombed it in February 1968 and during the Christmas bombings in 1972. Hanoi Hannah did not miss a beat, though. She was on the air right afterward.

Many years later I read that Hanoi Hannah was a Vietnamese woman named Thu Huong. After the war she became a TV personality on the Saigon TV station.

The Vietnamese voice abruptly ceased as Bill switched off his radio. My reverie broken, I went over to a chair next to the wall and sat down. We talked about the mission's chance of success, told war stories, and discussed, surreptitiously in sign language, the probable hiding places of the "bugs" we had been warned were here.

Strangely enough, none of us was affronted by the possible presence of hidden microphones. We accepted it as part of the atmosphere we were in as Americans in a Communist government guesthouse. One of the guys said the Minister of Internal Affairs would have thought it odd if his men had not bugged the rooms.

Afterwards we broke up to go back to our own rooms. I stripped down naked, eager to get my sweat-filled clothes off. My stump sock was saturated with sweat and a minor heat rash had broken out on the stump. The armpit on my good arm had a rash on it where my prosthetic harness strap lay. Being naked did not make me any cooler, though. The humid heat was worse than I remembered from the war. Not even New Orleans was this bad.

I stood in the old-fashioned tub and held the hand shower over my head, letting the tepid water dribble over my body to wash away the sweat. There was no hot water, but who needed it in that climate? The dribble of tepid water reminded me of those few times when I got to take a shower when I was in the South. A shower there was a wing tank or trashcan with a bunch of nailholes hammered in the bottom. The water pressure wasn't any greater with that system than with this system. But oh, it did feel good.

I carefully brushed my teeth, using the bottled water on the shelf above the sink. Routine habits are hard to break, and it was a challenge to not do the things I was unconsciously used to doing, like cleaning my toothbrush with water from the tap. I did not want tap water in my mouth.

Without my artificial arm on I was truly handicapped, as I had to figure new ways of doing things so none of my personal toilet items would come in contact with anything unsanitary. I held my toothbrush in my mouth, my soap against my chest with my chin, and used my hand to grasp anything else. I probably didn't have to be so persnickety, but the last time I left Vietnam I had carried a whole host of

99

parasites and infections with me. I did not intend to repeat those purging episodes again.

After that first day, I would relax my safeguards, except for the water. Vietnam just took getting used to again, at least up to a point. I would never want an open wound or sore in Vietnam. Not even a scratch.

I had brought my own toilet paper because I had read how scarce toilet paper was in Communist countries and its poor quality. It was a good thing I did bring my own supply. The toilet paper furnished by the guesthouse was like crepe paper; it stretched when you tried to rip it from the roll. That was no fun one-handed. It was not very good for wiping, but it would have been great to use in decorating a float if you didn't mind having a float the color of a 1950s American green kitchen-appliance display.

In order to cool off, I sat naked at the desk to write in my journal of the day's activities. On the desk in front of me was the American flag and a picture of my wife Mary and my two-year-old daughter Kate. Mary had been with me since the war.

On the corner of the desk was a picture of my twenty-one-year-old daughter, Teri. She had been ten months old when I left for Vietnam. After I was wounded, I had divorced her mother, at her request, when I was in the Army hospital. Consequently, Teri had grown up without me around. Although I kept in contact, I was a stranger to her, and she thought more of her stepfather than she did of me simply because I was not a regular part of her life. I was a thousand miles away when she was growing up. Her mother, stepfather, and I got along fine, and Teri was happy at home, so it wasn't a nasty situation at all.

I had lost my daughter at the beginning of her life. Having lost the tears and joy of raising her, and knowing she would grow old and die without ever feeling a closeness for me, was another wound I suffered from the Vietnam War.

Although I was saddened by that loss, there was a balance in the happiness I had shared with Mary. I was still in the hospital when I met her, and after seventeen years of marriage we now had a little girl. We had despaired of ever having children. But after I had an operation to close off a fistula caused by an old shrapnel wound that was threatening me with heart failure, something else was corrected during the long surgery and I was able to beget.

The experiences and wounds of Vietnam had indeed reached deep within me and had had a powerful influence on every aspect of my adult life.

I was part of Vietnam and Vietnam was part of me.

I pushed the chair, suddenly weary from a day of extraordinary events, roller-coaster emotions, and flashbacks. I put on shorts, set my travel alarm, and slipped beneath the mosquito netting. I turned out the light, tucked in the netting, and lay back on the hard straw pallet, resting my head on a spartan thin pillow and thinking how wonderfully strange everything was that I had seen so far.

August 26, 1987—The First Meeting

★ I awoke at that time in the early dawn when there is just enough gray light to make out what is around you. I lay on the hard straw pallet and took in the alien room. The mosquito netting draped over the bed enclosed me in a light gauzy cocoon, while the musty smell of the straw-filled pallet reminded me of my grandfather's barn, a pleasant smell, and relaxing.

The air conditioner ruined the effect with its roaring, which made the room sound like a B-17 bomber in flight. I looked at my travel alarm and decided I could stay in bed for one hour more. Breakfast would be served between seven and eight o'clock. I lay under a thin cotton cover, unable to go back to sleep, thinking about these alien surroundings half a world away from my home, and about the six other Americans sleeping in their rooms down the hallway.

All of us were here because out there in the Vietnamese countryside somewhere were the remains of eighteen hundred American servicemen who died in a war that ended thirteen years ago. On the other side of this planet were their families, still waiting to bury them. I never would have imagined I would be involved in anything like this.

I gave up trying to sleep, slid out from under the mosquito netting, and tried to put on the shower thongs provided with the room. My size-11 feet overwhelmed the small thongs. The Vietnamese were just too small-bodied for anything of theirs to fit us.

All seven of us met down in the dining room. A table had been set with four on one side and three on the other side. The Vietnamese were adhering to our wishes to keep us separated into two teams, even down to the breakfast table. We were served a Vietnamese breakfast of eggs, fruit, butter, and weevil bread.

Larry had brought along his small jar of instant coffee and we finally got the message across to the non-English-speaking waitress that we wanted hot water. When she brought it, it was a large dull metallic green thermos bottle, with a light bulb setting in the top as a stopper. As she set the thermos down in front of us, we stared at the light bulb like it was a joke. But it was no joke. In a land too poor to generate trash, everything is used and reused in a steady downward chain of devolution. Yesterday a light bulb, today a stopper for a thermos bottle, tomorrow who knows what.

We started relating stories of what we had seen in South Vietnam back in the war days when there would be hundreds of Vietnamese combing through the large dumps the Americans generated outside their bases. They did the most amazing things with our garbage. For instance, they would take the tin cans, melt out the solder, pound the cans out flat, resolder them into sheets, and then make things like suitcases. I have never forgotten seeing Vietnamese walking along carrying suitcases with the logos of the cans they had been made from: Coke, Budweiser, Quaker State Oil . . .

Those trash dumps must have been like mountains of treasure to the South Vietnamese. We all agreed an American trash dump would not last long in Vietnam today. In fact, someone said only half-kiddingly, with all the trouble the United States had getting rid of its trash, maybe a deal could be worked out with Vietnam to get the trash concession from America.

At 0830 the two teams went to their respective meetings on separate floors in the guesthouse. The Joint Recovery team met on the fourth floor, while the expert medical team met on the third floor. Our room was a small, unventilated space off of the staircase landing. I had noticed the maids watching TV in the room the night before. There was no air conditioning here and heavy curtains closed off the windows.

The Vietnamese Delegation was already in the room, standing and talking, when we climbed the steps onto the landing. Carl and I were very curious as to what these people would be like. They turned toward us as we reached the top of the stairs and came forward through the wood-framed double glass doors to greet us.

I looked closely at each one. There were eight men, all but two of them older than me. They were all short, small-boned, well-proportioned men, dressed in casual light clothing of slacks and open-necked shirts. We had taken our cue from Mr. Le Bang yesterday and we were also dressed in open-necked short-sleeve shirts. It was the only sensible way to dress in that oppressive heat.

We were introduced to the delegation. The leader was Dang Nghiem Bai, Director of Foreign Affairs, North American section. Dang was the family name and Bai the given name, but it is customary to call Vietnamese by their given name: Mr. Bai. We had been warned that if Mr. Bai was in charge of the delegation we would be in for a difficult time because Mr. Bai was a hard, tough, unrelenting man.

He certainly looked the part. He was about 5 feet tall, and his thin body looked as wiry as a piece of tough gristle left in the sun. He had piercing brown eyes, receding black hair, and ears that flared out from his head. He was smiling, and although he had all his teeth, they were stained and uneven. He was altogether a distinctive-looking man who projected an aura of confidence.

He shook hands and introduced his delegation. Dr. Bui Tung, Director, Prosthetic Institute; Nguyen Van Dong, Acting Director, Health Ministry; Bui Thanh Giang, Deputy Director, Ministry for Labor, Invalids, and Social Affairs; Le Bang, Assistant Director, Foreign Ministry; Nguyen Van Vinh, Secretary; Vu Khac Nhu, Secretary; and Tran Trong Hai, Rehabilitation Physician/Interpreter.

We filed into the narrow room and sat down opposite each other. The table was not very long, so their delegation took up three sides and we sat on the fourth with our backs to the door.

After both teams were seated, an Australian press group and a Vietnamese press group came in to take videos and still photographs. I wondered how this would play on the local news broadcast and I had a particular curiosity as to why there was an Australian press group in here.

They quickly took their pictures and departed. Mr. Bai got right down to business by reading verbatim a prepared statement which emphasized that this meeting was the first in the area of urgent humanitarian needs. We got the distinct impression he was specifically implying there would be more meetings to come. This perked our ears up as a positive sign they were sincere in this humanitarian issue.

Mr. Bai at first spoke through an interpreter, the rehabilitation physician Mr. Tran Trong Hai. However, Mr. Bai got exasperated after a couple of sentences at the mistakes the doctor was making in the translations. Mr. Bai kept interrupting to make corrections.

He specifically corrected the interpreter to emphasize the point about the "first meeting." It was at this point that he then directed Mr. Le Bang to interpret. Even with Mr. Le Bang, though, Mr. Bai would occasionally make corrections.

We were to discover Mr. Bai spoke English very well. He had been Vietnam's ambassador to Britain and he had been in charge of the Vietnamese mission to the UN in New York for three years.

When he was through with his opening remarks, it was our turn. Dr. Carl Savory formally introduced his team and made a brief initial statement. The gist of it was that General Vessey had sent us to Vietnam in a truly humanitarian spirit. Our mission was to gather facts and information, and to do an analysis of the conditions which affected the care and rehabilitation of the disabled in Vietnam, particularly in the area of prosthetic fitting and fabrication. We would report back to our government and to the nongovernment organizations (NGOs) on what we had found and what we thought the problems were. Consequently we had many questions that we would like to raise in order to present a clear picture of the situation here.

Carl ended by saying, "Our team sincerely would like to see concrete evidence of progress in this humanitarian area, progress that the American and Vietnamese people and the rest of the world can recognize as a result of people helping people. It is important to remember that a long journey begins with the first step."

The Vietnamese seemed to respond very favorably to Carl's presentation, and by their expressions and body language showed they were impressed by the reminder that a long journey begins with the first step.

I had been taking notes like mad and was thankful for the lull as Mr. Bai shuffled through an indexed sheaf of papers in an accordion file he had taken out of a much-worn briefcase at the beginning of the meeting. As the meetings progressed, this searching through the files after Carl spoke became a regular routine. We formed the impression he had a prepared statement for any contingency we would present. If we were hostile or insincere, he probably had a nasty index tab for us. If we were honest and sincere, which we always were, then he probably had a nicer tab. We were to experience a little of the nasty tab once in a while even when we thought we did not deserve it. But that was later.

All of us on both sides of the table took advantage of the lull to sample the refreshments on the table. There was strong black coffee and tea served in small, sturdy pots, bottled water of two brands, large bottles of warm beer, bananas, various fruits I did not recognize, and small squares of various types of sweets made from rice.

Mr. Bai found the paper he was looking for and we all prepared for his response. Now we would start getting into the real issues. Neither side up to this point knew the sincerity of the other side.

Mr. Bai read from his prepared statement at first, but as he got into it, the paper was used more as working notes to which he referred as he made his points. He started off by stating that Dr. Savory had not defined short-term goals. This statement turned out to be rhetorical in nature, as we would find out with later similar statements and questions.

Mr. Bai brought up prosthetics and orthopedics for the first time. He focused on a statement in General Vessey's August 20, 1987, message about the first important step. Mr. Bai talked extensively about "short-term goals," stating that if urgent problems were solved, "that will lessen suffering of our people," both in the Socialist Republic of Vietnam and the United States. He then went on to define "urgent needs," using examples of the care and rehabilitation of amputees and the spinal-cord-injured as areas with significant problems.

He and Dr. Bui Tung pointed out that currently only one third of the prosthetics needed for amputations could be met by the Vietnamese government's system. They went on to state that their goals in the area of prosthetic fabrication were to meet the needs of the other two thirds of the amputees. They wanted to be able to provide all amputees with lighter-weight prostheses. They were also concerned that the prostheses have a cosmetic appearance.

I was furiously taking notes, but at the same time I was

thinking how often I had heard the same refrain. In America, among the amputees I had met in twenty years of activism across the nation; in Mexico, from the amputees and staff at the rehabilitation center I helped their government set up; in Egypt, in my work with the Egyptian Army rehabilitation center in Cairo where disabilities are "as Allah wills"; and in El Salvador, where I assisted in developing an amputee center for victims of land mines, mostly children, from the guerrilla war.

Now here I was in Vietnam hearing the same thing within a few minutes of the meeting's start. I looked across at the row of Vietnamese. I did not trust them because I thought they were wily and conniving, but still, what they were saying was the truth. The concerns of an amputee were something I knew. Maybe this was a good sign. Maybe they were serious after all. Maybe.

They then talked about the needs of the spinal-cord-injured. Although artificial limbs were to be our main concern, we had the latitude to listen to any other problems they brought up. I was particularly interested in the needs of the spinal-cord-injured, and so I was pleased they wanted to include them in this first session. When they began to talk about wheelchairs, Carl and I could see they were talking about paraplegics and bi-lateral lower-extremity amputees who required the use of a wheelchair for mobilization. They specifically excluded quadraplegics and those confined to beds. We imagined those disabled did not live long enough to be helped anyway.

They made it very clear they were in desperate need of wheelchairs, but they also made it very clear they could produce wheelchairs themselves if they had enough raw materials to make them. They emphasized over and over the need for raw materials.

"We can build them ourselves if we have something to build with" was a statement we heard many times, but I must admit it did not click with us. We were thinking of how to solve the problem the American way—with technology and equipment—and the idea of raw materials wasn't part of that thinking at first.

As Mr. Bai continued, he stressed that he had been reminded by Minister Thach on the way to the meetings that it was very important to reach "concrete terms." Consequently our request to visit a rehabilitation center had been approved for the following day. We would be visiting the Center for Prosthetics and Rehabilitation at Ba Vi, one of the centers headed by Dr. Bui Tung.

The Vietnamese team emphasized that the center the American team would see was the biggest and the best, but was not representative of a typical center available throughout the country. All other centers were inferior. They pointed out that transportation of patients and general communication within the country was extremely difficult.

It was at this point that the meeting took a different turn. Mr. Bai began stressing the difficulties in the areas of previous "heavy bombing." He said he did not want to link the medical meeting with the POW/MIA meeting upstairs, but "sixty percent of the POW/MIAs came from these areas which had sustained heavy bombing."

I could not see Larry's face, but I could see Carl, and both he and I tried to remain poker-faced at this sudden turn in the meeting. Were all of our fears going to be justified? Was this a prelude to the Vietnamese going back to their old attempts to link humanitarian aid to political and economic issues? If they did, then the trip was for naught. I was disheartened as I prepared for the worst.

Then Mr. Bai began to lecture about American involvement in Vietnam since the war ended. He stated that for twelve years the Vietnamese had helped the Americans try to resolve the POW/MIA issue without any reciprocal help from the United States. He said this presented an ongoing problem for the Socialist Republic of Vietnam and at the last Party Congress it was the only area where the Ministry of Foreign Affairs was criticized. He underscored the fact there must be a two-way dialogue established. Mr. Bai said if the United States helped in the heavily bombed areas, "you will help yourself on the MIA issue." In order for there to be success in looking for MIA remains, the cooperation of the local people was essential.

He went on to define further "heavily bombed" areas. He became very specific and stated that one of the areas which had many invalids, disabled, and orphans was the panhandle area from latitude 20 degrees to 17 degrees. He also included latitude 13 degrees in the south of Vietnam as having urgent humanitarian needs. He said this was a very heavy combat area, with many, many MIA cases, and that perhaps there were more MIAs there than in the heavy combat area at latitude 20 to 17 degrees.

It was very important, Mr. Bai continued, that the United States convince the people who lived in these areas of two-way action. "The people of Vietnam have a long tradition on humanitarian issues, but cannot expect unilateral action on human issues to go on forever." "Frankly," he went on, "if the U.S. effort is big in the humanitarian areas, it is still minimal compared to the suffering of Vietnam." He quoted a figure of forty thousand dead or wounded caused from bombs and ammunition left behind after the war.

In conclusion, Mr. Bai said that efforts should concentrate on the disabled civilians and children. Long-term problems included orphans and "lonely people." (We found out later this was a term to describe individuals, usually the elderly and women, who had no one to support them or depend on other than the state.) He also mentioned in closing the 2 million people who were affected by Agent Orange and problems in providing health care and medical education. He reiterated that while Vietnam was communicating these needs to us, they were not to be construed as "war reparations or economic needs." This was just information to help us understand their problems.

As both sides were acutely aware, it was imperative that we maintain the distinction that humanitarian concerns were separate from economic and political concerns. The line was thin indeed and both sides would often take pains to remind the other of that distinction if an issue or statement was in doubt. Of such fine ink, diplomacy is written. Even so, our carefully crafted wording would later often be ignored by certain people or groups who saw any flexibility on our part as giving in to the Vietnamese demand for war reparations or economic aid. Everybody who supported the Vessey mission would come under criticism on this issue.

A break followed, and we all welcomed the chance to stretch. The note takers on their side and I, the note taker on our side, needed to straighten out our papers and read what we had written. This was the first time I had ever been involved in something like this. Mr. Bai spoke at a rate slow enough for me to copy, but I often wondered if what he was saying was translated properly. There were many times already where I thought I knew the point he wanted to make, but I was not sure he had translated it right. I could see where a word could make a big difference in meaning.

I walked downstairs to my room to refresh by throwing some water on my face and neck. The temperature in the room must have been over 100 degrees. It made me think about those hot days in the jungle when some of the men wore bath towels around their neck to wipe off the sweat. I chuckled at what they would think if I walked back in there with a towel around my neck.

Back upstairs, I talked to Carl and Larry. We agreed we thought it was going okay, but the language barrier was troublesome. Were we missing something? Larry said he did not think so, based on his experience from trips he had made before.

We went back into the room to begin the next session. Before sitting down we poured water into glasses and nibbled on the fruit. We were just shooting the breeze with the Vietnamese and the conversation got around to my artificial arm and how it worked. I showed everyone, including Carl and Larry, how I could peel a banana with my hook. They all gathered around at this demonstration and asked me a number of questions.

I asked them if they would like to see how it worked. Their eyes lit up and they said yes, they would. I had given this demonstration hundreds of times in the last twenty years because I had found that few people, including medical professionals, really knew or understood an above-elbow prosthesis. Even though they are dying to ask how it works, they do not want to embarrass me or hurt my feelings so they rarely will. Explaining the arm is always a great way to remove the fear from little kids and satisfy the curiosity of adults.

I unbuttoned my shirt and removed it. Meantime I kept up a running commentary on the purpose and value of such demonstrations in removing the fear and ignorance people have about prosthetics and disabilities.

All of the Vietnamese Delegation and my two partners watched in equal fascination as I pointed to various parts of my arm to describe how they functioned. First I showed the hook, which I opened with a cable attached to my harness. I pointed out the short, wide rubber bands which pulled the hook back together when I relaxed the tension in my harness. I showed them how the harness was attached to the prosthesis, and then I turned around to show how the harness crossed behind my back and looped under the opposite arm to support the prostheses, and how it was used to create tension on the two cables in order to make them operate. One short cable ran from the elbow and fastened to the harness parallel to the clavicle, and it locked and unlocked the elbow by a shrug of my shoulder against the snug harness. The other, longer cable was fastened to a projection off the hook and ran up along the arm around to the back, where it fastened to the harness near my shoulder blade. When I flexed my shoulders against the snug-fitting harness, I created tension on the cable, which opened the hook when the elbow was locked and moved the forearm up if the elbow was unlocked.

Using the hook, I picked up various items from the table and moved them around. I held a pen in the hook and used it to write Mr. Bai's name on the tablet in front of me. I peeled another banana and opened the wrapping around one of the small rice finger cakes.

Then I offered to show them the gripping power of the hook and asked for a volunteer to hold out a finger. Usually when I do this with people, there is always a slight hesitation. No one seems eager to stick their finger between the prongs of a metal hook for the purpose of testing its crushing ability. There is absolutely no danger, but still there is often a hesitation.

Not so with Mr. Bai. He grinned and without a moment's hesitation stuck out his finger to test the grip. I extended my hook out and opened it up to put around the finger. Then I gently relaxed the tension in my shoulder blades, letting the cable slowly play out so the rubber bands could pull the prongs together. Everyone was staring intently at the hook as it gripped Bai's finger. I let all the tension out in order to show him the full strength of the hook. Mr. Bai smiled to show everything was fine and I released his finger by opening the hook. Excited conversation broke out between them as others put their fingers out for a demonstration. I obliged them all, including my teammates.

My next move surprised them because I quickly removed my arm and handed it to them to examine. I took off my stump sock and described its function as basically a cushion and buffer. Then I described the stump, the importance of the placing of a proper surgical scar, the importance of a longer stump, and the personal hygiene a stump must receive.

Each member of the delegation examined the plastic artificial arm, turning it upside down, peering into the socket, checking out the harness, elbow, forearm, hook, and cables. After they were finished, they passed it over to Larry and Carl, who gave it the once-over and returned it to me. I put it back on, put on my shirt, and buttoned it up using my buttonhook.

I believed they were impressed with the arm. We talked about prosthetics before we started the regular meeting. The demonstration seemed to be a real icebreaker and the atmosphere seemed more relaxed afterwards. The Vietnamese are very informal. I think they regarded us as being too stuffy to give a demonstration like this. It seemed to be a turning point.

Carl Savory was first to speak at the next session. As with the earlier session, he would speak in short phrases and then wait until Mr. Bai or Mr. Hai translated into Vietnamese. When Mr. Bai spoke to us in English, there would be a pause while Mr. Hai translated what Mr. Bai had said into Vietnamese for the benefit of the Vietnamese in the delegation who did not understand English that well.

Carl said that the U.S. team had many questions, the answers to which would be very important in communicating the humanitarian needs of the Vietnamese people to the appropriate individuals upon the team's return to the United States. Carl emphasized during this presentation, as he did at all times, that our team was a "fact-finding" team.

When Carl got to the point of asking specific questions, I was finally allowed to speak officially for the first time. My role at this point was to expand upon each question for the purpose of getting as much detail as possible. What a relief it was finally to be able to speak! This was the longest I had ever gone in an important meeting keeping my mouth shut.

Often the meaning of a translation would not be clear. Then both sides looked puzzled as they tried to figure out what exactly was meant. One good example was our "questions." We found out later the Vietnamese interpreted the word "question" as "request." Bill Bell explained that the word "request" (*yeu cau*) also meant "demand" in Vietnamese. Therefore, when we were politely asking questions about information we wanted, they were interpreting that we were demanding information.

As Carl and I asked our questions that morning, the Vietnamese team took notes, but they had little response or comment. We explained the need for the answers to each question we asked. Even though we felt most of the questions were, from a professional viewpoint, self-explanatory, we were trying to be sensitive to what we perceived as a Vietnamese hesitancy to deal with our questions.

The questions we asked were as follows:

1. Amputees: how many are there? How many new cases per year? How many were traumatic? How many caused by disease?
2. How many of these amputees have prostheses?
3. Is there revision surgery? How much? Where is it performed? What are the problems encountered in surgery?
4. What is the system for providing an artificial limb to an amputee? What local, district, and regional systems are there, and who is responsible for the patient's training and evaluation?
5. How is fabrication of the limb accomplished? How is the prosthetist trained? How many prosthetists and laboratories are there and where are they located throughout the country? How many limbs do they fabricate? How long does it take for them to fabricate a limb?
6. What are the materials used in the fabrication of the limb? Are there any supply problems? What is the equipment used at each prosthetic shop?
7. Who is responsible for the rehabilitation of the amputee? Where does the rehabilitation take place —at the local, district, or regional level?
8. If rehabilitation is at the regional level, how do the

patients get there? How long do they stay? Do they receive vocational rehabilitation?

This was not all we asked, but the questions are typical. To us they were obviously the kinds of things that any consultant anywhere in the world would ask in order to develop a base of information from which to work toward solutions. After we were finished, we looked expectantly at the Vietnamese.

Mr. Bai put on his glasses, looked through his index file, stopped at one, pulled out sheets of low-quality lined tablet paper, and began to read from a prepared statement. But as he progressed through his statement, he referred to it only intermittently.

Mr. Bai reiterated that the priority humanitarian need was "to help the invalid children from the war." He emphasized that the number of individuals needing urgent care was high. He said the Vietnamese government was trying to concentrate on the individuals who had lost the capacity to work or provide for themselves. He mentioned again a "realistic" approach and stated what they were talking about was "three hundred thousand people being taken care of by the government."

Mr. Bai said these were the serious, urgent cases. He indicated that "the same category of serious cases was much higher at the end of the war," and that the Socialist Republic of Vietnam had obtained help from its friends in the Socialist countries and developing countries and a few Western countries.

He named some of the centers sponsored by these countries. One was in Haiphong Harbor and had been built by Norway. One center at Ba Vi (a center we would later visit) had been built by the German Democratic Republic. The American Friends Service Committee had built a center in Qui Nhon. Mr. Bai added that "all efforts would be extremely difficult without help from our friends. Technology in the North was trying to catch up to the Socialist countries, and in the South, we are relying on the old USA facilities."

Dr. Bui Tung spoke after Bai. He told us our questions revealed an obvious gap in technology between the two countries, and he made some statements about the differences.

Carl responded with some general remarks, essentially reemphasizing the fact-finding nature of our mission; that the answers to our questions were extremely important; and that it was necessary for our team to get a true feeling about the urgency of the Vietnamese problem. He repeated the points about needing specific answers and statistics, and communicated that the general feeling on our part was encouraging, based on this first plenary session.

Mr. Bai closed the meeting by stating it was too hot at 105 degrees to start the afternoon meeting before 1430 hours. He said that meanwhile they would work on getting the answers to the questions we had asked.

We went to our rooms to freshen up while they trooped downstairs and out to their cars, where the drivers had been waiting under the shade of the gigantic tree next to the guesthouse. We met downstairs in the dining room with the JCRC team, where we all sat together at the one table set up for us. We discussed the morning sessions and tried to get a sense of how it was going. As expected, the POW/MIA team's meeting had been nonproductive. Joe Harvey said the Vietnamese were friendly enough this time compared to some other meetings in years past, but they were not being any more forthcoming in answering any questions. Mr. Can, who worked for Mr. Bai and headed the Vietnamese Delegation meeting with Colonel Harvey, clearly was just going through the motions.

The key was the events taking place in our meeting. Carl told Joe, Paul, Johnie, and Bill that we thought our meeting was going very well and that it had been productive. Carl said we had been completely honest and sincere in our presentations and had shown them we were truly interested in helping them with their problems.

For their part, Carl commented, we had not been subjected to any attacks or propaganda or charges against America. In fact, we had the impression Mr. Bai was in charge of the humanitarian meeting because of its importance. He was there to gauge us and to ensure that there was no quibbling on the part of the Vietnamese Delegation. Whatever we wanted to know or see he would make sure we received a straightforward answer. Indeed, Carl said, we were constantly surprised at how open Mr. Bai and the delegation were. We found it hard to believe, but we felt the Vietnamese were telling us the truth. We certainly had not expected that to occur.

We all wondered what the Vietnamese were really up to. Did it mean they were sincere about the General Vessey agreement? It was far too early to determine that, but we all agreed that the morning had gone well.

After lunch, Carl and I went over to change U.S. dollars into Vietnamese dong at the Bank of Vietnam, the stone-columned, majestic building with the enormous billboard of Ho Chi Minh on the roof.

Although the ladies who changed our money were friendly and courteous, getting the money exchanged involved us in Communist inefficiency. In this case, four people were processing the paperwork required to change money. After watching them, I could see one person could have done it in half the time or less.

The official exchange rate was 80 dong to the U.S. dollar, but the black market price was 400 dong to the dollar and skyrocketing. Part of the laborious paperwork we went through was to enable the government to account for every dollar spent in Vietnam. The government was trying to control the black market and at the same time pretend it did not exist.

At the official exchange rate, whatever we bought with

dong was outrageously overpriced. All I wanted was to buy stamps and mail out souvenir postcards, but I would have to pay top dollar to do it. I did not even think about the black market, though. Only a fool would do something illegal in a Communist country, especially Vietnam. I had no desire to see the inside of Hoa Lo Prison the hard way.

Finally, we got the money we needed and left through the double side doors. Our wallets were bursting with the thick wad of dong. We stood out on the sidewalk discussing where to go. Carl said he was returning to the guesthouse, and I decided to go to the post office to buy my stamps.

It was only a block away. When I went up the broad marble steps and into the open king-size double doors, I had to stop in the lobby and look around to see which counter I should go to.

I turned around a couple of times and finally asked the next person to walk by me, a woman in her thirties, if she could speak English. Her eyes lit up and her face broke into a smile. She answered, Yes, she could speak English, but not very well. I thought to myself, That may be true, lady, but you speak a hell of a lot more English than I speak Vietnamese. She directed me to a counter and went on her way.

I was to be constantly amazed at the large number of people I met of all ages in the street who could speak some English. Vietnam bragged it had the highest literacy rate in Asia and the world at over 90 percent. Carl and I were skeptical of such claims, but there was no doubt the people we met in the street were educated. We wondered if this was true in the countryside. Also we wondered if it was real education or simply Marxist-Leninist indoctrination.

A wooden counter top ran the length of both sides of the stone-floored room. The post office looked like another of those massive French government spaces used to serve the public. There were individual counters down the middle of the floor where one could stand to write out addresses.

I stood in the line pointed out by the lady—actually more

of a group than a line. I did not want to be rude by pushing myself forward until it was my turn, but I wasn't sure how I could tell it was my turn. I decided I had better push forward or I would stand there forever. The middle-aged lady sitting behind the counter selling stamps did not speak English. But when I leaned my elbows on the counter to indicate to her and the people around me that I thought it was my turn, she and I used our hands, finger pointing, and pen and pencil to get our messages across to each other.

I laid one of my postcards out on the counter and stamped it with my fist. She nodded her head yes, but then shrugged her shoulders and pointed to a map in front of her of the world on an 8 by 11 sheet. I pointed to the USA. She smiled and said something, at which the Vietnamese crowd waiting at the counter looked directly at me. They perked up and became animated as they chattered among themselves. Open curiosity was in their faces. Some of them smiled and a couple even made noises of excitement.

I was surprised at their reaction. I had expected hostility in Hanoi, but I did not see it in any of the faces around me. I smiled back and wondered how could this be possible. We had been their archenemy, and in some ways still were, yet there was not a trace of that naked hatred I expected to experience from the people. I knew how I would have felt a week ago if I had encountered a North Vietnamese in my local post office.

My attention turned back to the matter at hand as the lady spread out four different stamps with different Communist themes for me to pick from. One with a picture of Ho Chi Minh on a red background caught my eye. I figured the best souvenir I could send my friends back in the States would be a postcard with a stamp of Ho Chi Minh and a Hanoi postmark.

I indicated I wanted to send thirty and was shocked at the price she wrote on a piece of paper. Each postcard was going to cost me about $3.50 to send. I counted through my wad of dong and came up short. I pulled out my U.S. dollars in

119

hopes of paying with them but to no avail. I had enough dong to send twenty postcards so I asked for that number of stamps.

She counted out the twenty Ho Chi Minh stamps and gave them to me. I already had three cards ready to go, so I went over to one of the counters to stick on the stamps. I licked the first one, but it did not have any glue on it. What the hell gives? I thought. Then I remembered when I was a new lieutenant in the South, I had brought a hundred stamps with me from home in case I could not buy them in Vietnam. Being the green troop I was, I did not know the military sent your mail home for free. When I pulled out my billfold after a couple of days in Vietnam, I discovered all of my stamps had stuck together because of the high humidity. The stamps were worthless. So naturally the Vietnamese post office would not sell stamps with glue already on them.

I did not know what I was supposed to do now. How would I get those damn stamps on my postcards? I took my three postcards back to the lady behind the counter, who took them and the three stamps from my hand before I could even open my mouth. She pulled a brush from a glue pot at the corner of her work space, carefully applied glue to the corner of the postcards, and just as carefully affixed the stamps to the glue. Next, she used an ink pad and hand stamp to affix the Hanoi postmark. She blew on the glue and smiled as she handed the three cards back to me and pointed to the front door where two mailboxes sat. I dropped the cards in what I hoped was the right slot and I thought there was no way they would ever get sent out of the country. Later on my friends reported that the cards started to arrive about three weeks after the postmark.

I walked out onto the front steps and paused in the blazing hot sunshine. I noticed the people hanging around the steps looking at me. I was a stranger in their midst and an object of curiosity.

Next to the curb were seven old decrepit bicycle rick-shaws. The drivers reminded me of soldiers with their faded olive-drab pith helmets and khaki trousers and shirts. Some of them were perched up on their bicycle seats and others were lounging in the passenger seat. Everyone smoked.

I crossed the street to walk along the Lake of the Restored Sword and meditate about these Vietnamese people. I had noticed yesterday and today something that struck me as unusual about the Vietnamese. At first they would ignore us and act coldly toward us, believing we were Russians, some of whom were around the city. But when the Vietnamese figured out we were Americans, they became friendly and curious.

This at first surprised me, for I believed the Vietnamese in the North to have an undying hatred of Americans. I had been reading in the American papers for years about the Vietnamese condemnation of Americans, of our "war crimes," and our failure to recognize Vietnam.

As I have said, I certainly knew how my buddies and I felt about the North Vietnamese. They degraded our dead soldiers by holding them for ransom for some ungodly reason. Mainly, I thought, to make America suffer for as long as they could by torturing the unfortunate families of these gallant men lost in battle.

So, I had hated the Vietnamese and I believed they hated us too. But here I was in the middle of Hanoi and I did not feel hatred toward these people. What was even more unsettling was that these people did not seem to hate us. In my mind's eye, I had pictured the Vietnamese people being as hateful toward Americans as those old World War II propaganda posters had portrayed the Japanese. Sinister and malevolent.

It wasn't so. As I walked around the lake in the humid heat of the noonday sun, I studied the people in the busy streets and I felt an odd sense of internal freedom. I was actually enjoying myself for the most bizarre of reasons.

I was not on guard for my life. When I was in Vietnam in 1967 and 1968, I had always wanted to be able to go for a walk and look around without having to worry about getting shot or blown up by these people. Now here I was smack in the middle of Hanoi, and I was safe. The people were friendly and I was having an enjoyable time. I could relax that old sense of danger.

The pleasure of walking peacefully among my former enemies and seeing them as people, after hating them all these years, seemed to release me from that hatred. The relief gave me freedom.

At 1430 hours we assembled back in the meeting room on our floor. Mr. Bai and Carl Savory resumed their conversations and cautiously explored the perimeters of what was possible between us.

Mr. Bai began with an overview of the humanitarian situation. He again brought up the importance of focusing on the "urgent needs." He then reviewed statistics he said were given to the United Nations "right after the war." These figures excluded the military and the 400,000 disabled of the "puppet regime"—the South Vietnamese.

The statistics of those Vietnamese needing humanitarian care were read from a list Mr. Bai pulled from his index file. They included the following: 300,000 disabled civilians: 1 million orphans, including 100,000 disabled children; and 1 million widows and people without means of support or assistance.

Mr. Bai made a point of telling us that since 1975, 100,000 disabled had died, and if there had been better care available many of them might have been saved. He looked up from his notes and directly at us with the clear implication America could have done something back then.

Carl, Larry, and I remained stoic throughout these barbed comments. Even though I had found freedom through loss of hatred for them as an old enemy, I wasn't in love with them, either. We were here to get facts, we weren't bleeding hearts. It might have been different for Larry Ward because his whole life had been one of humanitarian effort. He was deeply religious and had never harmed anyone in his life. The way Carl and I looked at it, the disabled and dead were part of the price of war. It was too bad for those people, but it was a fact of life.

War was not abstract to us. Both Carl and I had been combat officers who had personally killed Vietnamese, had led men in combat for the purpose of killing Vietnamese, and we had suffered personal wounds, in addition to seeing Americans and allies being killed and wounded by the Vietnamese we fought. That was our mission then. Now our mission was to gather facts objectively and report back to General Vessey. Whatever we reported would be the facts based on what we observed. There was no sense of guilt on our part for what America did or did not do in the past. That was war, and war is by its nature a cruel, capricious, unforgiving, indiscriminate form of death, and politics at its worst.

If Mr. Bai and the Vietnamese government thought they were going to lay a guilt trip on this team, they were wasting their time. Carl and I felt no guilt.

Mr. Bai shifted his focus to the most urgent cases needing humanitarian care. These were the 300,000 individuals who were described by him as disabled, incapable of working, and totally dependent on the state or others for their existence. The amputees made up a portion of this category.

It was at this point that Mr. Bai informed us our request to visit a prosthetic center had been granted. We would leave in a van the next morning to travel approximately 50 kilometers northwest to tour the center at Ba Vi, a village close to Son Tay. This would be the first time Americans had been allowed up there, we were told.

I believed it. Son Tay was where the Americans had conducted a raid during the war to rescue American POWs from a North Vietnamese prison camp.

The raid failed to rescue any POWs. The planning took too long, six months, and the situation changed. The POWs were moved and the planners did not heed intelligence information indicating the camp was empty. On the night of November 20, 1970, the rescue force, which had been training for months without knowing the mission until the last moment, left from Udorn Royal Thai Air Force Base, flying across Laos and into North Vietnam.

The fifty-six Army Special Forces volunteers flew in five Jolly Green Giant helicopters into the most dangerous combat area in the world at that time. They landed in Son Tay; were enveloped in violent firefights in which hundreds of enemy soldiers and advisers were killed; searched each cell in the prison; and only then after personally determining there were no POWs left in the prison did they pull off their own successful escape with just a few minor injuries. They were supported by Air Force and Navy pilots who flew them in, provided close air support, and conducted diversionary raids over Hanoi.

Although no POWs were rescued and the raid was a failure in that respect, the men who conducted it were no less brave than if it had been a success. The men performed brilliantly against great odds.

Another result of the raid was not known until years later. When these facts became clear, the "failure" of the Son Tay raid, in perspective, was not such a failure after all. The raid surprised the Vietnamese and caused a panic among their two strongest supporters, the Russians and the Chinese. Both countries were worried the Americans would conduct other pinpoint raids. But the most significant result from the raid was the Vietnamese decision to collect all the prisoners scattered through the war zones and put them into one place for safekeeping. That place was the Hanoi Hilton.

Men who had been kept in solitary confinement for years in caves and cages and small prisons were sent to Hanoi. There, many of these men saw other Americans for the first time and the will to survive was intensified. Their care by the Vietnamese improved somewhat. For all American prisoners everywhere, the Son Tay raid was to rank as one of their biggest single morale builders during their captivity, because it showed the American people had not forgotten them.

But, as with most things connected to Vietnam, failure was regarded not as a lesson to learn from but an embarrassment to forget. The military high command and the President's men wanted to sweep Son Tay under the rug as fast as possible. The man who led the raid, Colonel "Bull" Simmons, was passed over for general and retired six months later. The Army service schools never invited him to speak, although the Air Force service schools have. Citations for bravery were given to the men on the raid, but only after a great deal of pressure. In fact the medals were given, but the Army would not allow the citations to be written up and put into the men's records until more pressure was put on. (Most of the details of this sorry chapter in history are covered in *The Raid* by Benjamin F. Schemmer. I have also gleaned information from friends who knew many of the details from their military connections.)

All of this flashed through my mind when Mr. Bai mentioned Ba Vi. There was so much behind each word said at this table. He had so innocently mentioned Ba Vi, and yet the Vietnamese never did anything without a purpose. Mr. Bai went on to say that some of the questions we had posed to them in the morning session would be answered in the visit to the rehabilitation center at Ba Vi.

Dr. Bui Tung then made a presentation to us. He was not a pure politician like Mr. Bai, but he also spoke very good English. He was introduced as the director of rehabilitation and was both a professor and a surgeon. He was a robust-looking man in his fifties or sixties, bigger-boned and fleshier than Mr. Bai.

Dr. Bui Tung stated he was going to try to address the "demands" of the U.S. medical team. Dr. Savory was quick to take issue with the word "demand" and stated that we did not have demands, merely some questions that needed answering to better elucidate the problems and communicate the needs.

Dr. Bui Tung emphasized the point that he was a professional, but he felt he was expressing the opinion of his colleagues as well as the disabled people. He told us he wished we had come "twelve years earlier." After this morning's meeting, though, he felt the U.S. team was sincerely trying to make the first step, as was his team.

As to the assistance his country needed, Dr. Bui Tung said he had been thinking about this for quite some time. First we needed the statistics we had asked for, and he had them for us. As he gave us the numbers, he kept stressing that his statistics might differ from the numbers we had in our computers. He also paraphrased one of Carl's earlier statements that while the statistics were necessary, the overall concerns and needs of the people were more important.

It dawned on Carl and me that their side thought we had accurate statistics of their problems against which we would compare their statistics to see if they matched. They were worried because they did not have accurate statistics on their disabled.

He needn't have worried. No country in the world, including America, has accurate statistics on its disabled, but I did not think they needed to know that just then.

Dr. Bui Tung then described the general structure of prosthetic manufacture and rehabilitation services throughout the country. There were seven centers where artificial limbs were fabricated and patients rehabilitated. He emphasized the centers had the technicians with the expertise but they lacked the materials. He said they needed everything used in fabrication, including plastic, wood, metal, and leather. He said they were using aluminum for sockets as well as for calipers (leg braces).

The emphasis then shifted from our focus on prosthetics as Dr. Bui Tung began to talk about surgery for paralysis victims. He stated there was a general lack of X-ray film and antibiotics. Without the antibiotics, trying to achieve an acceptable standard of 2 percent infection rate was very difficult. It was at this point we found out that Bui Tung was a surgeon in addition to being a professor.

He talked about how the orthopedic center in the South had equipment that was twelve to fifteen years old, but the orthopedic center in the North was in even worse shape, with even older equipment. This answered a question we had been wondering about; namely, would the South be included in these humanitarian needs? Evidently it would be.

He emphasized there was a great need for vehicles to transport rehabilitation teams out to the countryside and to bring in patients to the centers.

Dr. Tung went on to address the question of training and continuing medical education. Most of the prosthetic technicians in the North had been trained by representatives from the German Democratic Republic, he said, and the prosthetic technicians in the South had been trained by Americans during the war. But all of them lacked the materials, tools, and supplies to work with. They had an on-the-job training program using the more skilled technicians to train the new technicians. Dr. Bui Tung shuffled his notes and reminded us that "training was not so much the worry." The most urgent problem was material.

Carl and I then asked a number of questions to try to clarify the statistics they had given us earlier. We finally determined that of the "urgent" population of 300,000 disabled, 60,000 were amputees.

I was tired from the suffocating heat in the room and the stress of such intense concentration. The effort of taking notes, the discussion back and forth on certain words or phrases as we tried to figure out if the translations were really saying what we meant to each other, the straining to hear every word, watch every facial expression, catch every movement of body language, and not miss anything, had exhausted us. On our part we had to guard ourselves from giving something away with our words, gestures, body language, or facial expression, and guard against being misunderstood or making an inaccurate statement or saying something they could later use against us.

As the afternoon wore on, I studied these men more intently. I explored my own feelings. What did I feel, sitting across from the Vietnamese Delegation? Even the sound of it, "Vietnamese Delegation," felt like a flashback to the Paris Peace Talks, when the media was full of the news of the different delegations sitting at the large round table.

The atmosphere then had been charged with contentiousness about every single thing—from the arguments over who should be represented at the peace table to the very shape of the table. (After weeks they decided on a round table.) It had finally come down to four representatives; the United States Delegation, the North Vietnamese Delegation, the South Vietnamese Delegation, and the National Liberation Front Delegation, or Viet Cong. Henry Kissinger said in his book *Years of Upheaval* that meeting with the Vietnamese tested his sanity.

Nineteen years had passed since the beginning of the Paris Peace Talks in 1968, and now only the American Delegation and the North Vietnamese Delegation faced each other across the table at the government guesthouse in Hanoi. The players had changed, the location had changed, and the stakes had changed. But problems remained.

There were parallels between the delegations then and those today. Back then the idea was a two-track approach to negotiations, to separate the military issues from the political issues. That way America could extricate itself from the war and let the Vietnamese figure out a political solution among themselves.

This time we were separating the humanitarian issues from the political and economic issues. Although the magnitude and urgency of what we were doing did not hold a candle to the importance of the task of the delegations back in 1968 through 1972, our goal was important nevertheless.

General Vessey and those of us on his team were trying to find ways to solve problems that still festered from the war. We wanted the return of the POWs and an accounting of the MIAs, and the Vietnamese Delegation wanted help for their disabled.

I wondered if both countries were finally prepared to finish this forty-year episode.

I had been watching the Vietnamese all day. In their eyes and faces were reflected our own inner emotions: yes, we were all suspicious, guarded, slightly paranoid, careful in our speech patterns, cautious in what we said. Mr. Bai and Dr. Savory were the paladins for each team. They were here because of their skill, determination, and sincerity. They faced off against each other and we backed our respective leaders. But neither side would show its hand to the other. Still, we had to make some progress, and certain words were used to tiptoe through the verbal minefield to our objectives.

Mr. Bai suggested a break and a stretch. I poured another glass of bottled water and thankfully drank it down. I was surprised to see the heat and humidity was as hard on the Vietnamese as it was on us. I had always thought since they lived here they were used to it. Obviously I was wrong.

After a few minutes we sat back down. The Vietnamese shifted focus to the spinal-cord-injured patients. As they talked, we became confused because of the high numbers of spinal-cord-injured they claimed needed a wheelchair. In a Third World country there should be relatively few spinal-cord-injured patients because most of them die of urinary-tract or other infections within five years after their injury. This was a common occurrence in America until after World War II, when spinal-cord-injured veterans banded together, formed the Paralyzed Veterans of America, and kept the attention of medical people attuned to their plight until some medical advances were made. Progress was slow, but the average life span of a spinal-cord-injured person in America was now only five years less than the average life span of other Americans.

We were skeptical of the high numbers we were hearing, until we realized they seemed to have included bi-lateral above-knee amputees as well as cerebral palsy and polio victims as part of their spinal-cord-injured group. They had estimated from surveys that thirty thousand patients needed wheelchairs.

But, they told us, their present productivity capacity was only three hundred wheelchairs a year. They lacked the parts and materials to construct the wheelchairs, which, they said, had to meet "Vietnam's standards." After further questioning we deduced what that meant. "Vietnam's standards" meant the wheelchair had to be rugged and heavy-duty to withstand the environment, the roads, and the treatment it would receive.

From what I had seen so far, not only did the wheelchair have to be rugged and heavy-duty to survive, the person using it in these conditions had to be just as rough and ready as his chair.

Mr. Bai and Dr. Savory agreed we were all hot and tired after a long, stressful day, and so they adjourned, for which the rest of us were thankful. Mr. Bai invited us to a dinner in our honor that night in the guesthouse and asked us to meet him in the entrance hall at 1800 hours (6:00 P.M.)

Thus the second plenary session ended. Worthy of note was that no POW/MIA issues were brought up all afternoon. This was important because it meant the Vietnamese were sticking to the rules by restricting our group to medical problems.

We each received personal invitations from Ong (Mr.) Dang Nghiem Bai. Mine was addressed to Ong (Mr.) Fred Downs. I put on clean-pressed trousers and a short-sleeved shirt. We met the JCRC team on the landing. When Bai had first invited all of us together to dinner, both Colonel Harvey and Dr. Savory had mentioned to Bai that perhaps we should dine separately since we were concerned about keeping our missions totally separate. But the three men quickly decided it was a lot easier for us to all eat together.

We went downstairs to the main foyer. We entered through a curtain-covered glass door into the large room where we had been welcomed the first day.

Mr. Bai was there with his delegation. He also introduced us to the Vietnamese who had met with the JCRC team. Mr. Bai had his deputy, Mr. Nguyen Can, in charge of that group.

The success of future JCRC meetings would very likely depend on the success of the humanitarian meetings. If we reported back to General Vessey that the Vietnamese needed humanitarian help and President Reagan agreed to whatever the general and policymakers decided, that would be a sign of good faith on the part of America and a sign of our sincerity.

The Vietnamese would then return these signals with ones of their own, namely, forward movement on resolution of POW/MIA and other humanitarian issues.

This was a cautious first step we were taking.

Both sides in the room were very aware of the importance of what we said and did while we were together during these four days. Not just formal things but the informal things that occurred—the things that make us human. What we saw and experienced, how we were treated and our impressions about each other, were all part of what would shape our conclusions as both sides later tried to figure out the dynamics of what had happened.

Both sides would worry about whether the other side had somehow tricked or manipulated them. Both sides would wonder if what they heard was the truth. Neither side wanted to lose face or be made a fool of, so each was cautious.

We began with a cocktail. The Vietnamese did not stand around and mingle; they sat down on chairs lined up on one side of the room and we sat in a row on chairs on the opposite side of the room, while women served us apricot brandy in delicate thimble-sized glasses. It was difficult, however, to carry on a conversation sitting like this, talking across the room.

After a bit of small talk, one of the kitchen staff came in and spoke to Mr. Bai. He nodded, then told us dinner was ready. We all stood, and he ushered us around the screens to where two round tables were set for dinner. The white tablecloths were laid with plates, silverware, and glassware. None of it was fancy. It was simple and functional.

Name cards had been placed showing where each of us should sit. After we sat down, various liquors were poured into the three stem glasses in front of our plates: vodka, apricot brandy, and a dark red wine. None of us, including the Vietnamese, drank the vodka. Mr. Bai led off with a modest toast with the brandy, wishing both sides success in solving our common problems. Dr. Savory returned the toast with one of similar hopes.

Everyone was friendly and the Vietnamese seemed to be comfortable. They drank little or no alcohol. There was plenty to drink, but I had no taste for the hard liquor. I tried the wine but it was terrible, so I drank beer. The bottled water had a smoky taste which I was getting used to.

As the evening progressed through numerous courses of very fine Vietnamese cuisine, I had a good opportunity to ask questions and observe these Vietnamese in more detail.

Mr. Bai, the leader, represented to me the quintessential North Vietnamese. He had been a prisoner of war under the Japanese; he had been shot in the stomach in 1952 when he was a Viet Minh fighting against the French; and he had been in charge of clandestine affairs in urban areas in the fight against the Americans.

As we relaxed and conversed in the comfortable setting, I thought to myself that Mr. Bai was no soft touch. He was one hard-core revolutionary who had been fighting for his country all of his adult life—over forty years of conflict. He had committed his life to fighting for his country. Although

I in no way agreed with his political philosophy, I found myself respecting the man for his determination and sacrifices.

But now that he had achieved all of his lifetime goals for his countrymen, I wondered what he thought about the present situation. The country was desperately poor, the UN statistics showed that. The Russians were pouring in $2 billion a year in assistance, but it was mostly military aid and oil. Meanwhile the people's health-care system was in dire need of assistance and the disabled needed help. The hospitals needed rehabilitation programs and a wide variety of medical assistance. Fourteen years of Russian, East German, and Cuban aid, and what was there to show for it in the health-care areas? What did we see out in the streets? Was there enough food? Was there any pleasure?

Vietnam's "friends," the Soviets and other Communist Bloc countries, couldn't run their own economies well enough to provide their own people with goods. So they damn sure were not going to be able to help the Vietnamese economy.

The Vietnamese cadre had fought all their lives to kick out the foreigners: the Chinese, Japanese, French, and Americans. They had succeeded, only to have them replaced by the Russians, who were also using Vietnam for their own purposes. Mr. Bai and his comrades had given their all and had achieved their goal, but it had cost them practically everything they had.

The signs of poverty were evident all around us. The dinner we sat down to was of many courses, plentiful and very well prepared. No problem there. But the condition of everything else—furnishings, clothing, paper—reflected what Americans used to call genteel poverty.

After the meal, I went for a walk alone. The hot, sticky night was uncomfortable to my unacclimatized body, but the sights and smells of the city overcame my sweat. The middle of Hanoi was unlike any capital city I knew. No neon lights, no cars parked along the street, no traffic lights, no one walking their dog, no public transportation at this hour, no eighteen-wheelers, hardly any motorized vehicles, no wailing sirens in the night, no cruising police cars, fire engines, or emergency medical ambulances, no stores with lit-up window displays, no flashing theater signs, no aircraft overhead.

I returned to the guesthouse, nodding hello to the young guard at the gate, and went up to my room. I stripped down naked, peeling off my sweat-soaked underclothes and artificial arm. I sniffed the socket and curled my nose. Eck! I would have to scrub it out tonight for sure. It was a relief to get all those sweaty clothes off. I vividly remembered on patrol in the Vietnamese jungle when we wore the same clothes until they literally rotted off of us. One patrol we were on lasted over thirty days. The only item we changed regularly was our socks.

God, we must have stunk.

After I finished showering and carefully brushing my teeth with the bottled water, I slipped under the mosquito netting and turned out the light. I lay on the hard straw pallet, thinking how strange everything was that I had seen and experienced so far.

August 27, 1987—The Trip to Ba Vi

★ The van picked us up after breakfast to drive us to the prosthetic, orthopedic, and rehabilitation center at Ba Vi. The three of us were excited at the prospect of seeing the center and traveling outside of Hanoi.

During yesterday's meeting I had asked Mr. Bai if I could take pictures on this trip. The other members of the delegation immediately frowned and said no, but Mr. Bai waved his hand in the air and said, "Yes, yes, of course he can. It is no problem. Besides, they have all the pictures they want from their satellites," pointing up to the sky as he spoke. Today I was loaded for bear with two cameras, extra lenses, and plenty of film.

Dr. Bui Tung had repeatedly pointed out yesterday that this center was the best in Vietnam. But he often called it a "paper elephant." We later discussed what he meant by this, and we came to the conclusion this center wasn't very functional. Now we would find out for sure.

The entire Vietnamese team, except for Mr. Bai, were going up with us. They were already in the van when we came out of the guesthouse. Dr. Tung had the passenger seat and the others sat in the rear, leaving the middle three seats for us.

The van had glass all the way around, with two doors up front and a sliding side door to load passengers into the two back seats. I was last in, so I could sit on the folding jump seat where I had more room to shoot pictures out the side windows.

The trip northwest for 50 kilometers was a kaleidoscope of Vietnam country life. The heavily traveled road was in terrible condition. The trip would take two hours over the roughest road any of us had ridden: it was narrow, two-lane, hard-packed, pot-holed, and a kidney-jolting ride. About an hour into the trip, as we crashed from one gigantic hole into another, I called out to the Vietnamese and told them we called these craters "potholes" in America.

Dr. Bui Tung answered back that they called them "hen nests." Dr. Dong in the back added that they called the really big ones "buffalo nests." I had grown up on the farm, so I understood how an agrarian society would come up with that term. A hen will scratch out a hollow in the earth to roost in during hot weather.

Whatever they were called, they kept the speed down very low and prevented many deaths. Those holes are probably the only reason thousands of people are not killed in wrecks every week, because the Vietnamese driver is reckless, arrogant, and drives at top speed, just like every other Third World imitator of the owner of Toad Hall. They also have a sincere belief that anyone else on the road is trespassing on their personal property. All pedestrians and all drivers think alike on this, and so they all refuse to give way to each other.

It was nerve-racking to see a bicycle or human seemingly being ignored by the driver and at the last moment slide by a molecule away. I never did get used to it.

The Vietnamese kept assuring us there was a short section a few kilometers long that was smooth. It was called "the Cuban Road" because they had done the construction. We would hit it right before the turn off to Ba Vi.

Ba Vi once was the site of a former French Army deserter colony. Over one hundred French soldiers and dependents raised dairy cattle there until they went back to France and Algeria in 1972 and 1973. The cattle were provided by the Cubans, who also built the road to the colony. The Socialist Republic of Vietnam's Public Security School and Police Dog School were nearby.

I was watching a lot of history pass by. At a bridge crossing or a formerly strategic spot along the road, there would be the remnants of an old French concrete bunker. The scars were still visible thirty-five years after an intensely fierce battle took place between the Viet Minh and the lonely post of a small squad of French soldiers. At one location a bunker had been split in half by an explosion of immense proportions. I had read somewhere that the French lost over 47,000 men fighting the Viet Minh. I wondered how many men on both sides had died along this stretch.

Regardless of its past, it was certainly peaceful now, with rice paddies and farming tracts. Every piece of ground was being utilized for farming; the sides of ditches, the edge of the road, the dams, every spare inch of dirt had a plant. I had read that the Vietnamese were desperate for food. From what I saw just on this road they must have been trying to raise enough food for themselves, plus enough export to pay off some of their debt to the USSR.

Water buffalo flourished here in this fertile country. The

big animals were used as beasts of burden in the truest sense of the word: they were the tractors of Vietnam. Plowing fields, pulling carts, alone or in double yoke, they were everywhere I looked.

As we left the city I had seen what looked to be a SAM site over in the rice paddies and called attention to it. However, one of the Vietnamese in the van kept pointing to a pagoda he thought was more interesting. The only other time I saw evidence of military activity on the way to Ba Vi was a huge 5-ton truck with a Soviet multiple rocket launcher set up on the bed. The tarp had blown off the load and a soldier was trying to recover it. The truck and the rocket launcher looked brand new. I guessed this far northwest it must have been heading for the China border.

On the trip Dr. Bui Tung, who traveled to Ba Vi three times a week to do surgery, related the plans to build a new in-patient facility at the hospital and the possibility of building another center closer to Hanoi. When we asked him why this center was so far from Hanoi, he insinuated it was for historical and political reasons.

Finally we arrived at a fork in the road and drove through a gate onto the grounds of what looked like a deserted complex of abandoned buildings spread haphazardly over 10 untended acres. The van drove up to a five-story structure that we were informed was the hospital.

The assistant director met us at the front door and escorted us up to the third-floor conference room. There we were given refreshments of bananas, fruit, coffee, peanuts, tea, and beer, while the director gave us a briefing on the hospital and its needs. Afterwards we were taken for a tour of the facilities. We began by going down the hall to the operating wing on the third floor. Through one open door we observed a surgeon scrubbing up for an operation that would take place in the adjoining operating room.

A small surgical team, consisting of a surgeon and four other individuals, was beginning corrective surgery on a seven-year-old girl who had a deformed foot due to crippling polio. They were going to move a tendon in an attempt to straighten out her foot.

To enter the operating room, we removed our shoes in the hall and put on old worn slippers lying there for that use. I was wearing cowboy boots; when I removed them, the Vietnamese did a double take and then talked among themselves while glancing over their shoulders at the boots.

I had been taking pictures and had stopped in the hall outside the operating room to change film before I went in. The others went into the room, leaving me alone for a moment while I worked with my camera. As I was transferring film, I noticed out of the corner of my eye a middle-aged Vietnamese couple and an old woman sitting on a bench nearby. They were dressed in peasant garb. Their faces were full of anxiety and they kept glancing at the door.

I stopped what I was doing and nodded my head at them in greeting. They nodded back. The hospital was empty of people, so I guessed the little girl was probably theirs. The old woman was clearly the grandmother. Everyone in our group had ignored them, but I figured they were like most parents who would be worried sick about a child going into surgery. A show of concern by the medical people would have been helpful.

In an attempt to show concern myself I pointed into the operating room, cradled an imaginary child in my arms, and then pointed at them. The couple's faces immediately lit up as they nodded their heads. I smiled and nodded to show I understood, then pushed my way through the door into the operating room.

What Dr. Savory and I saw was a notable lack of equipment and other features Americans feel are part of any operating room. There was no electricity and of course no lights. The operation was taking place next to an outside wall full of windows. There was no IV bottle or blood plasma. There was no monitoring equipment. In fact, there was no electrical equipment anywhere in the room. There were no screens on any of the windows or doors.

The surgeon waited until we entered the room. Then he proceeded to cut open the leg. The little girl's gown had been pulled up past her waist. There was no disinfectant on the skin or in the operating room. We had put on common slippers as our only precaution before entering. The surgeon operated without surgical gloves; he was using his bare hands.

As we left the operating room, I looked over at the family huddled anxiously on the bench awaiting the outcome. I put myself in their place. Parents of a child crippled by polio, operated on by a medical team lacking the most basic of equipment and supplies. How helpless they must feel! How their hearts must be torn with the plight of their crippled child. What desperate hope had led them to bring their child to this place?

Our group walked down the cement hall. The hospital was like a ghost town. It appeared to be practically vacant. Occasionally there would be a desk in a room with an administrative person sitting behind it, but most of the rooms were empty of patients. The hallways were empty of people. No doctors, residents, nurses, orderlies, technicians, or visitors were encountered as we walked from the operating room on the third floor to the physical therapy section on the first floor at the opposite end of the hospital.

When we reached the first physical therapy room, there were nine children undergoing therapy. Four female staff members were present. Upon our arrival there was a sudden burst of exercising started by the physical therapists with the children. The staff and the children stared at us as if we had come from the moon. Everyone was dressed in threadbare trousers and blouses.

Another small room with a table contained three children, two with polio and one with cerebral palsy. On the table were blocks and other devices for corrective therapists to use in training patients to use their hands. There was also a large, auditorium-sized room with a volleyball net and a few mats laid out on the floor, next to a wall to which weights with ropes and pullies were attached. Five children with polio sat on the mats. A fourth room contained sets of gymnastic parallel bars.

The few physical therapy devices in these rooms were old and covered with dust. The mats the children sat on were not dusty, but they were certainly old. Each room had a desperate, hopeless air about it. Trash, discarded equipment, and other types of junk were stacked along all of the walls and in the corners.

Overall, this almost vacant hospital was depressing. There were few patients, and the minimal staff were ill-equipped and seemed to be demoralized and poorly trained.

We exited through wide double doors onto a weed lot. The assistant director took us up a slight incline to a twin, three-story building 100 meters away. We were led into one ground-floor room containing three patients. The un-screened open door led into a dark, cell-like area with four beds. One woman and two men were patients. A small, unglassed and unscreened window was set in the wall opposite the door. There was an unpleasant sickroom smell. Except for this single occupied room, this complex seemed to be deserted too.

I had fallen behind while I was taking pictures. Attempting a shortcut, I came upon a man dressed in black pajamas maneuvering on crutches along the overgrown trail between the buildings. He was about twenty-three years old and his right leg was missing above the knee. He reminded me of a scene twenty years ago when I was patrolling Highway One south of Duc Pho. There I had seen another man dressed in black pajamas traveling the road, leg missing, swinging his body with crutches. I had felt deep pity for that man then, imagining how terrible life would be for him without a leg.

Now, as I watched a replay of that scene, I did not feel pity. I knew the inner determination that both that man and I, now an amputee as well, had to have to survive. I knew with the proper help he could learn to walk without

140

crutches. But he would need an artificial leg, and I had yet to see one here at this rehabilitation center.

He looked at my face as I paused to let him cross in front of me. He stopped a few feet away and rested on his crude wooden crutches, balancing on his foot and studying me. He was particularly interested in my artificial arm. I was wearing a red short-sleeve knit shirt in the hot weather, and he could easily see the plastic arm with cables and straps and hook. Naked curiosity showed on his face.

He gave me a puzzled frown. I pantomimed saluting and shooting a rifle to give him the idea I was a soldier. Then I stepped on an imaginary mine, showing the explosion blowing off my arm. He responded with urgent movements of his arms, pointing to himself, firing a rifle and making a sweeping action toward his empty trouser leg. I gravely nodded my head in understanding.

There was nothing else we could say to each other. I pointed to the group walking along the front of the hospital and the sounds of Carl hollering at me to catch up. I waved my hand in farewell and hurried away.

When I caught up with the group, I asked Carl if he had seen the leg amputee back on the path. He said he had and commented on what a healthy stump the man had. We talked among ourselves as to why he did not have a prosthetic device. This was a rehabilitation hospital and a prosthetic limb-manufacturing center, so it would be the place where an amputee should have a limb. We thought it was peculiar, but we would quickly have some answers because we were walking toward a group of buildings where prosthetic component limbs were made.

The building was an H-shaped, two-story structure that looked as if it had at one time been an old dormitory. It sat slightly downhill about 200 meters catty-corner from the front of the hospital. The track leading to it was unused and weeds grew in the middle and from the sides. As we got closer, I could see an old rusted boiler against one wall. A windowless van that looked like a Volkswagen minibus sat up on blocks with weeds growing around it. The cement walls were pitted and scarred from time and the weather. The whole place looked dilapidated from the outside; the inside wasn't much better.

Many rooms were bare and obviously unused, but there was activity in some of the others. What struck me about this place, which was the busiest of the buildings we had visited, was the lack of materials on the shelves, the ancient machines being used, and the old-style prosthetic component parts they were making. This was a system taught by the East Germans and it was miserably out of date.

After I looked in every nook and cranny, I decided that there wasn't simply a lack of materials—there were no materials at all. There was nothing to work on except for the few components the workers had in their hands.

A number of young workmen and women were in various stages of "finishing" prosthetic limbs by grinding, shaping, and smoothing the wooden sockets or hammering out the metal limbs. What was interesting was that although each worker was busy with one limb, there were no other limbs available to be worked on when that limb was completed. Finished limbs were stacked alongside the workbench, as if on display, but we did not see the next limb for them to start on.

In one corner of the building was a dark and dingy room smaller than the others. Everything here was covered in old axle grease, black with age and accumulated dirt. Two grease-covered men, sitting on their haunches amid a sparse clutter of sprockets, gears, and other aged parts, smiled up at us with betel nut-stained teeth when we stuck our heads in the open doorway. We were informed by our guides that this was a wheelchair repair area. I did not see any wheelchairs, but I thought to myself that if these parts were any indication, the wheelchairs were ancient.

Men and women worked industriously, but not safely. OSHA would have closed the place down immediately.

There were no guards on any of the equipment, belts were flying about freely, no one wore eye protectors, there were no safety kits, fire extinguishers, or even Band-Aids available. The hospital was next door, but from what we had seen, an accident victim would not have benefited much from its proximity.

Each room in the building specialized in a particular job. There seemed to be grinding and finishing work here, but most of the building was unused. Vacuum hoses were hooked up to the pieces of equipment to clean the dust, but a heavy layer of sawdust and plastic particles indicated the vacuum had not worked for a long time.

I came out of a room where a woman was sanding the socket on an above-knee limb and stood at the railing on the second-floor balcony to ponder what we were seeing. Out across the overgrown fence I saw, a couple of kilometers away, a short, jagged hogback of hills rising from the rice paddies. They looked blue in the heavy, humid air.

The land was so beautiful in contrast to this dilapidated rehabilitation center and surrounding buildings. There was something missing in what we were seeing here. But, like those hills, it wasn't quite clear yet.

We were loaded into the van for a short trip through the gate and around the block to a factory area consisting of a half dozen single-story buildings or sheds. These buildings contained heavy equipment used to pound, stamp, and cut out the initial prosthetic component parts. This was a relatively busy area, with dozens of workers spread throughout the grounds. Each shed we entered specialized in a different phase of manufacturing.

The workmen and women were all young, with a few exceptions, and friendly, and they answered all of our questions. Some of them wore those cloth caps with the little bill I always associated with the Communist worker. The smiling young faces of the workers seemed a little too contrived for me, but they appeared to know their machines and their work when we queried them.

The workers at each machine were surrounded by large piles of their work. Carl asked me why they piled 150 to 200 knee blocks in a huge stack. I answered that it was to impress us. At first glance, you would think these were some hardworking folks. But I had worked in steel mills and factory lines and something did not look right—just like the other place where the finishing work was taking place. Finally it came to me. I noticed there were no waste products around the machines. There should have been piles of shavings and wood or metal dust in proportion to the number of parts piled up. Also there was no raw material ready to be used in making the next part when the workman finished the part he was working on. It was as if they knew the VIPs were coming, so they brought a collection of finished products out of storage and piled them around the workmen. Then, when the "bosses" arrived, the workmen all commenced to work.

In spite of all the camouflage it was obvious the big pieces of machinery were old, worn out, and badly in need of repair or replacement. Some of the machines did not work and had not worked for years. It was all Russian and Eastern Bloc in origin and was probably old when it was given to the Vietnamese. There were no repair parts available, so the machines just sat there. A band saw had no band, a sander had no sandpaper.

The accident rate in the place must have been horrendous. There were no guards on any of the equipment, the machines were old and had many exposed working parts, the air was close and foul, the floors were dirt or cracked cement and the footing was treacherous, electrical wiring was exposed in various places, the working areas were dark and dim.

As I moved from one work area to another observing these conditions and Vietnamese workmen and women, I thought this must have been the way it was back in the middle of the Industrial Revolution, when men were not as valuable as machines and far easier to replace.

144

There were incongruous mixings of old methods with more modern techniques. Open-hearth forges were used to heat metal for shaping into braces. As we watched the worker showing off his skills, I was reminded of a blacksmith. The young man was solidly built. He pumped the bellows, forcing air over the coals and making them flare up with increased heat. With a pair of tongs he held a strip of metal in the coals until it reached the correct temperature. Then he moved the metal strip to an anvil and proceeded to pound it into shape with a hammer.

Other pieces, after being heated in the open forge, were passed to workmen at various presses to be pressed into a particular shape. This combination of using a human blacksmith to augment worn machinery to shape metal was a good example of "making do," as my farm relatives would say. A large electric oven was standing next to the forge. We were told it had broken down seven years ago and they had never been able to repair it or get a replacement part.

We saw many other examples of "making do" in their manufacturing procedures. One of the workmen was cutting old tires into long, narrow strips. He then weaved these on a square wooden frame to make seats for wheelchairs. Watching the old man's fingers nimbly weaving the tire strips, I was sorely tempted to ask him if he made Ho Chi Minh slippers during the war, but I didn't.

At another workbench a young man was truly proud, and rightfully so, of his ability to use a hammer and chisel, to notch metal burrs onto a fist-sized, egg-shaped metal ball. The ball was an attachment for the end of a router used to grind out the inside of an artificial limb socket. His finished products, lined up on the workbench where his vise was attached, looked just like the ones I was familiar with. He put a smooth, unmarked metal ball into his vise and in a rapid manner, starting at the apex, chiseled a spiral of burrs down the circumference of the ball. He proudly pulled it from the vise to show us. Although we were impressed with the quality of his work, we were not impressed with the quality of the metal. If an attachment to be used in grinding another material was so easily scored, then it would not be any time at all before it too was ground down.

There was a surprise for us in one shop. Ever since we had arrived in Vietnam, Larry Ward had been telling us and the Vietnamese about the load of five hundred wheelchairs his organization had brought in from India five years before. He kept asking about them; had they arrived safely? Did anyone remember them? Were they given out to the handicapped? And so on. But the Vietnamese had not given him any direct answers. According to Larry, though, these wheelchairs were just what Vietnam needed.

When we entered one of the shops, we saw the wheelchairs Larry had been talking about stacked unused over in a corner of the shed. Larry was taken aback and asked why his Indian wheelchairs were here and not being used. The shop foreman explained that these wheelchairs were not any good for Vietnam conditions. They looked like the wheelchairs we were used to seeing in America, but the foreman shook his head. He showed us the wheelchairs his shop made for Vietnamese conditions.

What we saw was a three-wheeled vehicle. The patient sat on a seat and flat board, with his legs straight out in front of him. He used one hand to steer a tiller bar attached to the front wheel, while with his other hand he propelled the wheelchair by push-pulling a lever sticking up out of the floorboard. It was attached to a ratchet gear assembly that drove the rear wheels.

We examined it closely. This was a durable wheelchair, built like a tank and weighing not much less. There was no doubt it was rugged, but it must have been a bear to handle with all that weight. The foreman told us this was good tough equipment and had low maintenance. If it did break down, anyone could fix it. He pointed over to the chairs from India and frowned. "These would never do in Vietnam," he told us. "They are very flimsy and would break down quickly. They are too delicate."

Finally the tour was over. We left the last shed and were directed back toward the van. There we gathered for group pictures. Afterwards as Carl was chatting with the shop manager, I stood near the rear of the van for a moment looking back over this complex of poorly constructed buildings within which the workers were scattered, busily going about their business. I thought about the open forge, the stamping machines, the basic methods they used to make prosthetic component parts, and I noted the disbursement of their manufacturing processes into single units.

I was looking at this militarily. You could never bomb all these types of places out of existence during a war. These little shops and simple manufacturing methods could be scattered all over the landscape, with no hope of stopping production by bombing. I was not thinking of prosthetic component parts but of rifles and other instruments of war that these machines could easily be converted into making. They could have scattered these damn machines under trees and in the ground and kept right on stamping out weapons.

I looked up at the clear sky and tried to imagine what this place looked like from a fighter bomber. During the war I had looked up at the sky hundreds of times, wishing for more air support. I glanced around the compound and with my mind's eye placed the antiaircraft guns that would protect a place like this. Then I thought about my pilot friends who had flown over this landscape and I imagined them attacking this complex. Even if they hit every machine, they wouldn't be destroying much. It was a hell of a risk for very little.

The machines we were seeing today were in sorry condition, but I bet during the war these machines got spare parts from the Russians and Chinese. Since the end of the war there probably hadn't been one replacement bolt sent.

The van rushed us around the block and through the gate back onto the hospital grounds. We went upstairs to the conference room, where we asked a few more questions pertaining to transportation and patient load.

The trip back was scheduled to leave at 1100 hours, so we were hurriedly loaded into the van after shaking hands with everyone. The assistant director and staff stood on the front porch waving goodbye as we drove out the gate.

We suspected everyone had played their role to the hilt. The whirlwind tour around the rehabilitation and manufacturing complex had taken a little over two hours. My impression of the place was that it was a backwater, way out in the country over roads that were the worst imaginable. I could only surmise that politics were responsible for locating what was supposed to be a leading rehabilitation hospital out in the sticks.

The drive back was just as jolting and miserable as the drive there, but this time our misery was worse because of the midday heat. Carl saw a mile marker for Son Tay and said it was no wonder the Son Tay raid had put the Vietnamese into such a panic. With the terrible condition of these roads, it would have been difficult to move reinforcements quickly into the area. A raid this close to Hanoi must have scared them pretty bad.

The Vietnamese were trying to fix the road in a few places; we could see the activity up ahead. When we came up on the small road jam caused by the work, we could study how they did it.

A pair of oxen were standing in the road, hitched to a wooden cart with steel wheels and spikes. Lying on the bed of the cart was a large, square, 500-gallon-size tank, which looked like an old oil tank that used to sit outside our farmhouse in Indiana. A smokestack jutted from the top. A grill underneath the tank held a fire fed by large branches and trunks of trees that hung out to the rear 10, 15, or 20 feet, dragging on the ground. The heat from this grate radiated outward and we could feel it in the van as we edged by. The tar stunk to high heaven.

One of the workmen, black with soot and streaked with sweat, pushed the trunks in as the fire consumed them. The continuous fire kept the tank above it hot enough to liquefy an oily tar contained in the open tank. The workmen drained off some of the tar from a tap in the tank, mixed in some rocks, and poured it into the potholes.

Most of the road crew were standing around while a few did the shoveling. This must be typical of road crews worldwide. The crew was working in the shade of the only group of trees on this section of the road. The holes out in the sun just would not get filled, we guessed.

After a couple of minutes we were past them and on our way. I wondered if our intelligence people during the war knew how bad these damn roads were.

Mr. Le Bang, our guide from the Foreign Ministry, pointed out the window toward a village across the rice paddies and told us it was a typical Vietnamese village. Carl and I had remarked on the villages earlier because they had reminded us of our combat tours in the South. Out across the wide expanse of rice paddies would be an island of trees. This marked the border of the village, which sat a foot or two higher than the surrounding rice paddies.

Mr. Le Bang informed us that trees were planted along the border and within the island where the homes were located. Palm trees, coconut trees, banana trees, and various other trees and bushes grew among the homes. Bamboo fish traps were wedged in all the streams and drainage ditches to catch the fish that escaped the fish ponds scattered through the rice paddies. Tobacco was planted in the ditches around the village and roads. Every square foot of land was utilized as much as possible.

The land was heavily populated. During the trip anywhere and everywhere we looked for as far as the eye could see there were people working, walking, resting. The countryside was rural but crowded with people.

We arrived back at the guesthouse in time for lunch. This was a mixed blessing, for even though we were hungry, we had gotten to the point where the Vietnamese food was just too spicy and odd-flavored for our taste buds. Carl was to the point of throwing up if he had to smell nuoc mam sauce much longer at our table.

Larry had brought a granola bar and he shared it at lunch. It was cut into pieces and eaten in honor of the "American Food God." Back in Bangkok, the JCRC guys had told us the tradition for the Americans returning from Vietnam was to eat their first big meal at Neal's, the restaurant famous in Bangkok for serving American-style food. We thought it was sort of a joke when we first heard it. After all, who wants to eat American food in a foreign land?

It was no joke. I could not wait to eat a steak with ketchup. I was staring down at my plate. There were two halves of a chicken head split right down the middle of the beak. I had never seen anything like this. It was interesting to see how the eyeball was hooked to the brain, but I didn't think I wanted to eat it.

The JCRC guys were having a great time watching our expressions. They pointed out there were ants in the rice I liked for its absence of flavor. And did we know, they gleefully informed us, that we were having eel soup for supper followed by fried snapping turtle? Bill, Joe, Johnie, and Paul loved this food. In fact, when they returned to Bangkok, they never went to Neal's. They always went to a grubby Chinese restaurant and ate more Oriental food and drank Singha beer.

They had all been very helpful in teaching us the ropes and acting as our tour guides. We hated to think what we would have done if we had had to travel into Vietnam by ourselves. It was strange being in a country where we were cut off from the outside world. When we got off the plane we had no way of getting a message out. There was no TV or radio we could understand or newspaper we could read. It was a scary feeling.

After lunch, Carl, Larry, and I discussed among ourselves what we had seen at Ba Vi. We thought the whole morning was a set-up deal, in that the staff and workers were making a special effort on our behalf. But we were used to those kinds of tactics. After all, there is not a rehabilitation center, children's hospital, or special interest group in the free world that doesn't know the value of impressing the visiting dignitaries with a dog and pony show. Jerry Lewis cries for the benefit of crippled children every year on national television, so if the Vietnamese wanted to operate on a little seven-year-old girl in order to prove their need for medical supplies, we knew it was just part of the show.

At 1400, after a short, hot walk, we sat down in the hot, stuffy room in the same seats we had before. Mr. Bai was again heading the Vietnamese team. He began by stating he was pleased the trip had been productive and that the U.S. team had seen the "reality" of the situation.

We surmised Mr. Le Bang had briefed him on the trip during the lunch period. He then changed tactics and began speaking about the short-term needs of the Socialist Republic of Vietnam. Then he began discussing the POW/MIA link. Mr. Bai said he understood we were not directly concerned with that issue, but he himself was "responsible for both meetings." He informed us he had told Mr. Can (heading up the Vietnamese POW/MIA team) to inform Lieutenant Colonel Harvey (the head of the American POW/MIA team) that the approach should be to solve the most urgent MIA cases. He indicated that the U.S. team wanted a more broad-based approach. He went on to say that solving the geographically wide range of cases would be difficult. There were twenty-eight cases in nine northern and seven southern provinces.

Mr. Bai stated he wanted to set a time limit for the resolution of the seventy most compelling discrepancy MIA cases for the end of the year, and that these seventy cases would receive maximum Socialist Republic of Vietnam efforts. He looked at us over the top of his reading glasses and said he had instructed Mr. Can in this matter. He added that many colleagues were hesitant about the difficulties to be overcome, but he had told them they must make it work: "Our spirit is our goodwill . . . we must put words into deeds."

Dr. Savory responded by stating his general lack of knowledge in the POW/MIA issue and that his team's role was not in this area. He said the team would communicate the problems at Ba Vi with accuracy and enthusiasm, and report on short-term concrete solutions that might be workable for the USA government organizations in addressing those problems.

Mr. Bai then reiterated that all wanted to see concrete progress in communications between President Reagan and the Socialist Republic of Vietnam's president, as well as between General Vessey and Minister Thach. They all wanted progress in the area of mutual "humanitarian cooperation."

Every once in a while Bai would refer to the "puppet regime" that used to be in the South. All my life I had read that Communists used phrases like "puppet regime," but I had never actually heard them spoken for real. There were a few other rote Communist expressions that cropped up once in a while, but I never sensed anything malicious in the use of the terms. It was as if they had used the words for so long they were a natural part of the language.

I smiled as I thought to myself that it was like our use of the term "Communist menace," "Communist plot," or "the evil empire."

It was getting toward the end of the afternoon when Mr. Bai started expanding the agenda, saying that there were "other proposals" to pay attention to. He referred to the "heavily bombed areas," emphasized the lonely old people, the disabled, widowed, and orphaned, and stated that they needed "facilities, medicine, drugs, nutrition, and a primary health-care network."

Another whole new topic was introduced when he began to talk about the recent typhoon and the epidemic of dengue fever, which Bai claimed was a humanitarian issue. He stated the U.S. government still maintained a hostile position toward the Socialist Republic of Vietnam and had missed many opportunities to help and show good faith and interest. Bai was quick to point out that none of this should be looked at as war reparations or economic aid.

He said the Socialist Republic of Vietnam was waiting to see if the United States responded with aid for typhoon victims. "It is my sincere advice that if this work is done . . . it will be very useful and significant." Dr. Savory responded he would communicate these other problems and asked for details about the dengue fever problem.

Bai responded by stating that based on good faith developed over the course of the meetings, he would give Dr. Savory a list of the specifics about the dengue fever problem, which represented the most urgent of all the urgent problems. Although this problem had been present in Vietnam before on an annual basis, this year the problem was much worse, serious, and more widespread. The meeting then concluded.

This was to be our last evening in Hanoi. Our side was hosting the dinner for the Vietnamese delegates this time. Both teams on both sides were attending. The humanitarian and POW/MIA teams would be together as they were when the Vietnamese hosted the dinner the night before.

Our meeting had ended at approximately 1600 hours. Carl and I were anxious to use the time until dinner to mail out postcards we had bought from the vendor on the corner. We felt these were some world-class cards. They were a mixture of Vietnam themes, ranging from scenes of the countryside to monuments from their wars. The single descriptive line on the back was usually printed in four languages: Russian, English, French, and Vietnamese.

When we went to buy the cards with the dong we had gotten at the bank, a crowd gathered around us as we stood at the vendor's stand. Carl, at 6 feet 2 inches, towered over me, and at 5 feet 10 inches I was a head taller than the

Vietnamese. So we were a prominent enough duo to draw a crowd. There must have been twenty-five to thirty people who stopped to look us over and talk among themselves. One of the men in the crowd got next to us and asked us in Vietnamese a question we interpreted as "Where are you from?"

When we answered in English that we were from the United States of America, his eyebrows raised and he excitedly relayed this information to people standing around him, who in turn relayed it to the perimeter of the crowd. They all looked closely at us. They talked to each other and started saying something to the vendor, who frowned, shook her head, and said something back.

We were just as interested in them. All people in Hanoi looked poor as church mice, but they always looked clean. The crowd consisted of mostly male adults of various ages. A few men dressed in civilian clothes were wearing the military-style cloth pith helmet of either green or tan, which seemed to be the leading choice for headgear among men. There were a few young soldiers standing close to us, but they carried no firearms. It was a typical cross section of Hanoi citizens.

Occasionally, a rider on a bicycle would stop to see what the crowd was all about. Someone would tell him, he would look at us in frank curiosity, then go on his way.

Our experience with the Vietnamese in the street was that they were always very open, curious, and forthright in asking and answering questions. And it seemed to me they were never shy about offering their opinion. A case in point: One of the men in the crowd must have offered his opinion about what we were looking to buy, because after he said something to the vendor, she reached under the stand and pulled out a set of delicately painted scenic postcards. He nodded his head. Then the vendor, the guy who came up with the idea, and the crowd close enough to hear what was going on all gazed expectantly at us as the vendor handed the pack of cards to us to look over.

By the most remote of coincidences these painted cards were exactly the type I had bought from a vendor on Highway One near Duc Pho in December 1967 to send back home as Christmas cards. My mom still had the card I had sent her. I naturally had to have these for myself. I nodded, said I would buy them, and asked how much they cost. The man who suggested she bring them out, the vendor, and the crowd seemed to be congratulating themselves on guessing correctly. Then more of them got into the act and started giving advice to the vendor as to what we wanted. Having succeeded once, she brought out more wares from under the counter for us to look over. We ended up buying forty postcards: the painted cards and a couple of packs of cards depicting military victories. Carl had spotted those first, so he got the lion's share.

In closing the sale the vendor did as all people do in Hanoi. Nothing went to waste, even in the most routine of activities. With an inch-long stub of pencil she wrote the cost in dong for each item on a piece of well-used scrap paper and showed us the total. The lady and her assistants wrapped our purchases in used newspaper and tied the bundle with a piece of string cut so short we did not believe she could tie a knot. But she did, leaving stubs of string so short you could barely see them.

The self-discipline of the North Vietnamese in these matters was impressive. Their years of deprivation from supporting the wars against the Japanese, French, Americans, Cambodians, and Chinese made them aware of the value of anything material, including a scrap of paper.

The same thing could not be said for utilization of people. That was one resource they had an abundance of—and they wasted it shamelessly. It did not take us long to see that the North Vietnamese did not or could not use people efficiently at all. Even at this tiny vending stand there were two assistants to help do what one person could easily do by herself. In any transaction involving the government it took at least three people to handle the money and paperwork. I think it had to do with the belief that to be more efficient meant fewer jobs.

Individual discipline was noticeable in a positive way in the matter of street crime. There was none to speak of in Hanoi. Carl and I remarked on how we were both guarded at first in pulling out our wads of dong because we both remembered the perils of flashing money in a crowd back in 1967 in the South. Our pockets would have been picked in a second by the hordes of kids that hung around GIs. We had begun to lose that feeling in Hanoi because the mood of the North Vietnamese people was different. There was no feeling of danger from lawlessness. The city, in spite of its poverty, seemed civilized. The crowd around us at the vending stand had been courteous, forthright, and friendly, but not suspicious or threatening in any way.

Carl and I walked down to the Dollar Store where we intended to buy gifts. The Dollar Store was owned and run by the Vietnamese government for the express purpose of selling only to foreigners. They would only accept U.S. currency, hence the term "Dollar Store." They would not accept their own money nor their allies' money. This was a surprise to us, but we were proud of the fact the American dollar was so strong.

Of course, in an economic sense the Vietnamese were so desperate for hard currency that every dollar counted. I had read how the drain of millions of U.S. dollars into Communist coffers put a hidden strain on our system, but I had never realized Communist countries refused to accept each other's money. It seemed strange to me that Communists kept thinking their system was better than ours in the face of this evidence of the continued failure of their own.

Everything in the Dollar Store was made by Vietnamese artists and craftsmen. The main room had glass counters on both sides. They contained jewelry made of wood, bone, ivory, silver, gems, and polished rocks. There were some silver tea sets, but the silver plating looked crude and poorly done. The room off to the left of the front room held the paintings by native artists; another room held lacquerware.

All the employees were female and could speak some English. They showed a general lack of enthusiasm for their jobs. The young ones were subliminally arrogant, and the older ones clearly did not give a damn.

I spent most of my time browsing through the stacks of paintings. Each artist's works were contained in one of those large foldover carrying cases common in art schools in the States. There must have been thirty or more artists' folders stacked in piles on tables around the room. There were a surprising number of good artists piled up here, I thought, as I pulled folder after folder from the stacks. The medium was watercolor and there were three themes: women, workers, and scenery.

I liked what I saw. There were quite a few good painters represented in these folders and some outstanding ones. The artists used pastel colors to bring a delicate lightness to the images of bamboo, water, mountains, and fields. Boats, water buffalo, people, and temples seemed to be only slightly more substantial in these traditional Vietnamese settings. Hanoi's buildings were the most modern images in any of the paintings. All of them were purely Vietnamese in what they portrayed: there were no images of war or machines or non-Vietnamese individuals or anything at all from the twentieth century.

I could not make up my mind which ones to buy; there were so many I wanted. When I asked the bored saleslady the price, she showed me a tiny tag attached to each painting with the price in dong and dollars. I did a double take when I saw that these paintings were selling for $3 to $5. I bought five. Back in the States it would cost me over $100 apiece just to frame each one. It would be the first time I ever put a three-dollar painting in a hundred-dollar frame. I was given my bill and told to pay in the back room.

While I was in the back I noticed a separate counter with

an advertisement for Heineken beer. Wait a minute, I said to myself, I had not been able to buy beer anywhere in Hanoi, and here in the Dollar Store they are selling an import. I had to admire the Heineken Beer Company's salesmen, though. I was always amazed how they marketed that stuff in the States and now I find the beer here.

I asked how much, and a lady in the back room told me beer was 60 cents a can. I said great, I would take a six-pack. She looked at me in puzzlement. "What a six-pack?"

She said, "I do not use change. It must come out even in dollars. For six dollars I can give you ten beers, but we do not have ten beers."

"Well, I only want a couple of beers anyway, and that is one twenty. Let me have two and you keep the change."

She shook her head, but told me to wait a minute. Then she went into the other room and talked to one of the jewelry saleswomen, who reached in the case and pulled out a silver filigree butterfly. The beer lady came back with it and told me it was worth 80 cents so I should give her $2 for which she would give me the two beers and the butterfly.

I thought that was a good deal, so I pulled another $2 out while she wrote up the two transactions separately in triplicate. This saleslady definitely showed initiative.

When we returned to our rooms, I took a shower and got dressed for the dinner at 1830 hours, then lay down on my pallet for a quick nap. All three of us on the humanitarian team were exhausted, and I was feeling particularly bushed due to an upset intestinal tract.

I fell asleep immediately and overslept by a few minutes. I was awakened by the lady who was assigned to our floor. She knew what our schedule was and she knew who was in their rooms and who wasn't. Evidently when I did not walk out the door of my room at 1830 hours, she came in to wake me. She stood in the foyer and knocked on the side of the wall to awaken me. I came awake with that sudden awareness of having screwed up. I thanked her, threw water in my face, and was only five minutes late.

Bill had ordered the menu for us and as a treat he had requested that the women serving us wear the traditional Ao Dai Vietnamese dress. They looked wonderfully feminine and lent a fine atmosphere to the room. Everyone on both sides seemed to be relaxed, and conversation ranged across the board. Two and a half days of intense meetings together had lessened our initially suspicious attitudes.

Carl, Larry, and I had already discussed many times before this dinner our thoughts and feelings about the Vietnamese Delegation, the people we met officially and unofficially in the street, what we saw, how we were treated, the atmosphere of the meetings themselves, and our general impressions of it all. We discussed these things with the old hands, bouncing our impressions and interpretations off their considerable knowledge and experience.

Our analysis was that the general atmosphere throughout the period of time we were in Hanoi was very cordial. The Vietnamese surprised us with their openness and frankness. The tone was set in the first meeting and continued to the end with increasingly free discussions.

We had no sense of hostility or antagonism toward us on the part of the Vietnamese. There had been little political rhetoric, and their team had adhered to the topics agreed upon by General Vessey and Minister Thach. We had halfway expected them to use the meeting to harangue us about the past, but they did not. The Vietnamese team projected what appeared to be a very sincere desire to communicate so as to establish these and future talks in what they call a "new improved spirit." It was our distinct impression that the Vietnamese viewed this meeting as a good opportunity to establish a meaningful dialogue and wished to prove or demonstrate their good intentions.

In addition to sticking to the issues, there was little overt effort by the Vietnamese to force the POW/MIA issue into the medical discussions. What references there were to the POWs and MIAs were clearly within the context of the dialogue at the time.

There was a definite trend for the Vietnamese team to emphasize realistic, concrete, rapid solutions to a finite number of problems, with the majority of discussions directed at the orthopedically disabled.

When we posed questions to the Vietnamese team, they listened attentively and answered enthusiastically. There never appeared to be any hedging and most of the questions were answered directly. It was our opinion they were not holding back or being evasive; their answers were honest to the best of their ability, and they truly might not have had accurate statistics in certain areas.

We had been prepared for much more closed, obtuse responses and political rhetoric, but all of this was notably absent from the discussions. Our consensus was that the Vietnamese had come to do business and, regardless of motivation, expected some progress and subsequent meet-ings to occur. By the end of the meetings both teams appeared to be quite comfortable in the various inter-changes between them. If anything, we had the opinion we were more cautious than the Vietnamese team. In a wrap-up, we felt very positive about our trip and they seemed just as pleased. Tonight's dinner was an affirmation of those feelings.

What had happened, I wondered, to cause the Vietnamese to soften the hard line they had held to for years? Part of the answer may have been in the room. Three members of the delegation working with us were young men who would have been teenagers or in their early twenties when the war ended, and so may not have been personally involved in the fighting.

I thought this was probably indicative of what was happening throughout the country. Maybe these young men and women did not have the same view of the past as did the older generation. Of course the old cadre were still in charge, although I had read that some of them were under heavy fire for not being able to wage peace as effectively as they had waged war.

My thoughts drifted back to these young men and women. I knew the older team members had fought in the wars, but how had the war affected this younger group? I asked Mr. Le Bang if he had lost anyone in his family during the war. He told me his grandfather's second wife was killed in an American bombing raid in December 1972. She was in a bunker with five railroad workers when a 1,000-pound bomb landed on top of the shelter. They all disintegrated in the explosion. But other than that, he added, he didn't personally know anyone who had been hurt or killed. The war had not touched him personally. His brother had been a captain fighting in the south, but he had survived the war.

Back in my room I contemplated his statement and his demeanor during our trip. It seemed to be indicative of the younger Vietnamese. The younger generation was not carrying so much baggage from the war. That had been their fathers' war and the Americans had been their fathers' enemies. The old cadre had sacrificed a lifetime, but the younger generation was just starting their lives. To them America was a hope, not an enemy.

August 28, 1987—Leaving Hanoi

★ We checked out of the guesthouse at 0800. Our rooms, including three meals a day, came to $50 a day. The rental for the van and driver was another $50 a day and the dinner we hosted cost $100. I paid for my room and Dr. Savory paid for the other items.

Checking out took a long time due to Communist inefficiency and mistrust. No one is entrusted to handle both paperwork and cash. In a large operation such as the Le Thach guesthouse, only one person will have the key to the safe. If he is gone you have to wait until he shows up. The cashier did not come to work until 0800 hours. When he did show up, he had to figure everything out by hand over in a partially constructed office across the driveway of the guesthouse. He had no change and everything had to be paid in U.S. dollars, so we traded bills around until we could make it come out even. Then the cashier had to make the bills out in triplicate. His assistant used an abacus to aid in the calculations. They were both young, as was Mr. Le Bang, who was translating between us. The driver waiting outside was young and the guards at the gate were young. The cooks, waitresses, and floor workers were young. How long would they put up with such stagnation? I thought with a little encouragement they all would gladly become America's allies.

I rushed down to the post office for one last mailing. The van picked me up from there and we were driven out to the Thang Loi Hotel on the West Lake. The night before at dinner, Mr. Bai had offered to have the van go out there so we could buy some souvenirs. The Thang Loi (Great Victory) is a Cuban-built resort hotel where many foreigners stay. There is a gift shop in the lobby.

Soon we would be leaving the city. I felt a pang of regret to be leaving so soon. Now that I had been in Hanoi for four days and had seen the people and walked the streets and lost my hate, there was more I wanted to know and see about Vietnam. While we were sitting in heavy traffic, I studied the throngs of people for the last time.

Out the side window of the van I saw a line of preschool children—little girls holding onto a colored ribbon while their teacher led them across a park. The Vietnamese call these "crocodile lines" because of the way the children are strung like sections in a crocodile tail. Looking at them, I knew these children were what the Vietnamese Delegation and the American Delegation humanitarian teams were all about. If we could make it work to help them, we would have done a good thing. After all, that is what we started out to do all those many years ago.

We drove past a number of embassies. The Soviet Embassy was a large, sprawling, French-colonial building painted the same green as the toilet paper in our room. A high, green-colored wall topped by barbed wire surrounded the complex. I noticed a similarity between this Soviet Embassy and the one in Washington, D.C. Every single window was tightly shuttered and all the doors were shut. Not a ray of light could enter that building. The one word to describe the Russians is "xenophobic."

The embassies of our allies were also on this street and the surrounding streets. Sitting in the relative comfort of the van, driving past these embassies, I wondered what our good friends the British must have felt like during those times when America was bombing the power plant or areas surrounding Hanoi. What must it have done to their psyche? Or was the diplomatic corps inured to such things?

We had been down this street yesterday on our return from Ba Vi and I knew the Hanoi Hilton was a block or so away. It bothered me to think of the years when Americans were sitting in prison and our allies were right outside the prison walls in their embassies.

There was a vivid basic lesson here on the tree-shaded streets of Hanoi for members of the Vietnam generation. Our fathers' enemies and allies during World War II had reversed roles, as some former enemies became allies, and vice versa. This we all knew as a matter of history. But as I watched the flags of these countries pass by, I realized that the intellectual knowledge of those facts was no match for the gut feeling of being in the country of my former enemy and seeing the flags of our friends flying from embassies on the street where our men were once held prisoner and tortured.

This is of course the way it has always been in the history of the world. But to have it laid out in front of my eyes made me think of the individual soldiers, sailors, and airmen whose lives are used up in these episodes between countries. They do what they are told is necessary for the well-being of their country. If they suffer because of it, then that is the price they must pay.

I accepted the idea; but as a soldier who had lost an arm pursuing this policy, I knew there was another aspect to it that people did not usually consider. No matter which side a person is on, it all becomes immaterial to the wounded individual. The only thing at stake then is his personal dignity as a human being, and if that is nothing in the great scheme of things, it is everything to that individual.

I had been involved with the disabled for twenty years. I knew how shabbily they were dealt with in America. The disabled did not have civil rights in my own country. A person's ability to have proper prosthetic appliance care was limited, and many did without.

The disabled person's lot in America was one of those shameful issues people didn't like to talk about because it did not fit America's image of itself. If things were that bad in America, then to be disabled in a Third World country must truly be hell on earth.

These were my thoughts as I mentally wrestled with the idea of suggesting we help the Vietnamese amputees. If the individual was just a soldier doing what his country asked, and if because of it he was disabled for the rest of his life, maybe we had a duty to help him regain his dignity as an individual. What about our former South Vietnamese allies, the ARVNs who had lost their limbs? Who was taking care of them? After all, this country could be our ally in the future, so what harm would occur to America in offering humanitarian assistance? And what if they remained our enemy for another generation? Helping the individual regain his dignity could not hurt America.

How many people behind those flags on this street had been personally affected by the good America did during World War II and afterward?

If America had thought it was so important to fight in Vietnam, then why hadn't all our allies fought alongside us against the common enemy?

My father's enemies were not my enemies and my children's enemies will be different from my enemies. My father's generation was magnanimous in helping both their allies and their former enemies recover. Germany and Japan were witnesses to that. The situation was different in our case because the Communists took control in Vietnam, and maybe we shouldn't do anything that could help them or their people. But maybe they wouldn't be Communist forever, especially if their children benefited from America's largesse.

Mr. Le Bang was pointing out the different embassies and then grew silent as we drove past the Hanoi Hilton. I tapped him on the shoulder and pointed at the prison. "The American Embassy," I said. Le Bang turned his head back around to see if he had heard right. We were all grinning. He interpreted for the driver, who looked at the prison, and both of them chuckled.

Little did I know that we were actually on the street where the American Consulate was located back during the time of the French. Five blocks east of the Hanoi Hilton, on Hai Ba Trung Street, the consulate had been in a French-style villa until it closed in early 1955. When I saw it later, our Vietnamese host pointed it out to me and said, "That is where your embassy will be." When he explained its earlier use, I asked him what it was being used for now and wouldn't they mind getting evicted? The reply was that it housed the offices of the Fatherland Front, an organ within the Communist Party. And no, there would be no problem when it came time to evict them for the Americans.

There was one more place to visit before we left Hanoi. The JCRC team had told us there was a monument with John McCain's likeness on it that we might like to see as a matter of interest. Anything to do with the war interested Carl and me.

On the return from the Thang Loi Hotel, the driver was instructed to drive back on the causeway between two lakes. The big western lake is the Ho Tay and the smaller lake the Truc Bach. The monument was on the tree-covered causeway next to the shore of the Truc Bach. Out across Truc Bach long tubes of 100mm antiaircraft guns clustered on the shore in a defensive position.

The driver parked the van off the road across from the monument and we crossed the road to look at it. It was like a stone slab standing on its edge, the flat side facing the road. It stood taller than a man and was about 6 feet long and half a foot thick. Carved on the left side as we faced it was a man-sized figure dressed in a combat pilot's uniform. The man was on his knees facing us, his head slightly bowed, his elbows pulled up even with his shoulders. There was writing on the stone to the right of the figure.

Bill translated it verbatim:

> *On 26 October, 1967, at*
> *Truc Bach Lake the military and*
> *the people of Hanoi City arrested*
> *John Sney*
> *MaCan, Major American Air Force*
> *pilot of an A-4 aircraft*
> *Shot down at*
> *the Yen Phu Power Plant*
> *This was 1 of 10*
> *aircraft that were shot down*
> *on this day.*

They had gotten some facts wrong: he was a lieutenant commander in the Navy, his middle name is Sidney, and his last name was misspelled.

Paul told the story of what happened at the lake. When McCain's A-4 Skyhawk got hit by a surface-to-air missile, he ejected upside down. The aircraft was tumbling violently, thrashing McCain about in the cockpit and causing his limbs to flail wildly. They were smashed against the edges of the cockpit when the ejection seat exploded him from the stricken fighter, and both arms and one leg were broken. His parachute opened automatically and he landed in the lake. He would have drowned, but a Vietnamese fisherman put out from shore in his boat and dragged him out of the water.

I stood on the shore looking over both lakes trying to imagine this place during that time. The sky above full of aircraft, missiles, the shrapnel from the antiaircraft guns, the horizon roiling with the smoke, explosions and dust from bombs and rockets hitting the earth, the cacophony cut through with the soul-piercing wail of air-raid sirens.

Up above in those aircraft were men who were my comrades in arms. On October 26, 1967, when John McCain was fighting the enemy in the sky above this city, I was in the South fighting the enemy on the ground. Neither of us ever dreamed how much the war would control our futures. He would become a prisoner of war and I would lose my arm. All of us involved in this war would be a part of Vietnam forever.

Standing in front of the monument that was intended as a tribute to the Vietnamese people reminded me that the meaning of an episode in history depends on which side you were on. This monument represented something glorious to the Vietnamese. But I identified with the man portrayed on the stone, knocked down but not out.

McCain almost died that day. His mistreatment as a prisoner of war exemplified the reasons why we hated the Vietnamese and why it was so difficult these many years later for us to deal with them.

John Hubbell's book *P.O.W.* tells McCain's story. When he had been brought ashore with two broken arms and one broken leg by that Vietnamese fisherman, "someone had smashed a rifle butt into his left shoulder, breaking it, and another had bayoneted a deep wound into his left foot." He had been taken to Hoa Lo Prison, the Hanoi Hilton, where he was beaten until he lost consciousness. For days he was forced to lie in his own vomit and waste. He was almost dead from his untreated wounds, beatings, and neglect when the Vietnamese discovered he was the son of an admiral and quickly took him out of the prison and into a hospital.

Reason enough to hate the Vietnamese, I reflected, but what did they think of us in those days? I noticed the face of McCain on the monument was fouled black from where cigarette butts had been rubbed as a sign of rancor. Some hate obviously still existed.

We piled back into the van for the drive out to the airport. We were happy to arrive at the airport and see our aircraft waiting on us. We were ready to go home. There were a few anxious minutes as we waited at the gate in the van for our passports to be cleared, and then we were driven through the gate out to the C-12.

UNITED STATES OF AMERICA was spelled out in big letters along the side of the white-and-gray-painted fuselage. The American flag was painted high up on the tail. The crew chief was sitting in the shade under the wing. He handed us a cold Coke each and shook our hands.

A gigantic Soviet aircraft was unloading Vietnamese and Russian passengers who looked over at us as they walked past on the way to the terminal. Our pilots were buying aviation fuel. They were standing in the blazing sun counting out hundreds of U.S. dollars in cash to a group of three Vietnamese who were busy filling out forms.

We threw our luggage in the rear of the twin-engine plane, shook hands with the Vietnamese, and got into the aircraft. The pilot, co-pilot, and crew chief loaded on board and welcomed us back to America. The crew chief handed us each another Coke from a cooler. We rejoiced with the crew about being back with our own kind. A wonderful feeling of euphoria swept through me. From the sound of his voice, Carl must have been feeling the same way.

The sweat ran in rivulets from our bodies; the inside of the cabin was like an oven. The pilots fired up the engines and we taxied out to the end of the runway where the pilots went through their checklist. We started to roll past the MiG-21 fighters and soon reached liftoff speed. The pilot rotated and flew outbound on the course given him by the Vietnamese in the tower.

My nose was pressed to the Plexiglas for a last view of the SAM missile site and the traditional Vietnamese village close by. How different this was from the last time I left Vietnam, wrapped in bandages and enclosed in the belly of a C-141 full of wounded soldiers returning home from the war.

It seemed like all of that had taken place only yesterday. A lot had happened in the intervening twenty years, but some things did not change. Vietnam was a strange and forbidding land, and we were still not friends.

Back in the States: The Report Is Published, October 13, 1987

★ Upon our return to the United States, we immediately reported to General Vessey and the Interagency Group. The Interagency Group had been developed to coordinate strategy within the various government agencies dealing with the MIA issue. They were curious as to the Vietnamese response to our trip. We stated that the Vietnamese were in desperate need of humanitarian assistance for their sixty thousand amputees. The amputees needed prosthetic limbs and rehabilitation. There was a need for material to build thirty thousand wheelchairs for the spinal-cord-injured, for amputees who did not have artificial limbs or could not use them, and for cerebral palsy and polio victims.

Identified needs included raw materials like plastic, aluminum, wood, leather, and steel, as well as equipment and tools used to fabricate prosthetic limbs and to manufacture wheelchairs. Physical therapy equipment and medical supplies were also needed, especially antibiotics and medicines to combat diseases. The report further stated that the Vietnamese required assistance in upgrading all of their rehabilitation centers, North and South. In the North were Ba Vi, Haiphong, and Tam Diep. In the South were Da Nang, Qui Nhon, Ho Chi Minh City, and Can Tho. We added the request the Vietnamese had made for assistance with the typhoon damage and dengue fever.

We agreed that Vietnamese needs were legitimate and recommended that help be provided. Most importantly, we reported that we felt the Vietnamese were sincere in their desire to work with the United States on common humanitarian issues.

The Vessey team had been infused from the beginning with the urgency of our trip and the need to react swiftly. The Pentagon provided secretarial help and we had a final written report ready in three days. We went back to our regular jobs expecting immediate action to follow on our recommendations, which had been approved by the Interagency Group.

To show their good faith, the Vietnamese, within days of our return, announced they were returning the remains of three MIAs. They also stated they were going to reopen other areas of humanitarian concerns—Amerasian children being one.

However, there was no immediate response from the Americans. We knew of nothing that was said or done about the recommendations in our report. Carl and I talked about it on the phone and we were mystified at what we perceived as a lost opportunity if America did not do something.

We did not know of the tremendous resistance from certain individuals both within and outside the government who were fiercely opposed to providing anything to the Vietnamese, including humanitarian aid. Their opposition was so strong they were effectively blocking or slowing down any official American government response. General Vessey and the Interagency Group were disappointed, but they were able to persevere and keep the humanitarian initiative alive. General Vessey flew to New York and met with Vice Premier Nguyen Co Thach, who was visiting at the U.N.

Finally, the Department of Defense and the State Department were able to publish our completed report, entitled *The Problem of the Disabled in Vietnam. A Report to Non-government Organizations Stemming from the Mission to Hanoi by Presidential Emissary, General John W. Vessey (Retired),* dated October 13, 1987 (U.S. Department of State, Washington, D.C.).

Due to America's policy toward Vietnam (trade embargoes, non-recognition), no U.S. government funding would be made available for assisting the Vietnamese. However, the report was to be a significant notice to the nongovernmental organizations (NGOs) that the U.S. government was encouraging them to provide humanitarian assistance to Vietnam. The U.S. government would facilitate the application of any NGO that applied for licensing to provide such help. Up to this time, the NGOs that had wanted to go into Vietnam since the end of the war had found it nearly impossible to receive licensing from the U.S. government to do so.

Because this would be a change from the official government stance, and in order to strengthen the signal to the NGOs that the U.S. government was strongly endorsing this report, arrangements were made for the team of Savory, Ward, and Downs, along with Larry Kerr from the State Department and Col. Bill Mayall, General Vessey's executive assistant, to present our report to a meeting of NGOs in Washington, D.C., in the latter part of October 1987. Thus, two strong signals were sent. One was to the Vietnamese, which indicated that the United States was sincerely pursuing its side of the agreement on humanitarian issues. The second was to the NGOs, which had been discouraged up to this point from assisting Vietnam, that the U.S. government had changed its stance.

We met with thirty or so representatives of nongovernmental organizations at the building of one of their members. It was a grand old structure behind the Capitol building in a block north of the Supreme Court. They had been planning to hold a meeting there and agreed to receive our group. Larry Kerr made the arrangements because as Vietnam desk officer he knew many of the representatives. As I walked through the hallways, I could see by the signs and posters that this building housed a multitude of groups that were involved with humanitarian projects all over the world. Some had a decidedly liberal political agenda. When I looked over the crowd of representatives, I got the feeling from their expressions that U.S. government employees were not their favorite people.

They did not have a clear idea what the Vessey mission was, nor exactly what we were doing there. After introductions were made and Larry Kerr briefly explained our mission, he handed the meeting over to Dr. Savory.

Carl did a superb job of presenting the report, and Larry Ward and I added extra information and facts as needed. In some ways, our enthusiasm for the project was as important as the report itself. The audience could sense we were sincere. That was good, because many had encountered red tape and obstacles at all levels of government over the years and had been stopped cold in assisting Vietnam. Thus, the NGO officers were initially skeptical and hostile toward us as representatives of the government. They asked some difficult questions of Larry Kerr, who was known by some of those who had tried to get permission in years past to assist Vietnam. Kerr also had the tough job of explaining to them that although the U.S. government was now asking their help in assisting in this humanitarian effort, they would not be able to request any money from the government. The U.S. policy toward Vietnam forbade any government money to be spent on Vietnam. I could tell by the comments that a number in this crowd did not like that policy. Some of the groups had been anti-war during the war and were still upset at America's role in the war. Some had been working in

South Vietnam on humanitarian projects at that time; others had been formed specifically to help Vietnam.

I had heard of two, the American Friends Service Committee (the Quakers) and World Vision, but others such as the U.S.-Indochina Reconciliation Project and William Joiner Foundation I knew nothing about.

Up until this point, I would never have dreamed I would be in the same room with the antiwar, help-the-Vietnamese types. But here I was, assisting in presenting to them an official State Department report stating that the U.S. government recognized the Vietnamese were in need of humanitarian assistance and would welcome their efforts to supply that assistance.

When George Washington defeated the British Army, General Cornwallis was so astonished at this turn of events that he had his band play "The World Turned Upside Down" as his troops stacked arms in surrender.

> *If ponies rode men and if grass ate cows,*
> *And cats should be chased into holes by the mouse*
> *If summer were spring and the other way around,*
> *Then all the world would be upside down.*

The world was certainly turned upside down from what I thought it had been.

Second Trip to Vietnam
★ November 1987 ★

UPI 11-6-87

Bangkok (UPI)—A team of three American doctors sponsored by the U.S. government are scheduled to arrive in Hanoi Monday to continue a survey of disabled Vietnamese, a U.S. State Department spokesman said Friday.

"Dr. Carl Savory and his team are scheduled to visit Hanoi Nov. 9 to Nov. 12," said Ross Petzing, spokesman for the U.S. embassy in Bangkok.

"While in Hanoi they will continue their survey on prosthetics and the disability situation in Vietnam," Petzing said.

The team started the survey during a visit to Vietnam Aug. 25 to Aug. 28.

Savory is accompanied by Dr. Frederick Downs, Chief of Prosthetics and Sensory Aids Service for the Veterans Administration, and Dr. Larry Ward, a representative of a private organization.

The findings of the team's first visit to Vietnam called "The Problem with the Disabled in Vietnam" was released to private organizations on Oct. 14 in Washington, D.C.

★ The news wire had got it wrong about me being a doctor and misquoted the title, but the rest was correct. We were going back to Hanoi on our second trip.

Our first visit had produced positive humanitarian results from Vietnam. The Vietnamese had returned three sets of MIA remains, including one set that was on the list of the first seventy discrepancy cases General Vessey had presented to them. These seventy were classified as "discrepancy" because they were men who had had a high probability of being captured alive or were alive when last seen in Vietnamese hands. The discrepancy was that America had thought these men would have been returned alive at the end of the war, but the Vietnamese claimed that they had no knowledge of some of the men. In other cases they claimed the men were dead, either killed in escape attempts or dying of battle injuries. America said if that were so, then where were the remains? The belief that the Vietnamese had refused to return the remains had fueled the suspicions of a lot of Americans that the Vietnamese obviously must be lying; if they could not return the remains, it must be because the men were not dead. Whatever other reason could there be for not returning remains? The Vietnamese had the answer, but no one knew what it was.

Another humanitarian issue the Vietnamese had addressed was to talk about releasing seven thousand South Vietnamese from the "reeducation" camps. These men, who had once been citizens of South Vietnam, America's ally, had been in the prison camps since the end of the war. They were the last of what had been tens of thousands of South Vietnam's military and government personnel thrown into the camps for years.

A third humanitarian issue was the resumption of talks between the Americans and Vietnamese on resolving the Amerasian children problem. Provisions were being made to allow the Amerasian children and their mothers to leave Vietnam for America.

The fourth humanitarian issue was the Vietnamese decision to begin discussions on reinstituting the Orderly Departure Program. This was the program whereby Vietnamese inside Vietnam could make application through their government to be allowed to emigrate to America where relatives were waiting for them. The procedure was an "orderly departure" from Vietnam, in contrast to the Vietnamese who escaped to become refugees.

With all of these issues, there were special interest groups in America that had to work through both governments, and the Vietnamese decision to allow these groups to proceed had a positive effect.

The Vietnamese had shown good faith in addressing America's humanitarian issues. However, America's slow response in return had caused them great concern. When they met with the JCRC team in Hanoi on October 28, 1987, they made it very plain that there would be no more talks until General Vessey's humanitarian team returned. So we did.

The period since our return from the first trip had been an education for me. Now that I had been to Vietnam as a team member of the Vessey mission on the POW/MIA issue I was suddenly in the middle of the issue. I began receiving a great deal of information from the various government and civilian individuals who had been working on these issues for more than a decade. These people collectively had more knowledge about the issues involving Vietnam and America than anyone else in the country. This did not mean they particularly agreed with each other on their interpretations of what that knowledge meant, nor what should be done with it.

I had a changed viewpoint now that I had more information. I still wanted to resolve the POW/MIA issue as much as ever, but I no longer hated the Vietnamese. Without the emotion, I was able to take a more rational view of what was going on between the two countries. The POW/MIA issue may have been the focus for most Americans, but the other issues involving American foreign policy and the interrelationships with the countries in Asia were incredibly more complex.

When we returned from the first trip there had been newspaper articles, news releases, and other activities concerning Vietnam and POW/MIA. There was a great deal of controversy in all of it.

The POW/MIA issue was an inflammatory subject in America, with charges and countercharges fired in broadsides from individuals and groups who had contrary opinions about everything connected to the issue. Even the humanitarian aspect was disliked by some people who thought the Vietnamese were trading MIA remains for aid.

Some believed the U.S. government was doing the best it could in resolving the issue; others distrusted the government and believed little or nothing was being done. There were some who believed a little of both. And, there were those who thought that our government knew there were live POWs, but was keeping it a secret.

Some congressmen had promised millions of dollars in rewards to anyone who could bring out a live POW. This idea was severely criticized by the National League of Families of American Prisoners and Missing in Action in Southeast Asia as complicating the issue: it generated false reports, encouraged extortion, and caused sources to withhold information in the hope of obtaining compensation.

Other congressmen took umbrage with the League, describing its criticisms as an attack on members of Congress who were trying to solve the problem.

A former prisoner of war and a congressional representative went to Thailand and floated plastic bags down the Mekong River to Laos and Cambodia with messages offering rewards for information on POWs. They were also going to send 2,500 balloons containing the message, but the Thai government stopped them.

A congressman released a list of seventy-six POWs he claimed were still being held by the Vietnamese, which was well publicized in the newspapers. The Vietnamese Army newspaper in Vietnam labeled the congressman's accusation "slanderous" and said the charge was nothing but "political provocation aimed at poisoning the U.S.-Vietnamese relations, which are being improved."

I thought of that line from the Kingston Trio song, "Nobody likes anybody anymore."

November 9, 1987—Return to Hanoi

★ We flew economy class from Washington, D.C., straight through to Bangkok in a twenty-eight-hour killer trip. There was no Defense Attaché aircraft for us this time. For the next hop into Hanoi the American Embassy arranged tickets for us on Vietnam Airlines (Hang Khong Vietnam). We were told by friends it would be bad. Hang Khong Vietnam would be an experience we would not soon forget.

We had gotten up early so we could allow plenty of time for checking in at the airport. The Thais and the Vietnamese have been antagonistic toward each other for centuries, but this had not stopped commerce between them. However, the Thai officials checking passports of passengers entering the Vietnam waiting area were not the usual smiling people we were used to seeing. These Thais were burly, rough-looking men who did not smile. They went to extra efforts to check the passports of the Vietnamese.

Up on the Thai-Cambodian border the Thai and Vietnamese armies were regularly shelling each other. There were many sections of the border in dispute and the two sides have fought hand to hand. The problem is that the Thai-Khmer border is not well marked. When the Vietnamese engaged and chased the Khmer Rouge (their real enemy in Cambodia), they sometimes chased them into Thai territory. This puts the Vietnamese soldiers into battle with the Thais, who are trying to protect their own territory against any incursions. As part of these battles the Vietnam-

178

ese intermittently shell the refugee camps in Thailand along the disputed border.

These events were happening concurrent with our trips, which made the missions that much more delicate because the Thais were our strong allies. Each trip we made involved close communication between American and Thai government officials so that the Thais were fully informed and reassured of their position.

I looked over the passengers gathered for the Vietnam Airlines flight. There were about thirty-five in total: we three Americans, three Italians with UNICEF, two British Embassy employees, one Swede, and a few Caucasians I could not identify. The remainder were Vietnamese, loaded down with all they could carry on board the plane. Carl and I thought they must have made a PX run into Bangkok's sprawling marketplace. In addition to what they were carrying with them, we had seen them check three to four cardboard boxes apiece through baggage. They looked like Christmas shoppers, they had so many packages. Most of them were men my age or older; few were women or young people. Carl and I supposed a Vietnamese had to have seniority or a high position in the party to be allowed to come to a non-Communist country. We found out later Bangkok was the only air-transit point to the Western world for all Vietnamese going in and out of the country.

When the bus pulled in at the terminal door to take the passengers the short, 100-meter trip to the aircraft, it was every man for himself. There was no seat assignment, so it was important to position oneself for the dash to the plane when the bus stopped. If there were not enough seats, one stayed behind or stood in the back of the plane. I did not take seriously the idea one would have the option of standing in the aisle, but I had never flown a Communist airline before. I discovered later they were not kidding about standing. Carl, Larry, and I politely shoved our way to a good position and were successful in boarding the plane when the bus stopped.

At 1400 hours we lifted off the Bangkok International Airport in a TU-134, a two-engine jet of Russian manufacture. I had never ridden a Russian aircraft before, especially one maintained by the poorest nation in the world. When we walked across the cement and up the portable stairs to board, I had noticed the paintwork of the airline's name on the fuselage was almost worn off.

Cobwebs hung down from the light fixtures, some of them non-functioning. The plane was extremely dirty. Every surface was smeared. The rug was frayed, torn, or bare in many spots, and grubby all over. A pile of rubbish and pieces of wood crates lay in the otherwise empty galley. The curtain between us and first class was open, and I could see no difference except the seats were wider. The cockpit door was closed.

I was sitting in the exit row. There were no seat assignments so you grabbed what you wanted, and I definitely wanted to be close to an exit. There was a band of steel encircling the inside of the fuselage to reinforce the body. In my row, the band extended to about half the width of the seat next to the window, so one was forced to sit sideways.

Carl was sitting in the aisle seat across from me. We took pictures of each other, not believing we were going to fly in this thing. Luggage was piled to the ceiling in the rear of the cabin. There must not have been a baggage compartment; the crew loaded baggage through the rear door and stacked it in the back of the plane on top of the seats. As it was being loaded, the pile edged forward until it reached the passengers, at which point the baggage handlers stopped.

No one seemed to have a working seat belt. I looked behind me at the luggage stacked to the ceiling and figured no one would survive a crash anyway. Later I was told there are some flights so full that Vietnamese stand in the aisle in the back of the cabin for the hour-and-a-half trip.

When we reached altitude, the cooler air mixing with the high humidity caused a fog to come pouring out of the air vents. Man, the last time I saw that happen was back during the war riding in C-123s and C-130s!

The three stewardesses were Vietnamese women dressed in slacks. One of them walked out of the fog with a tray of snack food. The two drinks offered were a bar-size glass of beer or a plastic cup of black tea. I took the beer, which was warm and tasted skunky; Carl took the tea.

After about an hour we started the descent. This Russian aircraft was designed to be converted into military use, so insulation was minimal. The noise inside the cabin became so loud during the descent that conversation was difficult.

The pilot made a long, low approach on final and a good landing. As we taxied over to the apron in front of the terminal, I could see a regular convention of Vietnam Airlines planes plus a Galaxy-sized Russian aircraft sitting close to the terminal.

Communists worldwide, we discovered later, had flown to the USSR the week before to celebrate the seventieth anniversary of the October Revolution. Now that the celebration was over, the aircraft were back and parked.

We unloaded down the steep, rickety portable stairs and crossed the cement ramp to enter the terminal, where we were given Customs forms to fill out. There was no VIP lounge for us this time, no sitting in air-conditioned comfort drinking bottled water and exchanging chit-chat. Instead, we were herded through Customs with the masses. Carl and I remarked to each other that we wished the official American government response to our report last trip had been quicker. Maybe we would have been treated differently, we joked.

This environment was more like the Communist countries I had read about. The tile floor was dirty; the walls were drab and badly in need of paint. A balcony on the back wall held five or six young men in uniform who were chatting among themselves while looking over the crowd. They seemed more curious than suspicious.

There was a uniformed young man in each of four wooden immigration booths, with a single glaring light bulb hanging from a frayed cord over his head. Carl put his passport on the shelf and the man did a double take when he saw it was an Official American passport and not the American tourist passport. He looked up through the thin bars of his cage at Carl's face and back at the passport. He called for his supervisor, who came over. After some conversation the supervisor went back to his desk and Carl was stamped through.

I was next in line, so for good measure I slapped my Official passport onto the shelf with my hook. My hook clung to the edge of the shelf while I looked innocently at the official and smiled. His face was expressionless but he craned his neck to look behind me to see if there were others. He checked me out against my picture, stamped the passport, and slid a board aside to let me pass. Carl and I remarked to each other on the absence of VIP treatment. We did not know if it was because our trips were now thought to be routine by the pragmatic Vietnamese, or if it was a signal they were displeased. We decided it was the former. After all, we were working for General Vessey, who was the VIP, and we were probably provided special treatment on our first trip just as a matter of courtesy.

A man from the Foreign Ministry was waiting with the Customs officials behind a counter; when he saw us filling out the forms, he came forward and introduced himself. It was Mr. Nhu, who had been a member of the delegation last time and was there as our escort officer. Carl, Larry, and I were especially happy to see him because up until that time the American Embassy in Bangkok had not heard back from the Vietnamese confirming the information about our arrival.

Communication with the Vietnamese was a constant problem. At first we thought it was because they were just being difficult, but we came to discover that the problem was their system of doing things. During their long years of war they had learned to keep everything secret so that it could not be leaked to the enemy. Information was not shared; everything was compartmentalized and rigidly controlled by a central authority. Therefore the message our government had sent to Vietnam about our pending arrival had, in all likelihood, taken so long to work its way through channels that the Vietnamese had not had time to compose and return an answer before our arrival. We had not learned it by this trip, but we would later learn that one message to one element of the Vietnamese government was not sufficient. The best way to communicate with the Vietnamese was to simultaneously send a message to the Vietnamese mission at the UN, the embassy in Bangkok, and the ministry in Hanoi.

When we took the Customs forms over to the officials, the Vietnamese penchant for inefficiency was clearly obvious as three or four young officials looked over the forms. Mr. Nhu was intently explaining to them we were important visitors, but they were not impressed. The more I learned about the Vietnamese, the more I realized they were not intimidated by anyone superior to them in rank. Finally everyone was satisfied and we went into the next room, where the luggage was coming through on a conveyor belt.

After walking past the luggage inspectors who waved us through—thanks to Mr. Nhu, who did have influence with them—we pushed through the waiting crowd at the front doors to where we could stand with a little breathing space around us on the sidewalk in front of the airport. I am always struck when I travel to Third World countries by the large masses of people waiting behind the barricades for their returning family members or friends. Going to the airport must be one of the few entertainments available, so it is an occasion in which as many people as possible participate.

In Bangkok, Carl and I had decided that a group of Vietnamese must pool their money and send one man to Bangkok to buy things for the group, including items used to set up businesses or to barter. All Third World countries I had seen did this sort of thing. I thought of the returning Vietnam Airlines flight as being like the resupply wagon train coming into the frontier post or a caravan arriving at the city gates.

I saw another group of Vietnamese who were disembarking from a Russian Aeroflot flight. A long line of Vietnamese streamed out of the plane carrying with them as many items as the Vietnamese arriving from Bangkok.

The Vietnamese returning from the USSR had gone there as part of an agreement to provide much-needed labor in the Soviet mines, factories, and other miserable work locations. I had read in the American papers that the Russians were using the Vietnamese as slave labor. As I became involved on a much broader scale with the history and present situation of Vietnam, I saw that matters were not that simple.

The conditions in Vietnam were such that unemployment was high—25 percent. There was no money and nothing to spend it on. People were on the edge of starvation; they had families to take care of.

Although I had read about these "slave flights" hauling Vietnamese to the USSR, the Vietnamese, I was to find out, were standing in line to sign up for work there. They fought over the chance to get chosen because that meant food on the table, medicines for the children, and luxuries they could buy and bring back home when they returned.

They were even called "heroes" because they were helping their country. When they signed up for two or three years of work in the Soviet Union, half of what they made went to pay off Vietnam's debt to the USSR, a quarter went to Vietnam, and the worker got a quarter for himself. It may have been slave labor from our viewpoint, but for the Vietnamese it was a straw to grasp, which they did willingly.

The driver of our van pulled up to the curb and helped us load our luggage into the back. We traveled light, with only one suitcase apiece. When we pulled onto the road from the airport, we drove past a large stone building that used to be a church. I had missed it on the first trip, even though it was the largest building in the area, because it blended in with the environment. The areas where the stained glass would be were either so dirty they matched the black stone blocks or there were dark gray faded boards over the window openings. From the appearance of the building, it looked abandoned.

I stared at it as we passed by. I guessed it would have been built sometime in the nineteenth century when the French were colonizing the country. A tremendous amount of labor must have been expended in its behalf.

The old church made me think of my friends married to Vietnamese Catholics, the children of other Vietnamese Catholics forced to flee the North in 1954 when the Viet Minh were victorious over the French. The children of those Catholics then were forced to flee in 1975 as South Vietnam fell to the Vietnamese Communists.

The forlorn church fed my recurrent doubts about whether anything good would ever come from what we were doing for the Vietnamese government. I now knew that some of the church leaders thrown into prison when South Vietnam fell were still in prison and were considered enemies of the state.

I pushed those depressing thoughts to the back of my mind. I truly was determined to do all I could to make the General Vessey mission a success. It was my duty.

November was harvest time and the people were busy in the fields. The rice was being cut and put into sheaves. The bundles of grain were then laid onto the road, to the consternation of the drivers, where vehicles would run over them, shucking the rice kernel from the husk. Rice sheaves lay for kilometers along both lanes of the road. Some of the sheaves were alarmingly big and the van bounced over them with a bone-jarring thud. The drivers of the various types of vehicles did not want to bounce over these bundles lying in the road, so they tried to avoid hitting them.

Our driver dodged and weaved his way past the bicycles, oxcarts, trucks, motorcycles, and other vehicles speeding along the road. They too were dodging and weaving around the sheaves of rice so that the whole scene looked like a piece of intricate choreography.

It was the beginning of winter in North Vietnam. We thought the 75- to 80-degree day was comfortable, but the Vietnamese were dressed as if for a winter storm on the American western plains: hats, earmuffs, scarfs, shawls, sweaters, coats; you name it, they were wearing it. We were comfortable in short sleeves. I was reminded of the time I visited Florida in November and was walking the beach with nothing on but a swimming suit and the other people on the beach were dressed in sweaters and coats. One of them said to me in passing, "You must be a tourist."

When we drove over the bridge crossing the Red River and entered the city, I immediately noticed more colors in people's clothes. I attributed this to the winter coats and sweaters.

The city was also bright with red banners from the recent seventieth anniversary celebration of the Russian Revolution. The Bank of Vietnam had long red streamers hanging the length of the building, and red banners crisscrossed the square in front of the bank. At the top of the bank, the billboard-size picture of Ho Chi Minh still smiled over the city.

We were again staying at the guesthouse, which was a positive sign. Dang Nghiem Bai, Director of Foreign Affairs for North America, was the head of the delegation again. We were informed he would have dinner with us at 1830 hours.

We went to our assigned rooms to unpack and take a shower. There was no hot water but I did not need it. Dinner was amicable enough. They gave us the schedule for the next three days. They also gave us an excuse about why we could

not visit Ho Chi Minh City as we had requested: there was a
trial in progress of the survivors of former South Vietnamese who had led a raid back into Vietnam. The force had
been betrayed and ambushed in Laos and two thirds of the
rebels were killed.

I had read about this raid in the papers back in the States.
Even though it seemed like a hopeless cause, there were
many Vietnamese exiles in America and other countries
who supported the belief that the Communist government
in Hanoi could be defeated by a counterrevolutionary force.
The former South Vietnamese civilians and military who
advocated this concept received money from the Vietnamese communities to support the activities of these groups.

Later on, when I began to ask questions around Washington, D.C., about these support groups, people told me that
although there were deeply felt anti-Communist sentiments,
there was also in some cases fear and intimidation in the
Vietnamese communities throughout the United States
about the tactics used by a few within these groups. Although not much attention was paid to these activities by
the American public, the FBI and RAND Corporation took
them seriously. Later, on January 28, 1988, the *Los Angeles
Times* would report that the FBI had begun an investigation
into political violence in U.S.-Vietnamese exile communities. From 1980 onward, the article reported, a pattern had
emerged involving politically motivated violent acts against
Vietnamese victims in many U.S. cities. Among these acts
were murder, assault, and arson.

I was unaware of all that on this trip, though I imagine the
Vietnamese probably would not have believed that we, as
government officials, were ignorant about such things.
Nothing more on the raid was mentioned during our stay.
Later on, back in the States, I read reports where the
Vietnamese charged that the majority of the financial
support and guidance for this group came from the United
States and Thailand. As proof of this, they pointed out that

the general, Hoang Co Minh, who was among those killed in Laos, had offices in the United States.

We were told by our sources that the North Vietnamese had intelligence agents infiltrated into all of the rebel groups operating in the refugee camps along the border, and that it was possible there could even be some who had made it to the States masquerading as refugees. The general was doomed from the moment he crossed the border with his guerrilla force.

The more I worked at this job and the more I discovered, the more amazed I became at the fierce undercurrents affecting the relationships between America and Vietnam.

Although the general may have had an office in the United States, that did not mean the U.S. government supported him. The point was that the Vietnamese government, in its heart of hearts, always believed that any person or organization from America that was hostile to Vietnam by action or deed was directed by the American government. As a police state it is probably impossible for Vietnam to conceive how much freedom people in America have to do what they want to do, whether the American government approves or not. The Vessey team, of course, had no control over these events, but their simultaneous occurrence was a painful coincidence.

After dinner, Carl went to bed with a rotten cold. I wanted to go for a walk and reacquaint myself with the neighborhood, and Larry said he would accompany me. We stood at the end of the park across from the Lake of the Restored Sword and watched the people pedal by. The air was heavy with the dense smoke caused by the soft coal they were burning to ward off what was to them the chilly air. Hard coal would not have polluted the air as much, but they did not have it.

It was a night for romantics. Strings of lights outlined the shapes of the Turtle Pagoda sitting in the middle of the lake at the south end and the Ngoc Son Pagoda at the northeast side of the lake. The Sunshine Bridge connecting the Ngoc Son Pagoda to the shore was also strung with lights. Pairs of lovers sitting on the park benches were talking intimately with each other, while other couples strolled on the walk around the lake.

At the north end we passed by six electric trolley cars parked for the night in the semi-darkness. As we walked past the ancient cars, dark and quiet against the backdrop of the French-colonial-style buildings across the street, I again had the impression we were in an earlier era.

When we reached the other side of the lake, the nearly full moon came out from behind the clouds and bathed the city in a soft wash of moonlight. The lighted pagodas in the lake and the quiet tree-covered city beneath the clear moon made the mythological story of the origin of Hanoi seem real.

In the year 1010, it was said, King Ly Thai To had been searching long and hard for a place to build the city from which he could rule the land. The legend said that late in the day, upon his approach to the Red River, a dragon burst from the ground and leaped into the sky, flooding the area with a brilliant light. The king believed such a place must be sacred and decided he would rule the land henceforth from there. The city was named Thang Long, which means the City of the Ascending Dragon. Later it would become known as Hanoi. On a night such as this, the legend seemed alive.

In a large municipal-type building across the road we could hear waltz music. We crossed the road to satisfy our curiosity and through the huge open windows we could see Vietnamese dancing a waltz. The music was a curious mixture of waltz music played on Oriental instruments. Three youngsters had climbed up the outside and were clutching to the window sill so they could watch what was going on inside the ballroom. Later on I learned that ballroom dancing was all the rage in Hanoi.

We walked on down the sidewalk until we found a well-lit café playing a Merle Haggard country-and-western music tape. The café next door was playing a hard rock tape. This was an astonishing thing for me to hear in Hanoi. When I told Bill Bell about it later in Bangkok, he smiled and told me he gives these tapes out whenever he is traveling in Vietnam. They make popular gifts, he added.

I was all for stopping at the one playing country-and-western and drinking a beer, but the woman behind the counter shrugged and waved her hand at the empty beer bottles. She was out of her beer quota for the day and could not sell anymore. The old men sitting at the tables out front smiled at me with betel nut-stained teeth and offered me a chair. I looked around and saw Larry was talking with someone down the block. He seemed to be in no hurry. I nodded thank you to the old men and sat down. The air around them was thick with cigarette smoke.

We quickly established where I was from. One of the men spoke English well enough so that I could understand him. He told the others I was an American, and they all perked up at that and gave me a real looking over. He asked me what I was doing in Vietnam and I told him. Then he asked if I had ever been to Vietnam before. I replied I had, and in fact, had lost my arm as an officer in the American Army fighting against the Communists in the South near Chu Lai.

He nodded matter-of-factly and said he had fought the American imperialists for many years in the South himself and the French colonialists before that. But too many years of wars were bad, and he was glad it was over. He asked me if my government compensated me for my service, and did they provide me with the arm I was wearing. I told him yes, and added I worked for our Veterans Administration assisting in providing artificial limbs and wheelchairs to all disabled veterans in America. He asked me how many disabled veterans America had, and when I told him approximately a million, he looked at me in wonder. I thanked him for his hospitality and said I must be leaving. My friend and I were tired and had to return to the guesthouse.

Next to the entrance of a well-lit building in the next block a Vietnamese newspaper was posted in a glass-fronted display case. The paper had the current date: November 9, 1987. A short, thin, rugged-looking old man, dressed in worn, mended clothes and a dark beret, was standing reading the paper, his hands clasped behind his back.

I stopped to look, curious to see the paper posted out on the street like this. The old man noticed me immediately and spoke to me first in French, so I replied I did not understand him. Then in bad English he asked me if I was British. I said no, I was an American. He asked if I had been to Vietnam before, which is the same question all Vietnamese must ask. I told him yes and repeated my story of when I was in the South.

He told me he was a teacher. He then told me he had a sister who lived in Anaheim, California, and asked me if I knew where it was. I replied I had been there many times and I understood there was a large Vietnamese community that lived there. He said wistfully that he hoped to visit her someday. I wished him good luck and bid him good night.

Even though the hour was late, there were a number of good-looking teenage girls out. They were walking in pairs or with larger groups or riding alone on bicycles. They were smiling, giggling, and having a good time together. They must have felt as safe as I did on the streets. I rarely saw a police officer in the day, and I never saw one at night except at the entrance to the police station.

The number of beggar boys had increased since the last trip, however. They looked like true beggars with their skinny, frail bodies, not like the well-fed beggars I had seen in the old days in the South. These kids were starving and they worked alone, not in packs.

One of the men we had dinner with the next evening was being transferred to the Vietnamese mission in New York

City. He was one of the younger members of the Ministry of Foreign Affairs and this was his first trip out of the country. We told him it was not as safe as Hanoi. We warned him about the city of New York. Muggings, robberies, assaults, murder, gangs, and every nightmare he ever had about the evils of capitalism were right out there to be seen and experienced if he was not careful.

November 10, 1987—The Morning Meeting

★ I was ready for breakfast at 0700, and Carl, Larry, and I went down together to the dining room. Soon six Frenchmen, four Russians, one Australian, one older American woman, and five Japanese came in and sat down at their respective tables.

The Russians sat next to our table. One guy looked exactly like the stereotype: heavyset, beefy, with a red face and short haircut. He was wearing ill-fitting cheap clothes and shoes of such poor quality they would have been on a bum in the United States. The Russians were sullen-looking and they were unfriendly. Their hostility was palpable.

Carl and I had never seen a Russian in person before. It gave us an eerie feeling to sit in the same room with our long-term Cold War enemies.

For each meal during the three days we ate in that room, the Russians would try to open the dining-room door the wrong direction, every time making a loud crash in that acoustically poor room. The door was set in a wall made of glass panels and wooden frames, and it reverberated loudly from any movement.

Carl and I had a difficult time not bursting out laughing because we began to anticipate the crash each time we saw a Russian head for the door. They did not seem to learn which way the door opened, nor did they try to be gentle with it. They just yanked. If they were entering from the other side, we knew it was one of them as soon as the door crashed into the jamb.

Carl and I figured the French, the Australian, and the Japanese were here on business, but we could not figure out what an older American woman was doing in a Communist country alone. However, Larry said he recognized her as a person who had been coming into Vietnam for at least ten years working for a private voluntary organization that helped the Vietnamese. He went over to her table to say hello.

Carl and I looked at each other in disbelief. The way we understood it, there were no Americans providing help to Vietnam; it was not allowed. When Larry returned he explained that there were a few Americans who had found ways to visit Vietnam and bring in a few items, even though it was frowned on by the State Department. This woman brought in medical supplies she purchased in Hong Kong.

We asked him, with some indignation, what kind of American would be in here helping the Vietnamese for the last twelve years. Larry told us there were Americans who were working in the South before it fell, and some of them tried to keep a few activities going under the present government. It was very difficult, though, because America did not recognize Vietnam.

We thought any activity by Americans in Vietnam not sanctioned by the U.S. government was somehow treasonous. Of course a lot of that kind of thing had gone on during the war and no charges had ever been filed against the people doing it. But that didn't mean we had liked it.

As old soldiers, Carl and I did not approve of those anti-American actions then or now. The memories of those bad times hurt. We talked about how we felt in those days when, as returning soldiers, we had been given a hard time by people. Especially galling were those Americans who traveled to Vietnam during the war, giving the Vietnamese all kinds of propaganda to use against us.

Now the irony was that some Americans thought we were

193

doing things just as bad because they claimed we were giving the Vietnamese propaganda to use in their efforts to gain recognition by America.

The meeting began at 0900. In keeping with the pragmatic Vietnamese way of doing things, the delegation was the same as before.

Mr. Bai opened cordially by going over our schedule and outlining some points. He said we would discuss the report Dr. Savory had presented to him at last night's dinner plus some other concerns.

In response to our specific request he had arranged for us to visit a hospital, the Bach Mai Hospital, in the afternoon. It was their finest hospital, the training hospital for all the doctors in North Vietnam. As an afterthought he added that this was the hospital bombed by the air pirates in Christmas 1972. At the time neither Carl, Larry, nor I thought much about this last statement. We would later find out the Bach Mai Hospital was a sore point with the Vietnamese; or at least their propaganda would have you believe so.

After the visit to the hospital, the Minister of Labor, Invalids, and Social Affairs would be waiting for us. He was very busy and the time arranged for the visit might change. Mr. Bai told us there was a problem with the four amputees we had requested be present for a demonstration, but Dr. Tung, the Director of Prosthetics, would settle the problem the following day.

Dr. Savory then made his statement: "It is good to be back. We have brought copies of the report to present to you. Much has happened since last we met. We are working diligently on these issues. We endeavored to minimize media attention until the report was published, so as to not prejudice nongovernmental attitudes. There was some media coverage and one or two articles reflected negative bias. But overall the feedback we received was quite positive.

"Mr. Kerr of our State Department introduced us to thirty executives of the nongovernment organizations and we presented the report in a positive light. It was well received and several organizations are interested in helping to provide humanitarian aid to Vietnam. You have read the report and you may have questions or need clarification. We welcome your comments on it."

Mr. Bai responded by saying they were glad to have the report and it showed our great effort and sincerity. He was concerned about our visit to Ba Vi because they had only shown us the place where they treated the children. He wanted us to understand that the reason why we did not see the adults who were invalids from the war with America was because they were concerned for our safety. I thought to myself that if I was responsible for a North Vietnamese visiting America, I would have the same concerns.

Dr. Bui Tung and Dr. Dong then made their comments, which basically said we had a positive spirit and it was obvious we wanted to solve problems.

Overall, the morning meeting seemed to go well, and the two delegations were much more relaxed and comfortable with each other. Our side talked a lot more, asking more questions as we tried to tie down specific numbers and information. We knew the Vietnamese did not have anything in material, supplies, and equipment, but what were their priorities of need? It was difficult to figure it out.

We had a hard time following their meaning at times and they had the same problem with us. Sometimes the flow of the meeting paused as both sides stumbled over a word not used in the same context in the other language. But the morning session ended on a positive note and we broke for lunch. Afterwards, we strolled over to the bank to exchange dollars for dong.

The visit to Bach Mai was a failure. We were confused, insulted, and infuriated by our treatment.

The driver drove us in the van to the south side of the city, where Bach Mai is located on a main street named Duong Giai Phong. We waited in the van at the front gate while our escort, Mr. Nhu, got out to explain to the guards who we were. A number of men who were loafing at the gate helped to open it when Mr. Nhu finished his explanations and climbed back into the van.

The hospital director and a handful of staff, all in white coats, were standing on the steps when we drove up front. Introductions were made out on the steps. Before we went inside, they pointed out the white cement two-story slab standing over to the side of the hospital as a monument to those hospital employees and patients who were killed when the hospital was bombed in December 1972 during the Christmas bombings.

We were invited to go look, which we did. There were twenty-eight names listed on the monument. The three of us discussed it among ourselves and finally remembered something about a hospital being bombed. We commented, "So this was the one." Carl and I were not overly concerned as it had been war, it had been an accident, and it had happened fifteen years ago. Although some of the hospital staff seemed to be agitated at our presence, we did not pay much attention. After all, we were here to help them.

I was later asked by a friend in Washington whether Carl and I had been overly callous and I was at first taken aback by the question. But then I realized that the questioner would never understand. I had killed many men and had seen my own men suffer and die. That was the way of it. It was burden enough on my soul to grieve for my own, let alone the enemy. Yet I could not dwell on it. That way lay madness. It was best to accept it and move on.

When we walked through the front doors of the hospital, the stench was overpowering. Carl and I were next to each other and we both expressed disbelief that this could really be their main teaching hospital. Not only did it stink, but it was filthy and as dark and dank as a dungeon.

We were led to a narrow room where a table was obviously used for staff meetings. We were expecting a briefing listing their medical needs and the problems they were facing.

There were three doctors dressed in white coats. They looked old and hard, and it turned out they were.

They launched into a diatribe against the American bombing of the hospital that lasted well over an hour. Each time they made a point they would lay a black and white picture of the damage on the table until shortly the whole surface of the long conference table was covered. Pictures of the rubble and the bodies were passed to us to look at. These doctors evidently had been here at the time and they described in excruciating detail the events of that day. Included in the diatribe were plenty of references to "American air pirates," "American air criminals," and "the dirty war waged by the imperialist forces."

This was like something out of a bad dream. Here we were, far from home in a stinking pest hole in the middle of North Vietnam, being berated by Communist cadre about an American air raid as if it had happened yesterday. I felt like a prisoner who had been brought down from the Hanoi Hilton for these people to beat up on so they could extract some sort of revenge and then send me back to the prison.

Christ, was I pissed off! Carl and I exchanged looks and I could tell he was just as pissed as I was. But we kept our mouths shut and our faces clear of expression because we were not sure of the purpose of this.

We asked ourselves afterwards if their purpose was to make us feel guilty. Were they trying to tell us they were still angry at us? This is a police state, and the Hanoi government never does anything without a reason. Was this a message from their government, or was it simply the Bach Mai routine that the staff put on for all visiting VIPs?

Carl and I were not into guilt trips, and we were not like those American apologists who travel over here to hear how evil America was. Maybe they did not know our purpose in being here?

As we sat there under this barrage of propaganda we became more than mad, we became perplexed. We were here to bind up the wounds and they kept pouring salt into them.

No American crew is ever going to deliberately bomb a hospital. We knew that, and for this doctor to keep harping at us about our comrades in arms was an insult.

The B-52s were bombing Hanoi as part of *Linebacker II*, the Christmas bombing in December 1972 designed by President Nixon to force the Vietnamese back to the negotiating table. Three of the targets the B-52s were striking—a North Vietnamese airfield, an air defense command center, and a petroleum storage area—were within hundreds of feet of the hospital.

The hospital may have been bombed, but it wasn't a target—it was a mistake. The Vietnamese claimed the Americans had purposely bombed the hospital and the world press agreed. America counter-charged that the hospital had not been hit by American bombers, but that the damage was probably caused by a SAM missile crashing back to earth or antiaircraft shells falling back.

Because of the adverse publicity worldwide about the American "terror bombing" of the hospital, the Pentagon ordered an in-depth photoanalysis of the raid. The painful truth discovered by Air Force photoanalysis was that a B-52 targeted to bomb the Bach Mai airfield had released its bombs too early and hit one wing of the Bach Mai Hospital.

I did not remember any of these details at the time we were receiving our lecture at Bach Mai. In fact, I did not remember reading in 1972 about this bombing which was so important to the Vietnamese then and obviously still so important today. Knowing the way I had felt about the enemy in those days, if I had heard about the bombing of the hospital, I would not have cared.

Finally the diatribe was over. We breathed a sigh of relief. They gathered up their photographs and stacked them in a file on the wall behind them. Now that they had done their duty, a transformation came over them. Their expressions changed from grim, forbidding masks to ones of professional concern as they slipped into their medical roles. They began to give us useful information about the mission of the hospital and its needs in terms of equipment, supplies, and material. After the briefing, during which they were gracious hosts serving us coffee, peanuts, and fruits, they took us on a tour.

The tour showed us something almost medieval. Dirt, filth, and unsanitary conditions abounded everywhere. Each room had a malodorous stench of its own. There were no screens on the windows or doors, all of which were standing open. Insects swarmed up from the floors and the patients when we walked by. Back in the dark, wet corners and cracks, the red, beady eyes of rats reflected, making my skin crawl with the thought of what it must be like here at night.

The smell from the toilets was putrid. Some patients were lying two or more to a bed; others would have three or four family members sitting cross-legged in bed with them. The beds were in wards, which was good because a patient by himself in a room at night would be in danger from the rats. The sheets on the beds were filthy beyond belief.

We asked each other why they could not use soap to keep things clean. The answer was there was no soap, and how could they trust the water used in a laundry even if there was soap?

There were a few donated electrical monitors, but they were covered with dust and there was no electricity to run them anyway. There were no medicines, no antiseptics, no bandages, no tape nor any other supplies. They told us they did not have any, and we had to believe them, based on what we saw ourselves. The three of us found it difficult to believe that a doctor could work under these conditions.

The tour was depressing. We talked among ourselves, discussing the place. This hospital was so bad, we wondered if this was real, or just a show they were putting on to gain sympathy. We concluded that while there were things they might not be showing us, the truth was that we were seeing the facts of life concerning health care in Vietnam. There was nothing of substance in the hospital. The head of

Infectious Diseases at Bach Mai said it all when he said, "All I have to work with are my hands, my eyes, and my brain."

We ended the tour outside, behind the hospital, and stood looking back at it. The hospital was a mess inside and outside. Most things were a mess in Vietnam, but the physical plant of this hospital was worse than anything else we had seen. I had the impression no one cared. For some reason this hospital was not coping as well as the other hospitals. We couldn't tell if it was because they lacked a sponsor, or it was terribly mismanaged. We felt strongly, based on the information and experience we were gaining, that it was probably both.

Our tour of Bach Mai was ended. There was no other scheduled stop. However, our escort from the Foreign Ministry said the medical people down the back lane behind the hospital had heard Americans were visiting Bach Mai and wanted to extend an invitation for us to visit their facility.

We said yes; we were anxious to see everything we could. The gate was only 100 meters down a narrow lane lined by crumbling cement walls. We walked the short distance. When we got to the gate, we asked what this place was.

Mr. Nhu turned to face us, "This place is what is called a—hummmm, what is the English word?—it is a leprosarium."

Carl and I looked at each other. "Hell, Fred, I don't think I've ever been to a leprosarium."

I knew I had never been to one. I did know there were lepers in Vietnam.

The director and staff came out to meet us and led us upstairs to a briefing room. We were introduced to a few other staff members, men and women, and were seated at another long conference table in a room with more light than the one at Bach Mai. We were extremely curious about the leprosarium and were looking forward to the briefing and the tour. This would be an experience few American medical professionals would have in a lifetime.

Consequently, we were disappointed when the director, a thin, elderly, hard-looking man with a pinched face and bad teeth, immediately launched a diatribe at us about the Yankee air criminals and bandits who bombed and strafed his leprosarium located north of the DMZ during the war. He pulled out a set of photographs and passed them around the table. Then he went over to a map and pointed out the locations of these institutions.

He claimed the leprosaria were attacked at least three times during the war, in 1965, 1967, and 1970. They moved the leprosaria from place to place to locations he indicated on the map. The area he was referring to was near Vinh. He listed numerous bombing raids, recounting in great detail the number of American sorties, types of planes, quantities of bombs dropped, et cetera, ad infinitum, ad nauseam.

I was angry, and I began arguing back in my head. I thought, You must be real dumb to have kept a facility in that area. The Vinh area was a big target during the war. In fact an oil depot in Vinh was attacked on the first day of the war, August 4, 1964, in retaliation for the North Vietnamese PT-boat attack against the U.S.S. *Maddox* in the Gulf of Tonkin. If Vinh was the area where the leprosaria were located, it was highly possible they might have been accidentally hit. If they were not easily identified from the air, they could have been attacked on purpose by aircraft believing they were legitimate targets.

Vinh was heavily attacked during the war because it was the key disbursement center for the war supplies going out on the Ho Chi Minh Trail. Materials, equipment, and supplies received from the USSR and China at the rail centers in Hanoi and the ports at Haiphong and other harbors were transported to Vinh in preparation for moving them down the trail to the Viet Cong and North Vietnamese Army in South Vietnam.

In early 1965, President Johnson approved Operation *Rolling Thunder* in an attempt to cut off those supplies. This was to be a series of air attacks in North Vietnam, the purpose of which was to intimidate the North Vietnamese with our airpower and to punish them in reprisal for their aggression in the South. The Communist forces were close to winning in the South and President Johnson, along with his advisers, thought attacking the North would stave off defeat. The Joint Chiefs of Staff believed that bombing the North would discourage the Hanoi government from continuing the war.

Supply routes for men and material south of the 20th parallel were hit the hardest from the first. Vinh and points south were within the approved attack area from the beginning. Because of its strategic position, Vinh was to remain a key target area until the end of the war.

From 1964 until 1973, Vinh and the southern part of North Vietnam were attacked by all manner of aircraft flown by the Americans and the South Vietnamese. F-100 Supersabres, F-105 Thunderchiefs, A-1 Skyraiders, B-57 Canberras, F-8 Crusaders, A-4 Skyhawks, F-4 Phantoms, and A-6A Intruders were all involved one way or another. A lot of planes had been shot down as a result of the high density of antiaircraft weapons deployed by the Vietnamese to protect those supply lines.

As the director was going over the number of people killed and the destruction incurred during those times in that area, I was thinking of what Mr. Bai had said once during our first meeting in August. He had referred to the large numbers of American MIAs south of the 19th parallel, and how important it was for the people who lived there to see evidence of American humanitarian aid. There were many orphans and widows and invalids who would benefit, and the cooperation from the people would be better in finding MIAs.

As Mr. Bai had pointed out, the areas where America had

the greatest numbers of MIAs were the same areas where the most destruction occurred from the intense air activity. The implication was that the people who lived in those areas had been badly mauled in the process and were not inclined to assist in retrieving American MIAs' remains.

Although this director was haranguing us for political reasons, there was no doubt in my mind that some of his anger was heartfelt. Anyone who had suffered in the war had good reason to harbor hard feelings about the terrible things that happened to them personally or to their family and friends. I certainly had.

Still, we did not appreciate the lectures. We did not feel guilty about any of the "criminal" charges, and having to sit through it was a waste of time. Finally he was through. As with the other diatribe, we refrained from making any comment and sat waiting for the briefing. We felt there was no sense in refighting the war.

The information he provided about lepers was interesting. There are about 36,000 lepers in Vietnam. Only a few hundred are institutionalized. About 13,000 are outpatients under a treatment program run by the leprosaria. Leprosy occurs mostly in tropical countries and the director felt Vietnam's leprosy rate was declining in relation to other tropical countries.

The center did not have sufficient medical supplies, bandages, alcohol for disinfecting, or medical instruments to do its work. The director and some members of the staff took us across the lane into a walled compound where the patients were housed. Carl and I quietly discussed the disease while we walked.

"Carl, leprosy isn't contagious, is it? I read where it wasn't." I was asking for reassurance.

"It is, but it is the least contagious of the contagious diseases."

"Damn, I don't care how least it is, it's still something you can catch."

"Well, I don't believe we have anything to worry about."

"That's nice to hear, but I'm not going to touch anything or anybody just to make sure."

In a courtyard at the corner of a low single-story dormitory we were introduced to staff members who worked with the patients. A covered walk ran the length of the building like a motel. Each patient lived in a single room 6 feet by 12 feet, with a cot covered with a thin mat of woven bamboo on one side of the room and a window in the back wall. Rooms were sparsely furnished but neat. There was no electricity, no water, and no bathroom.

We were led into various patient rooms to meet ten of the patients. They ranged from teen-aged to late-middle-aged. None of the patients had any amputations but there were dark splotches on the skin, and in a few cases there were ugly eruptions. One man looked as if his big toe would be going pretty soon.

The tour was quickly over, and we said thank-you and goodbye as we were loaded into the van. It was getting toward quitting time and everyone was anxious to have the guests leave. Some had to work at another job in order to feed their family, so they were worried about getting to the next job. We tried to be sensitive to that and did not allow ourselves to keep people overtime any more than necessary.

Back at the guesthouse, Carl gathered the team together to discuss our thoughts about the day. It had been a disappointing and a rather depressing one, partly because of the lectures we had received, but mostly because of the deplorable conditions of the Bach Mai Hospital.

It was similar in most of the countries of the Third World. The doctors do not receive continuing education and are frozen in time at the stage medicine was at when they graduated from medical school. They will not admit their deficiencies, however. They resent outsiders such as ourselves coming in and making suggestions as to how they can improve their facilities. That is universal to human nature;

no one likes to have his performance questioned. However, in the case of Vietnam they had to have our money, equipment, supplies, and material. So they told us and showed us things that hurt their pride, but they did it out of desperation.

We saw nothing today that impressed us positively. It was hard to believe this was Vietnam's best hospital. Where do the embassy people go when they need a hospital? A European would not go for medical care at Bach Mai; it would be like signing one's own death warrant. When we inquired about this, we were told the Europeans went to the Vietnamese German or Vietnamese Soviet hospitals for emergency care and then out of the country for more extended care.

The Vietnamese need so much you could devote your life and fortune to this country and not make a dent. They kept telling us about the help they had received from Holland, Sweden, the USSR, East Germany, Finland, and Cuba. We asked ourselves, where is evidence of this help? Other than a few pieces of unworkable equipment and some buildings we did not see this aid.

There is a great deal of jealousy between doctors, administrators, and government officials. They were generally negative, looking for ways to discredit each other and outside reviewers. The system forced the people to be at each other's throats because it was not designed to get them to work together. We could see mismanagement and little or no communication or cooperation between the various elements.

Carl wrapped it up by reminding us we could not change the way people do things. We could only report the needs of the disabled and assist in getting the message out. Maybe someday their system would change.

Before the meeting ended we discussed thoroughly why each director had put us through the haranguing and how we would handle it at the meeting with Bai. We did not know if this was a deliberate attack against us to show displeasure at

America's slow response with humanitarian aid—sort of a punishment—or the director's standard show for visiting foreigners to gain sympathy. Was this the director's chance to blow off steam at American government officials after all those years of being pissed off? It could have been done on orders of some of the hard-liners in the government, who were trying to queer the deal the moderates had made with the Americans. Whatever the reason, we decided Carl should not make a big thing of it, but he would tell Bai we did not appreciate the treatment and we would not expect it in the future because it was nonproductive.

We went out to shop, mail cards, and walk for exercise before dinner. After a pleasant dinner and conversation with the Vietnamese Delegation, whom we were getting to know better with each meal, we went for an evening walk to explore the city further. Finally we admitted we were tired and went back to our rooms at the guesthouse.

My room was softly bathed in the light from the small red-shaded lamp on my desk. The mosquito netting had been pulled out over my bed. The pictures of my family were out on the desk where I had set them earlier. The place was beginning to feel like a home away from home.

At 2200 hours I finished preparing for bed and sat down at the desk to write. The weather was pleasant, so I had the door to the balcony open. The city was quiet. I went out to stand on the balcony and look up at the sky. Few of the buildings are taller than the trees so I could see the sky in all directions with no breaks in the view. There was no radio, television, or newspaper in the guesthouse. I was reminded of my youth on the farm, when the only electricity we had were the dim bulbs powered by a weak power line strung on poles down a country road. This was a country on the edge of civilization, like our farm. It was self-sufficient, but modernization was creeping in.

It was very peaceful. I could hear an occasional vehicle far off in the distance. Once in a while a dog in someone's backyard or cage started barking, and others would take up the call and then stop. Lying in bed on the hard straw pallet under the mosquito netting, I listened to the peaceful night sounds. I felt a mystical experience. A full circle from the violence of the South twenty years ago to the peaceful setting of the North today.

November 11, 1987

★ While it was still dark, I became fully awake and restless. I had dreamed about the war—a time along the river when the enemy was all around and no matter how hard we fought, there were always more. I rarely had dreams about the war, but I guessed there were reasons for it to be on my mind. What an irony to be in Vietnam on that day. It was Veterans Day in America.

The sound of a cock crowing came clearly through the open balcony door. Soon there was a chorus of roosters crowing in the neighborhood around the guesthouse. I felt serene lying there, listening to sounds that came from my childhood on the farm. It was hard to believe I was in the middle of a city of 2 million people.

A light rain had fallen during the night. I went over to the balcony and stood looking at the courtyard below. A soldier walked slowly at his post, not as a guard but more as a ritual. He looked extremely young. There was no danger here . . .

When Mr. Bai opened our meeting, he asked us about our trip. Carl Savory answered on behalf of the team by telling Bai we had been offended and disappointed by the unnecessary recitals. Carl reminded them of the words of the Communist General Secretary of Vietnam, Nguyen Van Linh, quoted in an October *Time* magazine article, in which he stated it was time to forget the past and work for the future. Carl then said, "We found it hard to discuss the future with images of the past on the table before us," referring to the photographs they had laid on the table.

Carl added that this type of haranguing, if delivered to the non-governmental organizations, would be counterproductive. Then he introduced Larry Ward, who was going to present information and ask them specific questions.

We wanted to get across that we did not appreciate their making us a whipping boy, but we were not going to make an issue out of it or allow it to hurt our mission. Their faces reflected dismay at our anger, but we plowed ahead for an hour, proving we were as good as our word in wanting to gather information about the humanitarian aid Vietnam needed.

Among the proposals Larry presented was one for a nongovernmental survey group to come to Vietnam before the end of the year to focus on the problems of the disabled. Larry said he thought five or more people should make up the group. An important part of the response would be what procedure the group should follow in applying for visas, as this would not be an official government team.

When we were finished, Carl told them this was the end of our questions, and we prepared for their response. Mr. Bai went through the folders in his case, selected some notes from them to put on the table in front of him, and reached into his shirt pocket for his reading glasses. He adjusted them on his nose until he had them focused to his satisfaction. With both arms resting on the table, he quickly glanced through the yellow sheets he held in front of him. Then he looked at us.

"First of all, on your visit to Bach Mai. Our intention is to make you see some concepts of our public health service. It is not intended to take you there to see crimes of America in the past. My own brother was killed at Bach Mai that day and it is not something I like. But it is the past. We must heal the wounds. During your visit you could see that the public health service has a lot of trouble. When the United States permits NGOs to help Vietnam, they can see that equipment and medicine must be provided. Stress to them which should be the focus of help. The situation at Bach Mai is representative of public health hospitals in Vietnam. I propose you reiterate the needs of the public health service of Vietnam.

"As I tell you, it is the public health service which saved many American pilots. I remember when [John] McCain came to hospital, he believed he would die because of his wounds. I directed doctors to show compassion toward him. Recently we permitted him to visit Vietnam."

It was a fascinating experience to listen to a small piece of history told from the viewpoint of a man who directed it. It took a long stretch of the imagination to call the treatment McCain had received "compassion." In fact, some soldiers would call his treatment a form of torture.

The knowledge of that treatment fueled the flames of hatred that some Americans still felt toward the Vietnamese. But I noticed that my past anger at the Vietnamese did not flare up now.

The past was truly the past.

The rest of the morning was very difficult. It was not the fault of any of the members of either delegation, but rather of the diplomatic rules governing affairs between countries. The problem, as simply as I can put it, was that basically Vietnam wanted the U.S. government to give it direct aid, to normalize relations, and to remove the trade embargo. The United States refused to do so, and that would have been the end of it, except Vietnam had something America wanted very badly. And that something was an accounting of the POWs/MIAs from the war and other humanitarian issues. That gave Vietnam the only card it had to play, but it was an ace. There had been a standoff for nearly fifteen years, but the times had changed and events within both countries had forced them to try a different approach to solving their respective dilemmas.

Hence the humanitarian agreement. America would allow humanitarian aid to be provided to Vietnam by private money, not government money. In return, Vietnam would facilitate solving the human issues. There were a number of people in America and Vietnam who did not like the agreement, but both sides were willing to accept it, betting that in the future they could do better.

The problem we had to deal with was that allegations had been made in the U.S. press and some international papers since our first trip that Vietnam was using the remains of American military men as barter for aid. Both the Vietnam and the American governments denied the allegations. We had to reassure the Vietnamese that we understood they were acting in a purely humanitarian way on this matter.

We had to wrestle with other humanitarian points as well that morning: numbers and figures of disabled, materials and supplies needed, procedures involved with the pending NGO visit, the villagers' feelings about helping find Americans who had bombed them, plans for searches of crash sites. There was a constant reassurance by both teams that they were earnest and forthright in trying to solve these problems.

Mr. Bai brought up two new subjects: a second typhoon of the season that had caused much damage, and an outbreak of dengue fever that had caused many deaths.

Political issues were discussed: travel restrictions, derogatory statements by American officials and politicians about Vietnam, trade embargoes, resistance of some Vietnamese people to accepting these talks.

It was very difficult work, concentrating on each word and meaning and then phrasing an appropriate answer. By the end of the morning all of us were tired and drained.

We did get an answer to one question we had been wondering about. In the message to the Vietnamese informing them of our trip, we had asked if they could provide four amputees—two below-knee and two above-knee—for a demonstration that we wanted to put on. They had never answered, but I had brought along my equipment just in case, and it was in three cardboard boxes in my room.

Dr. Bui Tung added one final comment before the meeting ended: "The demonstration you have planned for us this afternoon. This is a new idea. We want to always see the new technology. We are prepared to observe. We listened to you earlier when you said you are prepared for discussion of idea to see if this technology will work in Vietnam. Do not think we are against technology if you hear criticism from our prosthetists."

On that note the meeting ended.

After lunch, Carl and Larry helped me carry down the three boxes I had brought from the States. They contained four sets of a new type of artificial limb I believed would be useful in solving the artificial limb problem in Vietnam. Midway through our second trip we were still trying to figure out how best to get those sixty thousand amputees fitted for a limb.

At least that is what we thought the problem was. Later we would deduce our approach was slightly off track. But for now we were exploring different solutions, and this was one of them. My idea was to get the leg amputee mobile by getting him up on a prosthesis that could be fitted quickly. Then he would have something to walk on during the three to five years it would take until the Vietnamese prosthetists were trained, the laboratories were established throughout the country, and the logistics of supplies and materials were solved.

Due to advances in technology and the ingenuity of some Americans, a device best described as an adjustable plastic pegleg with an adjustable plastic socket had been developed for use in countries where there were few or no prosthetic fabrication shops. It was not fancy or cosmetically appealing, but it was extremely functional and durable. It came in three different sizes: small, medium, and large. The socket and the length were adjustable with a few ordinary hand tools.

Roy Sneilson, a man I had known for ten years, had come up with the idea while fitting amputees back in the mountains and wild country in Mexico where there was nothing except what he could carry in with him. He had been a prosthetist since the end of World War II and did a lot of charity work. He knew that if he could give a man back his leg, he gave him back his life. Roy's idea enabled him to help a lot of people in a short period of time.

It was inexpensive enough that an American NGO could afford them. Of course, any price would have been too much for a Third World country, but we believed this was a good solution for an American NGO interested in the prosthetic problems in Vietnam.

This was not the final answer for Vietnam's amputees. The ultimate goal would be to develop a Vietnamese prosthetic program independent of outside help.

We walked from the guesthouse to the ministry, a three-story building half a block away. After a brief meeting with the Deputy Minister of the Ministry of Labor, Invalids, and Social Affairs, we were taken across the courtyard to a large, high-ceilinged room in which some twenty men were waiting for us. This was the group to whom we would demonstrate the new limbs. Four of the men in the room were amputees, two above-knee and two below-knee. The directors of several rehabilitation centers, some prosthetists, and others with political interests completed the group.

They chattered among themselves while Carl and I opened the boxes and spread the component parts out on a table, along with some tools included in the box. I had no fears about this demonstration not working. I had used these limbs very effectively in El Salvador for a program I was involved with down there. In about an hour or so an amputee could be fitted with this limb and be walking. We had fitted Salvadorian men, women, and children, and I was confident we could do the same thing here with the four amputees.

I studied the group before us. They were, with a few exceptions, older men with lined faces and a hard look about them. They were all dressed in mismatched dark, threadbare suit coats, sweaters, and trousers. A few more scarves, caps, or berets. They reminded me of a group of deadly serious dockworkers at a union meeting who had just come off the shift. They studied us with measured gazes.

These were men who had worked hard all their lives. Their attendance here today in the ministry was proof they were old cadre: men who had proven their worth during the war. Some members of this group were certainly here to get a feeling for the American efforts. There were those in this room with interests wider than prosthetics.

The room itself looked worn and tough. Faded paint, cement flaking from the walls. Like the rest of Hanoi, it had not had any touch-up since the French were defeated in 1954.

Before we started the demonstration, we made sure they understood we needed to hear their comments and criticism and questions.

The four amputees were introduced to us. They had all been soldiers. They stripped down to their shorts for the fitting; three had no prosthetic limb and got about on wooden crutches, but one was wearing a wooden leg. None of these men seemed in the least bit bothered to be used as demonstrators. They also were confident and evidently felt equal to the others in the room, as shown by their participation in the lively discussions afterwards.

First I gave a short lecture on the limb and how we thought it could be useful in quickly fitting large numbers of amputees in a short period of time.

Carl and I then asked for the first volunteer. The group looked toward a wiry man seated close to the wall. An above-knee amputee, he was the one wearing a wooden leg. He removed it, and as Carl and I examined his stump, we asked how he had lost his leg. He replied through the translator that he had lost it in a battle with the Americans in the South. He asked the same question of me, and I told him my arm was blown off by a bounding land mine when I was fighting in the South against the North Vietnamese. For the briefest second, we looked straight into the other's eyes. Had our paths crossed twenty years ago, one of us would have killed or wounded the other. I think in that microsecond we took each other's measure as to the worthiness of our former adversary.

My thoughts returned to the amputee I had seen at Ba Vi on our first trip. At the time I had seen him on the path and we had pantomimed how we had lost our limbs, there had been a distant memory of a poem I had once read but I could not place it. When I got home, I looked it up. It was "The Man He Killed," by Thomas Hardy, and it leaped to mind now as this soldier and I locked gazes.

> "Had he and I but met
> By some old ancient inn,
> We should have sat us down to wet
> Right many a nipperkin!
>
> "But ranged as infantry,
> And staring face to face,
> I shot at him as he at me,
> And killed him in his place.
>
> "Shot him dead because—
> Because he was my foe,
> Just so; my foe of course he was;
> That's clear enough; although
>
> "He thought he'd 'list, perhaps,
> Off-hand like—just as I—
> Was out of work—had sold his traps—
> No other reason why.

First trip to Hanoi, August 1987. JCRC and
Humanitarian teams in front of a C-12. From left to
right: the author, Paul D. Mather, Johnie Webb, Carlton
G. Savory, Larry Ward, Garnett E. (Bill) Bell, and Joe
Harvey

Carl Savory, the author, and Larry Ward flying out of
Hanoi.

The Vietnamese delegation, from left to right: Nguyen Hoang Giang, Nguyen Van Vinh, Bui Tung, Tran Lam Dong, Dong Nahiem Bai, Vu Khar Nu.

The author, Dr. Bui Tung, Mary Downs, Katy, and Abby at Dulles International Airport.

One of the "Hero" cemeteries along the road from the airport into Hanoi.

Residence along the road to Hanoi. Note the date, "1986," on top.

The monument commemorating the downing and capture of John McCain. Note the blackened face.

An amputee at
Ba Vi Hospital.

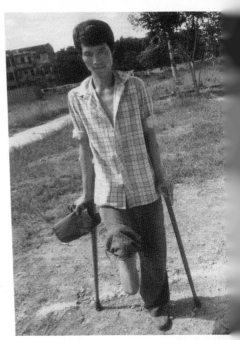

Patients in a room
at Ba Vi Hospital.

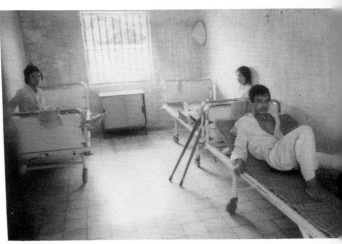

Street scene, Hanoi.

The Hanoi Hilton (Hoa Lo Prison), front wall.

Street vendors,
Hanoi.

Spinal-cord-injured
village resident,
Thuan Thanh.

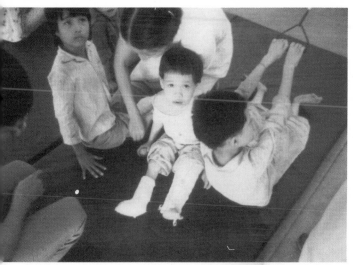
Crippled children receiving physical therapy at Haiphong Rehabilitation Center.

Ba Vi Hospital.

Wheelchair seat fashioned from strips of worn-out tires.

With many thanks to Fred Downs for important help —

Jack Vessey
General, USA (Ret)
President's POW/MIA

In a meeting in the Pentagon Office of the Chairman of the Joint Chiefs of Staff Admiral William Crowe, we discuss the usefulness of providing humanitarian aid to the Vietnamese. In attendance are: (from left) General John Vessey, Jr., USA (Ret.), Gerry Byrne, John Connor, Admiral Crowe, Andre Sauvageot and the author. *(Photo courtesy: Department of Defense)*

"Yes; quaint and curious war is!
You shoot a fellow down
You'd treat if met where any bar is
Or help to half-a-crown."

I was glad I had taken the time to look it up because Hardy's poem was so correct.

As our fingers probed the flesh of his stump, tracing the scars and feeling the end of the femur bone for smoothness from the surgeon's bone saw, I felt the nerves in my own stump tingle from phantom pain. This was a familiar sensation caused by nerve signals being sent along old nerve paths to limbs that are no longer there. At the point of amputation the disrupted nerve ends discharge the signals into the surrounding flesh, agitating it. This stirs up a distorted feeling of the old limb, so it feels twisted and cramped. Sometimes it is painful, but at all times it is uncomfortable. It is something an amputee learns to live with because it never goes away. Usually it can be kept at the subconscious level, but it is triggered into full awareness at the slightest provocation.

All of us amputees in the room were experiencing phantom pains. They had started, certainly, as we entered the room, thinking about our purpose in being there. None of us said anything because it was a fact of our existence and there was nothing to be said or done. It was a web that held all of us separate from the others in the room. We could never escape. It was a weird sort of bonding, not of our choice.

As we went through the business of fitting, the two groups became more comfortable with each other. The former soldier assisted us in adjusting straps and measuring stump size and matching length with his other leg. The other Vietnamese jumped right in by helping with the work; cutting, carrying, cleaning up. We were working together to solve this immediate problem, and for a while the politics were pushed to the back of our thinking.

The demonstration went fairly well. The small socket was

still not little enough for the thin Vietnamese stumps. A smaller size would have to be manufactured. I had brought plenty of stump socks which could be used to pad out the stump, so we were able to fit the above-knee but not the below-knee because that socket was too large.

They were concerned because there was no knee mechanism for the above-knee limb. I explained that this was a basic pegleg design to enable people to walk. They responded that the Vietnamese had to have a movable knee to ride their bicycle and also a movable ankle joint.

They were just getting warmed up for the criticizing session, which was started off by a gentleman who commented that there were some advantages to this limb. First, it could be mass-produced. Next, it was a quick fit for the masses. And the material it was made from was excellent. Oh yes, the socks were of high quality.

Next was a man who said frankly that in the case of the above-knee or below-knee, much depended on the socket. An adjustable height and width was helpful, but there was no size for the Vietnamese body.

Another man said that according to present technology on below-knee prostheses, we must take a mold of the stump. There are too many conditions which cause the stump to loosen in the socket.

Another person said he thought this idea would be useful for a new amputee to use in training.

One said the high humidity is bad for the use of plastic.

An intense-looking man whose brow was furled with wrinkles informed us the socket liner on below-knee prosthetics soaks up sweat. This was not useful in Vietnam.

Wooden prostheses were best for Vietnam, we were told. The wood is a natural product, and it breathes. There may be an allergic reaction to plastic sockets, someone added. This new technology was not suitable for women because the limb did not look cosmetic, another commented.

A tropical foot needs to be developed, they all agreed; a

foot that will work in high humidity and can be used in the rice paddy.

One of the men examining the limbs said that after three years, the plastic would become brittle and break.

Meanwhile the above-knee amputee we had first fitted was walking around the room, getting the feel of the limb. I asked him how he liked it. He told me it was too light, he thought the pegleg would not be good in the rice paddies, and he did not like the lack of a knee.

These were legitimate complaints, coming as they did from an amputee. But what about the principle of the idea, I queried. Maybe it has possibilities, he answered, but not for Vietnamese. He showed me his wooden leg with articulating knee and ankle. It was a beautifully crafted leg. Although it was stained and scarred from hard use, the skill of the craftsman was evident in the socket, knee, and ankle. When I looked at the ankle and foot, I was struck at how similar in size this was to a child's limb.

It was becoming obvious this group did not like the idea of using this immediate-fit limb in any capacity. We got the feeling they were satisfied with the system they already had. They did not want anything that had to be produced in some other country. They wanted to make the limbs themselves, and they could see right away the immediate-fit limb had all component parts made from advanced plastics with specialized equipment.

After they got through trashing the idea to their satisfaction, it was as if they had done their duty. Then Dr. Bui Tung, who may have thought the group was a little severe in their criticism, diplomatically remarked that perhaps the immediate fit would have certain usefulness in Vietnam. More study would have to be done.

I was disappointed at their lack of enthusiasm for the limbs I had brought from half a world away, but I was philosophical about it. At least we had tried.

At the beginning of the meeting we had told the group and

the amputees they were welcome to keep the limbs if they wished. At the end of the meeting they took everything, including the cardboard boxes. The three of us believed we had accomplished some positive goals by showing the Vietnamese we were sincerely trying to help them. By that criterion we judged the meeting a success.

After we walked back to the guesthouse, we were loaded into the van for a trip across town to the building housing the Ministry of Health. The building was part of a long row of twenty-year-old, graceless three- and four-story cement structures on the west side of Hanoi. Our escort explained who we were to the guards, who then pushed open the wire gate.

Our escorts took us up three flights of outside stairs and midway down a balcony to an open doorway. Inside was the typical low table used for entertaining guests, laid out with fruits, drinks, and cigarettes. The day was fading into twilight and the windowless room was dimly lit with one low-watt bulb.

The importance of the minister was indicated by the presence of Mr. Bai, who had accompanied us from the guesthouse in another vehicle. After being around Vietnamese who were barely the size of scrawny young American teenagers, we were slightly taken aback when we were introduced to Dr. Dang Hoi Xuan, the Minister of Health. He was almost as tall as Carl. His face was pleasantly lined from a constant smile. White, well-formed teeth flashed out from the smile, instantly reminding me of the Cheshire Cat.

He sat at the end of the table facing toward the open door and asked the rest of us to please sit down. Carl, as team leader, carried on most of the conversation in that dimly lit room.

Soon after we sat, Dr. Xuan began discussing his idea of giving more responsibility to the districts to provide local health care. In the middle of one of his sentences the power went out, plunging the room into darkness. Dr. Xuan did not miss a beat. He kept right on talking while we sat in the dark, politely listening to him.

There were no windows, and it was really dark in there. The twilight coming through the open doorway at the end of the narrow room had almost faded, but that was enough to highlight Dr. Xuan's teeth. With his big smile seemingly floating in the darkness, he looked more than ever like the Cheshire Cat.

In Hanoi, activity does not stop when the power stops. It was a weird experience to sit in darkness, conducting a formal meeting as if nothing was out of the ordinary. Soon the meeting was over and we groped our way to the balcony under the starlight.

We bid each other goodbye and got back into the van for a drive through the darkened city to the guesthouse. We were running late for a dinner our team was hosting for our Vietnamese counterparts.

This would be the fourth dinner we had eaten with Mr. Bai and the Vietnamese Delegation. The mood of both groups was good, and we were getting to know each other well enough that conversation ranged over a variety of subjects.

We were talking about the liquors served during our meals and the subject turned to traditional medicines. Mr. Bai explained the benefits of a certain wine used to help restore a man's virility. It came in three different strengths. There was Three Snake wine, Five Snake wine, and Seven Snake wine. Which one a man used depended upon his age and vigor. If he was relatively young, in his thirties and forties, then Three Snake wine would help him, but if a man was older or was having trouble of some sort, then the Seven Snake wine was the most powerful and beneficial.

I was skeptical. "Is this really true? You are not pulling my leg, are you?"

Bai laughed, "It's true. This has been proven many times. I know a man seventy years old who uses Seven Snake when he married young woman and he has many children."

"Just how is snake wine made?" I asked.

Mr. Bai held a fist up above the table. "You take three or five or seven snakes and hold them like this above the wine and cut their tails off so the blood drains into the wine."

"Are the snakes alive when this is done?"

"Of course."

"Oh."

"You should try some snake wine. It will be very good for you."

"Uh, you think so?" I said dubiously.

Mr. Bai leaned back and measured me with a cock-eyed smile and said, "I think maybe Seven Snake for you."

"No!" I laughed. All the men laughed good-naturedly at the interchange between us.

"There is also gecko wine." Bai continued. "A gecko lizard is put into the bottle. It is very powerful. Even better than snake wine."

"The only thing like that I've ever had was tequila with a worm in the bottle, but that didn't have anything to do with vigor. The worm just added a little tang to the liquor. I sure couldn't drink wine with a whole lizard in the bottle," I said.

"I have heard of this tequila," Bai replied, "but it is not as powerful as snake or gecko."

With that the conversation came to a close and Bai signaled it was time for them to leave.

November 12, 1987—Leaving Hanoi

★ The United States Embassy aircraft was scheduled to pick us up at the airport at 1200 hours. This gave us time to do a little shopping at the Dollar Store. Also we were informed the Minister of Health, Dr. Dang Hoi Xuan, wanted us to return to his office before we left Hanoi.

When the van pulled up to the Ministry of Health, the driver parked at the curb on the street out front. The escort officer asked us to wait while he ran in to get something from the minister's office.

We idled on the sidewalk watching the people go by. We took pictures of some children who were drawn by curiosity to the van. The sky was overcast but no rain was falling. It was a peaceful morning. Soon the escort officer returned carrying a sack. He put the sack in the front seat of the van, reached into it, and handed each of us a bottle wrapped in clear plastic.

"When Mr. Bai talked to the Minister of Health this morning, Dr. Xuan told Mr. Bai he wanted to give you this. His card is included in the plastic sack."

"Well, please thank them for us," Carl said politely as the three of us studied our bottles. "That is very kind of them. What is this?"

"It is a bottle of Seven Snake wine."

Things were happening in Hanoi. We had noticed an increased number of foreigners quartered at the guesthouse: Japanese, Russians, French, an American, and an Australian. We also had noticed an increased number of foreigners on the streets who looked as if they were tourists. And there seemed to be more shops open this time compared to our August visit.

As for us, with the exception of the Bach Mai incident, the spirit of our meetings had been positive. The meetings were less formal and more relaxed. There had been less rhetoric from their side. We had done most of the talking this time.

Back in the States, we decided there were some areas we needed to think more about in our report to General Vessey. It was apparent from statements made that there were some hard-liners within the Vietnamese government and outside it who were opposed to any cooperation with the U.S. government. We surmised these opponents were some of the old politicians, veterans, and war victims. Perhaps we needed to state more clearly that the humanitarian aid the United States was encouraging NGOs to provide would benefit everyone, including veterans and war victims.

Based on the recommendations in our final report, an offer was made to the NGO community asking them to travel to Vietnam. Six organizations then volunteered to go to Vietnam to review the humanitarian needs of the Vietnamese in the area of prosthetics: the American Friends Service Committee, NEED, Save the Children, the World Rehabilitation Fund, World Relief, and World Vision.

Approval was given by the U.S. government for these representatives to go to Vietnam on a survey trip from December 14 through 21, 1987, to focus on "The Problems of the Disabled in Vietnam." Larry Ward would be the tour coordinator. These six groups were going to be watched closely by the NGO community to see if the U.S. government was really sincere in its new policy. The Vietnamese were going to be even more interested in this trip for the same reasons.

There were still those who were against the idea. These people and organizations in the United States thought any intercourse with the Vietnamese was a major mistake and any concession by the Americans was a sign of weakness and a selling out. Some of them claimed the Vietnamese were trading bones for humanitarian aid.

Since I had been in that camp up until a few months ago, I understood just why they felt the way they did. I was in a real quandary because I thought helping the Vietnamese disabled was a good thing in itself and was in the best interests of the United States.

This new way of thinking was disquieting. It was true I was only a team member of General Vessey's humanitarian mission and we were part of an official mission of our government. We were doing what our government was sending us to do, which was reason enough for me.

I had a choice. If I had not believed in the humanitarian concept of helping the Vietnamese, I would have withdrawn from the team. But I did believe it was the right thing to do.

In combat it was easy: they were the enemy and you killed them. Simple, blunt, and final, no questions asked. Politics at its simplest.

Now it was hard. They were an enemy, but not in a military sense. They were an enemy because of their style of government. The arena of combat between the two countries was not on the battlefield, but on the world stage of politics, economics, and finance. I knew more about them now. They had an identity. They were people with children. They had mothers, grandparents, traditions, a way of life, a country, a history. They were not the mysterious "dinks" and Communists. They were Mr. Bai, Mr. Le Bang, Mr. Nhu, Dr. Dong, and Dr. Bui Tung.

By accepting them as a people, it became difficult to ignore the suffering of the disabled and the children. It could be done, of course, but our government had not sent us there to ignore those problems. It had sent us there to help solve them.

It was a policy decision with which I had no difficulty.

Third Trip to Vietnam
★ January 1988 ★

January 11, 1988 — Reflection on Twenty Years Ago

★ I was bemused by the coincidence that on January 11, 1988, I was once again preparing to leave for Vietnam. The Vietnamese had requested our return. Twenty years ago on this date my left arm had been blown off when I stepped on a land mine near Chu Lai, South Vietnam, while leading a combat patrol.

I had never wanted to see Vietnam again, and for almost twenty years I had not done so. Now I was preparing for my third trip in four months. In addition to these trips, I was reading as much as I could and having conversations with a broad array of people concerned with Vietnam. I was becoming involved with Vietnam to an extent I never dreamed possible.

The Vessey mission was being severely criticized by some conservatives for allowing the administration to have any relationship, humanitarian or otherwise, with Vietnam. The infighting was fierce and involved the administration, Congress, and the press. The magnitude of the battles was not large—more on the scale of small firefights—but they were deadly serious and bitter for the participants.

Public perception was critical. The Vessey mission

adopted a low profile regarding public relations, while the opponents projected a high profile in the press. The Vessey mission would get one small paragraph in the paper as a news release, whereas editorials countering it received full columns in papers such as the *Wall Street Journal* and the *Washington Times*.

As someone actively involved in carrying out the mission, I could not escape the crossfire. Those statements and charges of Vietnamese bad faith and exploitation were made to the country in a national forum—and to me on a personal level. The personal attacks were the toughest to take because they were coming from men I knew, Vietnam veterans, some of whom were friends whose opinion I respected.

Except in one or two cases these friends would basically say, "Downs, I think you are wrong as hell on this one and I'm going to fight you on it. But, you keep on doing what you are doing, I'll protect your backside." These are good friends to have.

However, the more I was learning about Vietnam—their war history, the changes they were struggling to initiate, their interaction, past and present, with the countries around them, their culture, traditions, and beliefs—the more I began to believe America's interests would be best served by developing a dialogue with them.

The major roadblock was, of course, the war history between the United States and Vietnam and the associated experiences: physical and psychological pain, tragedy, guilt, embarrassment, and the complexities of power politics. The Gordian knot of politics and history between the two countries would never unravel without attempting to pull a strand. In this case, the strand was humanitarian aid.

At this point, the Vietnamese were showing good faith on their part, and so the agreements between General Vessey and Minister Thach were being sustained. However, the initiative was under attack from elements within both countries, and it needed strengthening.

Hence, our return to Vietnam.

Carl Savory was also making this third trip. As we had agreed during our second trip, Larry Ward had taken the NGOs to Vietnam in December, so he was not a part of the team this time. Two new men were going in with us: Larry Kerr of the State Department, and Dr. Bruce E. van Dam, orthopedic surgeon at Walter Reed Army Hospital in Washington, D.C. Kerr had been with us on the first trip as far as Bangkok but this time he was going into Vietnam.

Bruce was coming along as a potential backup for Carl, if Carl could not make the next trip. Savory, Kerr, and I told war stories all during the flight to Bangkok.

January 15, 1988

★ Our flight to Hanoi on a Vietnam Airlines jet, a Soviet Tupalof 134A, was essentially a rerun of our previous trip: dirty, uncomfortable, and dangerous. Vietnam Air had clearly overbooked. Except for a few Vietnamese and Europeans, the flight looked like it could have originated out of Indianapolis, Indiana, there were so many Americans: fourteen journalists with their wives, thirteen members of a tour group; a group of fifteen students and four professors from Colby College in Waterville, Maine; and, of course, ourselves. We were all a little surprised to see so many Americans going to Hanoi. After all, America still did not recognize Vietnam and it was illegal for an American company to arrange tours to Vietnam. When we asked him what was going on, Larry said it was a mystery to him because he had been told by the U.S. Embassy that no Americans were going into Vietnam. He seemed kind of upset about it. (They were separate tour groups brought together by coincidence. Americans who travel to Vietnam arrange their tours through foreign travel agencies.)

As the pilot taxied to the Noi Bai terminal after landing,

we saw the U.S. government C-12 we had flown on our first trip, taxiing out from the terminal. It had just dropped off another congressional delegation visiting Vietnam. Congressmen Robert Mrazek from New York and Tom Ridge from Pennsylvania, a few of their staff, and an interpreter were going to visit Hanoi and Ho Chi Minh City. The night before, in Bangkok, we had met with a congressional delegation that had just returned from Vietnam. It was congressional recess time back home and the congressmen had taken the opportunity to scatter across the globe on their fact-finding trips. A bunch of them had chosen Southeast Asia and Vietnam.

Our escort, Mr. Nhu, was waiting for us as we cleared Customs. He helped load the luggage into the van waiting out front. I noticed the crowd was larger and I attributed it to the large Soviet aircraft that had evidently just arrived bringing back the volunteers with their loads of goods accumulated during their working period in Eastern Europe.

On the drive into Hanoi, I could see there were more brick homes under construction and I asked Mr. Nhu who owned these homes. He explained that a man applied to the village's "people committee" for a plot of land on which to build a home. When he was allocated the plot, he could then apply for a loan from the state for building material. Did the man have to be a member of the party and did the man belong to the people's committee, I asked. No, of course not. The homes we saw under construction belonged to the individuals. It was the dream of every Vietnamese to have their own brick home.

I had read that Vietnam was becoming deforested. It was easy to see why. The thousands of homes we drove by were not wired for electricity. Wood was used for heating the home and for cooking. The demand for wood to maintain those basics of life had to be increasing with the rapidly growing population.

I loved watching the Vietnamese countryside through the

window of the van as the driver bullied his way through the stream of traffic. I was studying and learning more about Vietnam, so the things I was seeing were starting to come into focus.

There are four traditional occupations in Vietnam: the woodcutter, the fisherman, the farmer, and the herdsman. These are an intricate part of the history and folklore of Vietnam, and embody the culture of the country. All of them could be observed during the drive into Hanoi.

I had seen all this twenty years ago, but did not associate an order to it. I was never in any of the cities, except in a truck passing through. I was only familiar with the Vietnam outside the cities and the military base camps. My platoon and I had spent most of our time in the countryside, patrolling through villages, fields, beside the ocean, up in the mountainous jungles, along rivers, guarding bridges on roads and next to lakes. The land and people were ravaged by war but life still went on. By necessity the South Vietnamese people and we soldiers lived and did our jobs while sharing the same ground. Although we had been allies, the potential for mutual distrust and hatred of each other was so easy and unavoidable that I could now understand how impossible our task as soldiers really was.

As I watched through the window, I matched what I saw with what I had learned, and it was a pleasant feeling. But my war experience was always at the back of my mind. I imagined myself leading my combat platoon from the airport through this countryside toward Hanoi, exactly the way I used to lead it through the countryside in Quang Ngai Province on a search-and-destroy mission.

The search-and-destroy concept was a tactic General Westmoreland developed to find the enemy, keep him pinned down, and destroy him with American superior firepower. In reality it usually meant that we foot soldiers patrolled until we found the enemy, and then we held on until other forces could come in to assist us. We were bait used to force the enemy into attacking us, giving away their position. A lot of times the enemy deliberately provoked us while we were in the midst of civilians, and those innocents paid the price in life and property.

If I were conducting that type of patrol along the road to Hanoi, a lot of people's lives would be horribly disrupted and their property destroyed. I had enjoyed being a soldier, but as I thought of those long-ago patrols I regretted what we had done to the civilians in the pursuit of the enemy.

I thought of how difficult it would be to lead a patrol through this countryside, and the remnants of French bunkers at every bridge we crossed underlined the truth of that. A few of the bunkers were split asunder, mute reminders of the men who died there. According to maps I had studied, this area was part of the De Lattre Line, established around Hanoi in 1951 by the French general Jean de Lattre de Tassigny, as part of a massive defensive perimeter to protect the Red River Delta.

I thought of the bridges like these that I had guarded in the South. There were three on Route 1 south of Duc Pho and I had divided my platoon into three elements, so there were about nine men to each bridge. When night fell, those nine men were the ones who were responsible for whether the bridge survived until morning. We built our bunkers of sandbags and wood. Occasionally there were fierce firefights for those passages over water and control of the road in between. Like the French soldiers, we controlled the roads only during the daylight hours. At night we controlled only what was inside our barbed wire.

The people and the land I operated in twenty years ago looked like the people and the land I was in today.

The wide, flat, multi-patterned fields spread out into the distance, cut by dams into thousands of small plots. The fields seemed to always have a season where work was necessary. The land never rested. It did not lie fallow here as it did in the South during the war. Black water buffalo pulled heavy, hand-carved wooden plows or rakes through the mud. Thin, sinewy farmers, whose bodies looked like cords of a rope, walked behind in the thigh-deep mud, guiding the buffalo from one side of the paddy to the other. Sometimes the man stood balanced on the rake, holding the tail of the buffalo with one hand and a switch in the other.

In the next field would be two men or women moving water from one rice paddy to a higher one with a wicker basket. Standing on either side of the basket, holding it with two 8-foot ropes, they would stand astraddle the dam and lean forward, dipping the basket in the water at the lower paddy. They would then pull on the ropes, swinging the full basket up and over the dam to the higher paddy, and tilt the ropes so that the basket upended, emptying the water. The two would swing the basket back into the lower paddy and repeat the whole procedure without stopping. They maintained this rhythm for as long as it took to fill the paddy.

Gaggles of white ducks by the hundreds would be driven along the edges of the ditches bordering the fields and the road by a man holding a 10-foot-long thin bamboo switch with the leaves still on the tip. Occasionally a child would be assisting, carrying his own shorter switch and skirting along the side of the duck herd, picking up the stragglers. Buffalo, oxen, pigs, chickens, ponies, and other animals were on the road, in the fields, in pens next to homes, or on their way to market.

Off the side of the road I would frequently see the brilliantly white shallow lime pits that were located in bare spots close to the villages. The 5-foot-square holes were dug so bones, shells, and limestone could be dumped into them to extract the calcium, which would be used to form components needed to make plaster, quicklime, and cement.

Men with axes worked on trees they had recently felled close to the road. The limbs would be trimmed off and then the trunk and limbs loaded onto an oxcart for transportation to wherever it was needed. The logs were half-again as long as the cart. The driver would be perched on top of them at the front of his cart, and the ends of the logs would often hang so far out the rear they would brush the ground. One place the logs were taken to was a pond next to a thatch-covered building on the outskirts of a village we passed through. I thought of this place as a sawmill. Dozens of logs covered the surface of the pond. Other piles of logs surrounded the pond and the lot where a dwelling stood.

Brick kilns could be spotted back from the road. The bricks were hauled by bicycle or cart from the kiln to one of the construction sites along the road or down one of the many side roads.

Vietnam's primitive agricultural economy has changed very little in a thousand years. Its 62 million people live mainly around the Red River Delta in the North and the Mekong River Delta in the South, making them the most populated deltas in the world. These rural people live a harsh, hard life, with the barest of essentials to keep them going. They are tough, clannish, and independent-minded: resistant to change and mistrustful of strangers. With a purpose in mind they can go a long time. These people had been the soldiers in the North and South. Poorly led, as they generally were in the South Vietnamese Army, they were poor soldiers. Strongly led, as they were by the cadre, they were good soldiers. And fighting for a cause made them even better. This was the land their forefathers had worked for countless generations in the same manner they worked it today.

I was watching them work in the twentieth century but it could just as well have been the fifteenth.

We soon arrived safely at the bridge across the Red River into Hanoi. The city looked quaint, as usual, and it was a comfortable feeling to be returning. We traveled the short distance through familiar streets to the guesthouse, where we checked in and then went for our orientation walk.

January 16, 1988—The Trip to Haiphong

★ We met the Vietnamese Delegation, as usual, in a meeting room in the guesthouse. Carl and I were encountering these men for the third time and we greeted each other warmly as associates. Mr. Bai was again in charge. We all shook hands and he introduced his team to us. It consisted of Dr. Bui Tung, Mr. Dong, Mr. Vinh, Mr. Giang, and Mr. Nhu.

Carl Savory made an opening statement and introduced the two new members of our team. In a positive and friendly atmosphere, the first session of the morning was spent discussing the successful visit to Vietnam in December of the six NGOs and the coordination of future meetings, the JCRC technical talks on POW/MIA, and the Vessey humanitarian initiative.

At one point Mr. Bai remarked that his government had read the American papers and they understood very well the difficulties we had to face. "The feeling of the USA people is that they classify us as bellicose. And some congressmen are out to say now we are the enemy. So we know it is very difficult for you."

Dr. Savory answered, "Yes, but it is our goal to move ahead regardless of what is said in the paper. We are committed to pursuing all routes with the NGOs in helping them to assist Vietnam. . . . The responsibility of the United States government has not been neglected. If not for the U.S. government we would not be here.

"As you well know, Americans are free to say what they wish, even if it is against what the government is doing. There may be Americans who are saying things against this effort, but the President and General Vessey are fully supportive of these humanitarian efforts between our two countries."

It was always interesting to us that the Vietnamese received American newspapers and articles and read them so thoroughly. Back in the States, a friend told me the Vietnamese mission at the United Nations had hired a clipping service to ensure they received anything written in America about Vietnam. These clips were then sent to Hanoi. In addition there were many Americans, some of them members of NGOs, who were extremely friendly with Vietnam, and on their own they made sure that they cut out and sent to the UN Vietnam mission all articles involving Vietnam.

These people and the clipping service were so thorough that there were times in our meetings when Mr. Bai would pull out an American article and quote directly from it. Sometimes we would not have the faintest idea what he was quoting until we returned to the States and asked about that particular reference.

The war had been so much a part of Vietnamese life that it had entered the language. When Carl asked them what size vans they needed for the mobile teams that drove out into the countryside to fit amputees with prosthetic limbs, Mr. Bai told us, "During the war on the Ho Chi Minh Trail, to explain to the Chinese the type of transportation needed, we used this description of a truck: A one-bridge truck, a two-bridge truck, or a three-bridge truck. The U.S. planes destroyed our bridges many times and they had to be replaced. The bigger the truck, the more replacement bridges it could carry."

During the break, Dr. van Dam and Dr. Bui Tung found they could speak German as a common language. They became fast friends. From then on, when Mr. Bai had trouble translating a Vietnamese word or term, he would discuss it in Vietnamese with Bui Tung, who in turn would discuss it in German with van Dam—who would then give the English meaning to us.

The remainder of the morning session was taken up with discussions of ideas and questions concerning equipment and material. I brought up the question of the needs of blind children and children with speech and hearing problems.

Mr. Bai said anything we were interested in doing for these children would be welcome.

In response to our request to visit prosthetic and rehabilitation centers, the Vietnamese Delegation had arranged an afternoon trip to the rehabilitation center at Haiphong. It was there, we were told, that we would see some more problems with the disabled.

Carl, Larry, Bruce, and I walked out the front door of the guesthouse just as our escort, Mr. Nhu, arrived with the van to take us to Haiphong. We crossed the Red River, heading east. From up on the Hanoi side of the levee I could look out across the homes crowded up right next to the river. They were made of dark red brick. Most had stained, red-tiled roofs, but there were a few with thatched roofs.

Boats of all types were tied to the bank or anchored out from shore. There were the traditional flat-bottomed wood sampans and, in sharp contrast, big steel barges and ships floating singly or tethered side by side against the muddy bank. The barges and ships left the sharp impression that they had been there for years. They were dark, dirty rusting hulks with uneven outlines, as if they were partially dismantled. I could see activity on some of them. Coal dust rose from one barge being unloaded so its load of coal could be distributed in Hanoi.

A long sandbar ran down the middle of the river. In keeping with the Vietnamese practice of letting nothing go to waste, crops were growing on sections of it. In another section close to the other side of the river a steam engine was loading sand onto a barge.

The road to Haiphong was a simple one, but its history in this century symbolizes the wars in this region. The road runs through land as flat as a table. Rice paddies spread out on both sides as far as the eye can see, along with regular fields with various other crops. It was better than most roads outside the city but it was still rough. The narrow paved strip was crowded with pedestrians, oxcarts, and vehicles of all descriptions.

We came to a traffic jam at a bridge across a river. Bridges were a key target for American war planes, and each one we crossed over was a replacement for another destroyed in the war. At places on both sides of the bridges the former locations of antiaircraft emplacements could be seen dotting the earth. The guns were gone, and grass or plants have taken their place.

Traffic jams are common at many bridges in the North because the usual narrow one-lane iron bridge is a combination railroad-and-car bridge. The vehicle wheels straddle the railroad tracks running the length of the bridge. Men at both ends of the bridge act as crossing guards. They stop the traffic going west so the eastbound traffic can cross. Then they reverse the process. When a train is scheduled to come along, vehicle traffic from both directions is put on hold. We spent about twenty minutes waiting for our side of the river to get its turn crossing the bridge. Finally we got to drive up the side of the railroad embankment onto the heavy wooden planking laid across the bridge for vehicular traffic.

My interest was drawn to a narrow-gauge railroad track that paralleled the road from Hanoi to Haiphong. A few cars sat on sidings here and there. The cars, like everything else in Vietnam, were old and well used.

After an hour or so we came to a slight curve, and a scene from my Indiana childhood sprang to life. Coming toward us was a string of railroad cars being pulled by a steam locomotive that looked like it was built in the 1930s. Black smoke bellowed from the smokestack and a south wind blew it in roils across the road in front of us and into the sky. The locomotive went charging by us and we could see the engineer, his elbow out the window, looking down the track. The fireman was busy shoveling in the coal.

The road we were on and the railroad track next to it was one of the most heavily defended strips of land in North Vietnam during the war. Haiphong Harbor was the largest port in North Vietnam and it was where the ships bringing war supplies to North Vietnam were unloaded. Ninety percent of the supplies arriving by sea landed at Haiphong, and much of that was moved inland by rail and road on this strip between Haiphong and Hanoi.

Although Americans were prohibited from attacking the ships in the harbor, they could hit targets on land. The U.S. government did not want the Soviet, Eastern European, and Chinese ships unloading war supplies to be hit by American aircraft for fear of starting a war with them. To keep civilian casualties to a minimum, there were restricted areas around Hanoi and Haiphong where attacks were not permitted except under certain conditions. The cities themselves were off limits to any attacks, except for very specialized targets. But targets outside those perimeters, such as roads and bridges, were hit hard and often.

The area encompassing Hanoi and Haiphong became one of the most formidable air defense systems in the history of aerial warfare. Thousands of surface-to-air missiles, thousands of various types of antiaircraft guns, and hundreds of MiG-17s and 21s made flying into the area extremely dangerous. Each day of the war that air defense system grew stronger. In addition to those dangers, every Vietnamese who carried a rifle was encouraged to shoot at the American aircraft. John Johnson (a pseudonym), who had flown three tours of Vietnam as a Navy pilot, had told me of the terrible strain on the pilots flying over the North. At one time the casualties were so high the commanders had trouble with some of the pilots refusing to fly.

Riding along this corridor in the relative comfort of the van, I looked at the peaceful sky and the pastoral land we were passing through, and I thought about the pilots who lie buried in the countryside somewhere beyond the horizon in all directions. John had known some of these men personally. A few had been close friends.

I studied the people we were passing on the road. How many of those Vietnamese we were passing had been a part of a gun crew or a SAM crew who had shot down one of our planes? How many of them had had relatives and friends who had been killed or wounded in the war? What had it been like in the countryside when one of our aircraft crashed? Bill Bell, Paul Mather, and Johnie Webb had given me a good idea.

Sometimes the aircraft crashed into a village, destroying a part of it and killing some people. More often it crashed in a field or woods. In practical terms, an American aircraft crash site was a bonanza to the Vietnamese, if they could get to it. They salvaged every piece they could. There are many exotic and common metals used in building high-tech aircraft: gold, silver, platinum, copper, aluminum, titanium, and other metals go into making instruments, wiring, weapons, the frame, engines, and fuselage.

These three men told me you could still see pots and pans made from American aircraft aluminum being used over the cookfires today. The Vietnamese used to brag about its source. When the JCRC team was coming into Hanoi in the 1970s, vendors on the street were selling combs made of American aircraft aluminum. The combs were fashioned in the silhouette of either a B-52 bomber or an F-105 fighter.

Sometimes there was not much to salvage at a crash site. If a jet augured in at high speed from a high altitude into a soft rice paddy, it would be buried under 30 or 40 feet of mud. The Vietnamese had no way to dig down that deep, and so that particular aircraft would remain where it was.

Johnie Webb told me about one such crash site they investigated. The American team had flown their own excavating equipment into Noi Bai Airport in the back of a C-141. Then they had driven with their Vietnamese counterparts to the crash site.

They had dug down 15 feet before they came to parts of the aircraft. While they were working at the crash site, the villagers gathered to watch the proceedings. After a week or so of excavating the American team had retrieved all that was possible from such a catastrophic crash: a few splinters of bones. In accordance with the agreement with the Vietnamese government, the American team filled back in the hole, leveled off the dirt, and did everything possible to restore the ground to exactly the way they had found it.

What no one had figured on was that the villagers would become upset when they discovered the gigantic hole was filled back in. They had been counting on being able to salvage the aircraft metals from the hole. Johnie said the villagers were pretty agitated about it.

I had asked Johnie, Bill, and Paul the question which had always been in my mind, even back during the war. "On those crash sites where the plane is not buried in the mud, what did the Vietnamese do with the bodies of the American pilot and air crews they found?"

"They would often bury the remains in a grave next to the crash."

I thought back on that conversation and reflected on the millions of men on this earth who have been killed in battle since time eternal, who were buried where they fell.

On a curve of Route 1 south of Duc Pho, South Vietnam, my platoon had buried the remains of three Viet Cong who had blown themselves up planting a land mine in the road next to a bridge we were guarding. I thought about them because they were part of the 300,000 missing in action the enemy had from the war. We had been glad they were dead, and we had just scraped the pieces into a hole and covered it over.

I had asked Bill Bell what the Vietnamese felt about their MIAs. Bill told me the Vietnamese believe that if they die in Vietnam, their souls return to the soul of the country, which is the mountains and rivers. If a Vietnamese dies outside Vietnam, his soul will wander until his body is returned to Vietnam.

A North Vietnamese I talked to later told me that when a Vietnamese dies away from his village, his friends always try to bury him so that he faces toward his home. He said there were many soldiers killed in the war far from home, but of course it was not possible to do these things except in special cases of friendship. He also explained that in the villages that lost sons during the war, the people built memorials to them outside the village gates. This was necessary so that they would always be remembered. I had thought of that conversation as we bounced along in the van because occasionally I could see in the distance a white pillar with a red star signifying a place of honor for the sons killed in the war.

As I learned more about the Vietnamese, I took hope that a people who believed such things would understand the anguish felt by Americans toward their fallen sons who were still missing in action.

I had talked to many Vietnamese who had told me they had hated the Americans during the war and for some time after. But enough time had passed now that they no longer felt that way. However, they added, there were still some people whose memories of the war had not faded, and they still had hard feelings toward the Americans.

One Vietnamese official in New York told me about one crash site they had taken the Central Identification Laboratory Hawaii (CILHI) and JCRC teams to in the middle of a village. An American aircraft had been shot down and had crashed into a home, destroying it, and killing one of the family members. Another home had been rebuilt over the crash site. The old woman who lived in it had argued with the Vietnamese officials who told her that her home would have to be torn down so that the crash site could be excavated in hopes of finding the American remains. She became very upset and cried a great deal. He was telling me this story to evoke sympathy for the plight of the villager, and to explain the difficulty the Vietnamese government had in dealing with its countrymen on eliciting their aid in reporting crash sites.

It was interesting to hear this story from the North Vietnamese because a year earlier I had been told about this same crash site by the JCRC team. This was what they told me: In December 1972, fifteen B-52 bombers were shot down around Hanoi and Haiphong. As part of the extensive intelligence gathering and tracking of every piece of information on MIAs, our side had a pretty good idea of the approximate location of most of the crash sites of these bombers.

In 1985, after a host of tedious meetings and negotiations, the Hanoi government finally agreed to let the CILHI and JCRC teams go to a suspected B-52 crash site 15 kilometers northeast of Hanoi at the village of Yen Thuong. The villagers claimed a large aircraft had crashed into their village in December 1972, killing a number of people.

When the teams arrived, they met a woman whose husband was allegedly killed when the aircraft crashed into her house. The team was directed to start their excavations in the garden next to the house. The Vietnamese had brought along a movie camera and filmed everything that happened. The American team dug deeper and deeper in the garden, expanding out as they went. The villagers directed them to dig closer to the house until it became obvious the house would have to be torn down before they could go any further.

The Hanoi officials and villagers then prevailed upon the woman to allow the Americans to tear down her house. She was assured the Americans would pay her for all damages. As the Americans dismantled her house, the woman cried bitterly, tears streaming down her face. The Vietnamese filmed everything.

The hole ended up being 100 feet long, 50 feet wide, and 40 feet deep. The digging started on November 18 and ended December 3, 1985. The team found large chunks of a B-52, but they were not able to find identifiable remains. The team was able to identify which B-52 it was. The big bomber had been struck by a SAM and had broken apart in its fall from 30,000 feet on that night in December 1972. Parts of it had scattered for miles, and this large piece had crashed to earth at a high velocity into this village. The crew was listed as missing in action.

The Vietnamese did a strange thing afterward. The CILHI and JCRC teams were later invited to a movie the Vietnamese wanted to show them. They took the Americans to a movie theater inside the former prisoner-of-war camp in Hanoi called "The Plantation." There the Vietnamese showed the Americans the propaganda film they had made at the crash site in the village of Yen Thuong.

Some of the Americans said it was the best textbook propaganda film they had ever seen, and that our military psy-ops should see it as an example of Vietnamese Communist propaganda at its most effective. It was filmed in black and white. It started with night scenes of flashing weapons and aircraft being shot down in flames. Then it switched to the village and showed the Americans tearing down the old lady's house and the tears streaming down her face. It was well done, and it was as anti-American as it could be. It perplexed the team. Why did the Vietnamese government show the Americans the film, and why did they show it to them in the old POW camp? Was it for revenge or just plain maliciousness?

No one knew the answer.

I turned my attention back to the road and thought about those Frenchmen who had fought for eight years before being defeated at Dien Bien Phu. This was the road down which the French traveled in October 1954 during their withdrawal from North Vietnam as per the Geneva Agreement of 1954. By May 1955, the French would all be evacuated from the port of Haiphong. In the eight years of the First Indochina War the French lost 44,967 dead and 79,560 wounded. In 1987, the remains of 10,000 French soldiers were finally returned home to France from Vietnam. René Cogny, the commander of French ground forces in the South, said it all: "Many deaths for few results, many deaths for nothing."

In Denver, Colorado, in 1970 I met a Frenchman who had been a soldier in Indochina, and he told me about a time when he and his men were cutting down some trees to clear a line of fire against the Viet Minh. A French plantation owner had flown out from Hanoi to rebuke him because those trees were part of the view from the front porch of the house and cutting them down had ruined the view.

"He did not care about my men at all," the former French soldier said. "When we returned to France, we were not welcomed and the people held us soldiers to blame for the war. It was a very bad time. You Americans should have learned from us."

As we entered the outskirts of Haiphong, I thought maybe it was not to late to learn something. This humanitarian effort certainly could not be any worse a decision concerning Vietnam than the decisions the top leadership of France and America had made before.

When we pulled up in front of the Haiphong Rehabilitation Center, we could see a difference in this center right away. It was a modern, single-level, functional building, with a flat roof. The staff came out front to welcome us. They took us inside the open, naturally lit building to a room where we were provided with refreshments and given a briefing. This rehabilitation center had been built by Norway, which explained its open, airy spaces.

The director of the center, Dr. Bang, was an enthusiastic individual who was proud of his center, and his staff reflected his pride. We were impressed with his attitude. Later on we would be impressed with what he had accomplished.

When he took us on a tour, we realized this was the busiest rehabilitation center we had seen. There were forty or fifty patients, most of them children brought there by their mothers. The center was located in the outer section of the city. Although it was difficult for mothers to bring their children because of the lack of transportation, many mothers were so anxious to have their children treated that they carried them on their backs many kilometers to the center, two or three times a week. We had seen some traveling on the road when we drove in.

Many of the children and mothers were in a large room about half the size of a basketball court, with lots of windows. Physical therapists were busy working with young children ranging in age from six months to three and four years old. The first thing that struck me was the pitiful crying of the babies and children whose crippled limbs were being gently forced to move through ranges of motion by the physical therapists. The mothers crouched or lay next to their children, attempting to comfort them with the touch of their hands and soothe them with their voices. The mothers' faces reflected the pain and fear of their children. Those mothers whose children were next for treatment stood nervously by, balancing them on their hip.

Carl and Bruce examined the children and asked a number of medical questions of the director and the staff about the causes of the diseases and the number of children affected. They said only 40 percent of the cases were caused by polio. We all took note of the adjective "only." The rest were congenital deformities and disease-related problems.

There were also ten or twelve soldiers in the room. They were in their late teens and early twenties, and all were wearing their green army fatigues. All of them were leg amputees. Some had knotted their empty trouser leg to keep it from flapping, while others just let the trouser leg hang.

They looked like any group of young soldiers with amputations. I had seen the same thing in El Salvador and Egypt. Twenty years ago in the American Army Hospital I had been a member of the same kind of group. It was no exaggeration to say I had now seen hundreds of soldiers from different countries who were amputees caused by war.

The children were the ones who broke my heart, though. None of these countries could afford to provide artificial limbs to the adults, let alone a growing child who would have to have the limb regularly replaced. The harsh reality was that if anyone got a limb, the priority was always the breadwinner, the adult who had to make a living. In El Salvador, the Knights of Malta had been able to provide limbs to children, but that was an exception to the rule.

As I watched these soldiers, I wondered how many thousands of soldier amputees there were in the world just from the wars now in progress. To my way of thinking it did not make any difference whether those amputees were Muslims, Christians, Jews, Communists, or whatever. They all went through the period these men were going through: freshly wounded and healing, and still among soldier buddies, with an unknown future as a disabled person looming like a mountain in front of them.

They felt out of place here among the women and children and stayed to the other side of the room pursuing their own activities. At one Ping-Pong table two above-knee, single-leg amputees were playing a fierce game. They were hopping back and forth and sideways on one leg, trying to keep the ball in play. Their empty pants legs whipped around like a distress flag. There were five leg amputee soldiers sitting on a mat, throwing a soccer ball disconsolately to each other. Other amputee soldiers stood nearby leaning on their crutches as they watched the activities. Everything about them projected their hopelessness.

One young man saw me watching him, and he hopped on his one leg through a doorway and then looked back through a window at us. I could see by the look of dismay on his face that he was embarrassed by his condition. He wanted to hide from us. He had probably not yet gotten over his shame at not being a whole man anymore. Hell, he looked so young he probably had not had time to discover what it was like to be a man at all.

The rest of the soldiers looked at us and went on with their activities. They talked among themselves as they watched us, and I remembered that twenty years ago, when the VIPs came to look at us in the Army hospital, we used to talk about the assholes who were staring at us. I figured these men were no different.

These young men were, for the most part, casualties from the war in Cambodia. A couple of them had fought on the China border. They all looked so young it was hard to believe they were soldiers. But I felt the same way when I saw the young men in the American Army. They looked so young to be in the military.

Later on, back in the States I would be asked by newspaper reporters and a few veterans: Didn't I feel any conflict in helping former soldiers who used to shoot at me?

My answer was, No, I did not feel any conflict. They had only been men who had done what their country had wanted them to do. When they became wounded and lost their limbs or the use of them, then they had lost part of their freedom, their independence, and their dignity as a human being. What we were doing in the Vessey mission was returning to them their mobility, their freedom, and their dignity. The politics between countries may change, yet that disability will never change.

Consequently I had no qualms about being here in Vietnam or anywhere else, doing what I could for the disabled. From years of working with so many disabled in America and elsewhere in the world, I had come to the notion that the disableds' personal misery took precedence over the politics of the country.

Bruce and I went outside through a side door to look at the training area used by the staff in rehabilitating the patients. This reminded us of a playground. There was a rubber tire hanging from a chain fastened to a frame. A raggedy-looking cloth was thrown over the frame and tire to protect them from the pending rain. Other poles and frames used for a variety of activities were positioned about the area.

Four training courses, each one representing a different type of terrain the individual would most likely encounter in Vietnam, were laid out in tracks, first over a flat stretch of ground and then up a small man-made hill about 4 feet high. Each track was about 3 feet wide. One was covered with rocks, one was made of mud, one was overgrown with weeds, and one was rough ground.

One young soldier, a leg amputee, was off by himself on one of the tracks, intently concentrating on going up the hill using his crutches. When he reached the top, he looked up and saw us, and then immediately hobbled to the side of the hill away from us and went behind a building. There were a few mothers shepherding their children around the tracks. One little six-year-old girl on crutches was attempting to walk on the rocky path. She looked determined; her mother looked apprehensive.

Some of the children and mothers gathered around us in open curiosity. One boy whom we guessed to be nine or ten rolled his wheelchair up next to us. He was friendly and was as interested in us as we were in him. The chair he sat in was an adult-sized American-type chair. There were no foot pedals, so his skinny legs dangled about 8 inches above the ground. His equally skinny child's body was way too small for the chair. His arms draped up and over the armrests and his hands could barely reach the wheel rims to propel the chair. The seat was narrow wooden slats positioned so that open gaps showed between each one. When I looked down at him, I could see the ground beneath the chair. He seemed happy to have what he had and showed off for us by pushing himself in a circle around us.

I looked around outside, and up on a bluff above the rehabilitation center was another reminder of the wars. Below the lip of the bluff a concrete bunker had been built back into the earth. The narrow, dark gun slit and smooth gray concrete stood out markedly against the rugged surface of dirt and rocks. It was probably an old French bunker, but it was hard to tell from where I stood. From old military habit I evaluated the fields of fire it commanded and what approaches I would use if my assignment were to knock it out.

I had done that kind of evaluation a lot in the twenty years since the war ended. It seemed to be a strong habit to check treelines or think about territory in terms of defending or taking it. It was not the kind of thing you talked about or people would think you were a little crazy. But every once in a while a close friend who had been in combat would let it slip out that he also had the habit of evaluating the terrain around him.

If those types of thoughts occupied my mind after only three years in the Army, then how had fifty years of constant warfare affected the thinking of the Vietnamese? The Vietnamese people were openly stating that their war leaders had taken the necessary actions needed to win the wars against the Chinese, Japanese, French, and Americans, but they could not win the peace. I could well imagine anybody who had fought in wars for their entire adult life would have a problem adjusting to leading in peacetime.

Americans were always trying to puzzle out the Vietnamese. We had been trying to do that most of this century and failing. On the personal level they were agreeable, but on an official level they would say one thing, but then do another thing that did not seem to make sense. They seemed to be so contrary. What was it they really wanted? Did they know themselves?

Thinking about my reaction to the bunker on the bluff caused me to consider the way the Vietnamese thought. Perhaps the key lay in their thousand-year conflict with the Chinese. The Vietnamese referred to it constantly in their conversation and in their literature. Maybe the Vietnamese were difficult to understand because in order to survive their thousand-year struggle, they had had to hide their thoughts and actions within one another like so many Russian Kachina dolls for so long that it was a cultural norm by now.

I went back inside the center and the director took us down a hallway toward the prosthetic workshop. On the way we detoured through a room the center used as its library. He was proud of his center and the library was no exception.

There were perhaps twenty thin books and fifteen health-care pamphlets on the small bookcase in the corner.

It reminded us that a need for medical books and journals was voiced in private by almost all health-care workers. In America we demand and are swamped by numerous journals and articles in each specialty and subspecialty, so it is something we take for granted. But in Vietnam and all Third World countries, only a few very lucky individuals received regular, timely, foreign journals or articles with information in their specialty.

Further down the hall we entered the workshop where limbs were made. There was a marked difference between this shop and what we had seen before. This was a Western-style shop in its layout of equipment and types of materials and components. Plastics, instead of wood, seemed to be the main fabrication material.

As the director explained how the rehabilitation center worked, it became clear to us that the center we had visited in Ba Vi was modeled after the East Germans, whereas this center was modeled after the Western Europeans.

There were a dozen workmen and women, professionally attired in white lab coats, who were busy fabricating limbs. Their workmanship looked good. We found it interesting the way the shortage of plastic affected how they made the limb. Narrow bamboo slats were used to reinforce the plastic on the same principle as steel rods used to reinforce concrete. The finished limb was fitted with a SACH (solid ankle cushion heel) foot. Carl and I looked at each other, because during our previous visits the other prosthetists we met said the SACH foot was not used in Vietnam. This was another example of why it was hard to understand the Vietnamese. Why would the other group say that?

There was a stack of finished above- and below-knee limbs standing in a corner of the shop, ready for the amputees to come in for the final fitting and adjustment. Some of them belonged to the soldiers we had seen in the PT room. Some would be taken out on the next trip made by the center. The director had explained that the center would send a truck or van out on a circuit through the villages in the surrounding districts. This trip could take several days because of the size of the area to be covered and the terrible road conditions.

During the stop at the district or village, casts and measurements would be taken of the amputee's stump. When the truck or van returned to the rehabilitation center, the workmen would fabricate the complete limb from those measurements and casts. If everything worked perfectly, the amputee would still wait months for the limb to be delivered back to him in the village.

Unfortunately for the amputee, nothing ever worked perfectly. As we were discovering, there was always a chronic shortage of fabrication materials. The resins and hardeners used to form the plastic had to come from foreign countries. The right type and number of component parts often did not always arrive at the center from the shop at Bà Vi, or from abroad.

Even this center, as well run as it was and with the high morale evident in the employees, could not keep its equipment running when the machinery broke down or parts needed replacing. In the workshop there was a band saw with no blade and a router with no sanding burr. The leather used in the thigh straps to hold the below-knee leg in place and the steel buckles used to hold the straps were also difficult to get.

This inability of the Vietnamese to replace these simple parts and acquire books, medicines, and thousands of other things made us realize how effective America's economic embargo of Vietnam was. It was one thing to read about it in the paper in the States, but quite another thing to see it in practice. The embargo had worked. When the economic and political issues were resolved between America and Vietnam, the humanitarian efforts would become a lot easier.

I was wearing a short-sleeve shirt and the prosthetists were obviously interested in my above-elbow prosthesis. We had never seen an upper-extremity limb being worn in Vietnam nor had we seen one being made. An artificial arm was rare in Third World countries. In fact, not many arm amputees wear them in the advanced countries either, because they can get along with one arm quite nicely and it is psychologically difficult to accept wearing such an alien device.

Carl noticed their interest and asked me if I didn't mind showing them how my arm worked. I told him no problem. He turned to the director and asked him if the prosthetists would be interested in seeing how my arm worked.

When the director translated this to the prosthetists, their faces lit up in eager smiles. They started talking among themselves and then sent a boy out on the run to bring back some more staff for the demonstration. The room was quickly crowded with men and women, while boys and girls peeked in the doors and through the windows.

I took off my shirt and explained how the cables and harness worked in relation to each other to perform the three functions of locking and unlocking the elbow, moving the forearm up and down, and opening and closing the hook.

Everyone asked questions. I did my favorite trick of asking for a volunteer and, with their permission, asked them to put their fingers into my open hook and then, gently closing my hook, lightly grasped their fingers. Then I took the arm off and passed it around, so they could all test its weight and examine it closer. Carl and Larry worked the crowd while Bruce took pictures. After they returned the arm, I put it back on and showed them how versatile it was. I noticed the kids at the outside windows had their faces pressed up against the glass so they wouldn't miss anything.

There were a variety of colorful toys on the tables and other items used by physical therapists in training patients in hand skills. A pegboard was within easy reach, so I used my hook to pick up different shapes and insert them into the corresponding hole on the board. Then I picked up a piece of chalk to write on a blackboard and discovered there was no longer any slate in the frame. One of the physical therapists explained to me they just wrote in chalk on the wood. I shrugged my shoulders and said if they can do it, I can do it. I held the chalk in my hook and started writing my name.

After I had done all that I could do with the available materials, Carl signaled a halt. I put my shirt back on while Carl and Bruce asked more questions about the center's activities.

When we left the room we noted, lined along the wall, the hand-drawn pictures of procedures physical therapists should follow in treating patients. The pictures had been drawn with colored pencils and pens on lined sheets of white tablet paper.

The patient rooms we were taken through were spartan but adequate, with two or four beds per room. The beds were solid wood and the mattress was a thin bamboo mat. This was the best center we had seen, and certainly the busiest. The director and his staff were impressive. They did not hesitate on any questions we asked, and they had volunteered useful information on Vietnam's rehabilitation operations. We felt we had had a productive day.

Finally, we bid them goodbye and loaded into the van. The driver and escort were anxious to finish the 100-kilometer trip back to Hanoi before dark. We had to stop for fifteen minutes about 2 kilometers down the dirt road to fix the horn—an essential for night driving. The driver pulled off the side of the road and we all got out of the van while he lifted the hood and proceeded to work on the horn.

It was very peaceful. We were in the suburbs of Haiphong and there were no motor vehicles around. The road was busy with people walking or riding bicycles in both directions.

A man and two boys drove a herd of cows past us. A fisherman was wading in one of the two ponds we were between, seining for fish with a net suspended from its four corners to a pole he was holding. Another fisherman standing in the pond on the other side of the road was throwing a net out over the water and pulling it in. A three-wheeled open-sided motorcycle bus we used to call a Lambretta putted by and it too, like its cousins in the South, was crammed with Vietnamese. Carl, Larry, and I really enjoyed seeing this vestige from the past. Bruce was too young to have served in Vietnam so he did not appreciate it as much as we did.

Two mothers coming from the center walked past us, carrying their crippled children on their backs.

The driver slammed the hood shut, signaling it was time to load up and continue.

We drove through what looked like the middle of Haiphong. The buildings were two or three stories high. We crossed a number of small concrete bridges over streams that ran through the town. The streets were jammed with people, many of whom were in colorful clothing.

Haiphong (*Hai* meaning "ocean" and *Phong* meaning "defend" or "protect") was built on marshy ground and lies along the Cam River. This main seaport for North Vietnam is also an industrial town. Some of the dingy side streets with their flat, gray, rust-stained warehouse buildings and cranes reminded me of Gary, Indiana, in the early sixties. On the way out of town we drove by the docks on the river. There were an incredible number of wrecked ships and hulks sitting half-submerged in the mud and water: ships, boats, barges, transports, freighters, patrol boats, you name it. There were boats pulled up into streams and tributaries of the river and lying in the mud next to Ha Long (Descending Dragon) Bay.

This graveyard of ships must have been the remnants of the vast, motley fleet the Vietnamese used during the war to unload the Russian, East European, and Chinese ships in the harbor. After the war, the craft were abandoned.

The ride back was a thrill a minute. The sun set soon after we left the city limits, but the traffic on the road remained heavy and the drivers did not slow down on account of darkness. At one point we came within an inch of crashing into a large sow. Even Mr. Nhu and the driver made a comment to each other about that. Larry and I remarked how happy we were to have two doctors with us.

Except for the occasional headlight—it was rare for a vehicle to have two—the countryside was completely dark.

January 17, 1988—Sunday in Hanoi

★ The next day we had some time off from our meetings and decided to take a short tour of Hanoi. Mr. Nhu and the driver escorted us. We always paid $50 a day for the van and driver whether we used it or not for each day we were in Vietnam.

In 1831, the name "Hanoi" first began to appear officially on maps. *Ha* means "river" and *Noi* means "inner" or "on this side," so the word *Hanoi* signifies "the city inside a bend of the Red River." The city had been known by other names; in the eighteenth century it was called the "Eastern Capital," *Dong Kinh* in Vietnamese, but European traders translated it phonetically as "Tonkin." The French called all of North Vietnam "Tonkin," and in American history books the Tonkin Gulf will always be a name to remember in relation to the war.

Our escort took us to a side street off of Ba Dinh Square. Ho Chi Minh's mausoleum faced the square, but that was one place we never wanted to get near because of the danger of a picture being taken. The propaganda from a picture of an official U.S. government delegation at Ho's tomb could destroy all that we were trying to do.

We were going to visit a famous Hanoi landmark located on a street behind the mausoleum, but the streets were blocked off so we had to walk. There was a block-and-a-half line of people strung out in orderly single file: old men and women, young couples and parents with their children, all waiting to view Ho Chi Minh's remains. This was contrary to Ho's will, because he left instructions that his body should be cremated and his remains scattered in both the northern and southern parts of the country. The fact that "Uncle Ho" (their form of endearment for him) was put on display like this underscored the stubbornness and power of the Communist Party of Vietnam. Their desire to make Ho Chi Minh an icon to the Vietnamese overrode his own wishes.

The fact that his remains were here made good sense to the Vietnamese who revered him, though. In August 1945 he had made a speech in Ba Dinh Square proclaiming Vietnam's independence. It was in that speech that Ho used the sentence he had borrowed from our Declaration of Independence: "We hold these truths to be self-evident, that all men are created equal, that they are endowed by their Creator with certain unalienable rights, that among these are life, liberty, and the pursuit of happiness."

Coming around the corner from a building nestled up close to the mausoleum was an honor guard of the best-dressed Vietnamese troops we had ever seen. There were six of them, and they marched by us on the sidewalk, executed a left turn, and marched down the street toward the front entrance of the mausoleum on the square. There they would go through the changing-of-the-guard ceremony.

As I stood there, I experienced a strange absence of hatred toward the man entombed in the square marble building. Even though Ho Chi Minh had been the driving force behind the revolutionary movement that had affected me so personally and my country as a whole, he was dead now and his country was united. That was the simple fact of it.

In the background, towering above the trees in the neighboring block, was a construction crane being used to construct the Ho Chi Minh Museum. He would probably have rolled over in his tomb if he knew that more than $20 million was being spent to build him a museum while his people were going hungry. This was contrary to the very frugal nature of this man, who lived in a simple house and carried a briefcase made of bamboo.

We walked on back to see what we had come to see: the Single Pillar Pagoda. It was built in the twelfth century by Emperor Ly Thanh Ton, who according to legend dreamed of a goddess sitting on a lotus flower who handed him a boy. At that time he had no children, but soon afterward a son was born to him. In thanks to the goddess he built a pagoda in the form of Buddha sitting on a lotus flower, placed on a single pillar raising from a small lake. The pillar represents the stem of the lotus flower and the lake represents human suffering.

The lotus flower is a central symbol in Vietnamese culture and the location of this pagoda added to the symmetry of Ba Dinh Square and Ho Chi Minh's mausoleum. The mausoleum's shape was meant to suggest a lotus flower, which the Vietnamese propaganda always associated with Ho Chi Minh. The name of his home village had been "Lotus Village." I was fascinated at the skill employed in symbolically establishing Ho Chi Minh as the father of his country.

The Single Pillar Pagoda had been here nearly a thousand years before events in this century overtook it. The French destroyed it when they withdrew from Hanoi in September 1954, but it was rebuilt by the Vietnamese a year later. The replica now stood in a garden-sized pond.

I wondered what it was with the French. This was the second historical artifact I had seen personally that the French had previously mutilated. When my wife and I visited Egypt, we had seen the Great Sphinx; one of Napoleon's artillery officers had used it for target practice and blown the nose off of it. From what I had read, the French had destroyed the Single Pillar Pagoda just to spite the Vietnamese for winning the war.

We walked back to the van for a quick trip out to the gift shop in the Thang Loi Hotel on the banks of the West Lake.

Other than a few war memorials spaced around the city, there was little to show that Hanoi itself had ever been in a war. From my first trip I had felt strangely relieved that we had not bombed Hanoi as severely as I had been led to believe from the news reports during the war. Both the Vietnamese media and the American media had given the United States, and most of the world, the impression that America had practically razed Hanoi and Haiphong to the ground. The facts had only come out after the war that the cities had not been systematically bombed.

Frankly, at the time I supported the bombings, and I wanted us to intensify them. I was a twenty-three-year-old soldier during my tour of duty and my gut feelings had nothing to do with world politics. Now I was forty-two. As I saw Hanoi, with its thousand-year history and its people, I struggled with the question of whether I could kill the people and destroy their cities if we went to war with this country again.

This was not an easy thing to contemplate. It was easier for me to kill and destroy when I was a young man and the enemy was a dehumanized thing. Could I do it again? The answer to myself was always yes. In fact, I strongly believed that because of my past combat experience I would be a better soldier, which meant I would be better at doing what an infantryman's job is, killing people and taking ground. It was a matter of pride and duty to my country and to the beliefs it stood for. Far from being a trite statement, this went to the very bedrock of what I believed myself to be. My home and my self were one.

In spite of this answer to myself, I was always saddened by the picture it brought to my mind of the misery, death, and suffering I had seen in our war, and the work I had done with the disabled in other countries' wars. It made me think that men who had been in actual combat would be far more sagacious and cautious if they had a voice in starting another war, whereas men who had never actually been in combat would be more reckless.

From the evidence, the Vietnamese people had had enough war after fifty years of it. They wanted to be done with it. Their government still had them in Cambodia and still fighting on the border with the Chinese, but the people themselves seemed tired of war. There was certainly no war atmosphere in Hanoi.

We explored on foot for the rest of the day. I had brought my video camera on this trip and was told by Mr. Bai there were no restrictions on what I filmed, so I was anxious to start filming the city.

It was Sunday, the day off for the week, so the crowds of people on the sidewalks and streets were heavier than normal. There were lots of one-man or one-woman business enterprises on the sidewalks. The women mostly sold foods: vegetables or meats, sugar cane, fruits; or sundries such as cigarettes, candies, bottled drinks, nuts, pens. The men did manual work. A solid wooden box the size of a vegetable crate would be carried on a man's back to a place on the curb. He would set it on end and open one side as a door. Inside would be the tools of his trade fastened to the door and to the shelves and walls of the box. One specialized in fixing bicycle flats. We watched as a man pushed a bicycle to the curb, negotiated with the tire fixer, and squatted to have a smoke while the tire fixer went to work. He knew I was watching him and he was proud of his work. He showed me what he was doing at each step of the process. In no time he had the tire off, the tube out, and was applying a patch to it.

Another shop-in-a-box belonged to a bicycle repairman. His box contained parts: gears, nuts, bolts, chain links, cables, spokes. They all looked old and well used, but they either worked or had been cannibalized for making other parts work. I watched the bike repairman squatting in the street next to the curb in a circle of parts from the bicycle he had dismantled. He was dirty and greasy, but his fingers moved nimbly over the part he was concentrating on.

A woman came toward us with her mobile shop. Her wares were carried in two bamboo baskets at opposite ends of a long pole she balanced in the middle on her shoulder. The baskets were filled with all types of knives, scissors, and sharp-edged kitchen utensils of all kinds. The utensils' handles were hand-carved of wood and the metal looked like forged steel worked by a blacksmith's hand. The weight of the two baskets bowed the bamboo pole but the woman just smiled as she walked by.

Another entrepreneur was the air-pump man. His equipment consisted of only an old-fashioned air pump used to fill inner tubes with air.

There was another sidewalk shop-in-a-box containing an assortment of teas in tiny containers. A lady, dressed almost in rags, squatted grimly on the curb waiting for a buyer.

Standing a little distance from her was a boy of eight or nine who was reading a comic book. It was in black and white and written in Vietnamese, so it was a local product. I remembered that Paul Mather told me he had once visited the Vietnamese model school and he had seen comic books in the school. The teacher explained the comic books were used as a teaching aid for the younger children. The stories were parables pertaining to Vietnamese culture.

Interspersed among the multitudes of vendors would be an occasional wretched-looking crone squatting on the curb. What these poor women sold were cigarettes. The difference between them and the other cigarette vendors was that their total inventory was only two or three cigarettes. They squatted for hours, I was told, waiting to sell their meager supply one at a time.

We walked down Hai Ba Trung Street past the former American Consulate and then the Hanoi Hilton. Midway in the block east of Ly Thuong Kiet Street, there was a double gate standing open on our left. An outdoor market ran the length of a street cut through the middle of the block. The street was closed off, and stands were set up down the middle and on the sides. It was a huge farmer's market, with the largest amount and assortment of food I had seen in

one reference in the entire book to the Chinese role in the war. I bought a copy for 1,600 dong.

North of the Lake of the Restored Sword is a section of Hanoi known as the Old Quarter. Even though the buildings were built at the end of the nineteenth century when the French took over Hanoi, the streets received their names in the fifteenth century. Artisans, craftsmen, guilds, and shop owners had gathered together at that time and the area became known as a "City with thirty-six guilds and streets." The short, narrow streets are named after the products made and sold in those times: Brine Street, Broiled Fish Street, Comb Street, Cotton Street, Hemp Street, Jewelers Street, Mat Street, Medicine Street, and so on. The district is still broken into specialty areas selling these items and more. In some cases, where I did not know the name, I still could have named the street myself. On one block the people made tombstones; on another, craftsmen were making wooden caskets.

The Dong Xuan (Winter-Spring) Market was at the northern edge of the area. It was a typical Oriental bazaar, with hundreds of shops and stands. The Dong Xuan Market's front entrance was through a French building that looked as if it had once been a large warehouse.

The intersection in front of the market interested me for military reasons. This was one area the French had shelled when they were driving the Vietnamese out of Hanoi in December 1946. French armored vehicles had rolled down this very street. Only a few blocks from here was Nguyen Thiep Street, which was accidentally bombed by one of our planes in December 1966 when trying to hit a railroad close by. The Vietnamese press had used the incident to their advantage in the propaganda war against America.

The intersection was crammed with shops now, though, with no hint of war. We stood for a moment in the street, enjoying the feeling of being there, before heading back to the guesthouse to prepare for dinner.

* * *

Before we left Bangkok, Bill Bell had written out a menu for us to give to the guesthouse staff as our suggestion for what should be served when we hosted the dinner. Included was a request for the female servers to wear the traditional Ao Dai, which was a blouse and slacks covered by a long dress with slits up both sides. We had to pay for any requests, but it added to the pleasure of the meal and was well worth it.

Both the Americans and the Vietnamese were in good spirits on this last night of our visit. Mr. Bai was his usual avuncular self at these informal dinners. The Vietnamese officials we met always seemed to prefer the informal setting. These dinners allowed more, and in many ways, better conversations than were possible in the more formal meetings held during the day.

I asked Mr. Bai questions about the war. He started off by saying he had been born in the Year of the Dragon, so he had been old enough to fight the Japanese when they came. He waved his hand and took a drag off a cigarette. "I smoke too much, but when fighting the Japanese and French I had to spend years underground and I was in tunnels on and off for seven years during the fight against the Americans. You know, there was nothing to do in the tunnels except smoke. It is very bad for me. My doctor tells me to quit, but it is very hard."

I found out from him that the reason the trees along the streets in Hanoi, and elsewhere in Vietnam along certain roads, were painted with white stripes was to help guide unlighted vehicles at night. This was a technique used in the countryside and on the Ho Chi Minh Trail during the war to avoid being discovered by American aircraft.

So much of what I have seen in North Vietnam reminded me of my youth on the farm in Indiana, when the modern conveniences of modern life were just becoming available. I asked him about electricity and phones.

"Only the high officials and doctors and men who have responsibility can have the telephone at first. They tell me I can have one, but I don't want one. If I have a telephone, I will get calls in the night for things that are not really important.

"Electricity will be good for the people, but we need better equipment. Someday electricity will be in every village in the countryside. We make some progress but it is slow."

I had seen that power was a problem. Our guesthouse was one of the few buildings that was allowed to have electricity twenty-four hours a day. In most of the city of Hanoi the amount of electricity was strictly rationed and the power was shut down at night.

Mr. Bai explained that the monsoons brought cold, wet winds in winter and hot, wet winds other times. There were eight to ten bad storms a year. The weather was very difficult for the people and often caused problems with the crops. If there was too much rain, the dams were washed away and the people suffered. Water was needed in Vietnam but the mosquitoes caused problems. He shook his head as he said, "Much dengue fever and malaria from all the mosquitoes are very bad."

Oh yes, the mosquito and Vietnam. Malaria had probably killed more people than all the wars. I had read where the soldiers sent south down the Ho Chi Minh Trail suffered as high as 20 percent deaths from malaria. It was a terrible problem in Vietnam, and every time I got bitten, which was often, I always thought about the very real danger of getting malaria and the slimmer chance of contracting dengue fever.

That bug was such a powerful factor in Vietnam's existence that Vietnam was the only country I knew of that had a folk tale about a mosquito. I thought about it as Bai talked.

A young, beautiful, and vain woman was married to a hardworking, loving husband. They lived a comfortable life, but the woman grew dissatisfied, so the husband worked harder in order to provide her with more luxuries. One day she died unexpectedly. The husband mourned her and did not bury her, but instead thought about how he could bring her back to life. He sold all his belongings except his boat. He put her body on board and then set off to search the waterways for the deity who held the elixir of life. He came to a high mountain next to a stream, tied his boat up at the bank, and climbed to the top, where he saw the deity. He dropped to his knees and begged for his wife to be brought to life again.

The deity said he could do that, but how did the man know if she would remain true to him? The man answered he did not care. The deity told the man to prick the end of his finger and let three drops of blood drip into his wife's mouth and she would come to life. However, if the wife should prove unfaithful, then she had to promise to return those three drops of blood.

The man agreed and returned to his sampan and, following the instructions, put three drops of his blood into her mouth, whereupon she came to life. Soon afterwards she ran off with a wealthy merchant. Her husband searched for her and after a year found her surrounded by luxury and asked her to return to his humble home. She refused.

The man remembered the instructions of the deity and told her he had brought her back to life by giving her three drops of his blood. Now that she was with another man, he wanted those three drops back.

The woman laughed and said, if that is all you want, I will give them back to you now. She pricked her finger, and as the first three drops struck the ground, she died. Her soul wandered until it was reincarnated as the first mosquito. Forevermore, whenever its descendants smell a human being, it steals some blood in the hopes of returning to human form.

When I asked Mr. Bai about this folk tale, he laughed and said that women and weather were both fickle and change rapidly.

Then I turned to Mr. Dong, the acting director of the Ministry of Health, who was always rather quiet but whose face was lined with pleasant wrinkles. Whenever I picture

264

him in my mind's eye, he is always wearing a light brown leather jacket. I think it was his proudest possession. It turned out that Mr. Dong had been a personal friend of Ho Chi Minh. We asked some questions about his friend, but all he would say was that Ho was a very great man, but also a good man.

The subject of Tet came up because it would be starting soon. Mr. Bai talked about the old days, in pre-revolution times, when the rich would take a whole month off to celebrate and the people would only get three days off. Nowadays, he smiled, everyone gets three days off. He explained that everyone went home: Tet is the time to visit parents and family. All the train stations and bus stations overflow with people heading home.

We talked about the things the Vietnamese did for pleasure, and one of those was reading. The men at the table all commented with pride on the almost total elimination of illiteracy. Virtually everyone in Vietnam had been taught to read. Books were always in demand, we were told. Dr. Bui Tung complained there were not enough English-language books available in Vietnam. There were Russian translations of English, he said, but they were not any good.

When I asked him what kind of writers the Vietnamese would want to read, he replied that he enjoyed Hemingway, O. Henry, Steinbeck, and all the other great American writers. I would have found this statement surprising and frankly, hard to believe, except for an extraordinary event that had happened when we went down to dinner that night.

When we first arrived on this trip, I had presented to members of their delegation copies of my two books, *The Killing Zone: My Life in the Vietnam War* and *Aftermath: A Soldier's Return from Vietnam*. Exchanging gifts was something we had always done, and our team felt my memoirs about the war would be an appropriate gift from me. The Vietnamese put a high value on books and writers, and the war was something we had in common.

They had all politely thanked us for our various gifts and

we thought that was the end of it. I believed they would probably put the books on their shelves without ever reading them. However, much to our surprise, when we had arrived downstairs for the pre-dinner cocktail, Dr. Bui Tung was full of questions about my books. He had read both of them completely and carefully.

They must have talked about it among themselves because Mr. Bai and the others were also curious about my answers. I was embarrassed when Bui Tung asked the meaning of the word "dink." "You use it many times but I do not know what it means. I cannot find it in here." He showed me his well-worn Vietnamese/English dictionary.

I had never even thought about the word "dink" when I was planning to give them the books. If I had been worried about anything, it was the scenes where I described killing enemy soldiers. I thought that would bother them if anything did. I looked right at him and replied, "Well, Dr. Bui Tung, it was a derogatory term we used to describe the enemy. You and your soldiers were called 'dinks' by us. Other terms were used by different American units to call the enemy. Names like 'gook.' Your soldiers probably had a derogatory term for Americans, didn't they?"

"Yes, now I understand what you mean by 'dink.' Our soldiers referred to Americans as 'dogs.'" In the Oriental lexicon, to be called a dog was the greatest insult.

Bui Tung had other questions for me that made me think twice. Never in my wildest dreams did I think I would be in Vietnam explaining to my former enemies what I had written about them. I was asked about the importance of a "body count." So I explained that our success was measured in the number of enemy bodies we could count after a fight. A question on my disparaging remarks about our South Vietnamese allies led me to explain that those were the true feelings my men and I had about the ARVNs.

There was one section in *The Killing Zone* in which I described a gunship killing four "dinks" in the open, and the Vietnamese were interested in exactly where that had happened. During the course of answering these questions I realized that I had not used the word "dink" to describe Vietnamese since my first trip in August 1987 to Hanoi. It had been an active part of my vocabulary from the war up to that time.

One of Dr. Bui Tung's questions was fun to answer.

"Tell me, Mr. Fred, what does it mean to have a 'lick on you'?" I explained that was an American slang expression we used to mean we were in trouble. "Sort of like now," I chuckled to myself. "It's a lick on me trying to answer these questions."

Sitting at the table after dinner, I asked Mr. Bai what he had done on the last day of the war. He stared off into the distance, the smoke drifting up from his cigarette, "I knew that morning when I got up that it would be the day. When I went into the office, I told everyone to expect good news. About midday we received word our army had captured the puppet palace and the puppet regime had surrendered. I told everyone in the office to go home. I had been keeping a bottle of wine in my desk drawer for years waiting for this moment. I took it out in celebration and went home to be with my family. It was a glorious day!" His face reflected the happiness of that moment twelve years ago.

In contrast, I thought of the moment when I heard on the radio that they had just received word that South Vietnam had surrendered unconditionally to North Vietnam. The war was over. I had been driving north on I-25, the Valley Highway in Denver, Colorado, when the announcement was made. I was astonished at the depth of sadness and loss I felt. The single thought that stayed with me, out of all the other terrible things that roared through my mind, was that my OCS roommate and friend, Bob Hutchinson, would probably be surfing at this moment if he had not been killed in Vietnam seven years before. Then the country-and-western radio announcer said: "In honor of the American men who lost their lives in Vietnam and to those men and women who served in Vietnam, this station will now play

'The Star-Spangled Banner.'" I had pulled off the road by this time and I cried unashamedly while our national anthem was played.

I remained quiet as that memory raced through my soul, but perhaps Mr. Bai read something in my face as I thought back on that day, for he reached for a bottle of beer and poured me a glass. "It is better the war is over," he said.

January 18, 1988

★ I was up bright and early to prepare for our departure. From the balcony I looked down on the park and watched the people exercising, playing badminton, or kicking balls around. I looked over at the magnificent French-colonial house in front of the guesthouse. I had been intrigued by it; it had been the residence of the French governor of Tonkin. The Vietnamese stormed the residence in 1945 during the August revolution and lost it when the French returned to reestablish colonial rule. Now the Vietnamese used it for state dinners and other formal functions.

Rain had fallen in the night and a strong wind and low clouds promised to bring more. I hoped it would not delay our flight out later in the morning. A monsoon was supposed to be coming in.

I leaned against the balcony and thought about what Carl, Larry, Bruce, and I had talked over last night after the dinner. We all agreed the Vietnamese were in desperate need of help. We had seen enough on these three trips to know they were honestly showing us the way it was. We were being equally honest in reporting it that way, but we were disappointed at the lack of help we were getting back home.

The Vietnamese were upset and worried that America was not responding quickly. They had told us they understood the difficulties we faced back home, but still they needed to show their people proof of progress, and there was nothing to show them. Meanwhile the Vietnamese claimed they had lived up to their end of the agreement.

The problem was, they were right; the response from our side *was* slow. There was a lot of resistance from some people to helping the Vietnamese, foot dragging by other people, sabotage, political infighting, an infinite number of critics, and just plain bureaucracy to overcome. The NGOs had responded slowly because they had already budgeted for the year when we had walked in unexpectedly and asked them for help. It was taking them time to come up with the money and to deal with the logistics of getting items to Vietnam.

Meanwhile, the Vietnamese were not getting anything on the ground but they had asked for us to return. There was an element of trust between the two delegations. We had shown America's good faith to the Vietnamese.

The one major responsibility we and the Vietnamese had, above all else, was to keep the lines of communication open and to continue to work on humanitarian issues in spite of the obstacles each side ran up against. So, judged within all the parameters in which we operated, we felt this had been a good trip. More importantly, we thought the Vietnamese felt that way, too. They considered the visit as a means to create a favorable climate between the two countries, which was very important.

But the nagging doubt we all had was that the thread between the two countries could easily break.

Fourth Trip to Vietnam
⋆ March 1988 ⋆

March 1, 1988—The Joint Casualty Resolution Center

⋆ I found it hard to believe but no sooner had we returned than I had to turn around and make a fourth trip back to Vietnam as part of the Vessey mission. I once read that according to a perverse law of international politics, hard-liners on opposing sides tend to reinforce each other's stubbornness and influence. This was nowhere more true than for the humanitarian mission between America and Vietnam.

If we had not made the fourth trip, the mission would have failed, which is what the hard-liners wanted. Although they were not the majority in either case, they did have powerful influence. And they were effective in manipulating the press and people by using misinformation, news leaks, and pressure. They tried desperately to stop our trips. What kept the Vessey mission from being killed off was the full backing by the National League of POW/MIA Families, Congress, and, of course, President Reagan. General Vessey was himself another powerful force for keeping the mission from faltering. All along he had felt a personal commitment to the families of the POWs and MIAs, and he was duty-bound to follow this through.

Even so, there were nasty attacks against individuals within the League, against the administration, and against the humanitarian team itself.

It was after the third trip that I became the most discouraged about my involvement in the Vessey mission. It was because of the intimidation tactics employed by those who had tried, and failed up to this point, to stop the mission. This period was definitely the low point of the mission for me. No matter how absurd or ridiculous the various charges were—that I'd been brainwashed by the Vietnamese Communists, for instance, or that I should be removed from my Veteran's Administration job—they hurt me. First, because some of them were coming from people I knew; second, in my naive way, I truly felt I had fought for the right to express my own opinion; third, I was doing this at the behest of my own government; and fourth, we had achieved some success: a number of MIA remains had been returned from Vietnam to America. The families of those men could now find peace.

I liked working for General Vessey. He was easy to talk to and always wanted to hear ideas or suggestions. He was a no-nonsense guy, and very supportive of us on the team. I felt I needed to talk to him now. I asked him what I should do. Was I hurting his mission? He told me to hang tough: he said I was working for him, and the critics didn't know what they were talking about. He shook his head at all the problems we had run up against and we both laughed. I felt very relieved.

And so we were called for our fourth trip. The agreement with the Vietnamese was that the humanitarian teams and the POW/MIA teams would meet every other month. If we did not show up, it would be perceived by the Vietnamese as bad faith on our part.

Another factor influencing the decision to make a fourth trip was that in spite of all our promises that "aid was on its way," nothing concrete had reached Vietnam. The presence of the Vessey team would help to allay any doubts the

Vietnamese may have been having about the promised aid. All of us on the team were extremely embarrassed and disappointed that things were going so slowly.

There were three of us on this trip. Larry Kerr from the State Department was the team leader; Bruce van Dam and I accompanied him. Carl Savory could not make it. Once again we endured the grueling flight and during our layover in Bangkok went to the embassy for meetings before going on into Hanoi.

I spent some time with Paul Mather and Bill Bell because by now I was beginning to piece together a lot that had been happening with them over the years and I wanted to find out about their involvement with the JCRC.

At various times in the past, they had come under heavy criticism by a few people for the way the American government conducted itself in trying to resolve the POW/MIA issue. The attacks on these men reminded me of the attacks on Vietnam vets when we returned to America. Many of the antiwar people who did not like what the government was doing in Vietnam had taken their wrath out on the veterans. Paul and Bill and other JCRC, DIA (Defense Intelligence Agency), and CILHI (U.S. Army Central Identification Laboratory Hawaii) members were in the same situation over this emotional issue. Some of those who did not like what the government was doing took their wrath out on these men. The unfortunate thing was that few Americans realized the dedicated work these people had put in on the issue since 1973. I certainly had known nothing about their work. It was important to understand because it answered a lot of the questions and put things into perspective.

The history and purpose of JCRC started on January 27, 1973, when the Paris Peace Accords were signed by the North Vietnamese, the South Vietnamese, the Viet Cong, and the United States. Article 8(b) included a specific provision dealing with the resolution of the fate of those from all sides who were still unaccounted for at the conclusion of hostilities.

It read: "The parties shall help each other to get information about those military personnel and foreign civilians of the parties missing in action, to determine the location and take care of the graves of the dead so as to facilitate the exhumation and repatriation of the remains, and to take any such measures as may be required to get information about those still considered missing in action."

A residual Four Party Joint Military Commission was formed for the purpose of carrying out Article 8(b). The two Communist parties (Viet Cong and NVA) made the two years until the end of the war in April 1975 a period of frustration, disappointment, and danger for the American and South Vietnamese parties.

The Communists had no intention of abiding by the Paris Accords, and this would include the carrying out of Article 8(b). Requests by the American and South Vietnamese members for information about specific cases of missing individuals were for the most part ignored by the North Vietnamese and Viet Cong members, or used as an excuse for polemics and diatribes.

Negotiations aside, though, the United States formed an operational element that was the first of its kind in military history. The Joint Casualty Resolution Center (JCRC) was established in Saigon on January 23, 1973, with General Robert C. Kingston, a former infantryman, as commander. The role of the JCRC was to carry out field searches, excavations, recoveries, and repatriation activities. Most of the personnel were search teams composed of Army Special Forces, who were the best trained and most effective in working on the ground, under dangerous conditions, and unarmed, as called for in the Peace Accords.

Because the Americans could only have so many military personnel in Vietnam due to the restrictions of the Paris Peace Accords, the headquarters of the JCRC was moved to Nakhon Phanom Air Base in Thailand.

Also located in Thailand was an important linkage necessary to the activities of the JCRC. In World War II Congress had made the Secretary of the Army responsible for returning the remains of servicemen killed in the war. This responsibility had been carried through to the present. Consequently, there had been two Army mortuaries in Vietnam that had identified all servicemen and women when processing their bodies during the war. When the U.S. forces withdrew from Vietnam, the two Army mortuaries were closed. The United States Army Central Identification Laboratory Thailand was then established in March 1973 at Camp Samae San, Thailand. Their responsibility was to examine and identify any remains recovered and repatriated in Southeast Asia.

The JCRC personnel were highly motivated and began their work with a great sense of purpose. Cases were reviewed and plans made up to search several likely sites where, evidence indicated, possible remains might be found. Of the approximately 1,700 MIAs in Vietnam, 1,084 had been lost in South Vietnam, so there was a lot of work that could be done.

However, the Communist delegates refused to allow any investigations on sites within Communist-controlled areas of South Vietnam, nor would they cooperate on site visits in South Vietnamese-controlled areas. The JCRC teams were on their own. They moved ahead with only the South Vietnamese to help them. Security at the site was of utmost importance, and so most site work was well within the areas controlled by the South Vietnamese government—or thought to be.

Once a site was identified and all parties, including the Communists, were notified, the JCRC teams went in. The teams included specialists such as crash-site investigators, grave registration experts, medics, explosive ordnance disposal technicians, and interpreters. The teams got into the site by walking, flying, driving, or in some cases of really rough terrain, rapelling in from a hovering helicopter.

The field teams were unarmed and, in compliance with the Peace Accords, traveled in helicopters marked with four broad orange stripes encircling the fuselage. Each team member was further identified by a bright orange armband and wore a uniform with bright orange pockets.

The work progressed in spite of the many obstacles facing them, especially the objections of the Communists.

On December 15, 1973, the third day of work at a crash site 20 kilometers southwest of Saigon, where seven years before a helicopter had crashed, the Viet Cong ambushed the team. They destroyed one helicopter and damaged two others, killed one defenseless American and one defenseless Vietnamese, and wounded four defenseless Americans and three South Vietnamese.

It was solid proof the Communists cared nothing about adhering to the Paris Accords, but there was proof enough of that throughout South Vietnam. The problem was, it did not make any difference. Even the killing of an unarmed team searching for bodies of Americans failed to receive more than a few lines in the American media. America was done with this war, and the North Vietnamese knew it.

But the JCRC continued to work until early 1975, when they were forced to stop because of the deteriorating conditions throughout South Vietnam caused by the advancing North Vietnamese Army. Their work had produced results, even under difficult conditions. They had recovered almost fifty remains, of which sixteen had been identified as Americans. But now they were assigned to help where they could as refugees poured into the cities and evacuation of personnel out of Vietnam began.

In the years after Vietnam fell, the JCRC avoided being disbanded, but it was severely cut in personnel and moved to Hawaii, along with the Army Central Identification Lab.

Meanwhile, during the first American congressional visits to Vietnam in December 1975, Vietnamese statements and actions sowed the first seeds of the suspicion and mistrust they would reap for years afterward.

First, they lied to the congressmen when asked if there were any Americans being held in Vietnam. Prime Minister

Pham Van Dong stated emphatically that all Americans had been returned to U.S. authorities in 1973. In fact an American citizen, Arlo Gay, a civilian, was a prisoner not 30 miles away from the congressmen. And although he was not a prisoner, U.S. Marine Robert Garwood was living in North Vietnam.

Then, the Vietnamese made it clear that they were linking progress on the MIA issue to U.S. economic assistance to help the Vietnamese "heal the wounds of war." They also specifically prohibited American involvement in the investigation of crash and grave sites, which was a blow to the hopes of personnel at JCRC and CILHI.

The Vietnamese exacerbated America's raw emotions from the war even more when they ghoulishly began to dole out a few remains over the years to various visiting groups or individuals. Many congressmen and citizens were deeply repulsed by this action.

Meanwhile the JCRC was not able to do field searches, but they did become deeply involved with interviewing the flood of refugees fleeing Vietnam. Vietnamese citizens, reeducation-camp inmates, and former Viet Cong could have information on crash and grave sites, and so leads emerged as a vast accumulation of evidence was developed and correlated. The Defense Intelligence Agency, the Central Intelligence Agency, the State Department, and the Justice Department also participated in interviewing the refugees.

In 1979 a series of events occurred that further soured the poor relations between America and Vietnam. When the deputy prime minister of China, Deng Xiaoping, was visiting in Washington, the Vietnamese Army was invading Cambodia and pushing the Chinese-backed Khmer Rouge out. Deng made threats from Washington that China would "teach a lesson to Vietnam." Within days of his return, China attacked North Vietnam.

Then, while China was in combat with the Vietnamese, the Chinese and Americans exchanged ambassadors and officially opened embassies in each other's countries. The Vietnamese saw this as U.S. hostility toward Vietnam.

In late 1979, an ethnic Chinese from Hanoi who had been expelled in a purge of Chinese residents claimed he had worked as a mortician for the Hanoi City Directorate of Cemeteries. He stated that in the conduct of his duties he had prepared or observed the remains of over four hundred American servicemen that had been warehoused in Hanoi. He was extensively questioned by American agencies and given a polygraph and other tests which gave conclusive proof he was who he said he was.

The Vietnamese denied they had stockpiled any remains; but they had already set the stage for Americans to disbelieve anything they said.

The JCRC held a few technical talks in Hanoi in the early 1980s, but nothing came of it as the Vietnamese continued to be obdurate on the subject.

President Reagan's election signaled the beginning of a new interest in solving the MIA issue. He initiated a series of bi-lateral contacts and diplomatic activities and sent a Deputy Assistant Secretary of Defense to Hanoi. He developed an Interagency Group to coordinate strategy within the government for dealing with the MIA issue.

Through all of this the JCRC continued to do the best it could. At every meeting with the Vietnamese Communists, rare as they were, the Americans concentrated on solving cases in the face of Vietnamese intransigence.

The Americans would provide a set of records with all the information on a case to the Vietnamese. The Vietnamese would then refuse to provide information from their records on any case, often saying they did not have any files. No one believed that, because the North Vietnamese had kept extensive files during the war. Field cadre had orders to send reports to Hanoi on all American crash sites, grave sites, and prisoners. Nor would they allow the Americans to go into the countryside to search for crash sites.

Neither statement was acceptable, but what could the

American side do? Nothing that already wasn't being done. Consequently what little progress was made in resolving cases was frustratingly slow. The Vietnamese were always sensitive to anything from the United States they perceived as "hostile" and would hold up cooperation at the drop of a hat.

The period from 1980 on had been difficult, but the meetings and cooperation had steadily improved, and the number of remains returned by the Vietnamese had significantly increased during the period since the Vessey mission started.

I was curious about the process involved when the Vietnamese handed over MIA remains. They were turning over twenty sets of MIA remains to America at Noi Bai Airport north of Hanoi the next day at about the same time we arrived on a commercial flight, and that made me wonder what the procedure was to transfer remains from a country we did not have formal relations with. Bill and Paul explained to me there was no set of procedures written down; they used the field manual for ceremonies and had modified it to fit the situation. This is how it would go:

The Vietnamese would send word through their embassy in Bangkok to our embassy in Bangkok that they were releasing remains. The Vietnamese would have each set of remains in a covered wooden box about 1½ feet wide and 3 feet long. They would be waiting in a hangar at Noi Bai Airport when the American C-141 arrived. The Vietnamese would present their documentation, paperwork, and any personal belongings, such as dogtags or ID card, they might have on the MIAs being returned. Aluminum caskets were unloaded from the C-141 and each wooden box, with the remains, was placed in one. A folded American flag was placed on each casket, then the honor guard loaded the caskets into the back of the C-141. The air crew and accompanying parties stood by the tailgate and saluted each set of remains as they were carried on board. The C-141 then flew back to Hawaii, where the remains were taken to the Central Identification Laboratory for an extensive evaluation. A set of remains could take, in some cases, six months or more to identify.

What the JCRC had been pushing for was to have the Vietnamese allow the Americans access to their records and to go into the countryside to search for actual crash sites. The evidence found at the crash site was important in helping to identify the aircraft and the crew: Serial numbers off the engines, weapons, and frame; whether the seat was still in the aircraft or the pilot/crew had ejected was all information useful to the JCRC team.

There were many crash sites the JCRC had a good fix on that they wanted to visit. On other sites where they only had an estimate of where the aircraft went down, they wanted to interview the villagers or cadre in the area to see if anyone knew about the crash in their area.

To do any of these activities, the Vietnamese government had to give its permission and support; and except in a couple of cases over the last fifteen years, this it had not yet done. If that ever occurred it would signal a breakthrough—the first time since the JCRC was formed in 1973.

There was an additional problem that the JCRC faced each day they were without access to the crash sites—Thai junk dealers. A friend of mine, a retired Air Force fighter pilot, told me U.S. aircraft losses in Southeast Asia from 1962 to 1973 totaled 8,588. That consisted of 4,868 helicopters and 3,720 fixed-wing aircraft. The majority had been found and recovered when possible, but there was plenty of aircraft wreckage spread across the landscape in Laos, Cambodia, and Vietnam that had not been recovered. The metal from these wrecks was worth a lot of money, and Thai junk dealers were paying top dollar for any wreckage brought to the Thai border. A thriving business had sprung up in the last couple of years as peasants began to sell pieces of wrecked aircraft, bomb casings, unexploded ordnance, and other scraps to roving dealers who drove around the countryside buying it and transporting it to the border.

One day one of the JCRC team, Bill Gadoury, was at a Laos border town where a ferry operated, when five flatbed trucks drove up loaded with pieces of wings, fuselages, and engines. Gadoury tried to get the authorities to stop the drivers, but they just shrugged their shoulders. As the trucks waited their turn to cross on the ferry into Thailand, Gadoury ran around copying down serial numbers from as many parts as he could, but that was all he was allowed to do.

Gadoury began to look through junkyards and found two data plates from a 105 that he was able to trace through the factory and get information about its assignment. As an aside, he said so many people were getting killed in the Thai junkyards while melting down the scrap that he was now seeing samples of live ordnance hanging from trees with signs warning workers to beware of this in the junk.

All of the JCRC team members I met were anxious to get into Laos, Cambodia, and Vietnam while there was still a chance of finding crash sites before junk dealers or the forces of nature had erased them completely.

As a foot soldier, I had a question for them; why did they concentrate on crash sites? What about the foot soldiers who were missing? Their answer was that aircraft crash sites got priority over soldiers just because the coordinates on lost soldiers were not that good, nor was there any machinery to mark the spot where they fell.

But in any case the best chance for success would be cooperation from the Vietnamese. They held the key.

Our talk concluded with the team saying that General Vessey's agreement with Foreign Minister Thach could be the best thing that had happened between the two countries, if it worked. Without General Vessey's agreement, there wouldn't be any cooperation at all between Vietnam and America.

Which was why the hard-liners wanted to kill it off.

We went downstairs to the embassy cafeteria and met up with Larry and Bruce. With Larry was a fellow State Department employee and friend, Harriet Isom, the chargé d'affaires in Vientiane, Laos. She was a tall, charming blonde who gave every appearance of being extremely professional in all facets of her job.

The American ambassador had left Laos in May 1975, but we had maintained a presence there through the chargé d'affaires, an official temporarily in charge of an embassy. She had been in the post for the last couple of years. Like most Americans, I did not know we had a mission in Laos since it had fallen to the Laotian Communists in December 1975.

After the takeover the Pathet Lao had removed the 650-year-old monarchy and installed a "people's council." They did not execute the royal family; they just let them starve to death. That way they could claim the family had not died at the hands of the Communists. The Pathet Lao Communist leaders ruled the country with an iron hand.

Harriet described Vientiane as a town where on a busy day at high noon a dog could sleep in the middle of the street without being disturbed. Neither she nor any of the American personnel, at the time, were allowed to go more than 6 kilometers from the edge of town. There were only twelve people in the American mission and only recently had couples been allowed to work in the mission.

I asked her if I could take pictures when we stopped over in Vientiane on the way out of Hanoi. She said no. The Lao Communists were very paranoid and suspicious about cameras. If they saw me taking pictures, one of the soldiers would rip my camera off me and throw it to the ground.

The Laotians were cooperating with America on the

POW/MIA issue at the same pace as the Vietnamese. There are 544 MIAs in Laos.

We took a Thai Airways flight into Hanoi. This was another new experience. Even though the Thais and Vietnamese are old adversaries, they had worked out an agreement a month or so earlier setting up Thai Air flights to Ho Chi Minh City. Thai Airways had already been flying to Hanoi for quite a few years. I found it odd that the Thais kept pressuring America to maintain its trade embargo against Vietnam while the Thais went ahead with their own business dealings with the Vietnamese.

March 3, 1988

★ During breakfast at the government guesthouse we were startled when a huge brown rat the size of a large cat came out of a crack in the wall between the dining room and the kitchen. It did not seem to be overly afraid of us as it explored along the wall toward the door leading to the kitchen. The son of a bitch caused the hairs on my neck to raise.

When the server brought us our breakfast of fried eggs, pâté, bread, pickles, and bananas, we pointed out the rat to her. She looked over at it and did not miss a beat. She just shrugged. Rats are a fact of life in Hanoi.

When the rat went back into the crack, I thought of the kitchen on the other side where our food was prepared. There was a Chinese saying that came to mind: "He who would enjoy his dinner must not look over the kitchen wall."

We met the delegation in the second-floor meeting room. We all knew each other quite well by this stage: Mr. Bai, Dr. Bui Tung, Mr. Vinh, Mr. Giang, and Mr. Nhu. Dr. Dong was unable to be with us at the meeting that day. None of us could know it at the time, least of all Dr. Dong, but Dr. Dong would not be making many more of these meetings.

Mr. Bai and Larry Kerr exchanged friendly opening comments and the meeting proceeded. Conversation revolved around the needs of particular rehabilitation centers and the relationship the nongovernmental organizations would have in working in Vietnam.

The Vietnamese were always asking questions to make sure the U.S. government was involved, and Kerr kept reassuring them that without the government's involvement in supporting the NGOs' actions to provide humanitarian assistance to Vietnam, there wouldn't be any help. Further proof of that, if proof was needed, was the official U.S. government team's presence on this fourth trip.

Bai and Kerr reminded each other of their respective governments' problems in addressing common humanitarian concerns within the limits of existing laws and policies and the feelings of the people.

At this point, Mr. Bai glanced at some sheets of paper, then put them aside to address us. "One of your congressmen made the statement in the press that Americans withdrew from Vietnam in 1973 but the war is still in their spirit. The war is still in the hearts and minds of both the Vietnamese and the American people. But lots of people in both countries recognize the suffering can be ended when two countries have friendly relations. And this is the main spirit of our policies.

"In the spirit of solving problems step by step, we have looked at a list of Vietnam's humanitarian concerns. We told General Vessey of these concerns: sixty thousand amputees, and three hundred thousand severely disabled from the war. But there are two other aspects of humanitarian issues we want to bring to your attention."

Bai had been doing all the talking while we listened. "The number of old people with no one to take care of them is large," he went on. "Our ways are not the same as other countries' in that we do not put them in old people's homes. The responsibilities are given to the authorities in the villages. It is the village chief's responsibility to put the old person with a family in the village. They become adopted into the family.

"In Vietnamese society, the son takes care of the parents when they become old. But the parents who lost their sons in the war and the widows who lost their husbands have no one to take care of them, and so this is the best way to care for them. Some assistance from the government is necessary so as not to put too heavy a burden on the family.

"The second point is vocational training for the handicapped children, orphans, and widows. Vietnamese policy is not to gather them into centers. All work is done at the village level. The problem is how to educate and provide them with training. We have done some of this, but there is much more to do."

Larry Kerr responded. "First some words from Mr. Schultz, our Secretary of State. 'Although Vietnam and the United States have some serious problems, they do not linger from the war.'

"At the same time," Larry went on, "war is not over until there is peace."

Bai interjected, "We would say, 'But not yet from enemy to friend.'"

Larry replied, "We know on both sides there are still people with old hatreds, but these past months and contacts between us have shown there is a great desire to help Vietnam. In looking at the two points raised by Mr. Bai, I will take these comments back to our government. But I will say the second one, vocational rehabilitation, is a U.S. strength best matched to your need."

The morning meeting was amiable, and both sides gleaned valuable information beyond the humanitarian issues. Each had confirmed that although there were obstructionists within each country to this effort, there were also many on both sides who believed it was a good thing and supported the effort to keep pushing forward.

At 1430 hours, we left the guesthouse for a short drive to the Olaf Palme Institute for the Protection of Children's Health, a showplace for the Vietnamese, their main pediatric hospital. It was an ambitious project built by the Swedes; it had not worked as well as they had hoped, but it was still the best the Vietnamese had.

We were taken upstairs to a library area and introduced to the dynamic director, Dr. Nguyen Thu Nhan. She was impressive, and showed professionalism and pride in the work her staff did. One of the first things I noticed about the room she gave us the briefing in was that it had a picture of the Swedish president Olaf Palme on the wall instead of the ubiquitous Ho Chi Minh.

She seemed to be full of energy and ideas, and believed in getting things done with whatever was available. She reminded me of the director at the Haiphong Rehabilitation Center, Mr. Bang, who also was a dedicated professional and ran an active program in spite of the shortages and bureaucratic obstacles.

As that center had done, this hospital had used available materials to make educational plans. Along the walls were hand-drawn and printed posters showing how mothers should breast-feed their babies. There were drawings of nutritional charts showing food groups, with information on prevention of diseases written in columns next to the food groups. They had made simple manuals explaining techniques in physical therapy.

Dr. Nhan had developed an educational program to teach mothers how best to feed and care for their children. With the help of the World Health Organization, using minimal resources, they had produced thousands of small plastic spoons with a big scoop on one end and a small scoop on the other end. Printed instructions tell the mother that if her child has diarrhea, she is to fill the small spoon with salt, the big spoon with sugar, and put them into a cup of boiling water. After it cools, she is to feed it to the child. Dr. Nhan only had enough resources to produce five thousand spoons a year and was unable to send this simple device to the millions of mothers in the country.

Twenty percent of infant and young children's deaths are attributable to diarrheal diseases because mothers in Vietnam still tend to reduce intake of solid foods during these episodes. Consequently the child loses the delicate balance of electrolytes and salts, and the kidneys stop working. It is hard to implement new ideas since the traditional method of treating diarrhea is to not give the child water or food, and of course this makes it worse. Another folk medicine remedy is to feed crushed dried grasshoppers to the patient —equally useless.

We were given lab coats to wear and then taken on an extensive tour of the hospital. As with everything else we had seen connected with health care in North Vietnam, the staff worked within severe limitations of medical supplies and inadequate medical equipment. They were swimming against the tide in an effort to cope with the endless number of childhood medical problems that plague the country.

There was no heat in the hospital. Hospital staff, patients, and families dressed warmly in coats and scarves. Children waited with their mothers in the halls. When we went into the rooms, Bruce asked the hospital staff what the mothers used for diapers at home. They replied that the mothers did not use diapers at home.

Mothers lay in the beds and held their babies, wrapped in colored blankets they had woven. Tiny caps made of colored cloth covered the babies' heads. The mothers had made those also.

Out in the hall bright mobiles hung from the ceilings. This was a Western touch added by the Swedish staff, who stayed hidden while we were there. We climbed to the seventh floor—there were no elevators—to visit the rooms. The

view out the window overlooking the city was worth the
climb.

As I stood beside one bed where a severely crippled child
lay with its mother, I thought about how seeing so many sick
and crippled babies and children numbed the senses. In a
way it was like combat. After a while you just got hardened
to what you were seeing. You had to if you were going to be
effective. This child was lucky. Some Vietnamese families
abandon disabled babies by giving them to orphanages. This
mother was trying to do the best she could in spite of the
bleak future for both the family and the child.

With the sad state of medical facilities and procedures in
Vietnam, the survival chances of a badly wounded flier who
fell into Vietnamese hands would have been practically nil.
There are some Americans who claim Vietnam is still
holding live prisoners. Their argument is that since none of
those who were badly wounded have yet been repatriated,
Vietnam must still be holding them. From what we had
seen, anyone badly wounded would most certainly have
died because of the poor medical situation.

With this fourth visit, and with later visits, plus information from the United Nations and the Centers for Disease
Control in Atlanta, the Vessey team learned the extent of
many disease-related problems of children and mothers.

Learning the facts, and seeing the children, stunned one.
But if we were going to help them, we had to understand the
problem, and that meant getting as many facts as we could.
Children's disabilities presented a grim picture. According
to UNICEF, there are over 25 million children under the
age of fifteen years old in Vietnam. That is 39 percent of the
total population—all born after the war with America was
over.

In this population there are approximately 70 deaths per
1,000, with the majority occurring in the first year of life.
Many women lose their babies because of tetanus and other
infections contracted at birth.

About 20 percent of the mortality among women in the

15-to-44-year-old age group is due to pregnancy or child-birth complications. Studies show that the maternal death rate may be as high as 500 deaths per 100,000 live births. The women are malnourished, work hard, and have multiple pregnancies, all of which weakens them and makes them more vulnerable.

The hard fact of life in Asia is that women have never been equal to men. There is a Vietnamese saying: "If you give birth to a boy, you have one child. If you give birth to ten girls, you have zero children."

Major causes of death among infants and children in Vietnam are malaria, diarrhea diseases, acute respiratory illness, measles, dengue fever and other forms of viral encephalitis, pertussis, viral hepatitis, and poliomyelitis. In most cases of child death, malnutrition is an aggravating factor.

Another paradox of Vietnam was that in the midst of this dismal environment, the health professionals we met at all the facilities we visited had received a good education and were familiar with recent advances in medicine in developed countries. Their frustration in not having the equipment, facilities, and money to face the substantial challenges presented to them was very evident by their comments and the evidence at hand.

What was exciting for our team members was the realization that the health-care problems in Vietnam were solvable with material resources. Vietnam itself had prepared the most important key to solving the problem by having motivated, adequately trained health-care professionals—who worked within a fully structured dedicated medical system, organized throughout the country from the national level down to the village level—already in place. The hardest part of solving any health-care problem in a Third World country is the decades-long process of training people and developing infrastructures from top to bottom.

The Vessey team recognized that the Vietnamese would benefit immediately from any resources they received. However, we were faced with the difficulty caused by the inefficient Vietnamese Communist system, which the Vietnamese themselves freely admitted "caused problems." The bureaucracy was bad enough, but the fact that there were no government resources to provide to the health-care facilities meant that each facility was basically on its own. The magnitude of the effort needed to solve even a part of all these problems was enough to depress anyone.

At dinner that night Mr. Bai was in an expansive mood. He was talking about the differences between war leaders and peace leaders. He said those who were highly respected during the war were not always the best leaders after the war. In fact, during the war no one dared to question them because they were so powerful. In war there was a strict line beyond which no criticism of the government could be tolerated. But in peace the line was not so clear.

Mr. Bai went on to explain. "At first there were many mistakes made after the war as some people tried to change everything very quickly. But the war had gone on for forty years and very few leaders knew how to deal with economics.

"And no one could speak out because everyone thought the same as they did in the war, which meant you could not criticize the leaders. That did not work. Russians and East Germans came in to teach the people at the grass-roots level how to do things differently, but they did not think about the reality of the people who had to continue living in those villages.

"Finally, in 1985 the thinking began to change as people were allowed to openly criticize the government and the bureaucrats. The people knew who was corrupt. The newspapers became the people's voice in criticizing and exposing the corrupt and the incompetent."

Bill Bell had told me on earlier trips that the papers he bought in Hanoi had editorials criticizing the government and people, so what Bai was telling us was true.

"Another problem was reconciliation after the war," Bai continued. "So many families were on different sides of the revolution that family and friends and neighbors were split. A neighbor who killed a man's son during the war, regardless of which side the other was on, could not have blood revenge taken out on him by the son's family. So there was a lot of work to be done in reconciling the differences between the two sides. Many people in the world predicted a bloodbath, but that did not happen."

Mr. Bai then gave an example of corruption. "A man goes into his local restaurant and spends twenty to thirty thousand dong every day. That restaurant owner knows the man does not make that kind of money legally. Therefore he must be doing something against the law. In the old days the restaurant owner could do nothing to criticize a more powerful man because it would look as if he were criticizing the war effort. Now the restaurant owner can write to the newspaper and expose the man."

All of this was an insight into the Communist way of doing things, but I wondered what happened if the man were innocent.

Dr. Bui Tung asked me some more questions about the meaning of terms and slang words I used in my books *The Killing Zone* and *Aftermath*. He wanted to know where we got the word "dustoff." I explained it was the term we used for the medical helicopter that we called in on the radio to carry away the wounded. I told him I thought it came about because the helicopter was "cleaning up" the battlefield by "dusting it off."

Larry Kerr, who had had two tours in Vietnam and spent eleven years in the Army, said the word "dustoff" was used because the first hospital helicopters in Vietnam used the code word "dustoff" on the radio simply because it was the next word in the codebook. After a while "dustoff" was used on the radio all the time, in the hopes the Viet Cong and North Vietnamese listening in on our radio frequency would recognize that the word indicated the helicopter coming in was a hospital ship and would not shoot it down. No one at the table mentioned the fact it did not work. The dustoffs were under fire as soon as they arrived on the battlefield.

The conversation turned to slang usage in all societies. Dr. Bui Tung and Mr. Bai lamented the shifting values of the younger generation and their lack of respect for their elders. Dr. Bui Tung, in obvious embarrassment at having to say what he was going to say, leaned across the table and told us one slang term which many younger Vietnamese were using was translated as "Fuck your mother." We were amused that so dignified a man as Bui Tung would use such language and that an American slang term was used in North Vietnam, although we wished the younger generation had picked a less offensive phrase. I wondered where they would have picked up that particular slang. "You motherfucker" was something we constantly used during the war, but American soldiers had not been around for fifteen years.

"No!" we chorused. "They really use such an expression?"

"Yes! They do, even in their own homes!" Both Bai and Tung grimaced and shook their heads at the effrontery of youth.

March 4, 1988

★ On previous visits we had asked to visit spinal-cord-injured patients because these are complicated disabilities, and we were interested in seeing how Vietnam handled these complex cases. We particularly wanted to see how they dealt with urinary-tract infections, bed sores, bowel evacuation, mobility, and independence.

From what we had already learned of the medical treatment and the infectious conditions in Vietnam, we knew we would see only a few old injuries from the war with America; the other patients would have died by now. The average life span for a spinal-cord-injured (SCI) patient in a Third World country was approximately five years. Most of them died of complications resulting from urinary-tract infections or diseases. Most of the SCI patients alive today would be soldiers recently injured in the present war in Cambodia and those injured in the skirmishes along the China border.

Mr. Bai had always politely rejected our request to visit SCI patients by saying, "It is not good. There are hard feelings from these men from the war. They would be upset to see you."

We believed these men could very well harbor hard feelings toward us. We had seen it many times among our own patients. Hatred and bitterness, among other emotions, were common feelings for those who were traumatically disabled. The feelings were part of the stages one goes through. Some patients got through them quickly, some took more time, and a few never got over their bitterness and hatred. There were psychological problems associated with any traumatic disability, but the SCI as a group had the most problems in learning to accept and cope with their injury because it was one of the worst to receive. Spinal-cord injury struck to one's core as a human being because it affected the most personal of bodily functions: sex and waste elimination.

There are basically two categories: paraplegics, who have lost function from the waist down; and quadriplegics, who have lost function from the neck down. Rehabilitation, access to prosthetic appliances, and employment of the handicapped are among the greatest challenges the disabled are facing in American society today. As rich as this country is, the problems are difficult. In Vietnam, where the per capita income is $150 a year, the problems are nearly insurmountable. What one must have when working with these problems of the disabled in Third World countries is the long view. A small step taken today starts a path toward the future.

We were told we would be driven out to where the spinal-cord-injured live in a village that had been built especially for them. The name of the village was Thuan Thanh. The last part of the 40-kilometer trip was over an extremely rough road. The government cannot keep the primary roads maintained and they must not even try to repair the side roads.

The trip through the Vietnamese countryside was something I never tired of. People were working everywhere: in the fields, along the road, hoeing, chopping wood, fishing, herding ducks, planting, making bricks, herding buffalo and cows.

The villages we drove by on these back roads always reminded me of the war. Villages had always meant Vietnam to me. During the war, my platoon and I lived next to villages and patrolled through them. In contested territory I had burned villages as part of search-and-destroy operations, searched through the "hootches" looking for contraband, made prisoners of anyone in the villages I suspected of being a bad guy, destroyed the stored rice we found if we thought it was being used to support the enemy. There were times we had fired into the villages because the enemy was there among the people. All of these actions were part of our job and we were rewarded for doing it well.

In fact, in those days I never thought of the villages as anything other than a cluster of meaningless primitive mud and straw huts. I knew people lived in the "hootches," but I never thought of them as homes. I never thought of myself as destroying someone's home.

I did not realize or care that the villages were the history, the guts, and the backbone of Vietnam. Evidently neither the President of the United States nor the Pentagon thought or cared much about it either. When America thought it was doing a good thing by removing the people from the villages in South Vietnam and setting them up in "secure areas," it was actually ripping asunder the thousand-year-old social fabric of the Vietnamese people. Removing the people from their homes in order to save the countryside was like what doctors used to do when they bled patients to get rid of disease: it took the lifeblood right out of them.

And to think the South Vietnamese government allowed such a thing to happen to its own people. I read that many of the former South Vietnamese officials blamed America for what happened to their country. But to my way of thinking they had allowed it to happen. Americans may not have known the cultural traditions of Vietnam, but the South Vietnamese government officials certainly did. Maybe they had gotten too far removed from the rural people to understand them anymore. They bought into the American way without protecting the Vietnamese way.

We slowed for a water buffalo standing in the road outside a village. I studied the village. It looked just like they always did. The difference was I understood a little more about what I was looking at.

The Vietnamese word for village is *lang*. The *lang* is where the roots of every Vietnamese are found. No matter where they go during their lives, they return during Tet, if possible, to visit their parents and relatives and the tombs of their ancestors. They use this time to introduce the children to their relatives.

There is an old Vietnamese saying that "The Emperor's rule stops at the village gate." The village society is a tight-knit group of families, where everyone knows each other and nothing can be done without common approval.

Around the village is a hedge of bamboo. The core of the village is the *dinh*. This is the hearthstone of Vietnamese culture, a communal house where all important meetings and ceremonies are held. The village elders and leaders meet there to discuss business and other matters affecting the village. Traditionally, the *dinh* is where the local heroes and deified souls of the dead are worshipped.

The *dinh* is carved with dragons and is the center of the traditions of the village. On New Year's Day, the most respected elder in the village opens the gates and digs the first hole in the ground while saying prayers to ask for blessings on the village for a successful year. During the year the *dinh* is the place for solemn and festive occasions: wrestling, swinging on ropes, chess games, fireworks, releasing birds, tugs-of-war, plays, dances, and other entertainments.

Traditionally, the parents of children reaching maturity give bricks to the village elders to be used for paving, or building wells, or other village needs.

Even the homes are traditional. They are composed of three sections and two lean-tos. The middle section is used for worshipping dead relatives. Joss sticks are burned on special days.

I thought a lot about all the homes we destroyed and the villages we burned. I was not going to shoulder the burden of America's or Vietnam's decisions in the war. It was history now; history is full of wars and the terrible and noble events that go along with them.

On the edge of the narrow wooded lane we were driving down, we saw the first SCI patient. He was sitting in a heavy three-wheeled chair looking out over the vast rice paddies through a break in the foliage. The chair was a type we had seen before: a triangular platform with two wheels in the rear and one wheel in front. When we passed by, he turned toward us with an expression one could assume the damned would have.

At the edge of the village the road became cement. It stayed cement through the village, then at the other edge became dirt again. There were a couple of dozen men in Vietnamese wheelchairs within the confines of the village. Dozens of children were running around as well.

We pulled into another narrow lane and stopped. Two

men came out from a one-room building to greet us. They were the director and his assistant, who were responsible for the SCI center at Thuan Thanh. The director's office was a tiny cramped space with a small table and a few chairs. The directors of these centers were assigned to their jobs by the ministry, and we thought this director must have angered someone at the top to receive his assignment.

After greeting us and ushering us into a room with a table holding coffee, fruit, and nuts, they gave a briefing on the center. It was built in 1965 especially for the spinal-cord-injured returning from the war. They pointed out that the paths within the village were cement to make it easier for the patients to move about.

When we asked them why it had been built so far out in the country, they replied that it was to keep the patients away from the populated areas because of the danger of bombings. But why were they still out here? Many of the spinal-cord-injured lived here permanently. These patients were warehoused in this one location. This is not unique to the Vietnamese; it is a practice in many countries. The families cannot take care of them and often do not want to.

In America, veterans who were spinal-cord-injured were kept in VA hospitals until the 1970s. At that time a movement started to push these patients out of the hospitals and into the community. Some of them had lived in VA hospitals since World War II and they fought to stay there. The spinal-cord-injured population who lived outside the hospital supported the idea of being outside because they knew how important it was to get back in the mainstream. The hospital is a protective cocoon against the outside world, which can be a scary place for someone who is paralyzed. Now the SCI have all kinds of opportunities that simply did not exist ten years ago. But in a Third World country it might as well have been pre-World War II.

The director informed us that the mission here at the center was in four areas: to provide vocational training, entertainment, nutrition, and medicine. The director's frustration came out as he listed the shortages and problems he faced. His was a difficult task. There were about two hundred permanent patients who lived in this village.

We were told that a big problem was the lack of parts, equipment, and raw material to train the men in repairing radios, the only rehabilitation activity available to them. In some centers the patients could open a shop to sell handicrafts, but here they did not have the wherewithal to repair or sell anything. The veterans here had many psychological problems, the director told us. His assistant mournfully nodded his head in agreement.

He told us that he had been trying to get paper and pencils so the men would have something to do. They could write or draw or make things out of paper to sell. If they could do that, they might be able to use the money to buy other things. But he seemed the most upset at his inability to provide the vitamins the men needed to supplement their diet.

We were taken on a tour. The village was small, with only twenty-five or thirty homes spaced around a U-shaped courtyard. Across the top of the U was a long shedlike building divided into stable-sized rooms. This building looked as if it had been constructed later than the rest of the village. When we walked past the open front doors, we could see the living quarters arranged in shotgun fashion through to the rear of the shed.

On both sides of the U were long buildings divided into living quarters that looked more like complete units. A cement path connected the U to each doorway so that the wheelchairs could move freely to any structure in the village.

We were following the path and were surrounded by children, who were excited at the strange visitors. Their excitement was counter-balanced by the dozens of men who watched us warily as they sat in their chairs scattered in spots around the courtyard. Although some of the men seemed interested in us, most of them projected an aura of indifference, and a few radiated hostility. Three or four moved their rusty, worn wheelchairs together to watch us balefully as they murmured to each other. I could not hear them but I knew what they were saying. We represented the enemy that had put them in this hell hole.

Larry and Bruce were sensitive to these men's feelings and did not want to take pictures or do anything that would cause embarrassment or mental anguish. They were uncomfortable with these disabled men. I was not uncomfortable. I was handicapped, so I understood it. There was nothing we could do to make the SCI feel any better or worse about themselves or us. The thing that would help them the most was for us to look around, take pictures and notes, and generally do those obnoxious things visitors do when they visit facilities for the handicapped. So I kept snapping pictures.

At the base of the U was the communal building used for meetings and entertainment. This would be the modern equivalent of the traditional *dinh*. We went inside and could tell immediately this was not a happy place. The TV was a dusty shell. The library did not have any books. The walls were cracked and featureless. This place was depressing.

As I walked out of the building past a group of men in chairs and down the cement slab toward the van, I thought about how little it would take to supply this village with one TV set, a VCR, a regular supply of films, radios for everyone, a steady supply of medicines and vitamins, a regular supply of books in Vietnamese, paper, pens, paints, a supply of parts and tools, vocational rehabilitation programs and the equipment to back it up . . . the list goes on. I thought about how easy it would be to equip a van with hand controls and give it to the villagers for their use.

These things were doable. Some were easier than others, but all were within the grasp of any American who wanted to do it. Yet I knew these men were doomed to spend the rest of their lives here dying of boredom and neglect.

Before we left the village, the director gave one more pitch for raw material. Paper and pens and cardboard boxes could be used by the men to make drawings and handicrafts to sell, he reminded us. Anything would be helpful; they would turn nothing down. He made another plea for vitamins and medicines.

We promised we would write it up in our report.

I for one was glad when we drove away. It had been a solid reminder that hell on earth can be worse than anyone can imagine. I thanked God that I had not been wounded worse than I was. Losing an arm was nothing compared to what could have happened to me.

There are times in one's life when one is thankful for an experience that shows him how fortunate he is. I thanked God I was in the service of America when I became disabled. My rich country fulfilled its duty to its disabled veterans to take care of them. The sign outside the entrance of the Veterans Administration where I work in Washington, D.C., has an 1865 quote from Abraham Lincoln which is the VA motto: "To care for him who shall have borne the battle, and for his widow and his orphan."

I looked at my artificial arm and felt lucky that America lived up to its responsibilities.

By the conclusion of the last meeting of the fourth trip, both delegations were working together very well. We more easily worked out problems and cleared up misunderstandings caused by translations; we were comfortable in freely discussing our political limitations and how we could best accomplish something within those perimeters; and our side felt confident with the accumulated facts on the medical situation. We agreed to expand humanitarian efforts into wider initiatives involving children, disabilities, and orphans.

Each delegation trusted that the other was doing the best it could under the circumstances. We made allowances for the reality that all of us were point men and that the governing decisions were made above us in the chain of command.

Mr. Bai's last comment was that they wanted General Vessey to know that Mr. Thach hoped the new year resulted in progression of our common interests. With that in mind, we left Vietnam.

Interlude: South Vietnam's Sacrifice

★ Ever since the war, I had hated the North Vietnamese and despised the South Vietnamese. During the four trips to Vietnam, my feelings about the North Vietnamese had changed, but of perhaps more significance to me personally was the recognition within myself of the sacrifice made by the South Vietnamese. My negative feelings toward them had also changed.

For years, America's mind had been focused on the North Vietnamese. But, as I had learned, the South Vietnamese deserved serious consideration as well. The strange thing for me was that it had taken my involvement with the North Vietnamese for me to realize it. The bulk of the fighting took place in South Vietnam, but Americans did not seem to grasp what that meant. I know for years I had not really thought about it.

There were probably fewer wounded former NVA in the North than there were wounded former ARVNs in the South. The American "dustoffs" had gotten the ARVNs to medical care quickly and then provided them with better medical treatment while they were healing. The result was that a larger percentage of ARVN wounded survived than did the enemy wounded.

I had always focused on the destruction of the North Vietnamese Army and the Viet Cong, and, strangely enough, never really associated that with the destruction of the South, the country we were trying to protect. As Vietnam came back into my consciousness, I would often reflect on the reasons for my long indifference to South Vietnam's plight.

North Vietnam's transportation systems and industry were hit hard but selectively by airpower during the war. However, the length and breadth of South Vietnam was the arena in which the war was fought for fifteen years. We fought on the ground in South Vietnam, and there is no worse kind of war than an infantry war.

The consequences of that ground war were staggering. To make it comprehensible to myself, I imagined what it would have been like if I had lived in a war zone from August 4, 1964, to April 30, 1975. I imagined myself on my farm (Vietnam's population was 80 percent farmers) with a war going on around me as I tried to work the land and raise a family. We were terrorized by the Communists at night. Our government failed to protect us. Our ally did not understand our customs or culture, had little respect for us as individuals (all Hoosiers look the same), and could not speak our language. But they patrolled our farms and towns, entering any dwelling at will to search and, at any provocation, unleashed the greatest military firepower in the world.

In thinking about the incredible difficulties the South Vietnamese endured in those years, I gained a great deal more respect for them. Millions of artillery shells were fired into the earth of South Vietnam. Millions of bombs, rockets, and bullets were fired. Millions of land mines were sown. Thousands of aircraft crashed in the South. Thousands of villages were uprooted and the villagers moved into resettlement camps: over 4 million South Vietnamese became refugees within their own country, and hundreds of thousands of acres of farmland were forced to lie fallow.

The economy was totally disrupted. There were 1 million South Vietnamese killed, hundreds of thousands wounded, tens of thousands of children left as orphans.

When South Vietnam fell, over 130,000 South Vietnamese escaped, but hundreds of thousands were trapped in the country. Approximately 13,000 Amerasian children were abandoned. All 1 million-plus members of the Republic of Vietnam's armed forces were thrown out of their jobs. Most of the ARVNs plus the former government employees were put into "reeducation camps," a euphemism for hard labor camps where the prisoners were brainwashed and deaths were common. The South Vietnamese people were subjected to an intense remaking of their society into a Marxist state where those who did not conform were ostracized, jailed, or disappeared. The Communists set up rigid controls over the society by establishing people's committees and police and security forces to monitor what each individual did. Arrests and jailings were common.

Although for some years after the war it was reported by many different sources there had been no bloodbath after the Communists took over, later evidence indicates that perhaps thousands of killings did take place. Getting even had a lot to do with it.

In the years afterward over a million boat people left Vietnam, some with the "help" of the Communist government, who exploited them in the process by demanding money from the families to allow them to leave.

The magnitude of the devastation of South Vietnam has never quite been grasped by most Americans. These people whom we helped for fifteen years by contributing billions of our dollars, our lives, and our national prestige were utterly on their own when we left. And when they were defeated, there was nothing much we could do about it.

We have dealt with "Vietnam" as an enemy country ever since. But a paradox exists because half the country was our ally and friend. America has a dilemma Solomon would have difficulty solving: By treating Vietnam as an enemy, we punish the half that was our friend; by treating Vietnam as a friend, we reward the half that was our enemy.

Back Home

★ Through the spring and summer of 1988, General Vessey sent two more teams composed of medical doctors who specialized in child care to Vietnam. The NGOs were starting to get geared up for their involvement and were contacting the State Department, indicating their interest in acquiring licensing so they could begin helping Vietnam.

The Vietnamese, for their part, had increased the rate of return of suspected MIA remains; they had also continued with the reestablishment of the Orderly Departure Program by which Vietnamese could legally leave Vietnam; with the processing of Amerasian children; and with releasing seven thousand reeducation-camp detainees.

The National League of Families of American Prisoners of War and Missing in Action in Southeast Asia continued their strong support of the Vessey mission and the President's policy on the POW/MIA issue.

Although both sides, the Americans and the Vietnamese, thought the other side should move faster, and despite the occasional glitches, all in all the humanitarian issue was proving to be successful and beneficial to both sides. So much so that in the latter part of November 1988, Dr. Bui Tung from the Vietnamese Delegation was invited to America for a visit.

Dr. Bui Tung Visits America
★ December 1988 ★

November 28, 1988—Bui Tung in Washington, D.C.

★ In March 1988, during our fourth trip, Dr. Bruce van Dam had invited Dr. Bui Tung to visit the United States in order to attend the annual meeting of the Society of Military Orthopedic Surgeons at Williamsburg, Virginia, in December of that year. The chairman of the society wanted Dr. Tung to present a paper to the members, many of whom had been military surgeons in Vietnam during the war.

The Vietnamese government had notified the U.S. government that it accepted the offer. In addition to the invitation from the military surgeons' organization, another group of NGOs invited Dr. Bui Tung and Nguyen Dinh Ngo, vice chairman of Binh Tri Thien Province, to a meeting in Boston.

Binh Tri Thien Province symbolized the reunification of North and South Vietnam into one country. It was a new province formed by merging three provinces that used to be separated by the old DMZ. The northern province, Quang Binh, was merged with the two southern provinces, Quang Tri and Thua Thien, to form Binh Tri Thien.

The meeting in Boston was being hosted by a number of NGOs that were working on providing rehabilitative assistance to Vietnam. Their meeting would be in mid-November 1988, a few weeks before the military surgeons' meeting in Williamsburg. This was fine with the Vessey team and the Interagency Group. It added to the importance of the trip.

On a more practical level, Bui Tung and his traveling companions did not have a dime to travel on. The Vietnamese government would not pay for anything. This was a people-to-people invitation. Therefore both the Boston and Williamsburg NGOs were footing the bills for their respective shares of the trip.

After the Boston meeting in November, Bui Tung was to fly on to New York, and then on to Washington by himself where he would meet with Bruce and me. During the free time before and after the Williamsburg meeting, Bui Tung would stay in Washington with either Bruce or me in order to help stretch out the dollars. Bruce would take him for a week and I would take him for a week.

This would be among one of the first visits to mainland America of North Vietnamese officials who would be allowed to travel outside New York City. There were Vietnamese who worked at the mission at the United Nations; Vietnam had been allowed to join the UN by a vote of the members in 1979. (In an attempt to improve relations, America had abstained from vetoing.) However, due to Vietnam's status as an unfriendly country, the Vietnamese in the mission were not allowed outside of a 25-mile radius of New York City.

In the case of Bui Tung, the State Department would provide the visas to allow him to travel anywhere he wished in the United States.

On November 22, 1988, Bruce called me to say Dr. Tung had arrived safely from New York. He said his presentation to the group in Boston had gone fine. Bruce had picked him up at the airport and had taken him to a hotel on Connecticut Avenue where he would stay first. The hotel was close by Bruce's home in northwest Washington. Dr. Tung would stay through Thanksgiving with Bruce, and I would pick him up on Tuesday morning, November 28. I would be responsible for him until Sunday, December 3.

On Monday night, the 27th, Bruce called to say Dr. Tung would be waiting for me in the morning. I asked Bruce how it had gone and he replied that it was like having an uncle visiting. Bruce said his two kids liked him, he had had Thanksgiving dinner with Bruce's family and friends, and he had attended church with Bruce and his family.

Bruce told me a story to give me an idea what Bui Tung was like. He said, "Remember when you were a kid, your mom always warned you to eat everything on your plate because if you didn't some little Chinese kid would starve?" When I said yes, I remembered Mom saying that many times, Bruce related how this had caused a funny thing to happen at the supper table during Bui Tung's visit. One evening when they were all gathered around the table, Bruce's little girl Debra was not eating her food. Bruce looked at her and said, "You know, Debra, there are children in Vietnam who would be happy to have that food to eat."

Bruce then turned to his guest and said, "Isn't that right, Dr. Bui Tung?"

Tung, with a twinkle in his eye, solemnly looked at the little girl and said, "That's right, Debra."

Bruce chuckled at the memory. "How often do you get a Third World person sitting next to your kid to verify that statement?"

I had been pleased by the story. But as I prepared for bed, my mind churned with thoughts of what all this meant. Imagine, I would be responsible for escorting a North Vietnamese Communist around Washington for a week! The State Department and Department of Defense had told both Bruce and me there were no limitations on what we did with Dr. Bui Tung—just show him America. Considering the circumstances of my twenty-year involvement with Vietnam, this experience was beyond my wildest dreams.

The next morning, after calling Dr. Tung from the lobby phone, I sipped a cup of coffee and thought how this lobby compared to our government guesthouse accommodations in Hanoi. I wondered what Dr. Tung thought about all he was seeing in America.

He was dressed in brown trousers and a tweed sports coat, white shirt, and tie. It was the same way he would have dressed for work in Hanoi. Although the temperature was hovering near freezing, he wore only a thin unlined raincoat to protect him from the cold.

We got into the car and drove to the Hill for a meeting with Congressman Sonny Montgomery. The congressman had made a number of trips to Hanoi in regard to MIA concerns and had an abiding interest in the issue. In the 1970s he had led two delegations to Hanoi, at the request of the President, to discuss POW/MIA issues with the leadership. Those efforts had led to controversy in the United States when the American Delegation reported to the President there were no live American prisoners left in Vietnam. There were a number of family members of MIAs and others who did not believe the delegation and claimed the American government was trying to wash its hands of the MIAs by writing them off.

Although Congressman Montgomery had been burned by the storm of protest that had arisen at the time, he was still very supportive of the Vessey mission almost ten years later. Congressman Montgomery and I knew each other because of his position as Chairman of the House Veterans Affairs Committee and my position in the Veterans Administration. When I was chosen for the Vessey mission, the congressman took more than a passing interest in its activities.

As we walked the vast marbled-floor halls of the Longworth House Office Building looking for Mr. Montgomery's office, Tung peered with interest into the open doors we passed. This was probably the very first time a North Vietnamese had wandered the halls of Congress.

We talked about the American system of electing senators and representatives.

When we reached the congressman's office, we were welcomed by him and made comfortable. We spent an hour talking with Mr. Montgomery about the humanitarian missions to Vietnam. The congressman had been of tremendous assistance to the Vessey mission by asking a friend of his, a vice president at a large chemical corporation, if he and his company could help. His friend helped in a big way by donating 30 tons of chemicals to be used to fabricate prosthetic limbs in Vietnam at the rehabilitation centers. This company then suggested two other large companies that would be interested in helping the Vessey mission, and those companies in turn donated 20 more tons of chemicals to be used in fabrication.

We discussed the impact those chemicals would have on the seven rehabilitation centers. Dr. Tung said very precisely that this amount would last one year and three months. He knew how much would go into the making of each limb, and he had calculated how far they could make it go. If the prosthetists used bamboo strips, they could make it go even further. However, Dr. Tung informed us, they would prefer to do it the proper way.

At the end of the meeting, the congressman's photographer took pictures of us standing and smiling. Then the congressman gave Bui Tung a pewter cup with the seal of the United States on the side. We shook hands and walked out of the office. Dr. Tung was quiet as we left, and I asked him what he thought. He replied, "The people in America have a strong voice here, I think."

I asked Dr. Tung where he would like to eat lunch and he told me he did not need anything to eat. I was to find out he lived very frugally and was spartan in his habits. I attributed it to his years of meager living as a soldier, and of being poor.

However, I needed food and suggested a good Chinese restaurant. He said it made no difference to him. It was only when we walked through the door of the restaurant and were seated by a surly waiter that it suddenly dawned on me that the Vietnamese and Chinese were traditional enemies. Maybe Chinese food was not such a good idea, after all. Dr. Tung pursed his lips and shook his head, telling me that of course Chinese food was good.

He ordered a large bowl of noodles and ate the whole thing. I learned that he never asked for anything special when it came to food, but if you put any food in front of him it would disappear. He never took seconds.

After lunch we went to my office at the Veterans Administration's Central Office, located across Lafayette Park from the White House. All of us in Clinical Affairs work on the medical services side of the hospitals. The nature of our work is such that we are divorced from politics and are only concerned with providing health care. Consequently, for my fellow program directors, being introduced to Dr. Bui Tung, a member of the Vietnamese Delegation, piqued their professional interest. They saw him as another doctor instead of a Communist.

I was concerned about my office, though. I had three secretaries and four technical staff. None of the secretaries was over thirty, so Vietnam meant little to them. It was ancient history. Of the technical staff, however, three were combat-injured Vietnam veterans. My deputy, Ed Nowak, a Marine corporal, had lost his left arm above the elbow when a Viet Cong soldier shot him with an AK-47 bullet while he was flying as a door gunner in a Marine helicopter. Don Babb, a West Point Academy graduate and a major in the artillery, lost his left leg above the knee and his right leg below the knee when a North Vietnamese Army mortar shell dropped next to him. John Clements, a Marine Infantry corporal, had both legs shattered when he stepped on a Viet Cong booby trap. The doctors had fused both his knees so he could walk.

These are great men, and usually very supportive of me. However, my involvement as a Vessey team member helping the Vietnamese was something they only tolerated. I was sensitive to their feelings and had called ahead from the Hill to warn Ed that I was bringing Bui Tung down to the office. We had agreed I would bypass their office and take Bui Tung right into mine.

Dr. Tung looked with interest at my office as I explained the purpose of the maps, charts, blackboard, and project boards I used to keep track of the Veterans Administration national Prosthetic and Sensory Aids Program.

On my desk were the routine accouterments of a modern manager: a Wang minicomputer, a Lanier dictation machine, a portable tape recorder, a telephone, ballpoint pens, paper, books, dictionaries, and files. In the other two offices I showed him the IBM terminal which hooked us into the VA national network and database, the Wang word processors at each of the seven desks, and the rest of the paraphernalia of a modern American government office. I could not help but think back to the Vietnamese "businesses" in refilling ballpoint pens, the hospital medical library devoid of books, the cheap paper found in books in offices. I looked at the material wealth that we took for granted and realized that within these three offices there was probably more technical equipment than the entire government of Vietnam had to run the whole country. I wondered if Tung was as astounded by our riches as I was astounded by their poverty.

We sat at the conference table while I outlined the mission and scope of my operation. In 1988, we furnished prosthetic appliances to approximately 1 million disabled veterans through a network of 172 medical centers, 292 outpatient clinics, and 233 nursing homes. The budget used to provide these items was $120 million.

Bui Tung used a map of Vietnam I had in my office to point out the locations and status of the rehabilitation centers, and the provinces and duties each was responsible for. There were seven centers, with no funding except salaries, to take care of approximately 500,000 disabled. In the North were Ba Vi, Haiphong, and Tam Diep; in the

South were Da Nang, Qui Nhon, Ho Chi Minh City Center, and Can Tho.

Every center suffered from a paucity of equipment, supplies, materials, and hand tools. Transportation to the centers was a major obstacle to the handicapped individual, due to appalling roads, lack of adequate public transportation systems, and too few vehicles.

What made it particularly bad for the Vietnamese soldiers was that although they were guaranteed a limb every three years, they had to get them from the rehabilitation centers, which were underfunded, had no materials or supplies, and therefore were often unable to provide enough limbs.

The soldiers came first in priority, and civilians next. Civilians had to pay for their rehabilitation. In the South, the former ARVN soldiers were treated as civilians.

As he talked, I mulled over the contrast between our resources, and it helped to bring into focus America's blessings.

Late in the afternoon we went to Bullfeathers, a bar on the Hill, where my wife Mary and two of my friends were waiting to meet Dr. Tung. Bullfeathers, located a block down from the Capitol Hill Club, is a Republican bastion. I thought Tung should see all sides of America, and the bar scene at Bullfeathers was definitely a side to see.

When we walked through the double oak doors, my friends were already waiting at a table reserved for us. Don Morrisey, a long-time friend who is politically to the right of Genghis Khan, works on the staff of a Republican congressman. Don makes no secret of the fact that he thinks the whole Vessey mission is a momentous mistake equaled only by Chamberlain's peace treaty with Hitler. Still, he is my friend and he stands by me.

Bob Kerrey, who had just been elected senator from Nebraska, is a below-knee amputee who lost his leg when he was on a mission as a Navy SEAL against a Viet Cong stronghold. He earned the Medal of Honor during the resultant battle. He had gone to war to fight against communism because he believed it was a repressive, dangerous form of dictatorship. Both of these men were curious to meet a North Vietnamese.

Bullfeathers was full of staffers from the Hill winding down after a day of innumerable crises and boring routine. Bui Tung looked around at the crowd of young enthusiasts and middle-aged cynics mingling in a cloud of cigarette smoke and loud talk, their drinks in front of them, and he remarked to me, "This is the same as we do in Vietnam." Yes, I thought, but the difference was this place did not have a daily quota of beer. There was no danger of running out.

Don and Bui Tung sat together across the table from me and compared the guerrilla wars going on around the world. These wars were invariably between a Communist-supported side and a democracy-supported side. Eventually the talk got around to the fighting in Angola. Bui Tung related how the Vietnamese prosthetists were in Angola helping the Angolan Communist government with their amputee problems resulting from the war with the rebels. Don, on the other hand, had been helping the Angolan Freedom Fighters with their amputee problems resulting from the war with the Communists.

I sat across the table, listening to them and trying to keep the astonishment off my face. The bizarre fact is I have been helping both Don and Bui Tung solve the amputee problems caused by the same war, on either side of the conflict.

Later on, Bob Kerrey asked Bui Tung where he had received his training as a surgeon. Tung answered, "Jungle."

We all looked at him, perplexed by his answer, thinking we had not heard him correctly. "Jungle?" Bob asked. "What do you mean, jungle?"

Bui Tung told us, "When I was a young man in the university, I left to join the Viet Minh to fight against the French. I was twenty years old. To become a surgeon, I studied during the rainy season at schools the Viet Minh operated in the jungle. During the dry season when we went into battle against the French, I would follow the soldiers and do surgery on the battlefield. Then when the rainy season started, I would go back to study in the jungle. I did this for five years until the war ended." We looked at Tung with respect. This small, pleasant, grandfatherly man had been forged of steel.

At the end of the evening Don asked me if I thought Bui Tung would like to tour the White House. I said sure, but it was kind of late to get tickets. Don said no problem, he would get VIP tickets for us. As we left for the night, Don told me, "Old Bui Tung isn't a bad guy. It's too bad he's a Communist."

November 30, 1988—Bui Tung Comes to My Home

★ I took Bui Tung to a private company to see centralized manufacturing, warehousing, and distribution of prosthetic and orthotic component parts. In the warehouse stood row after row of bolts, screws, washers, buckles, straps, parts, metals, plastics, leathers, chemicals—a huge cornucopia of everything a prosthetic and orthotic shop needs to fabricate limbs and braces. Bui Tung was very interested in the vast amounts of supplies available to the manufacturing process. In Vietnam, the few supplies are under lock and key, with three separate men holding the keys.

He remarked to me wistfully, as we left, that if he could put a complete shop with all these supplies and equipment in his seven rehabilitation centers, all the amputees in Vietnam would have a leg or arm. This was his dream.

That afternoon I drove Bui Tung out to our house in southern Maryland. My 1972 Volvo has 172,000 miles on it and looks pretty tired. However, it runs well enough. I explained all this to Bui Tung as we sat in rush-hour traffic caused by a backup on the Wilson Bridge. Bui Tung nodded his head and said, "Yes, it is an old car, but as you say it runs good so it makes no difference. The important thing is you have a car." This statement had powerful meaning coming from a man who was a doctor and a government official but had never owned a car.

My wife Mary is an excellent chef and she wondered beforehand what she should serve at dinner. I told her anything typically American would probably be okay. Tung had traveled and lived in East Germany, so he ought to be able to eat just about anything. Besides, I told her, he had spent years living in the jungle eating whatever was available, so her cooking wasn't going to kill him.

When we arrived, he gave the house the once-over as I unloaded some things I had brought from the office. Mary's Volvo was parked in the two-car garage, and of course the garage was lined with the numerous tools of the trade of all homeowners. The house is on a half-acre heavily wooded lot, surrounded by other homes and a golf course. I imagined there was no doubt in his mind that I was a capitalist.

Mary met us at the door with our one-month-old baby daughter Abigail in her arms and our three-and-a-half-year-old daughter Katie at her side. Katie was bubbling over with excitement at meeting someone new, plus she always met me at the door with enthusiasm. Coming home to my family like this always makes me happy, regardless of how bad the day has been. It is a pleasure I savor each day.

For the first time, I sensed, Tung felt enjoyment. Before had been all business, but this was personal. He did not let his guard down, but I could tell he was happy to meet my family.

Bui Tung took his shoes off when he entered the house. I had come to accept this as a common Asian custom. In my travels in Asia I noticed that even the most humble hotel would have slippers or shower thongs in the room right along with the towels. Mary was delighted because she preferred the "shoes-off" custom in the house. She told

Tung she would get him a pair of slippers, but he said no, he would just walk around in his stocking feet. When our nanny offered to hang his coat, he demurred and remarked that in his country he had learned to care for his own coat.

I had never expected to have a North Vietnamese Communist in my house. My home was the home of a soldier who had fought North Vietnamese soldiers and Viet Cong. I had memorabilia from our war with them all over my house, including war souvenirs I had taken from the bodies of men I had killed.

It suddenly hit me that this man was here as a friendly gesture on the part of the American government to show the Vietnamese we were serious about our humanitarian efforts. I hoped he would not be offended at some of the nonhumanitarian items he saw. Among the things spread around my office were a 122mm Chinese artillery-shell casing, an American tank-shell casing, a training hand grenade, a bayonet, pieces of shrapnel, and other odds and ends of a similar nature.

On the living room wall hung a vertical 5-by-1½-foot banner I had taken off the body of a soldier I had killed. It was red, bordered with yellow, and inscribed with four large yellow Chinese letters sewn down the middle and 1-inch letters embroidered with gold thread along each side.

I had been carrying it folded in my rucksack when I stepped on the "bouncing betty" land mine near Chu Lai on January 11, 1968. The banner had dozens of jagged holes torn in it from the shrapnel explosion. It was returned with my personal belongings to Fitzsimons Army Hospital, where it became one of my "best" souvenirs from the war.

A Chinese student translated it for me once. He explained it was a good-luck banner, sewn by a loved one and given to a soldier who was leaving on a long and dangerous trip. The soldier is like a bird who leaves the nest to venture out into the world. The bird is beset by storms and becomes wet and hungry, but returns safely to the nest. The small letters on the side told what village the man came from and something

315

about his family. China had ruled Vietnam for a thousand years, so it was not unusual to find the Chinese influence in items such as this.

I had always treated the banner with reverence because I believed it held part of the spirits of two soldiers and I always proudly displayed it. But as I stood in front of it with Bui Tung, I realized I could not tell him the story because it had come off the body of one of his comrades. If our roles were reversed and I was in his house, I would not be happy to be shown a souvenir taken from the body of an American. I would be saddened by the images such a thing would invite. I did explain to him that I was carrying it when I was wounded, and all those holes he saw in the flag were caused by shrapnel ripping through it into my body.

I did not elaborate further about the banner and guided Tung back to the foyer. Standing on a table commanding the entrance was Rick Hart's *Three Soldiers,* a cast of the model he used to design the large statue next to the wall at the Vietnam Veterans Memorial on the Mall. Tung politely listened while I explained what the statue and the Vietnam Memorial were all about. I told him that the wall had been paid for by the Vietnam veterans themselves and it had been very controversial. A number of people could not understand why Vietnam veterans needed a memorial or wanted a parade.

Dr. Bui Tung said he understood. He knew that soldiers in his country, who had returned as triumphant heroes to their villages, had commented on how they did not know how the Americans felt returning to their homes. The soldiers thought it must have been very difficult.

As always during these conversations with Tung, I was faced with the irony of explaining to a Vietnamese Communist why we were proud to be Vietnam veterans and why we had to fight so hard for recognition in our own country. I wondered how an American World War II soldier would have felt talking to a Japanese soldier if they had won the war and we were trying to retrieve MIAs from the islands they controlled, including Hawaii.

I took Tung downstairs to the recreation room and the bar. There on the wall were my medals, two swords, a rifle, artwork about Vietnam, a painting of the South Vietnamese Service medal, a large oil of me in Vietnam in combat fatigues, and a framed print of a "Hunter-Killer" team of two Cobra gunships and a smaller helicopter in Vietnam captioned: "Heading for Trouble."

I thought to myself, That's right on the money.

My library might put a more positive light on the tour, particularly the history sections on war. I got Tung a glass of water from the bar and suggested we go up to the library. Tung loved to read and had read quite a lot of American history. We asked him if he read for pleasure, and he replied that he enjoyed the classics but also mysteries and tragedies. I too love books, so I thought we couldn't go wrong.

As we looked through my Vietnam section, I had second thoughts about this great idea. Bui Tung slowly flipped the pages of a book filled mostly with photographs. There were a number of grim scenes of the Vietnam War. One was a full-page photo of dozens of NVA soldiers lying dead on the ground, another of dead Viet Cong soldiers who had been napalmed; there were many of refugees, aircraft strikes, and various scenes of war.

There were also pictures of the Communist atrocities of war, including a photo of a decapitated South Vietnamese. The terror campaigns waged by the Communists were brutal and widespread. The man standing next to me was a surgeon, and he had not done those things, but his government had as a matter of policy.

Neither he nor I commented on either set of photos.

Once again I had to turn away from the past and look toward the future, as did he.

Lined along the hall wall and in the bedroom and living room were the framed pictures I had bought in the Dollar

Store in Hanoi. Bui Tung told us they represented typical village life or scenes from Vietnam's past. On the end table in the living room he noticed the carving of a coal black water buffalo I had bought in Hanoi as a souvenir. I asked him how the craftsman got the carving such a coal black color; did he shellac it? "No," Bui Tung explained, "what you bought is made out of coal. It is its natural color. Coal is often used in making artwork."

We went into the kitchen and sat at the table while Mary cooked. She was cooking with one hand and holding Abigail, who was colicky and crying, on her hip with the other. Tung asked to hold Abigail and began to rock her and sing a lullaby to her in Vietnamese to try to calm her down. As he walked back and forth in the kitchen, Katie followed after, fascinated by the foreign language.

I watched this tableau from the doorway, measuring it against scenes from my past: the war, the angry college campuses, the harsh feelings toward Vietnam vets, the POW/MIA issue, my past hatred of the Vietnamese.

Watching this Communist singing to my baby dramatized the conflict within me, and in a broader sense between our two countries. As individuals, both of us could become friends. As individuals, we could share a common goal of trying to make life better for other individuals—in this case the handicapped and children. What was even stranger was that both of us adamantly believed in our own way of life and we were only working with each other at the orders of our respective governments. Even if we liked each other, neither of us would dream of working together if it was at cross-purposes to what our country wanted us to do.

Sad to say, I knew that if our countries went to war the next day, both Tung and I would dutifully become enemies again, even if it meant we would meet on the battlefield. The difference would be, now that I knew him, I would not take any joy in his death, only sorrow at the ways of man.

Before we sat down to dinner, Bui Tung presented each of

us with a gift. He gave Mary a watercolor of a Vietnamese village scene, painted by a friend of his who taught art to high school students. He gave me a small, 2-inch block of a green substance wrapped with a clear plastic. He said it was tiger bones and was very good for my vitality and virility. Bui Tung said tiger bone was very rare. It was made by taking the bones of a tiger and boiling them down into a gel. Then it was pressed and cut into blocks like this one. To prepare it for use, he told us, cut the block up into little pieces and put them into boiling water to dissolve them, then boil a pot of tea and mix them together. When it was thoroughly mixed, I should drink it. I put the block on my bureau to use in my old age.

Mary had prepared an elegant meal. All through dinner she carried on an animated conversation with Tung. She was as interested in Bui Tung as I. After all, Vietnam had changed her life as much as it had mine. When we met, I was a patient at Fitzsimons Army Hospital fresh from the war. The continuing effects of Vietnam on me had impacted on her as well over the last twenty-one years.

During dinner we talked about our Vietnamese friends in this country and remarked that one lady's name was Happy. Bui gave us the Vietnamese word for "happy" and told us his name meant "the East" or "Sun Rising in the East." The same as Mao Zedong. We asked him by what name he liked to be called. He said we were friends, so we could call him Tung.

Tung was interested in American culture and society. He asked many questions about our families and was particularly interested in our parents, where they lived and our relationship with them. He seemed surprised to discover we kept in close touch with them even though they lived hundreds of miles away. I got the impression it was not so good for the parents not to have a son or daughter close by to care for them. We explained that in America we felt the same way but often we were not able to stay close together because of jobs. Everyone, including parents, prized their independence and wanted to live by themselves. Also, parents did not want to be a burden on their children.

Unfortunately, I added, there were times Americans had carried the idea too far and many old people were left to live alone when they should be cared for by their family. But problems with the old people were being recognized and addressed, making many Americans reevaluate their responsibilities toward the elderly in our society.

Bui Tung had never visited America. He had spent three years in East Germany, some time in the Soviet Union, and of course a lifetime in the world created by hard-line Vietnamese Communist doctrine. Consequently he was thoroughly indoctrinated in the "failings" of American society. He was inquisitive, though, to find out the truth.

Our problem in explaining our society to him was the difficulty in reconciling the negative and positive aspects of that society. On the one hand, he saw riches beyond his belief. On the other hand, he was panhandled by the homeless and could read about the record number of murders, the drugs destroying our youth, the widespread pornographic shows, and more. All of this was reported in the newspapers and TV news shows numerous times during the day and easily seen on the streets around the White House and throughout Washington as I took him around.

Everything he had ever read and been taught about the evils of capitalism was right here, live and in color, in the capital of the United States. There was no avoiding it. For instance, in December 1988 Washington had the highest murder rate in its history.

I discovered during Bui Tung's visit that the greatest civics lesson for any American is to have to explain our way of life to a hard-line Communist. I am proud to be an American and proud of America, so of course I wanted to put our best face forward. But America's virtues are almost like religion: they have to be taken on faith in some cases. For instance, some of the murders in Washington that month were reportedly done by men who were out on bond for other murders they had committed. Now, try to explain to a foreigner how the murderer must receive all of his rights regardless of the rights of the society to be protected from him. It is the importance of the rights of the individual at the expense of everything else in America that makes us unique and hard to fathom.

The conversation turned to Tung and his family. He was proud to be from a family of scholars. His father was a scholar and his uncles too. In Asia the scholar is at the peak of respect in the society. He told us he had two sons, both of them doctors, one in Hanoi and the other in Ho Chi Minh City. His wife had died the year before. I remembered she had passed away in December 1987 between our second and third trip. Her loss had been a heavy blow for Bui Tung at the time.

As he sat at our table describing her, he told us that in the Vietnamese culture they believed the man was the pillar of the house. He made a motion with his hands signifying the pole holding up the roof of the grass-and-bamboo dwelling common to the Vietnamese countryside.

"But," Bui Tung continued, "when my wife died, I found that not to be true. She was the pillar of our home."

I was stunned to see tears well up in his eyes.

December 1, 1988—The *Washington Post*

★ I had asked Tung if he would like to visit the *Washington Post*. He said of course. Like so many things in our country on which he was well versed, he knew of the *Post*. He had been reading it every day and was familiar with its editorial format. Tung was an educated man and knew much of our history, especially the Revolutionary War, Civil War, World War II, and the Vietnam War. He knew the key names and their place in history: Grant, Lee, Eisenhower, Marshall,

Kennedy, Johnson, and the signers of the Constitution and our first presidents. He also knew the power of our press—as did all officials of the North Vietnamese government.

It was mid-afternoon when we arrived at the *Post*. I had arranged the visit through David Ignatius, editor of *Outlook*. He was curious to meet Bui Tung, surgeon and member of the North Vietnamese Delegation. I signed Tung and myself in, and we rode the elevator up to the fifth floor. This floor of the paper is impressive, with its vast unwalled space. The people are crammed elbow to elbow at long lines of desks, littered with work, and postered with clippings, cartoons, and other personal expressions of individuality to fight back the crush of their neighbor and the sweatshop environment. Glass offices claim the prime space along the wall, with windows as an executive privilege. Harsh, cold fluorescent lights glare down over the less privileged.

Bui Tung met David Ignatius, Curt Suplee, and the other staff members in the small *Outlook* section. David and Curt then took us over to meet with Dick Harwood, the ombudsman of the *Post* and its former number-three man. Dick was familiar with the Vessey mission and wanted to meet someone from Vietnam. All of us sat down in Dick's office while Bui Tung answered a wide range of questions about the humanitarian needs of Vietnam and the difficulties facing the Hanoi government.

Dick asked me how well the Vessey humanitarian effort was doing. I told him it was going pretty good and a continuing effort was growing among the nongovernmental organizations all the time. He then asked how many MIAs still remained. I answered about 2,400. About 545 of those were in Laos, 82 in Cambodia, 6 in China, and about 1,700 of them in Vietnam—600 in the North and 1,100 in the South. Fifty-four suspected remains had been returned since the Vessey mission in August 1987.

Dick asked Bui Tung how many MIAs Vietnam had from the war with America. Tung, sitting in a chair with his hands clasped in his lap, said he believed there were approximately

300,000 Vietnamese soldiers missing in action. After a moment's reflection he added the comment that approximately 1 million Vietnamese soldiers had been killed in the war against America.

I thought again of those Hero cemeteries in the North. The Vietnamese were meticulous in their record keeping. When a Vietnamese soldier died during the war, if at all possible he was buried in a well-marked and recorded grave if his remains could not be returned to the North. After the war, the Vietnamese grave registration teams had spent years recovering the remains from the graves alongside the Ho Chi Minh Trail and other battlegrounds to return to their family burial plots and Hero cemeteries.

I had read various casualty figures estimating that the loss in the North ranged from 400,000 to 1 million dead, so Tung was probably right.

The other figure that America did not pay much attention to was the fact that our allies, the South Vietnamese, lost approximately 1 million dead. This left hundreds of thousands of widows and orphans in the South to be cared for by the Vietnamese government. There were also the hundreds of thousands of disabled South Vietnamese soldiers to be taken care of. Although the Vietnamese government put its own soldiers and party members first, it had at least recognized the existence of its former enemy by allowing them to be treated along with the other civilians in the South. The problem was, there was not enough of anything to go around, so most people North and South were doing without.

These men had heard my stories about the problems in Vietnam, but here was an opportunity for them to talk to a North Vietnamese and get a feeling for what those numbers meant in terms of magnitude. I wondered what they were thinking. Were they suspicious of what Tung was telling them? Did they believe him?

When we left the *Post,* I asked Tung what he thought of the visit. He replied that the newspaper was good for the people because it told the leaders what the people think. In Vietnam, the newspapers reported what the people said and the people were free to write to the newspapers to report corruption and to complain against the government, just like the *Washington Post*.

When we arrived home that evening, Kate ran down the stairs to hug me and, much to Tung's pleasure, she hugged him also.

That night as we relaxed around the kitchen table, Kate surprised and delighted Tung, Mary, and me when she started talking her version of Vietnamese. She would babble out strange words and laugh at her success in getting our attention. Tung enjoyed playing the grandfather to Kate and Abigail while we talked each night. During lulls he would read the *Washington Post* and the *Washington Times*.

While he was doing this, I was looking through my Vietnam papers and found a photograph of an OSS Deer Team. In the picture the American team posed with Ho Chi Minh, Vo Nguyen Giap, and other Vietnamese. These OSS teams worked with the Viet Minh during World War II, and the presence of American senior officers attending Viet Minh functions when Ho Chi Minh took over Hanoi at the end of the war made it easy, according to Bernard Fall in his book *Two Vietnams*, for the Vietnamese people and the French to think America was giving its fullest backing to the Viet Minh.

It is often claimed that America lost a huge historical opportunity when Ho Chi Minh asked for (and expected to receive) the support of the United States but did not get it.

A closer look reveals that this was a time of duplicity, in varying degrees, on the part of numerous military, political, nationalist, and religious factions within the British, Soviet, American, French, Vietnamese, and Chinese nations. There was certainly more to what happened at that point in history than the Deer Team picture would indicate. But history is written from many points of view, with one's own biases shading the conclusions drawn from the evidence at hand.

It is a fact that there were Americans working with the Viet Minh and for a time many Vietnamese believed the Americans supported their nationalist aspirations. American officers believed France should not return to dominate Vietnam after the war. Roosevelt agreed, as he felt colonialism was one of the reasons the war had broken out in the first place. At his death he was trying to devise a trusteeship to keep colonialism out of Vietnam, but the idea died with him.

I showed the picture to Tung and asked if he knew about these teams who worked with the Viet Minh—in this case, Ho Chi Minh. Tung replied that, yes, he knew about the help the Americans gave during World War II. Then he told us a story about when he was a young man. He had entered the city of Hanoi in early September 1945, along with a crowd of hundreds of thousands, to hear the announcement by Ho Chi Minh of the formation of an independent Vietnam.

"Everyone was excited and we were crowded in the streets, when suddenly a military airplane appeared over the city. All of us became apprehensive, not knowing who it was, and we were afraid it would attack us. Then the fighter banked and we could see the markings showing it was an American fighter. We all cheered because we believed the Americans were our friends."

I asked Tung what he did during the war. He replied that he worked as a doctor in Hanoi until 1964. Then he was sent down to be in charge of a thousand-bed hospital north of the DMZ. This was the Military Region 4 forward field hospital, located near Kim Lien village in Nghe An Province, the birthplace of Ho Chi Minh. Tung was the chief surgeon there from 1964 to 1968. The hospital was spread out among seven villages of the "Viet-Trung" state farm, as a protection against the American aircraft. (Many American aircraft were shot down in the area where Bui Tung worked, and there were numerous last-known locations of MIAs there that the JCRC team wanted to conduct joint investigations with the Vietnamese.) He rode a bicycle from village to village, operating on the wounded who were brought in from the fighting in Laos, and the wounded who were brought back up the Ho Chi Minh Trail from the South. He operated on thousands of soldiers during that time. He was only able to go home to Hanoi for a short visit a few times during the four years he was assigned to the hospital.

Mary asked, "During all that time when you were operating and the wounded soldiers just kept coming, all those young men just kept dying, didn't you and the others ever become discouraged at so much carnage? Did you get tired of the war? Did you think it would ever end?"

Tung shook his head. "No. For us, the future was very gray. It was like a fog. Very indefinite. Our leaders had told us America was a very rich country, a very strong country, and it would take a long time to defeat them in war. We were prepared to fight a lifetime. In fact, we were surprised when the war ended as soon as it did."

I nodded. "You were surprised it lasted such a short time? We were surprised it lasted so long!

"What was one of the differences in running a hospital while fighting the French versus the Americans?" I asked him.

"When we fought the French, our hospitals were above ground because we could hear the airplanes in time to get into the trenches, and their bombs were not powerful enough to hurt us unless they landed on top of us. But with the Americans we had to have our hospitals underground because the planes flew so fast we would not have time to hide, and their bombs were so powerful that we had to be deep underground to be protected.

"After 1968 I returned to Hanoi, where I worked for the Minister of Health to struggle with the problems we faced with all of the wounded. Then in 1973, when we took over the northern provinces in South Vietnam, I was sent to be in charge of the medical treatment of part of our army. In 1975 as our army attacked south, I traveled with them behind the front lines to administer the medical care and perform surgery on the large numbers of wounded. I stayed with the army until we entered Saigon. Afterwards I was sent back to Hanoi to work in the ministry to be in charge of the rehabilitation centers and to perform surgery."

"Then you have spent most of your professional career as a battlefield surgeon. You must be glad it is over."

"Yes, of course. It is good it is over. There is so much misery in war."

Later on that evening our conversation got around to the changes occurring in Vietnam. One of those changes was television. Tung told us about Vietnamese TV. There was one station in Hanoi and two channels. One showed Vietnamese programs and one showed Russian programs beamed to them by satellite. Broadcast times were generally limited to a couple of hours a day.

The Vietnamese programming was practical and to the point, and sounded boring as hell to me. The first ten minutes of every day was to give the results of the lottery. A ticket cost 100 dong. Two numbers alike paid 500 dong, but the jackpot was to hit five or six numbers alike for a win of 3 to 6 million dong. Following the lotto would be fifteen to thirty minutes for the children with stories, magic, or puppets. Then fifteen to thirty minutes of local news, followed by fifteen to thirty minutes of international news. There would then be fifteen to thirty minutes of a program on special problems such as population control or child nutrition. Included once or twice a week in this time slot would be a program for the police, army, or Hanoi government. Next would be a local or international singing star or a film three or four times a week. The last program on Monday and Wednesday was a language and speech lesson in Russian; the last program on Tuesday and Thursday was a language and speech lesson in English.

When I heard that, I knew why I met so many people in Hanoi who could speak English.

On Saturday night there would be an extra bonus: a theater production, either traditional or modern.

The Russian channel was the sports channel. It was shown in real time, though, which was a problem. Tung said if a Vietnamese wanted to watch a particular football game, it might not start until 1:00 A.M., in which case a man would have to go to sleep early and get up to watch the game. Sometimes the Vietnamese channel would record a sport and rebroadcast it at a more decent hour during regular programming.

I thought Vietnamese television sounded like the pits, but Tung said people in Hanoi were crazy for it. Many people in Hanoi now owned a TV.

The Japanese TVs were expensive but they were the best because they were good for at least eight years. The East German and Polish TVs were cheaper but they were low-quality and broke down a lot. "A black and white Polish TV costs 400,000 dong—120 U.S. dollars!" Tung exclaimed.

Well, we asked, how does a Vietnamese family afford that?

Tung shook his head. "It is very bad. The children say to their parents they must have a TV set because everyone is getting them. The father must then sell something from his home to buy such an expensive thing. TV is bad for our families. There is no respect for the father unless he buys what his children want. I do not think TV is such a good thing."

December 2, 1988—Touring the White House

★ The next day we toured the White House. Don Morrisey had been successful in getting us two VIP tickets. This was the special tour run early in the morning before the regular tourists started through. The VIP tickets came from a congressman, and the tour included two extra rooms not on the regular tour.

The tour was a treat for me because I had never been there before. I was excited and in a mood to buy souvenirs. I offered to buy something for Tung, but he seemed uninterested in the idea. He was content to just look around.

The acoustics were terrible, and the group was large, so neither one of us heard much of the history from the guides. We just looked around at the different-colored rooms and shuffled along with the mass of people. All the rooms had been redone to show the White House at its best. Gold, silver, and china servings were on display, in addition to fine antique furniture, rugs, and magnificent paintings. Everything looked grand, and I was proud to show Tung through. He seemed strangely subdued, however, and did not comment on the splendor of the President's house. Soon we were through the front door and standing on the front lawn in the bright December sunshine. I took a picture of Tung with the White House in the background. Tung was probably the first North Vietnamese ever to tour the White House.

It was only later in the day, when we toured the Capitol, that I would find out why Tung was so quiet.

Jim Grady, a friend of mine, had offered to act as our tour guide through the Capitol building. Jim had been an aide to U.S. Senator Metcalf. Now he was a successful writer who still gave a great tour to his relatives and friends. When he heard that Bui Tung would be visiting, he offered to give us a tour in the spirit of building good relations between countries. Afterwards he said he would take us to an interesting bar and restaurant on the Hill.

He picked us up in front of the Veterans Administration building in his Jeep Cherokee and drove up Pennsylvania Avenue, pointing out the sights as we went along: the FBI building, the Old Post Office, the National Archives, the National Art Gallery, and of course the Capitol itself sitting on the little rise of land known as the Hill. Jim drove behind the Capitol to park next to the Folger Theater. Tung, being a practical man, admired Jim's Jeep more than the drive. "We could use this in Vietnam, Fred. We have many parts for Jeeps." "Yeah," I replied. "We left a slew of them behind."

We walked inside the Capitol, where Jim did a magnificent job regaling Bui Tung and me with stories about the building and the men and women who had served there. The Capitol is truly magnificent. The paintings, the murals, the statues—the history of the republic is evident in every nook and cranny. Within these rooms the men who formed our country moved as the ordinary mortals they were, and we can follow in their very footsteps both literally and figuratively.

Bui Tung, who had demonstrated his knowledge of American history many times during our dinners in Hanoi and during this visit, took great interest in Jim's tour. At the exit under the steps leading up to the House side of the Capitol, Tung stopped us. "This place I like very much more than the White House. This place shows of American people, is warm. The other place, cold." He explained that he thought the White House was too much like a palace, a place for royalty, whereas the Capitol was a place for the people.

While we were in the Supreme Court Chamber, Tung said, "The people of America should be proud to have raised up against the government, otherwise, the war would still be going."

"You mean our war with Vietnam?" we asked, confused because we at first thought he was referring to the Revolutionary War.

"Yes, of course. There is much history here which shows it is easy to see you Americans are revolutionaries and understand these things."

One of the things I had learned in talking to the North Vietnamese was the strange (to me anyway) belief that the American people were never their enemy, only our leaders.

At first I had ignored that as a Communist ploy, but I had come to think they really believed it. Tung's comment was in character with what they professed about America.

He thoroughly enjoyed the Capitol's democratic flavor, and he paid particular attention to the quotations above the doors on the House side, stopping to read many of them. I too took the time to read them and was struck by the power of our forefathers' ability to put forth such truth in so few words.

Tung identified with them, I could see, because they were from a people who had wrested their country from another in a revolutionary war. Our revolution was two hundred years ago, but the words struck home to the revolutionary standing before me.

I in no way confused our glorious revolution, which provided freedom to its people, with Vietnam's revolution, which repressed its people. But I could understand the hope for freedom from foreign domination that burned within the heart of the common North Vietnam soldier. Blasphemous as the thought was, it had to be true. Every man fights for freedom, or what he thinks will be freedom, and a better life for his people.

I looked at Tung who, with head craned back, was still reading the quotations. Then I looked at the quotes with new interest. They too held hopes for a better future and called for constant diligence against the repressor.

Next, Jim Grady and I asked Tung if he would like to visit the Vietnam Veterans Memorial. He said he would. I had fully expected him to decline because we on the Vessey team had been warned we could not go to Ho Chi Minh's tomb or the War Museum for fear the Vietnamese would take a picture of us and use it in their propaganda. Obviously Tung felt no such restrictions.

Jim drove us down to the west end of the Mall and parked his Jeep on Constitution near 21st. We stood in the bright chilly sunshine, looking over toward where the memorial melded into the ground. Between where we stood and the memorial was the self-appointed Vietnam Veterans POW/ MIA booth, which is open twenty-four hours a day. Three men dressed in camouflage fatigues and black berets were manning the booth, passing out literature demanding the return of POWs and an accounting of MIAs. They were collecting signatures from passing citizens on a petition to be sent to congressmen, calling for them to demand that the North Vietnamese answer the questions concerning POW/ MIA issues. Pictures of POWs were propped up on posters leaning against the booth.

There were T-shirts, buttons, bumper stickers, and other paraphernalia for sale sitting on the shelf in the front of the booth, along with a collection box for donations. American, South Vietnamese, and black and white POW/MIA flags were flapping briskly in the breeze.

My feelings about these men and their two booths (there was one at each end of the memorial) were decidedly ambivalent. I remembered when they had started as a movement designed to bring attention to the POW/MIA issue, and Vietnam veterans from different states took turns on a weekly basis manning the booths with high purpose. Through the years the effort to man the booths by states had dwindled, to be replaced by a small group of professional veterans who took it upon themselves to keep it staffed. At one time there had been some sort of confrontation with the Park Service, which attempted to throw them off the Mall, but through court action the booths were allowed to stay under set conditions. They were an indication of how the POW/MIA issue had become a crusade among the veteran community.

I explained to Tung what the booth was all about and why it was there. I told him the POW/MIA issue was important to the American people and efforts such as this went on across the country.

332

As we walked slowly past, Bui Tung curiously looked the booth over and stopped to scan a poster with pictures of Americans who were missing in action and POWs who were unaccounted for. Jim stood off to the side and I stood silently beside Tung. The Vietnam veteran in front of him exhorted a passer-by not to forget the POWs in Hanoi's jails. He would never know a North Vietnamese was standing a few feet from him.

The memorial consists of two polished black granite walls in the shape of a V. One arm of the V points toward the Washington Monument, the other arm toward the Lincoln Memorial. There is nothing inscribed on the granite except the date the war began and the date it ended—August 1964 and April 1975—and the names of over 58,000 men and seven women who died as a result of the conflict.

I automatically went to the directory to look up the location on the wall of men I had known who were killed in Vietnam. I explained to Tung what I was doing. Then we walked slowly along the slate pathway studying the rows and rows of names. There were flowers, wreaths, poems, and other personal items lying beneath the names, put there by friends or family members. It was just after Thanksgiving, so there were more of these things than usual. There was a picture of a young man taken during basic training. It was in a cardboard frame leaning against the black granite wall, on Panel 29 East. A note taped to the side was from a sister, who wrote she missed her older brother, as did Mom and Dad who still loved their son very much.

I explained to Tung that there were eleven Downs on the wall. I knew none of them but I felt the bond of kinship with them. I had come oh so close to having my name up there. I knew the spot on the panel where it would have been placed. The names were inscribed in chronological order of death, so I knew January 11, 1968, was on Panel 34E on line 29.

Each time I visit the wall with friends or relatives, I am struck by the sadness of the place. The personal items left along the granite always add a poignancy to the somberness of the wall. The impact of seeing 58,000 names of men who died in war is intensified by the statue of the three soldiers at the treeline, looking at their brothers lined up in death.

Bui Tung was quiet and contemplative. The three of us gazed out over the solemn patch of earth with its wall of recorded deaths and the statue of frozen youth.

I looked at the North Vietnamese studying the wall and then I glanced around. A memory of Bob Hutchinson, my old friend whose name is on Panel 39E, line 61, came to me. I visited him at his parents' house in California before we left for Vietnam in the summer of 1967. We were going to fight the Viet Cong and the North Vietnamese Army, and looked forward to doing it. Boy, we had a great time in those few days before we left California—we never really thought either of us would get killed.

Now here I was twenty years later, standing with a North Vietnamese, looking at Bob's name on a marble slab. I would have liked to have found some meaning in all that had happened to us, but nothing profound came to me. I just felt a sense of duty to keep trying to do the right thing. We did not know then it was going to turn out the way it did, and we do not know now how the present is going to turn out, but we cannot just walk away from it. Vietnam is still unfinished business.

When we were back home and sitting around the supper table, Mary asked Tung what he had thought of the memorial. Tung thought for a moment, then said, "It is good and it is bad. It is good because seeing so many names reminds all of us that peace is better. It is bad because it keeps the war in the minds of Americans and that is bad for Vietnam." Tung sat back and then leaned forward. "You know, even though I never held a gun or shot at an American, I feel somehow responsible for those names on the wall."

Both Mary and I were taken aback at this statement. There was nothing I could say, but I did think of those Hero cemeteries I saw out in the rice paddies on the road between Hanoi and the airport. My thoughts had not been nearly so charitable when first I saw them.

It seemed my former enemy was more compassionate than I. But then again, he was a surgeon and I was an infantryman. One's role is to save lives and the other's role is to take lives. At the end of war what a man has done will be a part of him forever, regardless of what he becomes.

Later we sat at the table discussing the POW/MIA issue and its importance to Americans. The subject had come up because while waiting in rush-hour traffic we had seen a bumper sticker on the car in front of us that read: "POW/MIAs—Hanoi Knows the Answer."

"There are so many reminders to the American people that Vietnam is bad," Tung ruefully commented. "We are trying to find these crash sites, but with some it is very difficult. Many crashed in the jungle and are unknown to us. Once we were attacked by an airplane and many of our soldiers shot at it but it flew away, seemingly unharmed. Six months later it was found accidentally in the mountains not far away. We think it was the same plane that attacked us, but even so no one knew it was there.

"In other cases, as Mr. Bai has told you, the people need to be convinced in the village as to why they should put forth effort to assist with crash sites. These planes caused much death and destruction in these villages. The village chief and district chief must answer to the people if they want them to cooperate. The people want to know what America will do to help them if you want them to help America. Of course, the humanitarian aid being provided now is good. It shows the people America is helping them.

"But so much attention to these missing Americans after all these years! In the war with America we lost over a million dead, and we have three hundred thousand missing and hundreds of thousands of wounded and widows and orphans and old people with no family to take care of them.

Yet that is the past. We must accept that. We mourn our great losses but we are ready to be friends with America."

"Yes, there are a number of us who can see that, but there are many obstacles," I replied slowly. "In addition to those our leaders have discussed, I think another reason there are still problems between us is the war was very divisive here, as you well know. There are still a lot of hard feelings here because we lost the war."

"But you did not lose the war!" Bui Tung adamantly shot back at me. "The American people and the Vietnamese people decided together to end the war!"

I was stunned by his comment. "What do you mean?"

"The American people and the Vietnamese people demanded the war should end between them. When they agreed on this, then the Americans left. Afterwards we knew the South Vietnamese government would be easily defeated because they did not have the will to stand against us. Without the Americans to do the fighting for them, they lost.

"As I told you in the Capitol building today, the American people should be proud to have raised up against the government. Otherwise the war would still be going on," Tung solemnly concluded.

The thought of Bui Tung not having any traveling money had never crossed my mind. But during his stay with us the facts slowly came out as to how frugally Tung made his way through each day. We talked about it at the dinner table.

Bui Tung left Hanoi with no money in his pocket. When he arrived at the Bangkok Airport, he had to convince a taxi driver to take him to the Vietnamese Embassy. Once there Tung had to go around to individuals in the embassy to collect enough money to pay the taxi driver, waiting anxiously outside.

Tung's airline ticket was paid for by the Society of Military Orthopedic Surgeons, as were his lodging expenses for the time he would spend at their conference in

Williamsburg. When he arrived in America he went first to Boston, where his lodging was sponsored by the William Joiner Foundation. He presented a paper to the group and was paid a small honorarium. That was all the money he had for the entire trip. Of course he had no credit cards, so in effect he was a penniless traveler.

The Boston group paid for his ticket to New York, where he stayed overnight at the Vietnamese mission at the UN, but there was a problem getting him a ticket from New York to Washington. This was solved when Dr. van Dam used his credit card to pay for Tung's ticket.

No Americans associated with Bui Tung's visit realized that he was traveling without any money. We assumed his government had provided some traveling money, but the government's philosophy was that if you were invited to travel outside the country, then the inviter had to pay everything. This was a typical Hanoi procedure, we were told later by the State Department. As this situation came to light, I asked Tung how he lived in East Germany and the other countries through which he had traveled.

He explained that in East Germany he would be given an apartment and a certain amount of money to use each day. It was up to him to see how far he could make it go. This way he could actually save some small amount to buy items for himself and gifts for the people back home. Tung said in Vietnamese culture it was very important to give gifts to relatives, friends, and fellow workers when returning from a trip.

In fact he was worried because everything was so expensive in America he could not afford to buy anything. He was going to hoard his honorarium until he got back to Bangkok. Then he would go to the large markets where he could get bargains.

It was important that he return with gifts for many people from this trip. Although it was an honor and a duty to come to America, there were people who were jealous and would want to receive a gift who ordinarily would not have expected one.

December 3, 1988—A Trip to the Smithsonian

★ Saturday, we went to the Smithsonian. To show off America, I chose the Museum of American History, one of my favorites. I felt Tung would enjoy seeing some of the history he had read about.

My guess was accurate. He seemed to be interested in the displays and took time to read many of the placards. For a scholar like Bui Tung, taking a tour through "America's attic" was a good method of getting an overview of who we were. It was doubly interesting for me because there were items in the museum I had always taken for granted until Tung questioned me on them.

He gazed with puzzlement at one of the new displays featuring "The Swamp Rat," a fuel dragster capable of obtaining a top speed of 220 miles per hour in a quarter of a mile. I had never tried to explain a drag race to someone who had never heard of such a thing. When I did, he seemed astonished that so much effort would be devoted to a task which had no outcome other than being the fastest vehicle in a quarter of a mile.

"Of what use is such a thing?" Tung asked me, his face wrinkled in a frown of puzzled wonderment.

I thought of all the serious answers I could give him about drag racing being a testing bed for improving automobile engineering ideas, but I thought the best answer was the reason we used to drag race when I was in high school.

"To see who can go the fastest," I answered.

Tung did not seem impressed with the dragster, but he took pleasure in the neighboring exhibit consisting of a series of bicycles ranging from nineteenth-century models made of wood to modern-day multi-speed racers made of high-tech lightweight metals.

We had an ice cream soda in the old fashioned ice cream parlor on the first floor. Tung had never had one before.

The section on the history of medicine was interesting in itself, but some displays gained in significance because items displayed as nineteenth-century implements were what Bui Tung had used during the Vietnam War. In the war he had used chloroform with a mask framework applicator just like the one shown in the display case. He shook his head and said, "Chloroform! No good! Very bad for the liver!" The exhibit at the Smithsonian could have been enriched by his experience.

Tung's ability to perform surgery under the worst of conditions had been acquired during his forty years of battlefield experience. They often had heavy casualties and few medical supplies; as a result many patients died who might have otherwise lived. Tung and his fellow doctors did not have the kind of material resources that the American surgeons had. The American surgeons had a pipeline from the States to provide them with the best equipment and all the supplies they needed. In the country they were supported by a medevac and all the other usual support elements. Consequently American surgeons were able to salvage a lot of wounded who would have died in earlier wars.

During the time he stayed with Dr. van Dam and his family, Bruce had taken Tung with him to Walter Reed. Tung attended surgery at the Army hospital and taught the residents some of the techniques he used during the war. He explained what they did in the field when they did not have anesthesia and they had to amputate a leg or debride a deep wound.

If the Vietnamese doctor was going to amputate a leg below the knee, he would take a long needle and inject a local anesthetic right into the spongy area at the end of the shin bone where it flared out toward the knee. He would then infiltrate that whole area at the top of the shin bone with lidocaine or novocaine and let it spread through circulation. The key was to have a tight tourniquet above the spot where the needle was inserted, so the local anesthetic had time to be absorbed, or it would spread to the heart or brain and kill the patient. Tung could then operate without the patient screaming, yelling, and carrying on. The soldier was conscious throughout the operation but did not feel the cut. Thinking about it made my stump tingle. Damned if I would have enjoyed being conscious and hearing the bone saw taking off my arm.

Their statistics on surviving a wound were surely a fraction of ours. In the American military, if you got hit in the head you had only a 10 percent chance of surviving; if you got hit in the chest, you had a slightly higher chance of surviving; and if you got hit in the belly, you had a slightly better chance. So, most of the people who survived wounds were those who received extremity injuries. They may have gotten their limbs blown off, but their vital organs were functioning, so they were salvageable. Consequently the vast majority of surviving wounded on the American side had orthopedic injuries. At one time it was estimated that if the soldier made it to the hospital, he stood a better-than-90 percent chance of surviving. These figures were so much higher than in previous wars because of the helicopter and the rapid transfer from battlefield to medical aid.

One of the hardships Tung had had to endure in the field was the need to be ready at a moment's notice to pack up and move out. This meant patients, equipment, supplies, and staff. They had to do this on occasion, often in the middle of the night, to get away from bombing raids or pending attack. The thousand-bed hospital, as big as it was, had to be moved. Even spread out among seven villages, some section or another would often come under attack and have to be moved. They lost a lot of patients each time they moved.

I told Tung during one of our conversations that Americans did not deliberately bomb or attack hospitals. The Vietnamese did not identify their field hospitals, so if they were attacked, it was because the Americans did not realize what they were attacking.

Bui Tung and the other surgeons had to learn a lot about how to make do. In talking to the residents at Walter Reed, he impressed upon them the philosophy that they may find themselves in a situation where they would not have all the resources they are used to or would like to have. They would then have to be creative in order to take the best care of the patient that is possible in the environment the surgeon finds himself in. If the stuff isn't there to do the job, the responsibility of the surgeon is not diminished. The patient still needs to be taken care of.

Bui Tung spoke with authority on this subject. Bruce and the rest of us who have visited Vietnam know that is what Tung and the other physicians are doing right now. They are making do because the equipment and materials are not there to do the job.

In fact, when Bruce went to Hanoi, he took bone screws, hip plates, and intermedullary nails designed for pediatric patients. These were common pieces of equipment Tung could use in his orthopedic surgery cases. The Russians are not great suppliers of medical equipment. The East Germans, where Tung had trained, are more supportive, but they are built like Americans and are big-boned. They would send equipment such as bone screws, hip plates, and nails, but they were designed for East German bodies and were not proportional to the small-boned Vietnamese. The equipment was just too big.

The Vietnamese surgeons are so strapped for equipment that they take out the pins used in bone fractures and reuse them. After the fracture is healed, they pull the pin out and use it again. They do not waste anything.

I thought of these things as we talked and continued our trek through the medical exhibit. One exhibit showed a large jar that was used by drugstores to hold medicinal leeches.

341

Tung said he was familiar with the application of leeches and had had them used on him to remove the blood from a serious bruise. He also believed many of the Asian medicines using herbs were beneficial.

On the second floor when we went through the Nation of Nations exhibit, Tung, who loved music, talked about how much he enjoyed the cartoons of Walt Disney, the music of Irving Berlin, and the singing of Bing Crosby. He did not like rock-'n'-roll music. "It does not have any pleasure in it," was his way of saying it.

Tung loved to play the violin. He owned three: one made in Italy, one made in France, and one made in East Germany. In the quiet of the evening, through the years of the war and afterward, he looked forward to playing. His violins were his only respite. I knew when I heard him speak lovingly about his violins that he would probably enjoy the music section of the Smithsonian.

The violin section is in a small area up on the top floor and I remember wondering as we looked for it whether it was worth the effort. But the joy in Bui Tung's expression when we finally found it told me I had done the right thing. I had not seen him this animated at anything else I had shown him all week. What we saw first were glass cases filled with violins. Oh, the pleasure of such a find.

We spent a good hour going slowly around the glass cases as Tung explained more to me about violins than I ever wanted to know. I found out the importance of the bow and the flow of the wood grain, the material that makes up the strings, the fingerboard and the turn keys, the shape of each section, and the country from which it came and the people who played it. And of course the most important element of a violin: its maker. Tung explained it all.

All week I had been carrying my camera, telling him to let me know what he wanted a picture of and I would snap it for him. There had not been one thing he had asked me to take a picture of until we found the violins. I shot three rolls of film on violins that day.

I learned a lot about violins, but my happiness was in leading Tung to this section of the Smithsonian. He was really enjoying himself, but the best was yet to come. Just when I thought we had experienced it all, we stepped through a door and found four Stradivarius violins in a special glass case.

Tung became positively ecstatic at seeing those violins. He told me he had read about the Stradivarius but he had never seen one in his life. Now here were four of them! He was absolutely delighted, and I received an education about the finer qualities of the Stradivarius violins and the man who made them.

To Bui Tung's way of thinking, a violin was the essence of happiness. He explained it to me this way: "You know, Fred, a woman can only give you pleasure for a few minutes, but a violin will give you pleasure forever."

At one of the last exhibits we saw before leaving, there was a Kentucky long rifle. I remarked to Tung at how the craftsman had done a superb job of working the wood. Tung looked at the beautifully textured hickory wood composing the stock and said, "It would be better used to make the wood for a violin."

Mary and I had asked Tung if we could give a small party so we could introduce some of our friends to him. There would be some friends attending who were married to Vietnamese. He hesitated slightly, but agreed to the idea.

As the time for the party grew closer, he did not seem comfortable. Finally I asked him, a few hours before it started, if he was worried about anything. Tung said perhaps not worry, but he did have a certain amount of anxiety. He did not think the Vietnamese Americans would receive him very well. But also he was not sure what to think of them, he honestly added.

Yes, I could well imagine. One of the Vietnamese women had been a child when her family escaped with her from South Vietnam as it fell. She was excited to be meeting Bui

Tung and he was pleased to be meeting her because as a child she was an innocent. But the others were young women who had worked with Americans, escaped from South Vietnam when it fell, and they were married to Americans. They were suspect in Tung's eyes simply because of that. He knew nothing else about them.

The North Vietnamese cadre believed the worst about these Vietnamese women who had married Americans. They considered them whores, or at best women who were used by the American men until they grew old and ugly, at which time the Americans would discard them. They believed the American men cared nothing for these Vietnamese women except to exploit them. Tung at first did not speak those beliefs aloud to me, but he alluded to them in his comments.

His attitude, however, was typical of the preconceptions that traditional Vietnamese families had about what would happen to their daughter if they had the misfortune to marry any foreigner—and an American in particular.

The negative preconceptions cut across politics. This belief was the same on the Communist side as it was on the South Vietnamese side. And during the war there was a basis in fact for this. There were many immature young American soldiers who married immature young Vietnamese girls, brought them to America, and then abandoned them. These girls would show up on the steps of the Vietnamese Embassy up on R Street NW off of Connecticut Avenue in Washington, D.C., looking for financial assistance to get back to Vietnam.

That was one reason the American bureaucracy in Vietnam, the military, and the embassy, erected so many administrative barriers to getting married. Before a couple could get married they had to have official MACV (Military Assistance Command, Vietnam) permission. That involved a long, arduous process, including religious counseling, counseling by the staff judge advocate, security clearance by the South Vietnamese National police, and so on. It was designed to slow things down. Some of these couples persevered, got married, had children, and were still living together after all these years. My friends were examples of marriages that had worked.

Despite Tung's initial misgivings, the evening went smoothly. The party in his honor was attended by countrymen who did not agree with him and who did not like his government. But I thought it would be good for him to meet Vietnamese who had escaped. As representatives of opposing political beliefs, he had as low an opinion of them as they did of him. But as individuals they could take each other's measure.

The people who attended the dinner at our house that night were Andy Gembara, my classmate from OCS, and his Vietnamese wife Happy; Paul Mather and his Vietnamese wife Loan; Jean Sauvageot, whose Vietnamese wife was too sick to come; and Lynn Doung, a Vietnamese who escaped from Vietnam when she was twelve years old.

Andy had been Special Forces and had been in Vietnam in 1967 and 1968 when he was severely wounded, almost losing an eye and suffering wounds to his shoulder and neck. He remained in Special Forces, returning to Vietnam in 1970, where he stayed until Vietnam fell in April 1975.

Paul had been one of the few advisers from the Air Force who was stationed by himself in a South Vietnamese village. He was in Vietnam from 1970 until it fell in April 1975.

Jean had spent eight years in Vietnam as a Special Forces Adviser. He had been the senior adviser to the Vietnamese at their National Training Center and was an adviser to the premier of South Vietnam. He also was in Vietnam until 1973 as an interpreter with the Four Party Joint Military Commission.

All of these men had stayed involved in one way or another with Vietnam through their jobs and their wives' families. They probably had a better feel for the issues involving Vietnam than most "experts."

Jean speaks Vietnamese so well that Vietnamese speaking

to him on the phone assume he is Vietnamese. He was particularly anxious to converse with Bui Tung and immediately sat him down for a long conversation.

The youngest Vietnamese woman, Lynn, was the most excited to meet Bui Tung. She was politely full of questions about Vietnam. She wanted to return to visit her family, and she talked to Tung about doing that someday. He replied she would be welcome.

The reaction among the older Vietnamese women was cordial but cautious. I was later told by the men that the Vietnamese women were not at first excited about meeting Bui Tung. But once they met him, they found him to be an interesting person. There was deference to him due to his age—Tung was fifty-nine—which is common among Asians. But there were also fundamental differences between the Communists and the non-Communists that made them distrust each other.

During the course of the evening, Bui Tung talked to them about the shortages after the war and the present suffering going on in Vietnam. Their hearts went out to him, for they knew the truth of what he was saying from the letters they received from their relatives still living in Vietnam. Although they were cautious about what he stood for, they could identify with the medical needs he was describing. Tung talked about the plight of the disabled veterans and their needs. He said he was here in America to gain support for the needs of all the disabled in Vietnam—veterans, civilians, and children. Vietnam was desperate for assistance. He made a plea for help from the people.

Later the men told me the ladies felt he was sincere but that they were also leery of the corruption within the Communist Party pertaining to goods and services. They had heard it was as bad in some respects as it had been in the South Vietnamese government, so they wondered if that was causing some of the problems with medical supplies. Because of the corruption, would medical supplies get through to the people if they were sent to Vietnam?

Afterwards, I asked Bui Tung what he thought about the evening. He expressed surprise that the American men seemed to truly care for their Vietnamese wives and remained married to them. Beyond that he made little comment, other than to thank me for an interesting evening.

After the party I drove him back to the hotel on Connecticut Avenue. I had enjoyed our week together and wished we could have had more time to talk and get acquainted. There were so many more questions I wanted to discuss with him, but the limitations of time had hemmed us in.

During the drive, I asked Tung what he thought about America now. At the time we were sitting at the traffic light on Indian Head Highway and Oxon Hill Road in Maryland, south of the District of Columbia, surrounded by the evidence of a vigorous, rich America. The lights from the long lines of traffic, the sounds of loud music thumping through the closed windows of automobiles on both sides of us, the muted roar of passenger jets whose bright landing lights shone through the darkness on their final approach to National Airport, new construction sites lining the road, hundreds of cars and dozens of trucks and vans speeding by on the Beltway in front of us: this was so much a part of my life I never thought twice about it. This crazed, headlong rush toward the future was routine for an American city.

Tung had been busy with his own thoughts, but finally he replied, "I had been told America was preoccupied with sex, had a high crime rate, was an unruly, violent country, and cared nothing for the family. I feel my visits with Americans in their homes have shown me the family is very important. American families truly seem to care for each other. I am happy to see the concern you have for your parents and children. This is a good thing."

He remained diplomatically silent on the other elements of America. I could not blame him. After a week of living in the capital of the United States at the height of a record murder spree, passing by the dozens of homeless who hung out at Lafayette Park next to the VA, seeing prostitutes

347

walking out to cars in front of us as we sat at the lights at Thomas Circle, watching the gangs of blacks dealing dope on 14th Street when we drove up to Walter Reed, and watching the hotel television and reading the *Washington Post* each day, Tung had seen plenty of things that were difficult to explain.

He had asked me, "Why, Fred, do you have so much of these bad things? This is not good for your country."

I always tried to explain that Americans too were disturbed at such things, but that there were intense disagreements on the best way to solve these problems. I told him I was a conservative, so I would take harsher measures against criminals. I would put more of our mentally incompetent into institutions and I would revise our social welfare system as a few items to start with. Of course, I told him, there are people of a liberal bent who are inclined not to blame those people for their shortcomings, but instead blame American society for their problems.

Meanwhile the situation got worse while those issues were hashed out between the two sides. I had no good explanations. I would have had trouble explaining America's failure to correct its cancers to one of our allies, let alone a Communist like Bui Tung.

The next day, a Sunday, Bruce picked Tung up and took him to church. Bruce had done this every Sunday and it did not seem to bother Tung. Bruce had asked him at first, of course, and somewhat to Bruce's surprise Tung had accepted the invitation and had gone each Sunday thereafter. Bruce said Tung was always attentive in church, observing everything and taking an interest in the activities. Tung seemed to have an understanding of Christianity and knew what was going on.

After church and lunch at the house Bruce drove Tung to Williamsburg, three hours south of Washington, D.C. At the meeting, Bruce and those who had invited Bui Tung were a little uncertain how the military orthopedic surgeons were going to react to a Vietnamese battlefield surgeon. After all, he was on the other side during the war, and there were quite a few battlefield surgeons who had served in Vietnam in attendance, including the present Surgeon General of the Army, General Frank Ledford.

Although Bui Tung did not visibly show it, Bruce was sure that he too was nervous about the meeting. However, Bui Tung was received as if he were an old buddy. Bruce said it was similar to when I went to Vietnam and met the old soldiers. I had more respect for them than I had for some bureaucrats in Washington, because we had both gone through a common ordeal as soldiers.

That was what happened between Bui Tung and the American battlefield surgeons. There were doctors who grabbed Tung and talked to him for hours about his experiences in the war. He was well received by everyone. He had spent most of his career as a combat surgeon and fit right in with this group. He presented his paper on "Orthopedic Care of the Disabled in Vietnam" and it was well received.

December 10, 1988—Bui Tung Leaves

★ The morning Bui Tung left was a clear, brisk, sunny December Saturday. He was taken to the airport by Bruce van Dam. Mary, the two girls, and I drove out to Dulles Airport to say goodbye. We met them at the midfield United Terminal. Bruce had his two children with him and we took a last round of pictures.

We had grown to like Bui Tung and we were going to miss him. He genuinely seemed to have liked us as well. We had promised to write each other. I felt there was much more that needed to be said between us, but we had from necessity and by nature kept our guard up. We both needed more time together in order to lower our defenses further. But frankly, as long as we represented our governments, we would be required to maintain that cautiousness with each other. We might say something to each other in all innocence that could be misinterpreted by our superiors as jeopardizing our country's position on an issue.

Bruce and I never felt Tung was "coached" to act as he did. He did not have to put on an act. He was comfortable with himself and proud to be a part of the revolution that freed his country. He did not hesitate on occasion to make criticisms about things in his country, but he did so no more than we did about our own. He obviously believed he was on the side that was right in the war. He had dedicated his whole life to supporting Ho Chi Minh's party. His party credentials after a lifetime as a battlefield surgeon must have been impeccable, and I am sure he was of that special group of old cadre who were highly respected by the other party members.

Bui Tung was amenable to reason. He was obviously a man of deep convictions, derived from where he was born and the historical circumstances in which he lived. He was, above all else, a man who had spent a lifetime healing other people. His goodness and sensitivity were sincere—his profession alone was proof of that. The frustration we saw in him as he tried to cope with the lack of resources was very real.

He is exactly the kind of man I would send out to represent my country if I was the Vietnamese government trying to put my best foot forward to the Americans.

If we chose to be cynical about the motives of a man who has operated on thousands of battlefield casualties over a forty-year span of his life, and who showed dismay at the long list of names on the memorial of one of his former enemies, perhaps we think too little of our own motivation: honor.

Tung entered the doorway of the DC-10 and waved at us one more time. As he turned to go down the entranceway, I felt a pang of regret at being unable to help this man more than we had. Although forces were gearing up and aid would be steadily increasing, there would always be a barrier between us, the one that separates a police state from a democracy.

The things I found abhorrent in the Communist system made me realize more than ever why we fought against it. If I sent a letter to Bui Tung, I had to send it through the Foreign Ministry. When I was visiting Vietnam, it was against the law for me to visit him in his home.

Tung and his comrades had won their country through force of arms, but they had adopted a system of government that was unable to provide services to the people. Even if our two countries normalized relations, the Communist system could not make effective use of the resources provided to them by this country. Yet to argue this point with Tung or any single individual was useless. Whether they liked their system or not was immaterial to solving the immediate problems. All we could do was to try to help and continue to build on the small foundation of humanitarian aid.

If we could keep building long enough, perhaps events would bring forth a political change beneficial to both countries. But whether that came to pass or not, we still had a responsibility to our leaders to make the humanitarian process work until they ordered us to stop.

As Tung disappeared down the passageway, I wondered what the next step would be.

Fifth Trip to Vietnam
★ May 1989 ★

May 21, 1989—Return to Hanoi

★ It had been over a year since my last visit to Vietnam. Many positive things had happened. True to our word to the Vietnamese, the NGOs had been building steady momentum in their efforts to provide humanitarian aid to Vietnam.

The State Department Vietnam desk officer and the staff in the Southeast Asia section were the single most important factors in making the Vessey mission a success. All we team members could do was make recommendations; the success or failure of those recommendations was the responsibility of the State Department staff, who had to dedicate themselves to the hard work involved in carrying them out. They had gone to extraordinary efforts in the past year, and the result had been that over thirty NGOs were now authorized and licensed, in one manner or another, to provide humanitarian aid to Vietnam. This was especially noteworthy in light of the incredible difficulty of operating within the parameters of America's nonrecognition policies, which included economic sanctions and trade embargoes. Not only did the State Department staff have to contend with those difficult issues; they had to coordinate the NGOs' licensing and activities in Vietnam with the Department of

Treasury and the Department of Commerce, who were responsible for enforcing these policies.

Of course obstacles were constantly being thrown up by the anti-Vietnam crowd. In Washington the cynical wisdom is: "It takes everyone to say yes to an idea to make it happen, but it only takes one to say no to stop it." And the anti-Vietnam contingent were effective in knowing how to say no. Although they had not stopped the Vessey mission, they had added to the difficulties of carrying it out. Even so, the mission had continued to overcome those difficulties and had grown more successful, due mainly to the efforts of the State Department at the working level and General Vessey and the Interagency Group's tenacity at the policy level.

The Vessey mission was working.

I had been busy in my role as General Vessey's team member, providing information to NGOs and working with them on possible resources that could be provided to Vietnam. In May 1989 General Vessey asked me to return to Vietnam once again.

Mike Marine, deputy director of the State Department, had replaced desk officer Larry Kerr as the responsible State official. This, in effect, upgraded the importance of the mission. He and I were the only ones going. We did not anticipate any problems, and the purpose behind this trip was positive. We were to confirm America's commitment to the continuation of humanitarian aid; allow Mike the opportunity to make a report to the Vietnamese on all NGO activities; and provide ourselves with a further review of rehabilitation centers.

This trip, I was carrying five human eyes, donated for cornea transplants by the Lions Eye Bank in Fresno for delivery to an eye institute in Hanoi. Tom Good, the president of that chapter, had worked out an agreement with the eye institute in Hanoi to ship them approximately five eyes every other week.

But Tom was having a problem setting up a voluntary and free logistical chain to make deliveries from the States to Hanoi. Time was of the essence because the eyes would go bad after ten days or if they got warm. It was necessary to keep them stored individually in little glass bottles, packed in ice. Tom asked me if I would carry them in with me, and I said I would.

The package was in a white Styrofoam container about 11 inches square. Inside were the five eyes packed in dry ice, along with twenty surgical Trephine blades used for the transplant surgery. On the side of the container was a 2-inch orange tape with the words HUMAN EYES written in black letters across the tape.

America is the only country in the world with an excess of eyes, Tom told me. It has about two thousand excess eyes a year. The European countries have enough for themselves and Third World countries have none. In the package were two eyes from a sixty-nine-year-old, two from a seventy-nine-year-old, and one from a sixty-two-year-old. Tom told me the age of the eye did not matter. The important thing was they worked.

Thus began another long trip to the Orient.

Mike Marine was an excellent traveling partner and a no-nonsense professional. Back in Washington, when he was first assigned to replace Larry Kerr, I was apprehensive about what kind of person he was. My fears were allayed soon after Mike arrived. I enjoy working with a man who knows his job, and Mike is such a man. About 5 feet 10 inches tall, with a stocky build, a short haircut, and glasses, he still looks like the Marine he once was. When I first met him, I asked what branch of the service he had gone into. He said with a name like Marine there was only one service he considered.

Mike had made arrangements for us to stay at the Imperial Hotel in Bangkok. The Imperial was a convenient place for us to stay; the Vietnamese Embassy was right next door. Directly across the street was the residence of the American ambassador. Down the street a couple of blocks was the American Embassy.

The morning after our arrival in Bangkok, we stopped at the Vietnamese Embassy to apply for our visas before walking on to the American Embassy. Applying for our visas was a new experience for me. Someone from the embassy had always done it for us on the earlier trips.

We entered through the green door into a small holding office. A square support column with a writing shelf surrounding it at waist height stood in the middle of the room. Through a window on the other side of a wall were two Vietnamese Embassy employees who accepted our passports and three head-shot photos.

After we filled out some paperwork, I looked around. In a stack next to my elbow were two types of travel brochures. This was interesting: I kept hearing that Thailand and Vietnam do not cooperate on many things, but there was always evidence to the contrary. These travel brochures had been put together by Thai travel companies, obviously in cooperation with the Vietnam Ministry of Tourism.

One was pink and one was beige; both had colorful scenes of Vietnam. The tours ranged from four days, three nights to eight days, seven nights. The brochures were printed in English, prices were quoted in U.S. dollars, and all tours included airfare from Bangkok to Ho Chi Minh City and back. The tours were all in the South: Ho Chi Minh City, Da Nang, Vung Tau, and the tunnels of Cu Chi. Included was a suggestion to bring small denominations of U.S. dollars.

Yes indeed, I thought, these are directed toward American tourists. We knew there were many former U.S. soldiers going back to Vietnam. It was certainly no secret. Although it was illegal for American travel agencies to set up tours because it was a violation of the "Trading with the Enemy Act," there were any number of ways for travel to be arranged outside the United States for Americans who wanted to visit Vietnam.

In fact there were so many Americans going into Vietnam and becoming familiar with it that I had heard some of them referring to Ho Chi Minh City as "Ho Ville."

One proof of the changing atmosphere was a white insert in all the brochures, a sheet entitled "Special Business Programs." It offered three-, four-, or five-day trips to Ho Chi Minh City with no special itinerary. This was for businessmen.

The Vietnamese told us to pick up our passports in the afternoon. We left and walked on down the street to finish our business at the American Embassy.

The next day Mike and I boarded a Thai Airways scheduled flight to Hanoi. The Thais had increased their business dealings with the Vietnamese over the last year and now had three regularly scheduled flights a week. We settled tightly into the tiny seats for the 90-minute flight to Hanoi.

I sat back and wondered what I would see in Vietnam this trip. I had heard and read that things were changing rapidly. The first change was evident while we were still in the air: Vietnamese Customs forms were given to us to fill out before we landed. This was much better than waiting to fill them out in Customs.

We landed at 1300 hours and our old friend Mr. Nhu was there to help us go through Customs. The difference in Vietnam was evident the moment I walked out through the double doors. There were three or four times as many cars and trucks as before. I counted three buses to boot. There were more people crowded around the exit waiting for friends and relatives. They were more vibrant and were dressed better than before, in much more colorful clothes.

Mr. Nhu and the driver had brought out a car rather than a van to pick us up. I noticed an American flag sticker on the dashboard next to the key slot. When I asked about it, the reply was that an American had given it to the driver, who had stuck it on the dash. He asked me if I liked it and I said sure. But privately I could not imagine a Vietnam flag on an American government car's dash. It was just another indication of the Vietnamese belief that the war was over. And of course an obvious ploy.

On the drive into Hanoi the road was bustling with activity. There were many new two-story brick homes in varying stages of construction. Scores of new little shops had appeared along the road where before there were none. More significantly, they were selling a variety of items, not just cigarettes as they had the year before.

We told Mr. Nhu we had an important package to deliver before we checked into the guesthouse. He looked puzzled at the mention of eyes until we explained their purpose. We showed him the address on the package and he said he was familiar with the location. After we crossed Chuong Duong Bridge into Hanoi, the driver drove straight to the Institute of Ophthalmology at 85 Ba Trieu Street.

We pulled into a driveway and stopped at the closed gate. Mr. Nhu got out to explain who we were and why we were here. A pedestrian doorway stood open next to the old iron double gate and through this came three men, who amidst much friendly chatter pushed the double gate open. Our driver drove through into the courtyard and parked at the rear near a stairway.

We were taken upstairs to meet the director of the institute, Dr. Nguyen Trong Nhan, who graciously bid us welcome. He accepted the package with many thanks and called for an assistant to take it away. He explained he would schedule operations to take place in the next couple of days.

He invited us to sit down on some chairs in front of his desk and an assistant quickly brought us water and fruit. As was usual with every medical professional in Vietnam, he was forthright in telling us about his problems. He was short of supplies and equipment needed to do the job. Mike had prepared well for the trip and was familiar with all the nongovernment organizations that worked in Vietnam, so he discussed how the NGOs could help the eye institute.

The two-story building was old and looked as if it had

been built in the nineteenth century. I did not see the operating equipment but I had been told it was outdated. Tom Good said that when he visited in November 1988, there were dozens of patients waiting for a cornea. The patients shared beds because of the overcrowding. He had gone into surgery where he had watched surgeons at several of the operating tables working without surgical gloves. I had seen all of these kinds of things before and did not expect the institute to be any different.

What *was* different about this office was the eccentric collection of equipment the doctor possessed. A videotape of eye surgery was running on a TV set on a table against the wall. I had never seen a working TV in a medical setting before in Vietnam. But the most incongruous thing was a toy I would have expected to see in the back window of a 1957 Chevy. As the doctor was intently describing his plight, my attention was drawn to a ceramic hula girl whose head and hips were held by springs. The piece was undulating silently on the table in front of his desk next to his right elbow. He must have banged into the table as he was handing us his business cards stating he was also the chairman of the Vietnamese Red Cross chapter.

During the meeting we discussed and clarified how eyes could most effectively be forwarded to him at the institute. He seemed confident the Vietnamese Embassy in Bangkok would successfully forward packages to Hanoi once the embassy received them from the Americans. His confidence, I found out later, came from the fact the wife of the Vietnamese ambassador in Bangkok was Dr. Le Mai, an ophthalmologist herself, who had practiced at the institute in Hanoi for twenty-nine years before moving to Bangkok. She was only too aware of the need for corneas for transplant.

Later, we learned that only three operations out of the first fifteen were successful. The lack of surgical gloves caused infections in twelve of the operations and the patients had remained blind.

After our short meeting, we drove into the tree-lined street and turned right for the drive to the guesthouse. On the way I noticed a sure sign of change from my previous trip, one that reminded me so much of South Vietnam when I was there in 1967 and 1968. There were dozens of new motorcycles on the streets, similar to the Honda 50s the South Vietnamese used to ride. These were about the same size, they went like a bat out of hell, and there were a lot of them, all bright red. The motorcycles I had seen over a year ago were few in number and all were ancient.

Another thing that was new for me were the brilliant red blossoms hanging from the Flame trees. It was spring, and they were out in all their glory, adding striking color to the earth tones of Hanoi.

When I saw the guesthouse at 2 Le Thach Street, I felt like I was seeing my home away from home. The young soldier on duty at the gate gave us a cursory glance as we drove through the open doors. The driver stopped in front and we hopped out to retrieve our luggage from the trunk.

But on entering the open double doors I was surprised to see major changes in the lobby. There was a table and chairs in one corner near the doors. A reception desk was set up next to the stairs and a smiling male receptionist greeted us. He even assigned us rooms and gave us keys from a set of blue or yellow tagged keys lying on the counter. We were given a card with our room number on it and, most amazing of all, he offered to have our bags taken up to our rooms.

I was astonished. On our other trips we had waited in the empty lobby while Mr. Nhu went off to another building to get keys and room assignments. In those days I had always felt like I was standing in a deserted hotel.

Another surprise was a push-button phone on the lobby desk. Behind the receptionist was a floor lamp and a fan on a pedestal, all brand new. A Roy Orbison song, "Pretty Woman," was playing on a big boom box. It was about the size of a medium suitcase and would have fit right in on the New York subway.

The receptionist saw me staring at it. He grinned broadly and informed me he liked black music like this song, but he really liked country music better. I did not have the heart to tell him Roy Orbison was white.

He assigned me to Room 111 on the west side of the guesthouse. I had never stayed on the back side before. From my window I could look out across the roof of the post office to the clocktower. Ho Chi Minh was not there to stare at me; he was on the other side.

There were some differences in this room from the ones I had stayed in on my four previous trips. The water bottle on the table was cut glass instead of the green tinted plain bottle. There were new foam rubber mattresses and pillows on the twin beds.

Over on the table I noticed a sheet of paper. As I read it, I wondered who the Vietnamese had hired as their marketing expert. There was evidence of a non-Communist mind at work here. It listed the prices and services available and started out with the heading:

Welcome to the Government Guest House

Attention: All bills must be paid in U.S. dollars and should be settled the evening before your departure. Prices do not include 10% service charge. Please do not hesitate to ask us for any special service.
Have a pleasant time in Hanoi!

Most of the services listed had not existed a year ago. The paper even mentioned a 10 percent service charge. What a difference! I had been told Communist governments frowned on tipping.

After unpacking, I went across the hall to knock on Mike's door to ask him if he wanted to go for a walk. He said he didn't but he would meet me at 6:30 P.M. in the room off the stair landing for the dinner.

Mr. Nhu had informed us when he dropped us off that Mr. Bai was inviting us to dinner especially for the purpose of introducing us to Mr. Nguyen Can. Mr. Can, Mr. Bai's deputy, was being assigned to the Socialist Republic of Vietnam's mission at the United Nations in New York. I had heard he was an urbane but difficult man.

Mr. Le Bang would be Mr. Bai's new deputy. He had been a regular member of the previous meetings and I remembered his grandfather's second wife had disappeared in a bunker hit by a B-52 strike.

I went downstairs and stood on the front porch soaking in everything. There were foreigners of all descriptions being driven up or driven away by their Vietnamese escorts— French, Russians, Japanese, and other Asians. In addition there were three separate groups of Americans. Former Ambassador William Sullivan was leading one of the groups; they had flown in on the same plane we had. Sullivan had been heavily involved in the 1968–73 Paris Peace Talks. He was now leading a study group to look at ways of helping Vietnam.

While I was standing there watching the parade, I heard a tentative "Mr. Downs?"

I turned and said, "Yes."

A slightly plump, middle-aged Western man standing about 5 foot 11 inches tall, dressed in light-colored trousers and a short-sleeve shirt, came forward to introduce himself as Thomas J. Vallely, Coordinator of the Indochina Programs for the Harvard Institute for International Development.

He started out our conversation by saying he was very familiar with my writing in the *Washington Post*. Vallely told me he was part of a group studying the economic situation in Vietnam and planned to develop a paper composed of proposals on how these problems could be overcome. While he was talking, an American woman in her late fifties or early sixties walked up, said she had seen my name, and she too was interested in meeting me. She introduced herself as

Virginia Gift. She said she had used my books in the college classes she taught in the States on the Vietnam War.

I wondered how they had known who I was. I discovered during the course of the conversation that both she and Mr. Vallely had noticed my name on the boxes of books I had brought, which were stacked next to the reception desk. When they had seen the name and then the one-armed guy standing on the porch, they figured it had to be me.

Ms. Gift had volunteered to come to Vietnam for a year to teach high-level Vietnamese officials English. She had gotten a job with the Ministry of Foreign Affairs, who had put her up in the government guesthouse and furnished her meals for the year she had been a teacher here. However, the Foreign Ministry had not renewed her contract and was now throwing her out of the guesthouse. She had subsequently landed a job with the Ministry of Tourism and was planning to stay in Vietnam indefinitely.

I wondered why an American would be motivated to do such a thing. It seemed strange to be standing here in Hanoi talking with an American who paid her own way to get here and who lived here for no other purpose than to work for the Communist government. It must have seemed strange to the Communists, too. I heard later they halfway suspected her of working for the CIA.

But she seemed like a nice person and I enjoyed talking to her. She knew a lot about the country. She answered one question I had been wondering about. She told me she was the one responsible for improving the guesthouse. She said the Vietnamese were working hard preparing for September 31, 1989. This was the deadline they had set for when they would finish pulling out of Cambodia.

"They think the Americans are going to flock into Vietnam on October 1, 1989, when it opens up. They expect America to normalize relations with them as soon as the pullout is completed. That's what the Americans have told them.

"I told them that if the Americans come to Hanoi, they

are going to expect to sleep on something other than straw mats and stay in rooms that are more comfortable," she went on. "And they were going to have to have service in the lobby."

The Ministry of Tourism should be happy they hired her.

While standing on the porch, I overheard a conversation about how the power grid that supplied Hanoi had increased in strength with the big dam constructed with the help of the Russians. However, the Soviet material and workmanship had been so bad that the large pipes through which the water flowed were leaking at the seams in torrents. The grid could fail at any time. The dam had had so many problems from faulty equipment and workmanship that the Vietnamese in charge of the project was in big trouble with the party.

It made me think once more of America's attempt to destroy the power station on the outskirts north of Hanoi twenty years ago. The effect of bombing seemed to have the same impact on the electrical grid system as the effect of Communist management. The end result in both cases was the same: intermittent power.

I thought it was getting crowded around the guesthouse with all the Americans these days. I was witnessing the end of a period of history. Shrugging my shoulders at the inevitability of the flow of events, I proceeded out the gate for my familiarization stroll.

The street scenes were the same, except for the motorcycles. Bright red JAWAs zipped along in traffic, weaving in and out of the slower bicycle brigades steadily pedaling away. The tattered men lounging in their dilapidated three-wheeled taxi bicycles were still in front of the post office, lined up along the curb waiting for a fare.

Old women with faces creased in networks of wrinkled brown skin, dressed in peasant garb of black pajamas and faded and torn blouses, squatted beside their tiny piles of produce on the sidewalk. What was different was that there was lots more produce in those piles than there had been on my earlier trips. The peasants looked better fed also.

Then I crossed the busy intersection and entered the big department store.

What a difference from the last time I was in this store a year and a half ago! There were more goods displayed than ever before. The prices were written in dong on the display signs, and at the official exchange rate of 1 dollar to 4,000 dong were pretty expensive. But there was no shortage of buyers. People were crowded around the counters, buying items as fast as the salespeople could get through the paperwork. This is no small feat in a Communist country that requires triplicate of everything and three times as many people as normal to do the smallest task.

Due to the raging inflation, another thing of interest was the large amount of bills involved in the transactions. Thousands of dong were needed to buy the least expensive item. Anyone who had money always carried a wad.

But the biggest surprise in the store was a new section for electronics. Crammed into one corner and sitting on dusty worn shelves were new 14-inch, black and white TV sets, with crudely printed price tags attached beneath. The price was 450,000 dong. I could imagine a family coming in to buy a TV set and pushing a wheelbarrow full of dong in front of them. The price translated to 112.50 U.S. dollars, which was not a bad price for an American, but which represented a Vietnamese's income for a whole year. I remembered Dr. Bui Tung's dismay in relating how families sold their possessions in order to buy a TV set for their youngsters.

After leaving the store I looked up at the rooftops and saw TV antennas protruding into the skyline. It reminded me of American cities in the late fifties when TV antennas were on every roof.

I had earlier passed by new shops selling electronic merchandise: tape players, portable boom boxes, and radios. None of these luxuries were to be found anywhere at any price before.

SONY and other Japanese companies were present in force. There was a Polish TV set, but I was told they were inferior to the Japanese. The brand of choice was Japanese.

Another thing that had changed was the price of Heineken beer at the Dollar Store. It had gone up from 60 cents to a dollar. Even worse, they had had a run on the Heineken and sold their quota for the day. Highly unusual. I thought about it: the Vietnamese did not buy anything in the Dollar Store, the embassies brought in their own beer, so this shortage must be a sure sign there were too damn many Americans coming into town buying up all the beer and driving up the prices. Surely this was a portent of things to come.

Mike met me in the hallway and we walked to the room where they were waiting for us. Mr. Bai introduced us to Mr. Can. We sat down at a round table and Mr. Bai talked Mike into relaxing by removing his jacket. Mr. Can looked dapper, with his smooth features and full head of white hair. He spoke very good English.

The meal was elegantly served. Mr. Bai told us the chicken and eggs main course was translated literally as "Mother and children get together."

The evening went very well. Conversation flowed smoothly, with lots of talk about the difficulties of living in New York. This dinner was, as Mr. Bai had stated, a good opportunity for Mike and Mr. Can to lay the groundwork for their future meetings in New York once Mr. Can arrived at his post in the UN. We were all relaxed, and I think both sides felt good about the progress being made. It had been slow going at first, but now the NGOs were getting well established and the Vietnamese cooperation on issues important to Americans had significantly improved.

Things could always be better on both sides, but at least we were moving forward. In perspective, we were doing very well indeed. From what I had read, relationships between the two countries were the best they had been since our embassy had closed down and left Hanoi in 1954.

All in all, the dinner was very successful.

May 23, 1989

★ The next morning, Virginia Gift was waiting to have breakfast with Mike and me. During our Vietnamese/ French meal of fried eggs, liver pâté, bug-filled bread (that had not changed), and thick coffee, I again noticed many nationalities sitting at the tables. There were two separate groups of Americans in addition to us, French, Japanese, and other groups of indefinite Western European origin. A constant stream of their companions entered and left the dining room. Vehicles and their drivers pulled up in a steady flow of Lada cars to whisk these people off to meetings.

There was a hustle and bustle here that had not existed before. A sense of expectancy permeated the air.

The first meeting was held in the room off the landing on the first floor. The Vietnamese Delegation was headed by Mr. Bai, and included Dr. Bui Tung, Mr. Nhu, and Mr. Vinh—the same group we had met with before.

The only person missing from their group was Mr. Dong. He had been killed in a Vietnam Air crash at the Bangkok Airport the previous August. I would miss him. He seemed to be a good man. In my mind's eye I always remembered his jolly disposition and the light brown leather coat he wore at the first sign of cold.

Also killed in the crash was the Minister of Health, Dang Hoi Xuan, the big man with the Cheshire Cat smile who had given us a bottle of Seven Snake wine.

After the preliminary pleasantries, Mike asked Mr. Bai if he had had time to review the report Mike had given him the night before at dinner. Mr. Bai said he had and he was pleased with it. The report, entitled *Vietnam's Humanitarian Concerns: American NGO Activity,* printed by the State

Department in May 1989, contained a synopsis of the NGO help provided to Vietnam to date. Or at least the help the State Department knew about.

Mr. Bai thanked Mike for the report and said he understood our problem in not knowing about all the groups that were in Vietnam. We were unsure of precisely what he meant by this, but we assumed he was talking about tourists who later decided to visit hospitals or clinics. As we progressed through the report, a few interesting facts came to light.

There was the case of an American nongovernmental organization from the Worcester, Massachusetts, area that wanted to help the Lien Hiep district hospital. This hospital in South Vietnam had been known during the war as the Living Memorial Hospital: it was a twenty-eight-bed facility originally constructed in the late sixties by a group of Americans from the Worcester area as a living memorial to American servicemen who had died during the war.

The same group who had initially raised the funds had now launched a fund-raising drive in support of the Living Memorial Hospital. However, the people's committee in charge of the hospital at Lien Hiep did not like the idea of this hospital being named as a living memorial to Americans killed in Vietnam. They thought that was inappropriate. They had named it the Lien Hiep Hospital after the fall of South Vietnam and they wanted to keep it that way.

The problem was the hospital needed the help, but they were not going to change the name. There was some doubt as to whether the Americans would go ahead with their project or not. Mike and Mr. Bai agreed the parties involved would have to work it out among themselves.

As I listened to this discussion, I could easily understand both sides. The Americans wanted to honor their fallen comrades in the best way possible. The political cadre and possibly the people did not like the idea of a living memorial to dead Americans within their midst.

I thought of the American reaction if the North Vietnamese had wanted to set up in South Boston a "living memorial" hospital in the name of Viet Cong and NVA soldiers killed in the war against America.

We went on to the next items. Mr. Bai told us they appreciated NGO assistance in the South, but they would be happy if more assistance could be directed to the North. Compared to the South, a very small percentage of the NGO aid was going to the North. The people in the North resented this somewhat, but they were willing to wait until the Americans felt happy with their renewed commitment to the South.

Specifically, they would like American NGOs to concentrate help in the four provinces in the North most affected by the war. He said the road system in these areas was terrible, which made it very difficult for women to get their children to the centers for help. That was why the help should go to them. Mr. Bai smiled and said, "The roads built in the South by the Americans are still the best."

Then he turned to another subject. Bai told us over four hundred American delegations, ranging in size from one person to a dozen or more, visited Vietnam in 1988. He expected both records to be broken this year. He told us he received many, many requests from Vietnam veterans wanting to return to Vietnam. Some of them simply want to be tourists; others want to help rebuild the country; and some return to settle their minds and are accompanied by their doctors (he was talking about Post-Traumatic Stress Disorder). Bai looked up from his notes.

"The trouble is they do not always fully state their intentions beforehand, and so when they arrive, they try to branch out on their own. This is very bad because the tours are not designed to deviate from their schedules."

There were also individuals and groups on humanitarian missions who made promises to other people they could not keep. There were some who promised to help a particular center and then failed to provide the promised resources. This was very bad for the medical people and the patients. For instance, one person was supplying Vitamin A to the eye institute on a regular basis and then without prior warning or explanation stopped. The problem was that the center and the people it provided care for had become dependent on the Vitamin A and had incorporated it into their planning.

Now they were perplexed as to why it had stopped. They did not know what to do, Mr. Bai told us. The patients still showed up, but there was nothing for them. I could understand the frustrations. It was so unfair for people to be careless in their enthusiastic promises, promises which in some cases literally meant life or death or disability.

An organization or an individual takes on great responsibility when they make a commitment to help another country. They become in effect the resource base for the people and partners in the health-care system. Thus, if they are to be effective and useful they must communicate regularly with the people providing the care, know their needs, provide for them on a regular basis. If there are to be any changes of resources, this must be communicated to the dependent groups in time so that they can prepare for its failure to arrive.

The long-term NGOs knew this, but the new groups, mostly veterans eager to do the decent thing, were less experienced and were thinking short term. There was not a thing wrong with this as long as everyone understood it up front.

A unique situation then came up. One of the NGOs trying to help was composed of former refugees—Montagnards who were interested in supporting three health clinics in Ban Me Thuot Province, their old home. Mike and Mr. Bai discussed the fact that although their medical supplies had arrived in Ho Chi Minh City, the group's request to travel to their homeland in the Central Highlands had not been approved.

A problem I knew they faced in getting permission to reenter Vietnam was the activism of a small, hard-core group of refugees in America who advocated and had supported guerrilla warfare against the Communist government. The Vietnamese government did not want those factions coming into Vietnam to stir up trouble or to make contacts. This Montagnard group was not composed of those types, but the Hanoi government had not had time to ascertain that. So the delays had happened, much to the dismay of the group.

Although temporarily stymied, the Montagnards were continuing their efforts to be allowed to travel home to accompany the next shipment of medical supplies. I could only imagine what the emotional reaction would be when the newly Americanized Montagnard met his Vietnam family back in the Central Highlands. How strange it was to realize that the refugees were returning as American citizens to the place they had escaped from as Vietnamese citizens.

The Central Highlands was my old patrol area, and the vision of endless mountain ridges fading into the green mistiness of a far horizon came into my mind.

Mike's list of the NGOs helping Vietnam showed that something unique had developed. In addition to the mainline NGOs such as World Vision and the American Friends, small groups of Vietnam veterans from across America had been independently forming their own humanitarian projects.

One group from California had formed an agreement with the Ho Chi Minh City authorities to carry out construction and renovation work at one of the city's polio orphanages. As well as providing medical supplies, they were going to repair the orphanage's therapeutic pool, build specialized toilet facilities, drill a new well, and construct a workshop for orthopedic equipment.

Another California group was supplying antibiotics, medical equipment, and surgical supplies to various institutions in the South. Yet another group from California built a fourteen-room, 2,400-square-foot health clinic in Vung Tau.

A veteran group from Chicago composed of Army Engineers went to Vietnam to work with the Vietnamese in clearing old land mine fields. A second group of veterans from Chicago delivered medical supplies and equipment to various health institutions in Hanoi and Ho Chi Minh City.

A group from Massachusetts was working on ways to strengthen the maternal and child-health and family planning facilities in hospitals and clinics in Hanoi, Ho Chi Minh City, and Ha Bac Province. A group of veterans from Boston delivered basic health-care kits to four prosthetic rehabilitation centers and two hospitals. This group also delivered medical supplies to the Institute for the Protection of Mothers and Children at the Tay Ninh Province hospital.

There was the Operation Smile group, composed of many veterans from New York and Washington, D.C., who funded a group of surgeons to travel to Hanoi, where they performed 140 operations on children to repair cleft lips and palates on 102 children. An old Army buddy of mine, John Connor, had been responsible for arranging their visit.

A group from the state of Washington had provided artificial limbs for twenty-five amputees in Hanoi. They were now working on a project with the Vietnamese in which one thousand amputees in North Vietnam would be fit with limbs by the end of 1990. The project would then be expanded into the South.

In addition to the Vietnam veterans starting new organizations, there were veterans who were members of the established NGOs and they were providing assistance to Vietnam. The president of one of these had flown fighter bombers against the Vietnamese.

So many Vietnam veteran groups and individuals were involved in the humanitarian effort. The humanitarian needs of our old enemy had touched the hearts of these Americans who had once fought in their land.

I had talked to quite a few Vietnam veterans who were doing these things. With a few notable exceptions, there was no sense of guilt driving these men and women. A few were millionaires; others were doctors, policemen, teachers, laborers, businessmen, government employees, military men, and decent men and women from all walks of life.

Those I had talked to had said it was "time to get on with it. The war is over." There was also, I think, a good feeling of doing something constructive.

Finally the review of the report was finished to our mutual satisfaction.

Mr. Bai summed up. "In this meeting we have reviewed our work to see where we can improve our work. There has been, as shown by the report, progress in this field with which both sides can be satisfied.

"This morning I reported to my superior about this report and he is happy. At first in August 1987 when you started to look at our problems, events moved very slowly, but we could see your efforts were sincere. There was a year of getting the attention of the American people to help the Vietnamese people, but now everyone's efforts are succeeding."

His comments were good news to us. From zero NGO help when we had made our first visit to over one hundred NGOs now in Vietnam, the Vessey mission had indeed made an impact. At last we seemed to have achieved what General Vessey had set out to do when he assigned the humanitarian team to its task. We had identified the humanitarian needs, the nongovernmental organizations were increasing in numbers and amount of aid, and the Vietnamese recognized our humanitarian concerns as genuine.

As for the American humanitarian issues, a lot of quiet progress had been made and more was planned for the coming months. A Department of Defense memorandum dated February 28, 1990, would show the results since General Vessey's August 1987 mission to Hanoi. The Orderly Departure Program had been allowed to proceed, with exit visas being issued to a total of 46,593 Vietnamese who wanted to leave Vietnam. This included 21,776 Amerasians and their relatives and 23,821 family-reunification refugees (those Vietnamese who wanted to leave and join their families living outside Vietnam). Ten thousand of our former South Vietnamese allies had been released from the reeducation camps, and they and their relatives were also allowed to leave under the Orderly Departure Program. The Vietnamese had agreed to a long-sought-after goal of the JCRC by allowing joint American/Vietnamese search-and-recovery teams to conduct investigations in the field; eleven joint teams had gone out or were scheduled for the next few months. Thirteen technical talks (official meetings between the JCRC and their Vietnamese counterparts in reviewing the case histories of POW/MIAs) had been conducted since August 1987. Eight humanitarian talks had been held. The Vietnamese had repatriated 230 MIA remains, of which 93 had been identified.

Although there were those on both sides who would say not enough had been done, the facts were that the American and Vietnamese governments were working in a better spirit than ever before.

The meeting ended before noon. It had gone extremely well.

The Xa Dan School for the Deaf and Dumb

★ After lunch Mike and I were scheduled, at our request, to visit two specialized schools for children with disabilities. There were no more meetings, and we were to fly out the next day. We wanted to take the opportunity to review two new areas in which to expand America's humanitarian assistance.

The driver and Mr. Nhu picked us up at one o'clock and drove the Volga through a twisted path of back streets and lanes until I did not have the slightest idea where we were.

Nhu and the driver did a lot of talking and peering at street signs, too, so the Xa Dan School for the Deaf and Dumb, our first stop, was definitely off the beaten path.

Finally, on a back street down a one-lane road, the driver stopped outside the gate of a large, L-shaped building. A fence boxed off the open sides of the courtyard. The gate was a ramshackle affair, as were the building and grounds. A man pushed open the gate and struck his head through to talk to the driver, who had gotten out of the car.

The driver jumped back in as the man pushed open the gate. We drove through and parked in the courtyard. Three people were waiting for us under an overhang next to a staircase. A light sprinkling of rain dotted the puddles of rainwater scattered around the grounds. We dashed from the car to the covered walkway and went upstairs to be seated in an open room by the director of the school.

Introductions were made and we quickly got down to business. As was usual when we interviewed any of the directors or their staffs at the facilities we visited, they were very open in expressing their opinions, needs, complaints, and criticisms about the government's lack of ability to get things done or provide them with resources.

As the director, Ms. Tuong, explained the school's operation, she painted a dismal picture of the "people's" failure to provide care to the people who needed it most, the children and the disabled.

The Xa Dan School for the Deaf and Dumb had been established in 1978. It was the only one of its kind in North Vietnam and was run by the Ministry of Education. Its capacity was 130 students, ranging in age from six to eighteen years. There are estimated to be three thousand deaf children in the Hanoi area.

We asked how the students were chosen from such a large number to take the few spots available at the school. Ms. Tuong told us the parents made application in July and a committee met in August to choose which students would be accepted. Some of the criteria: the students must reside in the Hanoi area; they must have some residual hearing; and children who have mental problems or additional disabilities are not acceptable.

The children do not live at the school, and no facilities exist for their transportation to school, so their parents must deliver and pick up the child each day. Most children are too poor to have clothes for winter, Ms. Tuong added.

The ministry paid the overhead, but from the sound of things that did not amount to anything. The school had no running water and no kitchen, so the children had to bring their lunch each day. The building needed to be wired for electricity; at present only one classroom had it.

She told us that one day Vietnamese television crews came to film at lunchtime. Those students who did not have lunches with them were hidden away from the TV crews.

There were eleven classes. Seven were devoted to vocational training in embroidery, sewing, carpentry, and weaving. There was one room used for rehabilitation. Half of the school day was spent on regular education and the other half on vocational rehabilitation. The small amount of supplies available were provided by the Church World Service, an NGO that had donated five sewing machines and five weaving machines, and by the Dutch, who had given them five sewing machines and ten weaving machines. The school provided a total of nine years' education for the deaf.

The method of treatment for the deaf was acupuncture. I thought to myself, so much for the healing powers of needles.

They begin school by teaching sign language. They stop after a number of months and teach lip reading from then on. Ms. Tuong indicated they were 100 percent successful in teaching students to read lips. Privately, we questioned this figure; in America, success at lip reading is not nearly this high, and English does not have six tones to every syllable as the Vietnamese language does.

The school was also responsible for teaching the child to speak. Ms. Tuong said they had only a 5 percent success rate. Vietnamese was a tonal language, so I doubted that anyone but the teachers and parents would be able to understand the 5 percent. I asked if they worked with the parents to teach them how to communicate with their children. They replied that they did.

This made me think of something else I had discovered in another Third World country. I wondered if it were true here also. I asked them if the hearing aids assigned to the student were theirs permanently. The reply was no. The hearing aids are given to the child while he or she is in school and then taken back when he leaves school.

There was a staff of forty teachers paid by the Ministry of Education. All teachers are given the same training as undergraduates. Those who are then assigned to this school are given extra training in teaching the deaf by experts from the Netherlands who come once a year.

I tried to think of a way to describe this place to Americans. Think of a schoolhouse without electricity and water that has been stripped and abandoned for years.

The school has received minimal support: a few hearing aids and tape recorders from Australia, New Zealand, and West Germany. All the equipment was old. Ms. Tuong told us the greatest needs of the school were for tape recorders, slide projectors, a 16mm film projector, and desks. They also needed funds to wire the school with electricity, dig a well, build a kitchen, and have a vehicle to use in picking up students.

There were no students there for us to observe. We were informed there was no class on Thursday. We had discovered after so many trips that it was a habit of some directors to hide their patients and students. The reasoning was that they believed the patients got in the way of visitors and detracted from the point the director was trying to make.

We were given a tour. There was a display room to show

what the students produced and the teacher gave each of us a colorful small bag. The classrooms were utterly barren. In one room the teachers were receiving training on lesson plans.

We were shown old hearing aids tucked away in cases. These aids were for the students when they were at school. I asked about the batteries and how they replaced them. They were rechargeable, we were told. That may be, I thought, but there was no evidence to prove it. Where were they charged? Only one room had electricity. The aids looked old and worn out. The director said she needed earmold material, hearing aids, and batteries.

I got the impression not all 130 students showed up at the school at the same time. It seemed as if these students were provided this school because the parents demanded it, but the ministry was not doing very much to help. They probably thought teaching the deaf and dumb was a lost cause. That is not to say the director and staff were not trying to do their job, because they were.

It must be depressing and frustrating not having the resources to do the job. When I asked what kind of journals or professional magazines they received at the school, I got the answer I expected, "None."

The Nguyen Dinh Chieu School for Blind Children

★ Next, we were taken to the Nguyen Dinh Chieu School for Blind Children. There was quite a difference; the school for the blind was large and attractive. It was on a main street, and when we drove through the gates we could see this was upscale compared to the pitiful place we had just visited. The three-story contemporary building looked relatively new.

The director and his staff met us at the front door and immediately ushered us into a room for refreshments and a briefing. Again the director was blunt in his statements.

He told us the school was founded in 1982 by the Christian Blind Mission (CBM), a West German nongovernmental organization. It built the new facility at a cost of approximately $1 million Deutschmarks. Unfortunately, the facility is underfurnished and underutilized. It needs electrical wiring and running water, and the Christian Blind Mission will not do any more. The director accused the CBM of building the school and then walking away.

We were told that there were 150 blind children in the Hanoi area. We did not believe that: it was contrary to everything else we had learned. (There should have been many more blind children according to the reports we had received from the various international health organizations working in Vietnam.) But only fifty of them attended the school because there were not enough teachers. These fifty lived at the school during the week; they ranged in age from seven to fifteen years old. In addition, 180 normal children also attended the school.

The Ministry of Education is in charge of the school, but it provides only the teachers, who are self-taught by spending one day a week for two years learning how to teach the blind. The capacity of the school is 150 blind, but they needed more staff before they could receive more students, the director told us. The Christian Blind Mission was training two teachers in India. The director was also planning to upgrade the quality of the training by trying to do an exchange program with a blind center in Ho Chi Minh City.

The school teaches electric appliance repair to the partially blinded. It also provides mobility training to the students. When I asked if the school provided white canes, the director replied there were no canes for children. This was no surprise to me as I had run into the same problem in other Third World countries, but still I was disheartened.

Even worse was the fact that there simply was not any

place in society for the disabled in these Third World countries. The director confirmed this by saying that "blind children are hidden away by the family." I had read that in the Orient it is considered a curse to have a blind child.

Because the ministry only provides the teachers, the families have to pay 17,000 dong a month for the blind student to attend. (At 4,000 dong to the dollar, that is a little over 4 U.S. dollars.) There are some cases where three children in the same family are blind but the family can only afford to send one of the children to the school. The director pointed out that friends and family must go out and raise funds to assist in sending the other children with their sibling. The director was proud to point out that all thirteen graduates from the first class had found jobs. This was the group that had started when the school opened in 1982.

The Director then took us on a tour of the concrete three-story building. It looked like it was still under construction, but work had stopped a long time ago. The floors, walls, ceilings, and roof were in place, but the rooms were barren and dusty.

Upstairs, we entered a classroom where the students were being taught music. We stood in back while the teacher had the students perform for us. A group of children of various ages sang a song. Then a quartet formed from the group and they sang. Next was a trio, then a duet, and finally a solo. I did not understand the words, but the sight of those little blind children invoked in me a deep sense of sadness and pity.

As I watched the little girls in their flowered white and yellow dresses move from their seats to stand in front of us, I was very moved. One tiny hand searched out to find the friend next to them and the other hand moved cautiously in space, searching for obstacles. Bright with excitement at the visitors, dressed in their best outfits, they held hands and moved in a conga line around their desks to the front and sang their songs.

One teacher played an acoustical guitar, accompanied by

a drummer who was an eleven-year-old boy with milky eyes. He was dressed in blue trousers and a pink shirt. His drums were cast-offs from God knows how many years ago, but he didn't let that slow him down as he enthusiastically drummed out the beat. Then there was a solo flutist who wore green-colored glasses. We applauded after each song, and if time had not been pressing we would have stayed for an encore.

We stopped at one room where blind students were working with sighted students in preparing materials for the classrooms. On this particular day they were preparing literature books for use in the second grade.

They had set up a sort of assembly line to make these books. A teacher would read a sentence to a blind girl. She would poke holes in a sheet of paper, spelling out in Braille what the teacher said. She gave the Braille sheet to two other blind students, who duplicated it for regular typesetting. Once the typesetting was completed, a partially blind boy took the form, ran a roller of printers ink over the type, then inserted the form into a small hand printing press. He used a lever to squeeze it down onto a sheet of paper to print the page for the sighted. In this laborious manner they made all of the books used at the school.

After the tour we asked the director what was the most pressing need. The reply was money. With money they could buy things locally to help the school do a better job of providing training to the blind students, and they could expand the program to include the rest of the blind children in the Hanoi area. They also asked for equipment for vocational rehabilitation training, particularly material for making lamps and other electrical equipment. It would be nice, one of the assistants said, if they could have toys, teaching aids, and chess pieces.

I thought the best way I could present the problem to someone back in the States would be to tell them to assume nothing exists at the school and then go from there in determining what would be needed.

There was one thing the director was proud of, and that was the fact they were digging a well 6 meters deep they could use for washing and other activities. At present the water supply they used was available only one or two hours each day, from midnight until 1:00 or 2:00 A.M.

Back at the guesthouse, Mike said he would like to go out to eat at a local restaurant on our last night in Hanoi. I agreed. Bill Bell had given me the address of the best restaurant in town, a real four-star place called Restaurant 17, located at 17 Ly Quoc Su Street, and we decided to go there.

By the time we had showered and dressed, it was dark. With instructions from the woman at the desk we went out the gate and went west around the Lake of the Restored Sword. This place was off the beaten path, so we stumbled down some pitch black streets looking for it.

Every few blocks in Hanoi the name of the street changed to something else and the address numbers, on hard-to-read ceramic tiles, started over at the beginning, which made it very difficult to find something in the dark.

We finally found the restaurant next to a pedestrian alley entranceway that looked to me more like the kind of place where you would get your throat slit if it was anywhere else but Hanoi. As I peered up the rough cement stairs, I thought this did not look like a four-star restaurant. We went up a short flight of stairs to a landing where the kitchen was located. Open fires were burning in grills. Blackened pots were scattered around on various surfaces, and the chef, holding a pan in one hand and a long knife in the other, smiled and nodded his head to us.

We went up three more stairs to a room with a couple of tables; one larger table took up an adjoining room, with six or seven men sitting around. They looked like old cadre and returned my curious glance with hard stares. A few had dark-colored berets cocked over their heads and that, coupled with the cigarettes they were all smoking, made the room look like a scene from a thirties movie. All of them were smoking heavily and the ashtrays were full. Bottles of beer and cups of tea were set on the stained, graying tablecloth.

I was enjoying every bit of the experience because this was the first time in five trips I had ever eaten away from the guesthouse. Mike was well suited to working in the State Department because he seemed to tread easily where this civilian's stomach feared to go.

We ordered fish dinners. They were served on chipped plates. We washed the delicious meal down with weak Chinese beer and strong hot tea. The only other table in the room was vacant. The group in the next room were conversing in a cloud of heavy smoke that drifted into our room. A bottle of apricot brandy sat in the middle of their table. The heat, the cook's chatter, and the smells from the kitchen a few steps away swirled around us. The atmosphere was ephemeral and we would soon be gone, but for a brief moment this tableau restored to me the romantic Orient of my long-ago dreams.

Finally it was time to go. We asked for the check and paid the total bill of 6 dollars U.S. We nodded to the cook and two other staff as we passed them on the way down the short flight of stairs. I regretted having to leave.

Walking back to the guesthouse on my last night in Hanoi, I pondered what I had seen this trip compared to my first visit two years ago. The transformation had been remarkable: the profusion of Western music and electronic equipment in the form of radios and televisions; the large number of new motorcycles; more food available in the street; the number of new stores carrying goods from other countries.

On my first trip I had compared Bangkok, a dynamic city of color, with Hanoi, a drab, sleepy city. Now Hanoi was like a peach blossom struggling to open. The potential beauty could be seen. But Vietnam was a police state, subject to a harsh Communist doctrine forged by war and deprivation. The men and women responsible were hard pressed to cope economically and politically with the aftermath of what they had striven for and won. Therefore, they could easily crush that blossom out of fear.

I thought Vietnam would do well to review its own tradition of dragons and phoenix birds, harmony and happiness. There needed to be a balance in Vietnam if it was to grow and prosper for the future. War and communism had got them what they wanted, but these factors needed to be balanced by peace and democracy if they were to enjoy it.

Communism was not the way to achieve harmony or happiness. The pragmatic Vietnamese must see this each time they compared themselves with the Thais, Japanese, South Koreans, and other non-Communist Asian countries.

The next morning, as we drove over the Flying Dragon Bridge I looked out the back window across the city of Hanoi for what could be the last time. The accomplishments of General Vessey's mission would be a small footnote in history and we, the foot soldiers, would all be quickly forgotten in the shroud of time.

But I always have believed the individual makes a difference to the future. Usually unheralded and unknown, they do make a difference, no matter how insignificant their efforts may seem at the time.

Watching Hanoi fade into the distance, I thought of myself in Vietnam twenty-one years ago, a proud infantry lieutenant leading men into combat. I had killed Vietnamese and they had nearly succeeded in killing me more than once. We had certainly made a difference in each other's lives.

My government had sent me there to fight for what I personally thought were good reasons: to help the Vietnamese achieve freedom and democracy by fighting communism. Many good men died on both sides, and the Communists ended up in control.

There had been a lot of pain and a lot of water under the bridge in the years since the war ended. But sooner or later America would normalize relations with Vietnam. Next would come trade, then aid, and then, who knows, we could be allies sometime in the future. It had happened in the past with America and many of our adversaries, and so it could happen with Vietnam. In spite of the grueling experiences we had been through and those yet to come, I found myself feeling good about being on the American team, working once again to help the people of Vietnam, including our old enemies. I wished them well.

May 27, 1989—The U.S. Army Central Identification Laboratory, Hawaii

★ It was a strange coincidence how so many significant dates had been a part of my trips to Vietnam. On May 27, my forty-fifth birthday, I was returning home through Hawaii so that I could take an authorized mid-trip break and use the time to tour the facilities at the U.S. Army Central Identification Laboratory in Hawaii. CILHI is the forensic laboratory where the MIA remains recovered from Southeast Asia are brought for identification.

Lt. Col. Johnie E. Webb, Jr., is commander of CILHI. He picked me up at the hotel in Honolulu for the short drive to the laboratory, located at Fort Shafter near the dock area that was the embarkation point for soldiers shipping out to Vietnam during the war. He gave me a briefing on CILHI, its history, and its mission in the recovery and identification of remains.

Identification of one's remains has always seemed very important to individual soldiers. A soldier does not want to die without his family knowing what happened to him. Death has been accompanied by solemn rites in all cultures throughout history. The individual must be properly disposed of, as dictated by his society, and honored by his family. To die as an unknown soldier buried in an unmarked grave goes against the very soul of man.

In America's Civil War, for example, men going into battle would write their names on a piece of paper and pin it to their shirts, so if they were killed their bodies could be identified and their families notified of their death. However, many men who fell in battle were interred where they fell, with little attempt at identification.

I thought back on our own experiences in the Vietnam War. One of the first things the drill sergeant had us do in basic training when we entered the Army was to etch our names and serial numbers inside each boot and belt, helmet and cap. When we asked the sergeant why we had to do that, he looked at us with a deadpan stare and said, "'Cause when you get blowed to shit, there will be something to help identify what's left of you." He had just returned from Vietnam, and we did not know if he was kidding or just trying to scare us. Later on when I was in Vietnam and saw what happened to men who had been "blowed to shit," I knew he had not been joking.

On a more formal level, identification of remains is important to the military. They are entrusted with the welfare of millions of personnel and our society expects them to account for every single one in peace or war. Consequently, the first items issued to us upon entering the service were our two dogtags. We were told to wear them at all times and never take them off. The dogtags had our name, religion, serial number, and blood type stamped on them. There were two dogtags because when a man is killed in battle, one is left on the chain around his neck to identify the body and the other one is available to be taken back for identification if his body has to be left behind.

In today's military, there is an elaborate system set up to recover and identify remains of men killed in war, but it was not always so. Not until the Spanish American War did the U.S. government develop a policy of disinterring remains from their graves in Cuba and returning them to the United States for permanent burial.

In World War I, a Graves Registration Service was established by Congress to find, recover, and identify soldiers killed in the war. The remains were to be returned to America if at all possible.

In World War II, the Secretary of the Army was made responsible for the program of recovering, identifying, and returning to the United States the remains of men killed in the war. The various Army laboratories involved in this program were shut down, by an act of Congress, five years after the war ended.

During the Korean War, one Army laboratory was established in Japan to process the war dead.

During the Vietnam War, the U.S. Army had two mortuaries in Vietnam to identify the dead and process the bodies or remains. One mortuary was in Saigon and one in Da Nang. In March 1973, when American forces were withdrawing from Vietnam, the mortuaries were moved and combined into the U.S. Army Central Identification Laboratory at Camp Samae San, Thailand. In May 1976, the laboratory was moved to Honolulu, Hawaii, where it has continued to operate.

Colonel Webb told me CILHI's mission had been expanded to conduct search-and-recovery operations not only for the dead from the Indochina War but the dead from the Korean War and World War II. The laboratory also provided worldwide support for the search, recovery, and/or identification of remains of servicemen and women killed or missing in current operations such as the Arrow Air crash in Gander, Newfoundland, at Christmas 1985, and the Beirut, Lebanon, Marine barracks terrorist bombing in 1983. The Arrow Air crash was a military charter flight returning U.S. military personnel from their base in Germany back to the United States.

CILHI's personnel are uniquely suited to the task, as the organization has collected together a range of specialists found in no other place. These include search-and-recovery teams trained in archeological excavation techniques, laboratory teams consisting of physical anthropologists and

386

forensic odontologists, and casualty data-analysis teams who collect personnel, medical, and dental files on those servicemen still missing, and develop location maps of their last-known position when lost.

Using state-of-the-art computers, microscopes, and radiographic equipment, the staff studies and analyzes available remains to determine identity.

As a matter of curiosity, I asked Webb how many MIAs from World War II and Korea were still unaccounted for. He told me there were approximately 79,000 missing from World War II and 8,000 from the Korean War. I compared those numbers to the approximately 2,400 missing from the Vietnam War, and I wondered what was different about those earlier wars that the families of those missing had not demanded an accounting as the family members of Vietnam's missing had.

I thought it was because no one trusted what the U.S. government told them anymore. The anger for the POW and MIA families stemmed from the Johnson years, when the word from the White House was to not tell the families of POWs and MIAs anything and to keep them quiet. After years of suffering and not knowing what happened to their men, the families themselves finally broke through the government muzzling, but there was forevermore a mistrust between the government and those families who had been cheated in the vilest way.

The attention now paid to the American POW/MIA issue will have an impact on the next war. No longer will POW/MIAs be afforded the low priority accorded to them in the past. They will become an important factor in the psychological and public relations strategies developed by both sides. In any war we fight in the future, our enemies will know the value of American prisoners, but more importantly, the American government will know their value, too.

Johnie Webb then took me to the laboratory where the remains were examined. When we walked into the large, well-lit room, my eyes were drawn to the thirty gurneys set in five straight, orderly rows, taking up more than half the space in the room. Remains were on the gurneys and each one was covered by a white sheet. An American flag was hung on one wall.

The remains are treated with dignity from the moment they are received by America at the airport near Hanoi until they are identified and buried according to the family's wishes. Webb pointed out five gurneys that held remains from a B-52 that had exploded after being hit by a SAM. One of the crew had escaped, but these five had gone down with the plane. The skeletons from this crash were relatively whole, but there were some gurneys where only a few bits of bone were lying under the sheets; there had been very little to retrieve from the crash. I could easily imagine the terrible scene inside each aircraft as it tumbled to earth. The families of these men had waited a long time to put these men to rest, and their wait would now be over.

If there was more than one man on board the aircraft, the remains will usually be commingled. The first task in the identification process is to separate the remains into individuals. The condition of the remains depends on a lot of factors—speed of the aircraft and the angle it hit the ground being the major ones.

The task the CILHI has is a difficult one, as the staff analyzes everything they can about the returned remains: the location of the crash, the date of the crash, serial numbers off the aircraft and weapons, records of the people manifested on the aircraft, and of course all of the scientific evidence that can be gleaned from a study of the remains matched against medical and dental records of the missing personnel. Also included in the return of remains are any personal effects found at the crash site. These include identification cards, dogtags, and in the case of one set of remains I saw, a battered flight helmet.

But what was truly remarkable were the remains from World War II which shared this room with the remains from the Vietnam War. Johnie had told me about all the World War II crash sites that CILHI had investigated and the mammoth task still remaining to be done. Over three hundred crash sites were identified by location in New Guinea alone. I was astonished when Webb explained that they had recovered the remains of a crew from a B-24 Liberator that had been lost in 1944. They had been able to identify these remains due to their location in the aircraft, which was relatively intact, and the personal effects found in each location: an ID card with a thumb print, and in one a silver dollar with the man's initials scratched into it, a common practice for air crews in the Pacific.

I gazed at the personal effects and remains of an air crew from a war my father had fought in almost fifty years ago. I had no idea this sweep of the battlefields was a continuing effort worldwide. The enormity of a project involving the retrieval of remains from a world littered with the dead from the battlefields of World War II, Korea, and Vietnam was staggering. I pictured in my mind the individual soldier killed at a moment of battle. The clash of nations always comes back to the loss of one man.

In a back room Johnie showed me the files of over 55,000 men killed in Vietnam whose mortuary records had been moved to CILHI. I felt a dark wind blow inside me. I asked, "Would you have the file of James S. Yoder, my point man, who was killed when we were ambushed around Thanksgiving, 1967?"

Johnie got them for me. In Yoder's file I stared at the Defense Department form showing the outline of the human body where a mortician twenty-two years ago had marked the places in Yoder's body that the ChiCom machine gun's bullets had entered. I read the coldly stated facts about the wounds, and I saw and felt the heat of the terror that day when we had been ambushed and Yoder had been killed before my eyes.

As I stood there amid the remains of those men in the process of being identified and the files of 55,000 men who had been killed, my thoughts returned to the faces of Yoder, Hutchinson, Iding, and others I knew who had died. I thought of the disabled American men from the Vietnam War I knew today—the blind, the spinal-cord-injured, the amputees. And I thought of the 1 million Vietnamese killed on both sides, the thousands of disabled Vietnamese, North and South. I thought about our efforts to retrieve remains and the efforts of the Vietnamese to remember their war dead with the Hero cemeteries outside each village.

I realized that the real tragedy was that, despite everything that had occurred, neither the Americans nor the Vietnamese were happy with the end result. Since all else had failed, perhaps the humanitarian issues would be the catalyst on both sides to resolving the differences between the two countries.

Any soldier who has been in combat knows that there comes a time after the battle, when the smoke has blown away and the dust has settled, when you must lean down and give your foe a hand. For in that moment of generosity, the war is truly over.

Index

attitudes toward Americans in, 87, 89, 119, 121, 153–55, 169, 190–91

attitudes toward Russians in, 87, 89

ballpoints refilled in, 57

banking services in, 117

beer sales in, 65, 72, 86, 87, 88, 89, 93, 94, 96, 132, 158, 190, 365

cafés in, 88–93, 189–90

Christmas bombing of, 41–42

cigarette smoking in, 71, 86, 89, 90, 190, 258

Cuban-Vietnamese hospital in, 84

department stores in, 63, 364

dogs in, 83–84

Dollar Store in, 156–58, 220, 365

drinking water in, 51, 52, 61, 99, 106

electricity lacking in, 93–95, 218–19, 263, 363

English speakers in, 118, 157, 190, 327

flat tires in, 58, 257

foreign embassies in, 163, 165

foreigners in, 192, 221, 260, 361–62, 362, 363, 366

former POW visits to, 76–77

French influence in, 48, 60, 74, 84, 94, 255, 261

government guesthouse in, 48–52, 64, 96, 99–101, 128, 134, 161–62, 186, 204, 207, 218, 221, 262, 263, 359–62

guesthouse meals in, 65–67, 102, 130–33, 149, 219–20, 282, 366

heat and humidity in, 50–51, 54, 60, 67, 71, 86–87, 96, 129

Hoa Lo Prison in, 73–76

Ho Chi Minh's mausoleum in, 253

jazz club in, 85–87

Lake of the Restored Sword in, 53, 55, 56, 59, 60–61, 62, 63, 84, 121, 188–89, 381

lipstick smears sold in, 57, 71

mythic origin of, 189

newspapers in, 67, 87, 191, 289, 324

Old Quarter in, 261

outdoor markets in, 258–59, 261

postal services in, 118–20

postcards in, 153–55

poverty in, 54, 56–57, 58, 59, 70–72, 83–84, 90, 93–94, 258

radio broadcasting in, 96, 98

Restaurant 17 in, 381–82

soap shortages in, 70–71

soldiers in, 53, 63–64, 68, 133, 154, 254, 359

street conditions in, 72, 82

street crime in, 156

street scenes in, 48, 53, 54–55, 56–57, 60, 61, 63–64, 71, 72, 77, 84, 133–34, 154–55, 162, 257–58, 358, 363–64

television in, 95, 327–28, 364–65, 375

Thang Loi Hotel in, 41, 77, 162, 166, 255

traffic in, 47, 54, 55–56, 60, 63, 72, 74, 82, 162, 359, 363

Hanoi Hannah, 96–98

Hanoi Hilton, see Hoa Lo Prison

harassment and interdiction (H and I), fire, 38, 46

Harvard Institute for International Development, 361

Harvey, Joe, 11, 21, 25, 46, 50, 66, 74, 76, 83, 95, 150
  as JCRC team leader, 13–14, 22, 29, 116, 130–31, 151

Harwood, Dick, 322–23

Hero cemeteries, 40–41, 323, 334–35, 390

Hoa Binh Hotel, 93–94

Hoa Lo Prison (Hanoi Hilton), 45, 73–76, 79, 118, 163, 165
  U.S. POWs in, 73, 76, 77, 78, 79, 80, 82, 124, 163, 167, 197

Hoang Co Minh, 188

Index

Index

Official American passports, 182
Olaf Palme Institute, 285–87
Operation *Homecoming* (1973), 2
Operation *Rolling Thunder*, 202
Operation Smile, 371
Orderly Departure Program, 3, 176, 303, 372–73
Oriskany, U.S.S., 80
orphans, 4, 63, 109, 122, 284, 370

Palme, Olaf, 285
Paralyzed Veterans of America, 129
Paris Peace Accords, 272–73, 275
Paris Peace Talks, 19, 67–68, 128, 272, 361
Pathet Lao, 281
Pat Pong Street, Bangkok, 14–17
Patrick, Pat, 78–80, 94
Paul Doumer Bridge, 26, 46–47, 76–77, 80, 94
Peking Sally, 97
Pentagon, 42, 170, 198, 293
people's committees, 227, 302
Petzing, Ross, 174
Pham Van Dong, 274–75
"Plantation, The," 76, 241
plastic peglegs, 211–14
  fitting of, 215–16
  Vietnamese response to, 216–17
polio, 60, 130, 138, 139, 169, 243, 288, 370
P.O.W. (Hubbell), 167
POW/MIA families, 2, 7, 270, 307, 387
  see also National League of Families
POW/MIA issue, 2–5, 176–77, 209, 303, 307, 334, 387
POW/MIA negotiations, 232, 271–72, 277–78
  accounting for POW/MIAs and, 3, 5
  agreement on, 4–6, 281–82
  humanitarian vs. economic concerns in, 2–3, 19, 108, 109–10, 128, 131, 151–52, 159–60, 175–76, 209–10

JCRC team in, *see* POW/MIA team, U.S.
  location of remains and, 108–09
  meetings on, 108, 116, 141, 151, 271, 278, 373
  repatriation of remains and, 2, 4, 102
  separation of teams in, 5–6, 19, 29, 31–32, 50, 65, 66, 102
  surveillance of teams in, 50, 99
  U.S. delegation in, *see* POW/MIA team, U.S.
POW/MIA team, U.S.:
  attitudes toward Vietnamese within, 13–14
  Bangkok-Hanoi flight of, 21–27
  Bangkok meeting of, 18–20
  JCRC members of, 5–6, 11, 13, 21, 22–23, 31, 40–41, 48, 50, 53, 65, 66, 67, 76, 85, 93, 96, 130, 150
  non-JCRC members of, 6
  prior Vietnam experiences of, 52, 64, 67–71, 73, 76–77, 94–95
  war stories told by, 25, 98, 102
prisoners of war (POWs), 2, 25, 176–77, 209, 307, 332, 334
  Hanoi Hilton and, 73, 74, 77, 79, 80, 81, 124, 163
  release and return of, 41, 81, 129
  Vietnamese treatment of, 45, 79, 124, 167–68
Problem of the Disabled in Vietnam, The, 171–73, 174
Prosthetic Institute, 104
prosthetics, 5, 7, 67, 99
  amputees and, 106, 114, 141, 169, 211–18, 233
  cosmetic appearance of, 106, 216
  demonstrations of, 110–13, 212–18
  fittng of, 215–16
  harnesses and, 99, 111, 112
  humanitarian negotiations over, 105–15, 126–27
  materials needed for, 107, 114, 126, 127, 142, 169

Index

Index

FREDERICK DOWNS is the director of the Prosthetic and Sensory Aids Service for the Veterans Administration. He received eight awards for his courage during the Vietnam War, including the Silver Star and four Purple Hearts. He is the author of two previous books, *The Killing Zone: My Life in the Vietnam War* and *Aftermath: A Soldier's Return from Vietnam*. He lives in the Washington area with his wife, Mary, and their two daughters.